LIBRARY OF SECOND TEMPLE STUDIES

93

Formerly the Journal for the Study of the Pseudepigrapha Supplement Series

Editor
Lester L. Grabbe

Founding Editor
James H. Charlesworth

Editorial Board
Randall D. Chesnutt, Philip R. Davies, Jan Willem van Henten,
Judith M. Lieu, Steven Mason, James R. Mueller, Loren T. Stuckenbruck,
James C. VanderKam

ABRAHAM IN JEWISH AND EARLY CHRISTIAN LITERATURE

Edited by
Sean A. Adams and Zanne Domoney-Lyttle

LONDON • NEW YORK • OXFORD • NEW DELHI • SYDNEY

T&T CLARK
Bloomsbury Publishing Plc
50 Bedford Square, London, WC1B 3DP, UK
1385 Broadway, New York, NY 10018, USA
29 Earlsfort Terrace, Dublin 2, Ireland

BLOOMSBURY, T&T CLARK and the T&T Clark logo
are trademarks of Bloomsbury Publishing Plc

First published in Great Britain in 2019
Paperback edition first published 2021

Copyright © Sean A. Adams, Zanne Domoney-Lyttle and contributors, 2019

Sean A. Adams and Zanne Domoney-Lyttle have asserted their right under the Copyright, Designs and Patents Act, 1988, to be identified as Editors of this work.

For legal purposes the Acknowledgements on p. vii constitute an extension of this copyright page.

This work is published subject to a Creative Commons Attribution Non-commercial No Derivatives Licence. You may share this work for non-commercial purposes only, provided you give attribution to the copyright holder and the publisher.

Bloomsbury Publishing Plc does not have any control over, or responsibility for, any third-party websites referred to or in this book. All internet addresses given in this book were correct at the time of going to press. The author and publisher regret any inconvenience caused if addresses have changed or sites have ceased to exist, but can accept no responsibility for any such changes.

A catalogue record for this book is available from the British Library.

Library of Congress Cataloging-in-Publication Data
Names: Adams, Sean A., editor. | Domoney-Lyttle, Zanne, editor.
Title: Abraham in Jewish and early Christian literature / edited by Sean A. Adams and Zanne Domoney-Lyttle.
Description: London; New York: T&T Clark, 2019. | Series: Library of Second Temple studies, 2515-866X ; volume 93 | Includes bibliographical references and index.
Identifiers: LCCN 2019021449 (print) | LCCN 2019981054 (ebook) | ISBN 9780567675521 (hardback) | ISBN 9780567692542 (epub) | ISBN 9780567675538 (pdf)
Subjects: LCSH: Abraham (Biblical patriarch) | Abraham (Biblical patriarch–In rabbinical literature. | Abraham (Biblical patriarch)–In the New Testament. | Abraham (Biblical patriarch)–In literature.
Classification: LCC BS580.A3 A3734 2019 (print) | LCC BS580.A3 (ebook) | DDC 222/.11092–dc23
LC record available at https://lccn.loc.gov/2019021449
LC ebook record available at https://lccn.loc.gov/2019981054

ISBN: HB: 978-0-5676-7552-1
PB: 978-0-5677-0152-7
ePDF: 978-0-5676-7553-8
eBook: 978-0-5676-9254-2

Series: Library of Second Temple Studies, 2515–866X, volume 93

Typeset by RefineCatch Limited, Bungay, Suffolk

To find out more about our authors and books visit www.bloomsbury.com and sign up for our newsletters.

CONTENTS

ACKNOWLEDGMENTS

We are grateful to Dominic Mattos at Bloomsbury, who has responded to our queries with grace, efficiency, and patience. Our series editor, Lester Grabbe, has been responsive and supportive. Our thanks also go to our colleague, Sarah Nicholson, who read several chapters. A special word of thanks goes to Michael Mulryan and Merv Honeywood for providing editorial assistance, proof-reading, and referencing support.

We owe a great debt of gratitude to our spouses, Megan Adams and Simon Domoney-Lyttle, who not only allowed us to spend many hours on this project, but had to endure innumerable conversations about it. It is to them that we dedicate this volume.

Sean A. Adams
Zanne Domoney-Lyttle

Glasgow, UK
February 2019

ABBREVIATIONS

AB	Anchor Bible
AB	*Assyriologische Bibliothek*
ABD	*Anchor Bible Dictionary*
Abr.	*De Abrahamo*
Adol. poet. aud	*Quomodo adolescens poetas audire debeat*
Adv. Marc.	Tertullian, *Adversus Marcionem*
AGJU	Arbeiten zur Geschichte des antiken Judentums und des Urchristentums
AJ	*Antiquitates Judaicae*
AJEC	Ancient Judaism and Early Christianity
ALGHJ	Arbeiten zur Literatur und Geschichte des Hellenistischen Judentums
AnBib	Analecta Biblica
Ant.	*Antiquities of the Jews*
Anth.	Vettius Valens, *Anthologia*
Apoc. Abr.	*Apocalypse of Abraham*
Apoc. Zeph.	Apocalypse of Zephaniah
AYBC	Anchor Yale Bible Commentary
b. Sanh.	*Babylonian Talmud: Tractate Sanhedrin*
Barn.	Barnabas
BBR	Bulletin for Biblical Research
BCE	Before Common Era
BDAG	Greek-English Lexicon of the New Testament and Other Early Christian Literature
BDF	A Greek Grammar of the New Testament
BETL	Bibliotheca ephemeridum theologicarum lovaniensium
Bib	*Biblica*
BIS	*Biblical Interpretation Series*
BJS	Brown Judaic Studies
BZAW	Beihefte zur Zeitschrift für die alttestamentliche Wissenschaft
BZNW	Beihefte zur Zeitschrift für die neutestamentliche Wissenschaft
C. Ap.	*Contra Apionem*
CBET	Contributions to Biblical Exegesis and Theology
CBQ	*Catholic Bible Quarterly*
CE	Common Era
CEJL	Commentaries on Early Jewish Literature
Cher.	*On the Cherubim*
CJAS	Christianity and Judaism in Antiquity
CP	Classical Philology
Congr.	*On the Preliminary Studies*

DCH	*Dictionary of Classical Hebrew*
DCLS	Deuterocanonical and Cognate Literature Studies
Deus Imm.	*Quod Deus sit immutabilis*
Dial.	*Dialogus cum Tryphone*
Disc.	*Discourses*
Dig. Puls.	Galen, *De Dignoscendis Pulsibus Iv*
DJD	Discoveries in the Judaean Desert
Ebr.	*De ebrietate*
EKK	Evangelisch-katholischer Kommentar (Vorarbeiten)
ExAn	*Exegesis Animae*
Exc.	Excerpts from Theodotus and of the so-called eastern doctrine of Valentinianism
FAT	Forschungen zum Alten Testament
Firm. Mat.	Firmichus Maternus
FRLANT	Forschungen zur Religion und Literatur des Alten und Neuen Testaments
Fug.	*De fuga et inventione*
GAP	Guides to the Apocrypha and Pseudepigrapha
Gen. Apoc.	Genesis Apocryphon
Gen. Rab.	Genesis Rabbah
Gig.	*On Giants*
GLAJJ	Greek and Latin Authors on Jews and Judaism
Gram. et Rhet.	Seutonius, *On Grammarians*
Haer.	*Adversus haereses*
HCS	Hellenistic Culture and Society
Hist.	Thucydides, *History of the Peloponnesian War*
HTR	*Harvard Theological Review*
Hom. Luc.	*Homiliae in Lucam*
HUCA	Hebrew Union College Annual
Inst.	*Institutio oratoria*
JAOS	*Journal of the American Oriental Society*
JBL	*Journal of Biblical Literature*
JCPS	Jewish and Christian Perspectives Series
JJS	Journal of Jewish Studies
JPS	Jewish Publication Society
JSJ	*Journal for the Study of Judaism in the Persian, Hellenistic and Roman Period*
JSJSup	Journal for the Study of Judaism in the Persian, Hellenistic and Roman Period, Supplements
JSNT	Journal for the Study of the New Testament
JSNTSup	Journal for the Study of the New Testament Supplement
JSOT	Journal for the Study of the Old Testament
JSOTSup	Journal for the Study of the Old Testament Supplement
JSP	Journal for the Study of the Pseudepigrapha
JSQ	*Jewish Studies Quarterly*
JSS	Journal of Semitic Studies
JTS	Journal of Theological Studies

KJV	King James Version
LAB	*Liber Antiquitatum Biblicarum*
LCL	Loeb Classical Library
Leg. All.	*Legum allegoriae*
LHBOTS	The Library of Hebrew Bible/Old Testament Studies
LNTS	Library of New Testament Studies
LS	Louvain Studies
LSTS	Library of Second Temple Studies
LXX	Septuagint
Marc	*Adversus Marcionem*
Meg.	Megillah 14[a]
Migr.	*On the Migration of Abraham*
MS	Manuscript
MSU	Mitteilungen des Septuaginta-Unternehmens
MT	Masoretic Text
Mus	*Muséon*
Mut. Nom.	Philo, *On the Change of Names*
NHC	Nag Hammadi Codex
NHS	Nag Hammadi Studies
NIGTC	New International Greek Testament Commentary
NovT	Novum Testamentum
NovTSup	Novum Tetamentum, Supplements
NRSV	New Revised Standard Version
NT	New Testament
NTS	*New Testament Studies*
OCD	Oxford Classical Dictionary
OT	Old Testament
OTL	Old Testament Library
Pan.	*Panarion (Adversus haereses)*
Phld.	Ignatius, *To the Philadelphians*
Poet.	*Poetica*
Porph.	Porphyry *Hom. Quaes Homeric Questions*
Praem. Poen.	*On Rewards and Punishments*
Poster. C.	Philo, *De posteritate Caini*
Praep. Ev.	*Praeparatio Evangelica*
Princ.	*De principiis (Peri archōn)*
Procopius of Gaza	*Comm. Gen Commentary on Genesis*
Ps-Plutarch *Lib. Ed*	*De liberis educandis*
QG	*Questions and Answers on Genesis*
QE	*Questions and Answers on Exodus*
Ref.	*Refutatio*
RevQ	*Revue de Qumran*
RSV	Revised Standard Version
Sacr.	*De sacrificiis Abelis et Caini*
Sanh.	Sanhedrin 58b
SAPERE	Scripta Antiquitatis Posterioris ad Ethicam
SBL	Society of Biblical Literature

SBLDS	Society of Biblical Literature Dissertation Series
SBLEJL	Society of Biblical Literature Early Judaism and Its Literature
SC	Sources chrétiennes
SCS	Septuagint and Cognate Studies
SHR	Studies in the History of Religions (supplements to Numen)
Sib. Or.	Sibylline Oracles
SNTS	Society for New Testament Studies
Somn.	*On Dreams*
SPB	Studia postbiblical
SPCK	Society for Promoting Christian Knowledge
SPhA	Studies in Philo of Alexandria
Sphilo	*Studia Philonica*
STDJ	Studies on the Texts of the Desert of Judah
Strom.	Clement of Alexandria, *Stromateis*
SVF	*Stoicorum veterum fragmenta*
T. Abr.	*Testament of Abraham*
T. Benj.	*Testament of Benjamin*
T. Isaac	*Testament of Isaac*
T. Job	*Testament of Job*
T. Jos.	*Testament of Joseph*
T. Jud.	*Testament of Judah*
TBN	Themes in Biblical Narrative
Theon, *Prog.*	*Progymnasmata.*
ThLZ	Die Theologische Literaturzeitung
Thuc.	Thucydides
TU	Texte und Untersuchungen
TynBull	*Tyndale Bulletin*
UCLA	University of California Los Angeles
Vett. Val.	Vettius Valens *Anthology 2.28*
Virt.	*De virtutibus*
VisAmrbar	Visions of Amram manuscript b, in Aramaic
Vit. Mos.	Philo, *De vita Mosis*
VTSup	Vetus Testamentum, Supplements
WJK	Westminster John Knox
WUNT	Wissenschaftliche Untersuchungen zum Neuen Testament
ZAW	*Zeitschrift für Alttestamentliche Wissenschaft*
1 Clem.	1 Clement
2 Clem.	2 Clement

INTRODUCTION: ABRAHAM IN JEWISH AND CHRISTIAN AUTHORS

Sean A. Adams and Zanne Domoney-Lyttle

Abraham the father. Abraham the patriarch. Abraham, the founder of monotheistic faith traditions. Abraham, the recipient of God's covenantal promises in Genesis. Abraham, the husband to Sarah, Hagar, and Keturah. Abraham, the father of nations. Abraham the exalted. First introduced in Gen. 11:27, the figure of Abraham has been given these titles as well as many others throughout the reception of his character in ancient Jewish and early Christian texts. His name has become synonymous with the foundations of Israel in the biblical texts, with covenantal promises made between God and Abraham the chosen one, with claims to land, identity, and personhood, and with themes of righteousness, sacredness, hospitality, and inheritance.

From where did these constructs of Abraham's character arise? Why is Abraham considered the ultimate father rather than a strong warrior or political leader? What aspects of his character are illuminated and remembered, and which are forgotten or suppressed? Furthermore, *how* is he remembered? This volume traces the diverse ways that Jewish and early Christian authors discussed Abraham, adapted his Hebrew and Greek Bible narratives, and used Abraham imagery in their works. The individual essays tease out the various ways that the character of Abraham was described, viewed, understood, and used, both within the Hebrew Bible and across different collections of ancient texts, including the Apocrypha, Pseudepigrapha, rewritten Scriptures, and texts produced by Philo, Josephus, New Testament authors, early Church Fathers, Gnostic writers, and Greek and Latin outsiders.

Across these chapters, several themes have emerged concerning the representation and memory of Abraham across Jewish and early Christian texts. Most prominently, Abraham is paired with his descendants, Isaac and Jacob, forming a triad of patriarchs through whom God's covenant promises are given and reinforced. The patriarchal triumvirate is drawn upon in diverse ways, and many of the ancient authors discussed in this volume view Abraham through both a theological and an historical lens, recognizing him as a central figure of their spiritual belief and as the founding patriarch who lived in history. For Jewish authors in the Hebrew Bible, for example, Abraham is the father of their people and the person to whom God made his covenant promise; a promise transferred and rearticulated to Jacob and Isaac. For Christian authors, such as Paul and the early Church Fathers, Abraham retains his central position, but is reinterpreted in light of the authors' understanding of the Christ event and the relationship between these two figures. A similar interpretive framework is applied by Gnosis authors, but for them Abraham is not a positive figure that needs to be incorporated into a new theological scheme, but someone who needs to be excised from the pure revelation of the true God that was offered by Jesus.

In general, depictions of Abraham are positive, with the patriarch presented as a model for emulation, the progenitor of the Jewish people, and a friend of God. This positive characterization is not surprising in that most of the people who discuss Abraham are Jewish. Some non-Jewish authors also present Abraham in a positive light, either because they are writing a history that is dependent on Scriptural texts, they are positively predisposed to Judaism (e.g., Hermippus), or because they are in the employ of a Jewish king (e.g., Nicolaus of Damascus). A majority of negative depictions come from non-Jewish authors, either historians who are writing polemical works (e.g., Manetho) or Gnostic authors (e.g., Marcion, Valentinus) who, for theological reasons, want to distance Jesus and their understanding of God with the creator God and characters from Jewish Scripture. This diversity of presentations provides a good example of the malleability of Abraham's depiction and how an author's starting point strongly influences, and perhaps even determines, how s/he will portray an individual.

Another finding of this volume is the tendency by authors, both Jewish and Christian, to expand the Abraham narrative. For example, Philo (*Rer. Div. Her.* 27, 29; *Congr.* 151–52, 156; *Abr.* 71, 248–52) and the authors of *Jubilees* (19:26–22:30) and *Genesis Apocryphon* (2.3–18; 19.17–21) use constructed speeches to emphasize specific theological elements pertinent to their argument. Crafted speech is not limited to Abraham and human characters, but statements can also be attributed to God (e.g., *LAB* 7.4; 10.2; 12.4; 14.2; 18.5; 23.5–7). In contrast, Josephus significantly abridges God and Abraham's extensive dialogue about Sodom's fate in Gen. 18:16-33 (*Ant.* 1.199–200), likely because this was not relevant/useful for Josephus' literary purpose.

In addition to creating speeches, ancient authors also sought, on occasion, to make changes to Abraham's story. One practice was to fill in narrative gaps; Abraham's early life and post-mortem activities are subject to this approach. Scenes from Abraham's youth are infrequent, but are found in a few texts that attempt to show how Abraham deviated from the practices and ideas of his father Terah (e.g., *Apoc. Abr.* 3.2–4; 8.3–4; *LAB* 6.1–18). These narrative expansions fill gaps within Abraham's narrative and help explain why Abraham was chosen by God. Depictions of Abraham's post-mortem activities are less expected, but are prominent in Testament and Apocalypse texts and absent in most other genres. Here we find Abraham as one of the people who will be raised at the resurrection of the dead (*Sib. Or.* 2.245–49), who has escaped from Hades (*Apoc. Zeph.* 9.4–5) or, alternatively, who exists in the presence of God continuing his intercessory work, pleading before God on behalf of his descendants and sinners (3 *En.* 44.7; *T. Isaac* 6.9–23). For many of these authors Abraham is a person who continues to exist (cf. Mt. 22:29-32).

Another practice was to downplay awkward passages and reinterpret them in order to make the actions of Abraham or God less problematic. A good example is found in 4Q225 2.i.9–10 in which the Prince of the Mastemah accused Abraham before God regarding his son Isaac, an incident that is presented as the catalyst for the command to sacrifice Isaac. Regarding the relationship between Sarah and Pharaoh (Gen. 12:10-20), certain texts minimize the event by making Pharaoh the active character (*Jub.* 13:12-13), while others indicate that calling Sarah his sister was the necessary action to preserve his life (i.e., through a dream *Gen. Apoc.* 20.14–22).[1] These changes relate to the exemplarity of Abraham and the need to ensure that what could be construed as morally questionable acts are properly understood.[2] The downplaying of awkward narratives highlights the tension felt by ancient authors between being faithful to the text and taking creative license. Most authors use Abraham in a way that aligns closely with the Genesis text. The *Testament of Abraham* remained true to the Genesis narrative by not creating a death-bed testimony for Abraham, but added the scene in which Abraham asks to see the entire created world before his death (*T. Abr.* A9.6) and all the faces of Death (A19.5–6).[3] The rationale for such an alignment is not always clear, but could be linked to the authority of the original text, the (likely) widely-held knowledge of the Abrahamic narrative by the intended readers, the piety of the author, or a combination of the above. Nevertheless, ancient authors did not feel absolutely constrained in their handling of the character of Abraham.

Reading Abraham in light of, and in relationship to, other Scriptural passages or characters was a prominent way for ancient authors to engage with the Abrahamic narrative. The most common example is how authors throughout our chapters grouped Abraham, Isaac, and Jacob together as a triumvirate of Jewish patriarchy. Although Abraham can be, and regularly is, referenced individually, his association with Isaac and Jacob is significant as it both traces the succession approved by God and acts as a shorthand for a theological perspective on the land and God's

1. The parallel, sister-calling narrative of Gen. 20:1-18 is even less prominent and is regularly part of the omitted material.

2. On the exemplarity of Abraham in specific corpora, see A.Y. Reed, "The Construction of Subversion of Patriarchal Perfection: Abraham and Exemplarity in Philo, Josephus, and the Testament of Abraham", *JSJ* 40 (2009): 185–212. Cf. Sir. 44:19-21; Tob. 4:12; CD iii.2–3; Heb. 11:8-12; *1 Clem.* 10.1–2. In contrast, the author of the *Testament of Abraham*, although depicting Abraham as faithful, also recounts how he refused a request from God (9.4–6) and goes back on a promise he made to Michael (15.1–10).

3. Cf. Origen, *Hom. Luc.* 35.3 in R. Bauckham, "The Dispute over Abraham. A New Translation and Introduction", in *Old Testament Pseudepigrapha: More Noncanonical Scriptures,* Vol. 1, eds. R. Bauckham et al. (Grand Rapids: Eerdmans, 2013), 58–62.

promises. The reading of these lives together is not only important for tracing the history of the Jewish people, but could also be viewed symbolically (e.g., Philo, *Abr.* 48–51), with the triad offering more than the sum of each part.

Abraham's relationship to Sarah, Hagar, and Keturah is less prominent than his pairing with Isaac and Jacob, and within the Hebrew Bible and Gnostic texts these women rarely feature. In a number of other corpora, the women are infrequently mentioned, and when they are, they are used as part of a wider argument about Abraham (e.g., Gal. 4:22-31).[4] In contrast, certain authors, such as Philo, understand Sarah, and, to a lesser extent, Hagar as important figures in Abraham's life (*Abr.* 245–54) and as symbolically meaningful in an interpretation of the Genesis text (e.g., Philo, *Congr.*). Similarly, Josephus appears bothered by Sarah's absence from the *Akedah* narrative, and because of this, he adds that Abraham concealed God's command from her (*Ant.* 1.225).[5]

The association of Abraham and other individuals is not limited to biblical characters who appear in his narrative. For example, in the Commentary on Genesis A (4Q252), the interpreter read the life of Abraham through a wider scriptural lens, especially the book of Deuteronomy. In works of rewritten Scripture, actions attributed to Abraham mirror those of other biblical characters,[6] and in the Gnostic *Second Discourse of Great Seth* the author viewed Abraham as following the path of Adam in contrast to that of Seth (cf. NHC VII.2 62.27–63.3). These points of contact imply a more unified reading of the biblical texts in which the character of Abraham is not read in isolation, but as part of a wider theological and literary narrative.

Ultimately, and perhaps unsurprisingly, the interpretation of Abraham is characterized by diversity. The theological or ideological perspective of the author substantially influences and often determines how they engage with Abraham and handle his narrative. In general, ancient authors, when evoking Abraham, highlighted one or more of his character traits (e.g., faith, hospitality, fatherhood, etc.) or read his story through a specific interpretive lens (e.g., allegory). When rewriting his narrative, authors regularly filled gaps, reordered events, expanded reported speech, and even made claims about Abraham's current state in the afterlife. All of these actions show that Abraham was an important character for these ancient readers, and that they saw his narrative as particularly fruitful for interpretation and relevant to their lives.

4. For a wider discussion, see J. McDonald, "Searching for Sarah in the Second Temple Era: Portraits in the Hebrew Bible and Second Temple Narratives", PhD diss; Brite Divinity School, 2015.

5. Another example of the expansion of Sarah's character is seen in *Gen. Apoc.* 20.1–8 and the description of her beauty.

6. E.g., Abraham's escape from the fiery furnace by the Tower of Babel (*LAB* 6.3–18; cf. Dan. 3:1-30); Abraham unlike Noah and his family (CD iii.2–3); Abraham tested like Job (*Jub.* 17:15-18); cf. b. Sanh. 89b; Rab. Gen. 55.4.

Chapter Summaries

This volume contains eleven chapters in which each scholar evaluates how the character of Abraham is employed in their specific author or corpus. We recognize that this type of division is not always beneficial and is regularly arbitrary (esp. Apocrypha, Pseudepigrapha, Gnostic, etc.), based on later reader or scholarly categories (e.g., canon) that were unlikely to have been germane to their ancient authors. Our volume structure is not an attempt to endorse the siloing of these texts, but is a concession to practicality.

The starting point of the author determining a certain portrayal of the patriarch is only one relationship which affects how Abraham is portrayed and perceived; another is the relationship between Abraham and the characters he is often seen interacting with in the texts of Genesis. Reading Abraham in the context of husband and father, for example, can impact how a reader may understand and receive the patriarch.

This argument is drawn upon by Zanne Domoney-Lyttle in her chapter concerning Abraham in the Hebrew Bible. In this chapter, Domoney-Lyttle traces the reception not only of Abraham, but of his partners and the mothers of his children Sarah, Hagar, and Keturah throughout the texts of the Hebrew Bible. Domoney-Lyttle argues that, as the reader progresses through the Hebrew Bible, Abraham's name becomes greater while the memory of his partners is erased, a move on behalf of the authors which indicates Abraham's name is used to reinforce patriarchal ideologies concerning themes of land ownership and patrilineal descent; in short, the covenantal promises. Abraham's name becomes a metaphor for those promises, a metaphor which would be threatened with the inclusion of Sarah, or Hagar, or Keturah. Thus, by selectively preserving certain parts of Abraham's history, the writers of the Hebrew texts present a counter memory of Abraham, which supports a political agenda of land ownership and a social agenda of correct family lineage.

Though an important figure in the Hebrew Bible, Abraham is not one of the central figures; David, Moses, and even Solomon have stronger claims to this title. One of the emerging themes in this volume is that, despite Abraham's lack of centrality in the Hebrew Scriptures, he actually becomes increasingly popular in the ancient texts which follow. In Géza G. Xeravits' chapter concerning Abraham in the Old Testament Apocrypha, he traces common themes of Abraham's story which suggest that Abraham was not only a popular figure, but that there is strong evidence of a rich tradition of literature and history built around the patriarch. We can see this for example in the way that Genesis 22 is recalled and re-presented in various apocryphal books such as Judith, 1 Maccabees, and the Book of Wisdom, which suggest not only that the memory of events in Abraham's later life is still important, but also that he grew in popularity specifically because his name could be used as a model of faith and trust in God through the invocation of narratives such as Genesis 22. Finally, Xeravits draws attention to the malleability of Abraham's character as well as thematic variability within his biographical narratives, noting again the approach of authors who selected and re-presented aspects of Abraham's life to reframe his character according to need.

Jared Ludlow's chapter traces the use of Abraham in Old Testament Pseudepigrapha. In this chapter, Ludlow also draws the reader's attention to the creative approach of ancient authors to gaps in Abraham's life which add color and intrigue to his character, but which also remain consistent with more traditional approaches to his biography. In the *Testament of Abraham* for example, Abraham's refusal to follow the angel Michael to heaven (Recension A) almost presents him as a stubborn and disloyal character, the opposite traits which readers usually associate with Abraham. To rectify this, Ludlow discusses how Recension B of the same story foregrounds Abraham's intentions as an explanation for the trouble he causes in the text. This short example demonstrates the importance that Abraham's character should be remembered positively, and with the traits that many Jewish and early Christian communities had come to recognize him for.

Moving away from characterization, a number of the chapters identified a possible relationship between the genre of a work and how the Genesis narrative was used. In her chapter on Rewritten Scripture, Susan Docherty identifies specific approaches to Abraham's Genesis narrative by authors of Rewritten Scripture, two of which we have seen in the above chapters: 1) selective abridgement or omission of specific narratives in Abraham's story, and 2) the provision of a new context for episodes from Abraham's life. Other exegetical techniques highlighted by Docherty include: 1) the reordering of some events in the Abraham narrative; 2) the introduction of minor difference from the Genesis accounts; and 3) the inclusion of supplementary material in which the author's own emphases can be developed. On this last point, Docherty argues that it is the addition of material which reshapes the figure of Abraham rather than the tweaking of Genesis narratives. Unlike the previous chapters which have highlighted the ideological concerns of authorship in the presentation of Abraham, Docherty argues that rewritten Scriptures are exegetical in their focus (i.e., concerned with clarifying the texts) and less concerned with propagating political or social concerns.

In his chapter on Abraham in the corpus of Philo of Alexandria, Sean Adams adopts a character theory approach, and evaluates how Philo reads Abraham's life in light of his relationships. Adams argues that modern theories about how character is developed in narratives can be profitably applied to Philo's interpretation of the Genesis narrative. In particular, an interfigural approach, which identifies relations between characters within or from different texts, highlights how Philo defines Abraham through his engagement and relationship to other characters, especially, but not limited to, Sarah, Isaac, Lot, and Pharaoh.

Michael Avioz argues in his chapter on Abraham in Josephus' writings, that they should be considered an exegetical project as well. Avioz' categorization of Josephus' writings as exegesis differs from Docherty's taxonomy; instead, Avioz argues Josephus' reputation as exegete is concerned with translating the Hebrew biblical text into Greek, with reconciling contradictions in the Hebrew Bible, and with addressing problematic ethical issues which might have troubled Graeco-Roman readers.

Joshua W. Jipp considers the role of Abraham within the Gospels and Acts of the New Testament. In this study, Abraham's memory is invoked inconsistently across NT texts, and Jipp draws out both the similarities and differences across the handling of Abraham's narrative to demonstrate once again that his name and memory is called upon to endorse or suggest social or political ideologies. In the Gospels (excluding Mark), Abraham is used as a link between God's covenant with Israel and the person of Jesus, through genealogical descent (e.g., the genealogical material in Matthew), but also through his acting of the deeds of Abraham (e.g., in John), for example. Abraham as model of faith, hospitality, and fatherhood is prevalent within these texts and indicates not only how the patriarch was understood, but also the qualities which were of most importance to those ancient communities.

The role of Abraham as exemplar is also debated in Pauline scholarship and is typically viewed as falling upon interpretational lines; for scholars who advocate for the "Old Perspective" Abraham represents a model of faith (esp. Romans 4), whereas, for "New Perspective" scholars Abraham is not interpreted primarily in those terms. In his chapter on Abraham in Paul's letters, Chris Tilling has argued that this classification dichotomy does not accurately represent scholarly positions, and dampens the nuance proposed by scholars in their reading of Paul.

Seth Ehorn's chapter on Abraham in the Apostolic Fathers highlights the importance of Abraham's family line (both literally and spiritually) in forming identities for early Christian writers. Ehorn here notes that these ancient authors often selected and/or modified specific narratives from the life of Abraham to support and suggest their own political and social agendas, a theme prevalent across many of the chapters. These agendas may be minor (i.e. using Abraham as a model of hospitality in *1 Clement*) or have wider significance (i.e. Ignatius Christianizing Abraham, diluting his Jewish origins in his *Letter to the Philadelphians*). Ehorn's chapter suggests the continued importance of Abraham as a character in faith traditions, but only when the invocation of his name can be used in specific ways.

Another finding of this volume is the relationship between the depiction of Abraham and the context of the author who employed him. For example, among non-Jewish authors, the depiction of Abraham changed from that of a militaristic and monarchical individual to that of religious founder knowledgeable of divine lore. This shift paralleled the rise in Christianity within the Empire and the importance of Abraham in religious discussions, an argument proposed by Margaret Williams in her chapter on Abraham in Greek and Latin authors.

Csaba Ötvös traces the reception of Abraham in the ancient Gnostic systems. As noted by Ötvös, Abraham is not a central figure in the Gnostic texts, and does not often appear in primary or secondary sources regarding that literature. Where Abraham's name does appear, it is often used allusively to suggest a connection with biblical material. In this context then, Abraham's name is used to legitimize the authority and knowledge of the writer rather than invoking the patriarch's name to highlight an agenda or suggest the moral implications of Abraham's life story. This suggests that invoking Abraham's name is a way for ancient Gnostic authors to claim their own power and identity, a move which is arguably a step beyond the reception of Abraham discussed in the previous chapters.

The figure of Abraham has lived many afterlives throughout the texts discussed in this volume. This volume is not only a testament to the importance of the patriarch, but also adds to the living story of Abraham whose name continues to pervade religious and cultural traditions, and whose afterlife continues in these new texts which center on his character. By presenting a more thorough outline of the impact of the figure and stories of Abraham, we have created a more concise and complete idea of how his narrative was employed throughout the centuries, including how ancient authors adopted and adapted received traditions. This study only traces a few avenues of reception and there are many more paths to investigate. In particular, investigating the reception of Abraham in other faith traditions and in subsequent time periods and texts would be fruitful lines of inquiry in their own right, but would also shed more light on how Abraham was understood in the corpora discussed in this volume.

Chapter 1

Abraham in the Hebrew Bible

Zanne Domoney-Lyttle

Like much of the Hebrew Bible, Abraham's narrative is entrenched in a patriarchal structure of creation and reception. It was written by men, for men, and is mostly about men. Where women are represented, they exist as secondary components within an androcentric narrative, allowing men to continue moving, talking, fighting, procreating, establishing dynasties, and even dying.[1] Rarely are women given their own stories, and rarely are their perspectives represented in any meaningful way.[2] The patriarchal narratives in Genesis 12–50, stories in which Abraham is a key figure, exist only because there were women who enabled the lineage of Abraham firstly to come into being, and secondly to continue growing. However, within the Hebrew Bible as a whole, it is Abraham's name, along with his son Isaac and his grandson Jacob, which are repeatedly remembered and which are invoked to reinforce patriarchal ideologies concerning covenantal themes of land ownership and patrilineal descent, mostly through the concept of Abraham as the father to his people.[3]

The near complete erasure of women, and in particular of mothers in the reception of the patriarchal narratives, is not particularly surprising given their androcentric origins and history.[4] However, it does lead to a quandary for readers

1. For example, Delilah weakens Samson by finding out his strength is his hair. She shaves his head and hands him over to the Philistines, an action which arguably leads to his death (Judg. 16:17-30). Delilah disappears after handing Samson to his enemies.

2. With the exception, perhaps, of Ruth and Naomi (book of Ruth), Esther (book of Esther), and Judith (book of Judith, in the Apocrypha).

3. J.C. Exum, *Fragmented Women: Feminist (Sub)versions of Biblical Narratives,* 2nd edn. (London: Bloomsbury/T&T Clark, 2016), 81–2; F. Stavrakopoulou, *Land of our Fathers: The Roles of Ancestor Veneration in Biblical Land Claims* (London: T&T Clark, 2010).

4. As Ackerman suggests, "Ancient Israel was a kinship-based society, with kinship defined through the patriline, so that both genealogies and rights of inheritance were, with only a very few exceptions, [. . .] traced through patrilineal lines of descent." See: S. Ackerman, "Women in Ancient Israel and the Hebrew Bible", *Oxford Research Encyclopedia of Religion,*

as, outside of the book of Genesis, they regularly encounter Abraham as a father of descendants who have no meaningful connections to their mothers. I argue that, as the reader progresses through the books of the Hebrew Bible, the memory of the mothers is so thoroughly erased and subsequently forgotten that it can appear to the reader that Abraham's descendants are in fact "motherless" children. At least, the sons of Abraham usurp the figure of mother completely, taking her place in the texts. These fissures in the text are problematic and lead to assumptions that mothers are firstly non-essential characters in the patriarchal narratives, and secondly, that they are a disposable component in the shaping of Israel's future. Again, this outcome is unsurprising in a text concerned mostly with presenting and preserving male perspectives, but it does lead to a lopsided view of the relationship between fathers and mothers within the Bible as a whole. Further, the lack of attention paid to the mothers of the Abrahamic narratives shapes how the reader views and understands the figure of Abraham-the-father in the Hebrew Bible outside of the book of Genesis.

This chapter is concerned with tracing the reception of Abraham across the books of the Hebrew Bible outlining Abraham's identity and reputation as "father", specifically with regards to the collective social memory of Abraham as father, juxtaposed against the erasure of his three wives/partners within the books of the Hebrew Bible. I also discuss the implications those representations may carry for the reception of Abraham in the Hebrew Scriptures more broadly. To begin, I turn to the texts of Genesis to explore the characterization of Abraham as father within the patriarchal narratives, before turning to examine the development and proliferation of that characterization throughout the books of the Torah, the Prophets, and the Writings.

Abraham the Father

Father of Isaac and Ishmael and the sons of Keturah, husband to Sarah, Hagar and Keturah, Abraham is the recipient of the promise of countless descendants, an area of land and a blessing bestowed by God. Unsurprisingly, the language used to describe Abraham throughout the Hebrew Bible is based in masculine pronouns and male-dominated word-choices, mostly through the use of "father" as a title. In Deut. 1:8, for example, Abraham is referred to as "father" to his people (לַאֲבֹתֵיכֶם), who are now charged with claiming the land that was promised to them through him: "See, I have set the land before you; go in and take possession of the land that I swore to your fathers, to Abraham, to Isaac, and to Jacob, to give to them and to

http://religion.oxfordre.com/view/10.1093/acrefore/9780199340378.001.0001/acrefore-9780199340378-e-45 (last accessed 17 September 2018). The patrilineal structure, which affected families, law, inheritance, etc., probably meant that space for women was restricted or limited to specific roles within the community. Ackerman discusses this in her outline on gendered roles in the Hebrew Bible in the above work.

their descendants after them." In Isa. 41:8, the reference to Abraham's fatherhood is brought up again: "But you, Israel, my servant, Jacob, whom I have chosen, the offspring of Abraham, my friend." The connotation behind the use of זֶרַע, which is regularly glossed "offspring" (NRSV) and sometimes "seed" (KJV, for example), is linked to male virility, and appears only once in relation to female fertility in the Hebrew Bible.[5]

Even the name "Abraham" is linked to concepts of masculinity and fatherhood. Abraham's pre-covenantal name "Abram" means either "exalted father" or "father of elevation", and "Abraham" can be translated as "father of a multitude".[6] Abraham's identity as both "man" and "father" is not only central to his narrative and impact in the Hebrew Bible, it is also used to provide an identity and voice to his descendants. Throughout the Hebrew Bible, references abound to Abraham as father,[7] or to God identifying himself as the "God of your father(s), Abraham, (Isaac, and Jacob)".[8] Mostly, invocations to the patriarchal triumvirate are bound with appeals from the people of Israel to be remembered by God through his covenant with Abraham. The ability to trace their genealogy to Abraham their father is a method of classifying themselves against other groups in the land, as well as for staking a claim on their promised land,[9] and defining social functions, juridical powers and religious imperatives associated with the genealogical system of the Israelite community.[10]

For such an important figure who is literarily the father of all of his descendants, it must also be acknowledged that Abraham is not even one of the most recognized figures in the Hebrew Bible.[11] "Abram" is mentioned fifty-nine times in the book of

5. זֶרַע relates to sowing seed, semen virile, offspring, and sprouts or shoots. In relation to women, זֶרַע appears only once in Gen. 3:15 in connection with Eve. However, J. J. Collins persuasively argues that syntactical features potentially distinguish between זֶרַע meaning the singular "seed" or the plural, "seeds", concluding that in Genesis 3:15, the "seed of the woman" indicates a single descendant rather than multiple descendants, as is the case whenever the word is used in connection with Abraham. See: J. J. Collins, "A Syntactical Note (Genesis 3:15): Is the Woman's Seed Singular or Plural?", *TynBull* 48, no. 1 (1997): 139–48.

6. R. Hendel calls the naming of Abraham in Gen. 17:5 "a performative utterance in which God makes Abraham the ancestor par excellence." R. Hendel, *Remembering Abraham: Culture, Memory and History in the Hebrew Bible* (Oxford: Oxford University Press, 2005), 33.

7. For example, see: Deut. 9:5 or Isa. 51:2.

8. For example, see: 1 Kgs. 18:36 or 1 Chron. 29:18.

9. For more on this, see: T. Römer, "Abraham Traditions in the Hebrew Bible Outside the Book of Genesis", in *The Book of Genesis: Composition, Reception, and Interpretation*, eds. C.A. Evans et al. (VTSup 152; Leiden: Brill, 2012), 159–80, here 178–79; Stavrakopoulou, *The Land of Our Fathers*.

10. Hendel, *Remembering Abraham*, 34.

11. J. Blenkinsopp, *Abraham: The Story of a Life* (Grand Rapids, MI: Wm B Eerdmans, 2015), 1.

Genesis and a further two times outside of Genesis (1 Chron. 1:27; Neh. 9:7). "Abraham" is mentioned 117 times in Genesis, and only forty-two times outside of Genesis, and the name "Abram" or "Abraham" appears in isolation (i.e., without reference to his descendants),[12] or without reference to the title of "father", only seven times outside of the book of Genesis.[13] From this brief quantitative study, it can be surmised that the connection between Abraham and "father" is consistent throughout the Hebrew Bible.

This indicates that Abraham's significance extends beyond the role of a character in a series of legends, using descriptions of Abraham that normally include a patriarchal element. However, this count of Abraham's name also suggests he is not as important a figure as other biblical men, such as Moses, David, or even Solomon, whose names appear in the biblical texts much more frequently,[14] and unlike these men, he is far more likely to be linked with the concept of father, rather than the idea of his being a great warrior, king, or leader.[15]

Most current scholarship on the reception of Abraham in the Hebrew Bible is concerned with his identity and role as father and how that relates to possession of territories as promised in his covenant with God.[16] It is mostly men who have thus far undertaken such scholarship, and the results, though fruitful, challenging and rigorous, are steeped in androcentric perspectives, often reflecting the social location of the scholars. As Frances Klopper notes in relation to biblical studies in general, "[t]raditional male commentators wrote under the guise of neutrality but imposed their assumptions on the text and failed to question its moral difficulties."[17] This is true with regards to the reception of Abraham in the Hebrew Bible as well as in other ancient texts.

12. By this I mean descendants in any form, including references to children, seed etc., named or unnamed, preceding or succeeding the name of Abraham.

13. See: Josh. 24:2; 1 Chron. 1:27; Neh. 9:7; Ps. 47:9; Ps. 105:42; Isa. 63:16; Ezek. 33:24.

14. Moses' name occurs 764 times in 702 verses; David's name occurs 1,018 times across 859 verses; Solomon's name occurs 287 times in 260 verses. While it is not the most scientific way to explore the influence of these figures on the rest of the Hebrew Bible, I argue that charting the number of times their names appear does give some indication as to how memories of their names and their deeds are invoked.

15. Granted, Abraham is also associated with characteristics of a great leader, and occasionally a warrior (see Genesis 14, for example), but I maintain that the strongest association with Abraham is as a father.

16. See for example: Römer, "Abraham Traditions in the Hebrew Bible"; ch. 1 in Blenkinsopp, *Abraham: The Story of a Life*; Hendel, *Remembering Abraham*; E. Noort, "Abraham and the Nations", in *Abraham, the Nations, and the Hagarites: Jewish, Christian, and Islamic Perspectives on Kinship with Abraham*, eds. M. Goodman et al. (Themes in Biblical Narrative Jewish and Christian Traditions 13; Leiden: Brill, 2010), 3–31.

17. F. Klopper, "Interpretation is All We Have. A Feminist Perspective on the Objective Fallacy", *Old Testament Essays* 22, no. 1 (2009): 88–101.

The emphasis on interpreting Abraham as a father figure in Genesis and beyond is so well-established, that considerations of how Abraham achieved that title in the first place—namely because his wives and sexual partners,[18] Sarah, Hagar, and Keturah, became pregnant and gave birth—have been more or less lost in scholarship. As noted, there are a number of studies on Abraham as a father,[19] and there are a number of studies on motherhood narratives in Genesis.[20] However, little consideration has been given to the reception of Abraham in the Hebrew Bible in relation to his wives/partners,[21] and how the erasure of the mothers throughout the Hebrew Bible impacts the reception of Abraham as father.

18. It is understood that Sarah is Abraham's primary-wife (the Hebrew אִשָּׁה is used in Gen. 11:29 for example), while Hagar is described as שִׁפְחָה meaning female slave or a maid-servant in Gen. 16:1, though is once called "wife" in Gen. 16:3 before her status reverts back to slave in Gen. 16:5. After the death of Sarah, Abraham marries Keturah (Gen. 25:1) and she is described in the same language as Sarah, אִשָּׁה in the text of Genesis. However, Keturah is then called פִּילֶגֶשׁ (concubine or paramour) in 1 Chron. 1:32, a demotion from the position of primary-wife which she occupies in Genesis. The insinuation taken from these word choices is that Sarah is Abraham's primary-wife, Hagar is a handmaid or slave-girl belonging to Sarah but given to Abraham by Sarah, and Keturah assumes firstly the position of primary-wife after Sarah's death, but her reception in later biblical texts is as a concubine because she does not embody the same status as Sarah, who has produced Abraham's heir to the covenantal promise. The legal status of concubines is still contested among biblical scholars, so it is unclear whether Keturah enjoyed the same privileges as Sarah, or if she was treated differently legally or otherwise. Collectively, I will refer to them as wives/partners. For more on the legal status of women and wives see: I. Hamley, "'Dis(re)membered and Unaccounted For': פִּילֶגֶשׁ in the Hebrew Bible", *JSOT* 42, no. 4 (2018): 415–34; S. Démare-Lafont, "The Status of Women in the Legal Texts of the Ancient Near East", in *The Bible and Women: An Encyclopaedia of Exegesis and Cultural History—Torah*, eds. I. Fischer et al. (Atlanta: SBL, 2011), 109–32.

19. See, for example: C. Delaney, *Abraham on Trial: The Social Legacy of Biblical Myth* (Princeton: Princeton University Press, 1998). There are further examples above.

20. See, for example: E. Fuchs, "The Literary Characterisation of Mothers and Sexual Politics in the Hebrew Bible", in *Women in the Hebrew Bible: A Reader*, ed. A. Bach (New York/London: Routledge, 1999), 127–40; Exum, *Fragmented Women*, especially ch. 4: "The (M)other's Place". It should be noted that there are proportionally fewer studies on Keturah than exist on Sarah and Hagar.

21. There are, of course, a few sources which deal with the theme of Abraham and his partners in relation to the covenantal promises. For example, see: U. Bechmann, "Genesis 12 and the Abraham-Paradigm Concerning the Promised Land", *The Ecumenical Review* 68, no. 1 (2016): 62–80, https://doi.org/10.1111/erev.12199 (accessed June 11, 2019).

Abraham and His Progeny

To be a father, one must have offspring. Generally speaking, to produce offspring one requires a female, and Abraham had three women in his life: Sarah, Hagar, and Keturah.[22] Sarah was his first wife and the reader is told she was very beautiful, but infertile.[23] After a period of time and significant events including the Hagar-Ishmael episode (Genesis 16), Sarah eventually becomes pregnant following a divine proclamation (Gen. 18:10) and gives birth to Isaac in Gen. 21:1-3. Hagar was Sarah's slave and appears to have no difficulties bearing children, giving birth to Ishmael in Gen. 16:15 after Sarah offers her to Abraham as a way to procure a child. Keturah was married to Abraham after the death of Sarah and was also seemingly fertile as she gave birth to six sons before Abraham died (Gen. 25:2). It is through these women that Abraham is made a father, a patriarch, yet they do not figure in the narratives of the Hebrew Bible which call upon Abraham's name in remembrance, except for on three occasions.

In contrast to Abraham's recurring title of "father" in the Hebrew Bible, Sarah is only called "mother" twice in Genesis (Gen. 17:16; 24:67) and her association with motherhood occurs only once outside of Genesis, in Isa. 51:2: "Look to Abraham your father and to Sarah who bore you". That is also the only instance that her name occurs outside of Genesis. Keturah is never given the title "mother" but is named as bearer to Abraham's children twice in the book of Genesis (25:1; 25:4) and twice outside of Genesis in 1 Chron. 1:32-33. Hagar is given the descriptor of "mother" once within Genesis (21:21) but is not mentioned again in the Hebrew Bible.

Abraham's identity of father is strongly reiterated throughout the Hebrew Bible as we have seen, yet the handful of references to the mothers who bear his children suggests both that they are unimportant characters within the covenantal narratives, and, as such, they are not significant factors in the future of Abraham and his descendants. Sarah, Hagar, and Keturah do not need to be remembered. Because of this, the memory of the mothers is erased as the reader progresses throughout the Hebrew Bible, so I will now examine the texts of the Hebrew Bible which support this view, and argue that the erasure of motherhood impacts on the characterization of Abraham.

Abraham the Father in Genesis

The identity of Abraham as "father" pervades the texts of Genesis. He is first introduced to readers of the narrative as part of a genealogical line connecting

22. Following an ancient rabbinic idea, Rashi suggests that Hagar and Keturah are the same person, but there is no textual evidence to suggest this. See: R.E. Friedman, *Commentary on the Torah* (New York, NY: HarperCollins, 2001), 85.

23. See Gen. 12:11 and 11:29-30, respectively.

Noah's son Shem to Abraham's father Terah (Gen. 11:10-26), indicating to the reader that Abraham and his brothers, Nahor and Haran, are descended from righteous stock. The genealogical recantation ends with Abraham and his brothers, signaling the beginning of a new narrative which introduces the wives of Abram and Nahor, Sarai and Milcah (Gen. 11:29-30), and tells of Terah's death (Gen. 11:32). Terah's death marks the shift from Abraham's historical family line to his future line in Genesis 12.

In the beginning of his story, Abraham is promised land, a blessing, and descendants who will become a great nation (Gen. 12:1-3).[24] The text is ambiguous here; it is unclear if this promise refers to direct descendants born to Abraham through his wife Sarah, who is described as infertile in Gen. 11:30, or if the reference is to descendants born through his kin: his brother Nahor, or his nephew Lot, for example. As the narrative progresses in Genesis, Abraham raises this point when he questions God in Gen. 15:3: "You have given me no offspring, and so a slave born in my house is to be heir." God responds in the negative, reassuring Abraham that "no one but your very own issue shall be your heir" (Gen. 15:4), which Abraham believes, making him righteous in the eyes of his God.

A solution to Abraham's lack of offspring is presented in Genesis 16 when Sarah gives her slave-girl Hagar to Abraham in order that Sarah may "obtain children by her" (Gen. 16:2). Abraham lies with Hagar and she falls pregnant, but Sarah expels her from the community after Hagar "looked with contempt on her mistress".[25] Quite what this means is unclear; suffice to say Hagar has harmed her mistress enough for Sarah to expel the only chance Abraham has had at this point to father a child.

Arguably, Abraham has thus far been central to the covenantal story between himself and God. Sarah has been by his side for the most part but is a secondary character, and Hagar is only introduced at the beginning of Genesis 16. This structure of power in the narrative alters in Genesis 16 as, arguably, Sarah leads the narrative in this chapter. It is her suggestion to use Hagar as a vessel for a child

24. J.N. Oswalt notes that these promises are "mundane" because they were "neither spiritual nor transcendent" but based on material things that Abraham potentially could have gotten by himself. He also suggests there is nothing "religious" about these promises which were made to Abraham seven times (see: 33–34 of his chapter). However, this misses the point, because a combination of descendants, land, and blessings from God would give Abraham's name immortality among the people, and is one of the factors which allowed "religious" traditions as we understand them today, to form around the father-figure. See: J.N. Oswalt, "Abraham's Experience of Yahweh: An Argument for the Historicity of the Patriarchal Narratives", in *Perspectives on Our Father Abraham: Essays in Honour of Marvin R. Wilson*, ed. S.A. Hunt (Grand Rapids, MI/Cambridge: William B. Eerdmans, 2010), 33–43.

25. Van Seters discusses this episode further in: J. van Seters, "The Problem of Childlessness in Near Eastern Law and the Patriarchs of Israel", *JBL* 87, no. 4 (1968): 401–8, here 403.

(Gen. 16:2), and it is her demand to banish Hagar (Gen. 16:6). Overarchingly, it is Sarah who takes control of ensuring Abraham becomes a father and fulfils God's covenantal promise, even though Abraham is the character most concerned with his lack of progeny (Gen. 15:3).

Sarah's initial plan for Hagar to fall pregnant is successful but, as noted above, Hagar's new status of the bearer of Abraham's child causes friction between her and Sarah, and Hagar is expelled into the wilderness. Here, she receives a divine visitation from a messenger of God, announcing that she will have a son called Ishmael because God has "heard" her plight (Gen. 16:11).[26] Abraham is not party to this declaration, and this scene marks Hagar as the first woman in biblical text to receive a divine proclamation from an angel of God. That it is Hagar, a lowly Egyptian slave-girl who receives reassurance and a promise from God concerning her son, and not Abraham—who is partly responsible for banishing her to certain death even though she carries his long-sought after progeny—indicates two things. Firstly, Hagar as mother is the parent concerned for the wellbeing of her child and herself, and requires comfort from God,[27] but Abraham as father is missing from both the text and the proclamation, which suggests he is seemingly unconcerned with the fate of both mother and child. This reflects the passivity of his response to Sarah expelling Hagar in 16:6, as well as his general passivity in resolving the problem of a lack of children despite covenantal promises (cf. Gen. 15:3). Secondly, this suggests that Ishmael's fate will never be the concern of Abraham the father but only of Hagar the mother, foreshadowing what is to come in Gen. 21:8-21. The expulsion of Hagar and Ishmael in Gen. 16:6-14 demonstrates that Hagar-the-mother is central to the survival of Abraham's child, whereas Abraham-the-father is accountable for the near-death of his unborn son. Hagar returns to the family and gives birth to Ishmael in Gen. 16:15, and Abraham becomes a father for the first time. Despite his reputation in the Hebrew Bible as being the ultimate father, he has not shown many fatherly attributes thus far.

The Hagar-Ishmael episode in Genesis 16 is somewhat reversed in Genesis 18. Whereas it was Hagar/mother who received the promise of a son from God without Abraham, in Genesis 18 it is Abraham/father who receives the promise from God that Sarah will bear him a son. This time Sarah/mother is not privy to God's promise; instead, she must eavesdrop at the door of her tent in order to hear that she will fall pregnant. In this episode, Abraham receives the promise from the visitors in silence, but Sarah is heard laughing, an action which foreshadows the name of her miracle child, Isaac (i.e., "he laughs").[28] Sarah's response of laughter juxtaposed against Abraham's silence suggests either her disbelief and Abraham's acceptance or Abraham's disbelief (he is too shocked to speak) and Sarah's joy—the text is unclear.

26. Ishmael's name is a play on words, often translated as "God hears", referencing that he heard Hagar's distress. See: N.M. Sarna ed., *The JPS Torah Commentary: Genesis* (Philadelphia: The Jewish Publication Society, 1994), 121.

27. Sarna, *Genesis*, 120–1.

28. Sarna, *Genesis*, 127.

Sarah becomes pregnant and gives birth to Isaac in Genesis 21 and, unlike Ishmael who is named by the divine messenger in Gen. 16:11, it is Abraham who names Isaac (Gen. 21:3). This action emphasizes the different treatment of each child by Abraham as father; one child is left to the care of God, the other is cared for under the protection of family with Abraham as head. The banishment of Hagar and Ishmael into the wilderness for a second time follows the birth of Isaac (Gen. 21:10), but not before Abraham displays emotion for the first time towards one of his children:

> [11]The matter was very distressing to Abraham on account of his son.[12] But God said to Abraham, "Do not be distressed because of the boy and because of your slave woman; whatever Sarah says to you, do as she tells you, for it is through Isaac that offspring shall be named for you.[13] As for the son of the slave women, I will make a nation of him also, because he is your offspring."

Abraham's distress at the thought of banishing Ishmael potentially demonstrates that an emotional bond has developed between father and son since the first time Hagar was cast out while carrying her child.[29] He is now physically and psychologically unwilling to cast out his son, who he has seen grow up before his eyes. From a contemporary perspective, this suggests Abraham acts as a father to his children only after birth when they are able to interact with him, to play with him, to learn and to grow in front of him, but this bond appears to be either non-existent or much weaker while his children are in utero. However, through the lens of high infant and female mortality rates in antiquity, distance between unborn child and father could also suggest that Abraham did not develop a bond until he knew his child was born safely and healthily. In Gen. 21:12-13, God placates Abraham by promising him that Ishmael will thrive and become a great name if Abraham follows Sarah's instructions. This reassurance is enough to override any emotional distress Abraham is feeling, and he acquiesces to Sarah's demand, sending his son and his partner Hagar into the wilderness for a second time.

The display of emotion in that narrative contrasts with the infamously emotionless scene of the *Akedah* narrative in Genesis 22. Described by Erich Auerbach as "fraught with background",[30] God's command that Abraham sacrifice his son, "his only son, Isaac" (Gen. 22:2) is met with silence from Abraham and a

29. Sarna suggests that it is "fatherly love" and "moral considerations" which make Abraham hesitate in carrying out Sarah's orders. Sarna, *Genesis*, 147.

30. In Auerbach's comparison between Genesis 22 and the *Odyssey*, he describes the biblical text as a text which purposefully lacks details and emotions, in order to accumulate suspense as the reader progresses, as well as to encourage the reader to fit into the world of the Bible rather than fit the Bible into the reader's world. See: E. Auerbach, *Mimesis: The Representation of Reality in Western Literature*, trans. W.R. Trask (Princeton: Princeton University Press, 1953), esp. ch. 1, "Odysseus' Scar".

resolve to carry out the instruction. Many different interpretations of the *Akedah* have been written that cover whether or not Abraham was being tested, whether he knew God would intervene and not allow Isaac to be killed, as well as discussions on Isaac and Sarah's role in the narrative.[31] For the purposes of my argument, I draw upon it to highlight the disparity between Abraham's treatment of his sons to reveal how his reputation as a father developed from the texts of Genesis.

As noted in Gen. 21:10, Abraham is reluctant to expel his son for fear that he will not survive. In contrast, when God instructs Abraham to kill his remaining son in Genesis 22, Abraham shows no emotion but sets out to commit the act directly by his own hand. Finally, when the traumatic scenes in Genesis 22 culminate in a reprieve from God and a reiteration of the covenantal promises (Gen. 22:11-18), it appears that Abraham and Isaac go their separate ways, never appearing together again in the texts of Genesis from this point forth.[32] Viewed through the lens of trauma, it is fair to surmise that such an event would create an irreconcilable rift between father (and would-be killer) and son.

For the ancient reader as much as the modern reader of the Genesis texts, Abraham's inconsistency in the treatment of his sons creates an awkward and unflattering image of his foray into fatherhood. From a narratological perspective, there appears to be a lack of emotional bond between father and sons except for the single occasion in Gen. 21:11, which is quickly overridden, and there is no reason to suggest that his identity as father is contingent upon developing a relationship with his progeny.[33] This is further emphasized when his third partner

31. For example, see: Blenkinsopp, *Abraham: The Story of a Life*, in particular ch. 7, "In the Land of Moriah" (140–58 of his book); P. Trible, "Genesis 22: The Sacrifice of Sarah", in *Women in the Hebrew Bible: a Reader*, ed. A. Bach (New York: Routledge, 1999), 271–90; G.W. Coats, "Abraham's Sacrifice of Faith: A Form-Critical Study of Genesis 22", *Interpretation: A Journal of Bible and Theology* 27, no. 4 (1973): 389–400, wherein Coats discusses how the theme of obedience often read into Genesis 22 can be understood as a reaffirmation of the covenantal promises through Isaac's salvation; H. Gossai, *Power and Marginality in the Abraham Narrative*, 2nd edn. (Eugene, OR: Pickwick Publications, 2010), 102–21.

32. Gen. 22:19: "So Abraham returned to his young men, and they arose and went together to Beer-sheba; and Abraham lived at Beer-sheba" suggests that Isaac did not return with Abraham, nor did he live with him. Similarly when Sarah's death is announced in Genesis 23, it is only Abraham who goes to mourn for her and attend to her burial; Isaac is missing from the story.

33. However, one could also argue that this claim presupposes an idea of fatherhood which is characterized by emotional connection, and it does not consider other elements such as providing food and income for the family or ensuring the safety of children, etc. I have not defined what I understand fatherhood (or indeed, motherhood) to be, purposefully so that the text might speak for itself with regards to the kind of father Abraham is portrayed to be, from a literary perspective. However, I understand this is a problematic approach as I, a modern reader, can only highlight literary aspects from a modern understanding of fatherhood.

Keturah gives birth to six more sons in Gen. 25:1-2, although this could reflect what the ancient author thinks is important for the reader to know, rather than presenting the reader with a more complete picture of Abraham as father.

Here, the biblical text is no more than a short genealogical note and an explanation that before Abraham died, he "gave all he had" to Isaac, but to the sons of his concubines he gave gifts and sent them away from "his son", Isaac (Gen. 25:5-6). It is Ishmael and Isaac who bury Abraham,[34] but again the biblical text suggests no emotion connected with the event. To summarize, Abraham's reputation of "father" is based on confusing interactions with his children, and a difficult relationship which does not appear to be typically that of a father who is good to, or who cares for, his children. This suggests his legacy of father is not about his emotional or physical capabilities, but something else entirely.

Mothers in Genesis

Of Abraham's three wives/partners, Sarah is given the most space in the texts of Genesis. This is not particularly surprising given that she experienced the longest relationship with her husband out of the three. We do not know Sarah's age when she marries Abraham, and though we know she dies at the age of 127, the text is unclear with regards to whether or not Abraham and Sarah still lived together at the point of her death (Gen. 23:1-2).

Sarah's introduction to the reader is as Abraham's wife, who is infertile (Gen. 11:30). The text does not indicate if she is troubled by her lack of childlessness, nor does it suggest Abraham is particularly concerned either. As previously discussed, some thought is given to the issue in Gen. 16:1-2 when Sarah decides that her slave-girl Hagar could be the one to provide Abraham with an heir, an endeavor which is, as we have seen, not altogether successful in how the situation concludes.[35]

34. The two sons burying their father is another "matter-of-fact" event, which likely took place because the responsibility and duty to bury one's family fell on the shoulders of the children. See J.A. Callaway, who discusses burial rituals in relation to family duties in ancient Palestine in more depth: J.A. Callaway, "Burials in Ancient Palestine: From the Stone Age to Abraham", *The Biblical Archaeologist* 26, no. 3 (1963): 73–91. One could suggest that by bequeathing all of his possessions to Isaac, Abraham is demonstrating some affection to his favored son; after all, there is some suggestion that inheritance laws in ancient Israel stated that the firstborn son should legally acquire the estate of their father (see for example: E.W. Davies, "The Inheritance of the Firstborn in Israel and the Ancient Near East", *Journal of Semitic Studies* 38, no. 2 (1993): 175–91. Abraham disregards this law by ignoring his firstborn Ishmael and favoring his second born, Isaac. This is a decision which would normally have been made only if the firstborn son had "committed a serious offence, usually against his own family" (Davies, "Inheritance of the Firstborn", 191). See also: Stavrakopoulou, *Land of our Fathers*, particularly chs 1 and 2.

The practice of using a slave or servant in place of a woman unable to have children was common practice in ancient Near Eastern laws, as demonstrated by scholars such as J. van Seters and N. Sarna, for example.[36] Any resulting children would belong to the slave-owner and though the status of the slave would be elevated if she bore sons (daughters did not achieve the same status), it could just as easily be lowered if the slave started to act as equal to her mistress. In Genesis 16, then, Ishmael would belong to Sarah, and according to those laws she would be his legal mother.

The biblical text does not recognize this in any capacity: "Hagar bore Abram a son; and Abram named his son, whom Hagar bore, Ishmael" (Gen. 16:5). Sarah has little to do with this birth or the child, and indeed is not mentioned in association with Ishmael at any point in Genesis, except for when she observes him playing with Isaac (Gen. 21:9). She has no motherly feeling towards him, despite the fact her husband now has a legitimate heir to the covenantal promises. When Sarah gives birth to Isaac, she acts to prevent Ishmael from sharing in any of Abraham's inheritance by again asking Abraham to cast out Ishmael and his mother.[37] Hagar does exhibit emotion toward her son, casting him under a bush because she cannot bear to watch him die (Gen. 21:15-16), and when they are both saved, she continues to care for him and finds him a wife from her own country (Gen. 21:20-21).

Sarah's experience of mothering Isaac is similarly demonstrative of love, nurture, and emotion. She celebrates with joy, reflected in her son's name, and in disbelief at finally becoming a mother (Gen. 21:7). She protects Isaac's future by asking Abraham to cast out Hagar and Ishmael (Gen. 21:10) and God agrees with the matriarch, marking Isaac as the successor to Abraham's covenant with God. Though no other word is written on Sarah's relationship with Isaac, these short texts arguably demonstrate a parental connection demonstrably stronger than Abraham's bond with either of his sons.

Keturah is the anomaly in the characterization of mothers; to her, no narrative is given only to say that she was taken as a wife, and she bore Abraham another six sons (Gen. 25:1-2). There is one other short verse which suggests Keturah's role of parent was more enduring than Abraham's to their sons: following the end of a short genealogical list, the writer has concluded "All these were the children of Keturah" (Gen. 25:4b). Similarly, in 1 Chron. 1:32 Abraham's sons by Keturah are

35. Gen. 16:2. J. van Seters has argued that this narrative is not concerned with providing Abraham with an heir, because any child born through a slave belongs to Sarah: "the wife of the patriarch gives her maid to her husband in order that she herself may have children through her maid" (p. 403). Van Seters continues that Abraham's need for an heir obscures this stipulation, but is clear that the child would not belong to the patriarch. Van Seters, "The Problem of Childlessness", 401–8.

36. Van Seters, "The Problem of Childlessness", 403; Sarna, *Genesis*, 146–7.

37. Sarna suggests Sarah is asking Abraham to grant freedom to Hagar and Ishmael so that they forfeit any right to inherit his estate, a legal clause in the laws of Lipit-Ishtar. Sarna, *Genesis*, 147.

described as "the sons of his concubines" suggesting Keturah was the main parent of her children.

Parenting in Genesis

Abraham's actions, emotions, and behavior as a father in the texts of Genesis do not suggest he was regarded as a particularly good, loyal, or responsible father. His reputation in the rest of the Hebrew Bible, as we will see, suggests he is remembered particularly as a model father figure, regardless of his arguably poor relationships with his own children. There exists, then, a discrepancy between Abraham's characterization of fatherhood discussed above, and the reputation he develops later. In contrast, narratives of motherhood in Genesis suggest that each of Abraham's wives/partners *are* characterized as steady, possibly loving mothers, though they are given far less space in the text which makes it difficult to draw out their characters fully. It follows then, that Abraham is not remembered as a model father because of his actions in life, but because of the legacy given to him through the covenantal promises with God. Likewise, Abraham's wives/partners were not part of those covenantal promises, and their reputations as good mothers in life are not as important for the future destiny of Abraham's lands, territories, and descendants.

Parenting after Genesis

As noted above, Abraham's name appears only forty-four times outside of the book of Genesis, and the majority of these references are to the patriarchal triad of Abraham, Isaac, and Jacob. As Römer points out: "the triad is used to characterize YHWH as the 'God of Abraham, Isaac and Jacob (Israel)'",[38] or as an "allusion to the divine land promise" made to Abraham and inherited by the succeeding patriarchs.[39] The use of Abraham's name in Exod. 2:24, for example, creates a connection between the covenantal promises in Genesis, and the plight of the Israelites in Egypt—God remembers the Israelites because of Abraham and his descendants. Similarly, in 1 Kgs. 18:36, the prophet Elijah is the one to remind God of his earlier promises by naming him "God of Abraham, Isaac and Israel". The invocation of Abraham's name in these passages serves as a connection between the ancestral father and his millions of descendants, but does not appeal to the fatherliness of Abraham's character.

Römer is among a group of scholars who make the link between Abraham's memory in the Hebrew Bible and the date of the texts which recall him.[40] He

38. Römer, *Abraham Traditions in the Book of Genesis*, 177.

39. Ibid.

40. Ibid., 159–60, 177; See also H.G. Williamson, "Abraham in Exile", in *Perspectives on Our Father Abraham: Essays in Honor of Marvin R. Wilson*, ed. S.A. Hunt (Michigan: Wm. B. Eerdmans, 2010), 68–80.

argues that Abraham's name appears in biblical texts which can be dated to the exilic period. As such, communities exiled from the land promised to Abraham appealed to God to remember his covenant with their "father" Abraham and restore them to their territories. His name is not recalled as frequently (or at all) in texts written pre- or post-exile, because God had already remembered his people, though there are of course exceptions to this.[41] Hugh G. M. Williamson develops this premise noting that it was not only exiled communities who called Abraham's name in times of need, but also the communities who remained in Judah during the exile who needed "reassurance and reorientation".[42] I will turn now to an examination of these texts to discuss this in more detail.

Ezek. 33:24 is potentially attributed to the non-deported Judean population during the exile, and it can be read as either a call upon God to restore their land to the Judean population by expelling the Edomites, who occupied it during the years in exile, or as a message to those in exile that they are not the true heirs of Abraham because they left the land promised to him.[43] Clearly, the collective social remembrance of Abraham's name in this passage is not linked to his fatherhood, but to his claim on the land promised to him by God in Genesis: "Abraham was only one man, yet he got possession of the land" (Ezek. 33:24a). The land is claimed by Abraham, and, as descendants of their patriarch, the Judean population may claim that land in his name. Though there is an indirect reference to Abraham as father through the reminder of the text—that the population in Ezek. 33:24 descends from him—his name is used to reinforce the patriarchal ideology concerning land ownership *through* patrilineal descent and physical occupation, rather than through descent alone.

Hendel calls this a counter memory of Abraham; that is, the recasting of a memory which refutes, revises, or even replaces an accepted memory of the past,

41. Abraham's name appears in post-Exilic literature, including: 1 Chron. 1:1; 1:27-28; 1:32; 1:34; 16:16; 19:18; 2 Chron. 20:7; 30:6; Neh. 9:7. Examples of pre-Exilic literature include proto-Isa. 29:22 and potentially, Mic. 7:20.

42. Williamson, "Abraham in Exile", 68. Examples here include: Ezek. 33:24: "Mortal, the inhabitants of these waste places in the land of Israel keep saying, 'Abraham was only one man, yet he got possession of the land'; but we are many; the land is surely given us to possess."; Jer. 33:26: "would I reject the offspring of Jacob and of my servant David and not choose any of his descendants as rulers over the offspring of Abraham, Isaac, and Jacob. For I will restore their fortunes and have mercy upon them." There is a suggestion that Jer. 33:26 is a late addition to the literature, potentially meaning it is a post-exilic insertion designed to reassure the exilic community by invoking Abraham; and Ps. 105:6: "O offspring of his servant Abraham, children of Jacob his chosen ones", vv. 8-9: "He is mindful of his covenant forever, of the word that he commanded, for a thousand generations, the covenant that he made with Abraham, his sworn promise to Isaac," and v. 42: "For he remembered his whole promise, and Abraham, his servant."

43. Römer, "Abraham Traditions in the Hebrew Bible", 162–4; Hendel, *Remembering Abraham*, 42.

usually as a means of recasting a memory in light of a new political or social agenda.[44] In the case of Ezek. 33:24, the Judeans who remain in the land after the destruction of Jerusalem reconfigure their collective memory of Abraham to claim that it is no longer enough to be descended from Abraham's genealogical line; one must also be resident in the land to be considered a legitimate child of Abraham.

There is a similar theme in Jer. 33:26. The motif in this passage is primarily concerned with the restoration of Israel, both physically (i.e. a rebuilding of the city), politically, and religiously.[45] In this verse, Abraham's name is remembered by God, who uses it to remind his exiled people (and arguably, himself), that their destiny is rooted in an ancient covenant that he made between himself and the patriarch.[46] C. Lombaard calls the inclusion of Abraham and his succeeding patriarchs in this verse an unexpected occurrence,[47] arguing that the text brings together separate but "parallel-running" theological streams, including patriarchal kinship, covenantal promise, the kingship of David, and elements of Creation theology.[48] Lombaard suggests that Jer. 33:26 is a late addition to the biblical text, possibly making it post-exilic. If this is the case, then the inclusion of the patriarch in this verse is potentially designed to carry over the covenantal blessings received by Abraham into the kingship of David, and the priesthood.[49]

Jer. 33:26, then, is not a recollection of Abraham as father, but a counter memory of Abraham as the receiver of a blessing from God, which must be carried over and married into the political state of his descendants in post-exilic Judea. Brueggemann writes that "the oracle appeals to memory and tradition in order to assert a theological reality that overrides present historical circumstance",[50] implying that the tradition of Abraham as father is the key to overcoming the political crisis. Invoking both Abraham and David in the same speech is a powerful political move which speaks to each man's relationship with God, rather than their status as either father or leader (respectively).[51]

44. Hendel, *Remembering Abraham*, 41.

45. R.P. Carroll, *From Chaos to Covenant: Use of Prophecy in the Book of Jeremiah* (London: SCM, 1981), 207.

46. W. Brueggemann, *A Commentary on Jeremiah: Exile and Homecoming* (Grand Rapids, MI: William B. Eerdmans, 1998), 321–22; See also S.A. Adams, *Baruch and the Epistle of Jeremiah: A Commentary Based on the Texts in Codex Vaticanus* (SCS; Leiden: Brill, 2014), 89.

47. C. Lombaard, "The Strange Case of the Patriarchs in Jeremiah 33:26", *Acta Theologica* 35, no. 2 (2015): 36–49, here 36.

48. Ibid., 44–5.

49. Ibid., 45.

50. Brueggemann, *Commentary on Jeremiah*, 322.

51. One might also suggest that Matt. 1:1 invokes the names of both Abraham and David to discuss messianic ideas, again drawing on the special relationship between them and God to highlight themes of the chosen people, rather than drawing on Abraham's status as father or David's status as leader.

Psalm 105 does not follow the trend of calling upon the memory of Abraham to reinforce claims on land and covenantal blessings. Marty E. Stevens calls Psalm 105 "the *cliff notes* of the Torah", arguing that the psalm is concerned with reciting God's actions towards his people, including the Abrahamic covenant.[52] Ted Hildebrandt notes that it is unique among psalms, being the only one to refer to Abraham directly (as opposed to Psalm 47 which mentions the "God of Abraham" in v. 9).[53] A lack of reference to David or Zion is also troubling to Hildebrandt, who argues that the inclusion of Abraham reconnects the people of Israel to the patriarchs during the troubling time of the exilic period. Like those in exile and the disparate few who remained in Judea, the patriarchs were "few in number when they first came into the land; they arrived after wandering from one nation to another; and they were protected by God from the kings who already occupied the land."[54] The exiled/remaining communities could identify with parts of Abraham's history, which offered them hope and reassurance for their uncertain futures.

Though Hildebrandt also suggests that Psalm 105 is a reaffirmation of the Abrahamic covenant by God (for example, the word "land" is repeated ten times in the psalm,[55] calling to mind that element of the promise between Abraham and God), the main assertion is that Abraham was used as a model to help guide the diasporic communities through their exile until they could return to their land. Though still not recalling Abraham's memory of his fatherhood, Psalm 105 is concerned with reminding God of the covenantal promise of land, but it seems the poet-writer was most concerned with recalling Abraham's history as a model/guide for moving forward. Erik Haglund supports this concept, noting that Abraham's whole history is recalled in Psalm 105, as opposed to just his name. Further, the following themes can be read from the psalm, all of which serve to reinforce the connection between Abraham and land: 1) proclaiming God's deeds to his people; 2) reflections on God's deeds; 3) memories and traditions of God's deeds; and 4) a reminder to keep the commandments.[56]

52. M.E. Stevens, "Between Text and Sermon: Psalm 105", *Interpretation: A Journal of Bible and Theology* 57, no. 2 (2003): 187–9.

53. T. Hildebrandt, "A Song of Our Father Abraham: Psalm 105", in *Perspectives on Our Father Abraham: Essays in Honor of Marvin R. Wilson*, ed. S.A. Hunt (Michigan: Wm. B. Eerdmans, 2010), 44–67, here 45–6. Ps. 47:9 claims that non-Jewish nobles gather as the God of Abraham's people. The author did not use Abraham's name leading up to this, nor did they need to use Abraham's name in this verse, so one could argue that invoking Abraham's name here is meaningful, especially in its ethnic implication.

54. Hildebrandt, "A Song of Our Father Abraham", 61.

55. Ibid., 58.

56. E. Haglund, *Historical Motifs in the Psalms* (Coniectanea Biblica, Old Testament Series 23; Uppsala: CWK Gleerup, 1984), 22–3.

The use of Abraham's name in post-exilic texts is mostly to reinforce and claim covenantal themes of land ownership through patrilineal descent. Abraham as father is a symbolic invocation rather than a genealogical affair.[57] Patrilineal descent is most important in these texts, because it establishes the legitimacy of the father and rules out the idea that the child does not belong to the father. Further, matrilineal descent would make the mother too important in the text, potentially de-legitimizing and removing power from the father.[58]

This androcentric concept is at work in the above texts where Abraham is recalled as symbolic father, but the names of the mothers are not mentioned, expect on two occasions. Sarah is mentioned in Isa. 51:2, and Keturah appears twice in 1 Chron. 1:32-33. In the latter instance, possession of Abraham and Keturah's children belongs to Keturah as indicated in the language of the texts of Genesis and 1 Chronicles: "All these were the *children of Keturah* (Gen. 25:4); 'The *sons of Keturah*, Abraham's concubine: *she bore* Zimran [. . .]' (1 Chron. 1:32); 'All these were the *descendants of Keturah*' (1 Chron. 1:33).[59] The word-choice here indicates to the reader that the children belonged to Keturah which means they are not 'right' children—i.e. they are not legitimate because they cannot inherit Abraham's status as patriarch/become party to the covenantal promises—because Keturah was not the 'right' mother; that status belongs to Sarah alone (Gen. 18:15-19).[60] By aligning the children with Keturah rather than Abraham in this way, there can be no questions raised as to who the true heir of the covenantal promises is.

However, the inclusion of Keturah in 1 Chron. 1:32-33 signifies that God has kept the promise of descendants with Abraham. Even though Isaac (born through the "right" mother Sarah) is the only heir, Abraham has other children who will procreate to expand his lineage. Along with Isaac and Ishmael, Keturah and Abraham's children are evidence that the promise is being delivered upon, but the continued emphasis on Keturah as parent means they cannot interfere with patrilineal claims on land. That part of the promise belongs to Isaac alone. Invocation to Keturah, then, is another way of claiming the covenantal promise by the righteous heir as opposed to the wrong descendants, and links this passage with themes discussed above.

Isa. 51:2, which is the only time Sarah is mentioned outside of Genesis in the Hebrew Bible, is unusual when considered against the above passages. Williamson suggests that the purpose of this (potentially)[61] post-exilically-authored chapter is

57. One could argue that this idea is represented through the ritual of circumcision which physically marks the male as a descendant of Abraham and an adherent to the covenantal promise of Gen. 17:11, but I would argue it does not necessarily mean the male is biologically descended from Abraham.

58. Exum, *Fragmented Women*, 84.

59. Emphasis my own.

60. Exum, *Fragmented Women*, 81–2.

61. Römer rightly suggests there are divergent claims among scholars about whether or not Isa. 51 is a post-exilic text. Römer, "Abraham Traditions in the Hebrew Bible", 164.

not concerned with claims to land; rather, it is concerned with the development of the community of Israel.[62] Williamson suggests that the restoration of Zion (the people, not the land) and "the formation of the character of the community is also prominent"[63] in this text, and that is the reason Abraham and Sarah are remembered. Interestingly, there are also intertextual connections with Ezek. 33:23-24; each of the texts present Abraham as "one" from whom "many" descend. But Römer proposes that Isa. 51:2-3 serves as a correction to Ezek. 33:23-24 in the way it suggests overcoming conflict between the remaining Judean population and the exiled communities of the diaspora.[64]

The solution to the conflict lies in developing the community, an action that begins with looking "to Abraham your father and to Sarah who bore you" (Isa. 51:2). The invocation to Sarah in this passage, then, is about reinforcing the idea of the "right" descendants who are born through Sarah's bloodline because she was the recipient of God's covenantal promise, and she alone of the mothers can deliver legitimate children.[65] True descendants of Abraham must come from Sarah's lineage as well, and only in that genealogical line can a true community develop and claim the promises granted to them from God.

Conclusions

In the introduction to this chapter, I argued that Abraham is recalled throughout the Hebrew Bible to reinforce patriarchal ideologies concerning land ownership and patrilineal descent, rather than as a model father figure, which is what he is most remembered for in the texts of Genesis. I also noted that the lack of references to Abraham's partners in the Hebrew Bible leads to a quandary for readers of the texts, because the memory of the mothers is so thoroughly erased and subsequently forgotten that it can appear that Abraham's descendants are "motherless" children.

The texts I have discussed above support the idea that Abraham's name is remembered mostly in connection with claims to the promised land, and the title of father is used to suggest that those claiming the land are descended from Abraham, as his children. Likewise, invocations to the patriarch are concerned with establishing the identity of those who call his name; a signifier that they are the "right" descendants. I have not considered in-depth any texts where God recalls Abraham (such as Exod. 2:24), but there is a general consensus among scholars that these instances are about God reminding himself or his people of the ancient covenant he once made with Abraham. In this respect, Abraham's name is another way of referring to the covenantal promises made in Genesis, not a remembrance of a father-figure.

62. Williamson, "Abraham in Exile", 76.

63. Ibid.

64. Ibid., 167.

65. Exum, *Fragmented Women*, 81–3.

The connection between Abraham, covenant, and especially land is of primary importance to his descendants who wish to claim the land promised to them; the promise that Abraham will have many descendants is already being fulfilled and is of lesser importance than physical space. Claiming this space through Abraham's name turns his memory into a metaphor for a geographical location, an idea that manifests itself when Jacob is re-named Israel (Gen. 32:28; 35:10) and is remembered dually as Jacob/Israel throughout the Hebrew Bible (e.g. Exod. 32:13). Abraham as metaphor for land does not require the mothers, because it is a conceptual idea created in a community who practiced patrilineal descent, a practice which does not require mothers for anything other than giving birth since the children are traced through the father's line.

However, as we have seen, there is such a thing as a "right" and "wrong" mother, and the reader is alerted to this both through the fact that the mothers of Abraham's children are mostly erased from the Hebrew texts, and because, when they are recalled, it is with the intention of highlighting the correct and incorrect lineages. The author's explicit word choices in 1 Chron. 1:32-33, which suggest that Keturah's children primarily belong to her (i.e. not relating them to Abraham in a clear line) indicate that the sons of Keturah are not true descendants of the covenant because Keturah is not the mother who was part of God's promise in Gen. 18:10. Sarah received that promise, and only a son born from her can inherit Abraham's status and promises. Invoking Sarah's name in Isa. 51:2 alludes to this proper lineage by suggesting descendants born of Abraham and Sarah must remember their history and build their community again post-exile. Thus, the lack of attention paid to the mothers in the Abrahamic narratives impacts how the reader understands the figure of Abraham-the-father; his name is moved away from concepts of fatherhood and fatherliness, which are attributed to him in Genesis, and instead, it becomes a metaphor for covenantal promises—mostly in terms of land—made to the patriarch all those centuries before.[66]

66. With thanks to Sean A. Adams and Sarah Nicholson for their comments on earlier drafts of this chapter.

Chapter 2

ABRAHAM IN THE OLD TESTAMENT APOCRYPHA*

Géza G. Xeravits

The patriarch Abraham is one of the most pre-eminent figures of the Old Testament. The "first Jew," beneficiary of God's promises and covenant is an exciting personality already according to the primary epical source where he first appears (Genesis). It is no wonder that later biblical texts and the authors of the literature of early Judaism were heavily interested in Abraham, and developed a rich tradition around him.[1] This contribution intends to explore texts that belong to a rather artificial category, the Deuterocanonical books or the Old Testament Apocrypha. These late Second Temple period writings do not appear in the Hebrew Bible, but found their way into the Septuagint and its parent versions.[2]

The evidence might be categorized into four distinct groups. The only text of the first group, Sirach 44:19-21, is a complex unit that draws on various themes. Texts belonging to the second group center on the story of the *Akedah*, the "binding of Isaac" (Genesis 22). The third category has the common *Leitmotif* "inheritance of the land," whereas the fourth group does not have a central unifying theme.

* The author is indebted to the editors of the volume for their helpful comments on the first draft of this paper.

1. R.S. Hendel, *Remembering Abraham: Culture, Memory, and History in the Hebrew Bible* (Oxford: Oxford University Press, 2005), 31–43; M. Goodman, G.H. van Kooten and J.T.A.G.M. van Ruiten, eds., *Abraham, the Nations, and the Hagarites: Jewish, Christian, and Islamic Perspectives on Kinship with Abraham* (TBN 13; Leiden: Brill, 2010); J.D. Levenson, *Inheriting Abraham: The Legacy of the Patriarch in Judaism, Christianity, and Islam* (Princeton: Princeton University Press, 2012); G.A. Anderson and J.S. Kaminsky, eds., *The Call of Abraham: Essays on the Election of Israel in Honor of Jon D. Levenson* (CJAS 19; Notre Dame: University of Notre Dame Press, 2013).

2. See e.g., L.T. Stuckenbruck, "Apocrypha and Septuagint. Exploring the Christian Canon", in *Die Septuaginta und das frühe Christentum—The Septuagint and Christian Origins*, eds. S. Caulley et al. (WUNT 277; Tübingen: Mohr Siebeck, 2011), 177–204.

Sirach 44:19-22

I begin this chapter with the most complicated witness, the book of Ben Sira. This book—collecting together rich and multifaceted traditions of early Judaism—was written in Hebrew at the beginning of the second century BCE and was translated into Greek by the author's grandson in 132 BCE, according to the Prologue of the Greek version.[3] The book has two main parts: the first is a collection of sapiential sayings (chapters 1–43), while the second is a detailed *encomium* of the high priest Simeon that evokes many important figures from Israel's past (the Praise of the Ancestors, chs 44–50).[4] The latter section contains a passage on Abraham.[5] Below, I quote the entire passage according to the longer, Greek version[6]:

> Abraham was the great father of a multitude of nations,
> and no one has been found like him in glory.
> [20]He kept the law of the Most High,
> and entered into a covenant with him;
> he certified the covenant in his flesh,
> and when he was tested he proved faithful.
> [21]Therefore He [God] assured him with an oath
> that the nations would be blessed through his offspring;
> that he would make him as numerous as the dust of the earth,
> and exalt his offspring like the stars,
> and give them an inheritance from sea to sea
> and from the river to the ends of the earth.

This passage alludes to various texts from Genesis.[7] The opening title "father of a multitude of nations" (πατὴρ πλήθους ἐθνῶν) is taken from Gen. 17:4, the story of the covenant of circumcision between God and Abraham. The idea of covenant

3. On the dating, see e.g., P.W. Skehan and A.A. Di Lella, *The Wisdom of Ben Sira* (AB 39; New York: Doubleday, 1987), 8–16.

4. On the latter, see, e.g. T.R. Lee, *Studies in the Form of Sirach 44–50* (SBLDS 75; Atlanta, GA: SBL, 1986); O. Mulder, *Simon the High Priest in Sirach 50: An Exegetical Study of the Significance of Simon the High Priest as Climax to the Praise of the Fathers in Ben Sira's Concept of the History of Israel* (JSJSup 78; Leiden: Brill, 2003).

5. See P.C. Beentjes, "Ben Sira 44:19-23—The Patriarchs: Text, Tradition, Theology", in *Studies in the Book of Ben Sira*, eds. G.G. Xeravits et al. (JSJSup 127; Leiden: Brill, 2008), 209–28; B.C. Gregory, "Abraham as the Jewish Ideal: Exegetical Traditions in Sirach 44:19-21", *CBQ* 70 (2008): 66–81; M. Marttila, *Foreign Nations in the Wisdom of Ben Sira: A Jewish Sage between Opposition and Assimilation* (DCLS 13; Berlin: de Gruyter, 2012), 165-71.

6. The Hebrew MS B does not have a parallel text for bicolon 21cd. For the differences in the textual traditions, see Beentjes, "Ben Sira 44:19-23", 209-12, 227.

7. Beentjes, "Ben Sira 44:19-23", 215-16.

appears in the present context of Sirach twice, in cola 44:20bc. Colon 20c continues the allusion to Genesis 17, when speaking about the bodily sign of the covenant ("he certified the covenant in his flesh," ἐν σαρκὶ αὐτοῦ ἔστησεν διαθήκην), because this chapter speaks about the circumcision. The more general formulation of 44:20b could refer either to Genesis 17 or to Genesis 15—both chapters deal with the issue of the covenant. The fact that Abraham is called "faithful" (πιστός) in colon 20d might suggest the impact of the latter passage, for the verb "believe" (πιστεύω) is its *Leitwort*.

Colon 20d of this text reminds the reader of the *Akedah*, when alluding to Abraham's test ("when he was tested he proved faithful," ἐν πειρασμῷ εὑρέθη πιστός). The creative combination of elements from Genesis 22 ("during testing," ἐν πειρασμῷ) and Genesis 15 ("faithful," πιστός) is worth noting, for this aspect places the *Akedah* into the perspective of covenant. Ben Sira is thus the first witness of a longer interpretative tradition, which will be seen later in this chapter (1 Macc. 2:52), and which occurs also in the New Testament (see Jas. 2:22-24).[8] Most of 44:21 alludes to the continuation of the *Akedah* story, in some cases quoting verbatim Gen. 22:16-18.

Gen. 22:16-18	Sir. 44:21a-d
By myself I have sworn, says the Lord: Because you have done this, and have not withheld your son, your only son, [17] I will indeed bless you, and I will make your offspring as numerous (πληθύνων πληθυνῶ τὸ σπέρμα) as the stars (ὡς τοὺς ἀστέρας) of heaven and as the sand that is on the seashore. And your offspring shall possess the gate of their enemies, [18] and by your offspring shall gain blessing (ἐνευλογηθήσονται ἐν τῷ σπέρματί) all the nations (ἔθνη) of the earth for themselves, because you have obeyed my voice.	Therefore He assured him with an oath that the nations would be blessed through his offspring (ἐνευλογηθῆναι ἔθνη ἐν σπέρματι αὐτοῦ); that he would make him as numerous (πληθῦναι) as the dust of the earth, and exalt his offspring (τὸ σπέρμα) like the stars (ὡς ἄστρα).

The idea of Abraham's numerous offspring resonates with texts from the "inheritance" group (below), and the closure of verse 21 develops further this theme. The verb "inherit" ([κατα]κληρονομέω) recalls the vocabulary of Gen. 22:17, but what follows is in fact nearly exactly borrowed from Ps. 71:8 (MT 72:8),

8. E. Kessler, *Bound by the Bible: Jews, Christians and the Sacrifice of Isaac* (Cambridge: Cambridge University Press, 2004), 38, 60–62. Late antique Jewish and Christian exegetical traditions on this chapter are treated in G. Stemberger, "Genesis 15 in Rabbinic and Patristic Interpretation", in *The Exegetical Encounter between Jews and Christians in Late Antiquity*, eds. E. Grypeou et al. (JCPS 18; Leiden: Brill, 2009), 143–62.

a psalm which relates the duties of the ideal king and his splendid rule over Israel and the nations.[9] The use of a royal psalm with reference to Abraham shows another interesting exegetical combination of different sources. Although nothing explicitly indicates that Ben Sira would interpret Abraham or his descendants in connection with the idea of kingship, here again the impact of Genesis 17 is probable.[10] In 17:6 God promises to Abraham that "kings shall come from you" (βασιλεῖς ἐκ σοῦ ἐξελεύσονται). The image of Abraham as a progenitor of rulers is complemented here by the view that he himself was a kind of royal personage. In the Septuagint version of Genesis, this view is reinforced by a reading of 23:6. Here Abraham intends to acquire a burying place for Sarah, and the sons of Chet label him: "a king from a god among us" (βασιλεὺς παρὰ θεοῦ εἶ σὺ ἐν ἡμῖν). This feature reflects the idea of the exaltation of figures of the past, a common trend in Second Temple Jewish literature.[11]

The Akedah *Group*

Abraham's sacrifice, as related in Genesis 22, is one of the most important biblical legends. After his extreme obedience to God—which might have included the sacrifice of his beloved son, Isaac—Abraham got the promise of numerous offspring.[12]

In the Book of Judith, written during the Hasmonaean period,[13] chapter 8 contains the introductory address of the heroine. In her speech Judith warns the leaders of Bethulia to trust in God, and do not surrender the city to the enemy. She rebukes them not to test God ("who are you to put God to the test today," τίνες ἐστὲ ὑμεῖς οἳ ἐπειράσατε τὸν θεὸν ἐν τῇ ἡμέρᾳ τῇ σήμερον: Jdt. 8:12). At the end of her address she evokes the example of the forefathers (Jdt. 8:25-27). The key term of this closing exhortation is, again, "to test" (πειράζω); nevertheless, in this case, it is God who tests the patriarchs. In Judith's approach, God deserves thanks for testing humans ("let us give thanks to the Lord our God, who is putting us to the test as he did our ancestors," εὐχαριστήσωμεν κυρίῳ τῷ θεῷ ἡμῶν ὃς πειράζει ἡμᾶς

9. See, e.g. F.L. Hossfeld and E. Zenger, *Psalms 2: A Commentary on Psalms 51–100* (Hermeneia; Minneapolis: Fortress Press, 2005), 202–20.

10. Gregory, "Abraham as the Jewish Ideal", 78–79.

11. In this connection it is enough to mention Moses, who is also presented with royal treats in a number of sources. See W.A. Meeks, *The Prophet-King: Moses Traditions and the Johannine Christology* (NovTSup 14; Leiden: Brill, 1967), *passim*; on related issues in the Pentateuch, see D. Matthews, *Royal Motifs in the Pentateuchal Portrayal of Moses* (LHBOTS 571; London: T & T Clark, 2012).

12. On the *Akedah* see e.g., E. Noort and E.J.C. Tigchelaar, eds., *The Sacrifice of Isaac: The Aqedah (Genesis 22) and Its Interpretations* (TBN 4; Leiden: Brill, 2002); Kessler, *Bound by the Bible*; Levenson, *Inheriting Abraham*, 66–112.

13. D.L. Gera, *Judith* (CEJL; Berlin: de Gruyter, 2014), 26–44.

καθὰ καὶ τοὺς πατέρας ἡμῶν: Jdt. 8:25). Judith's speech thus uses the idea of testing as a kind of frame, which creates a sharp contrast between her contemporaries (who test God in their ignorance) and the patriarchs (who remained steadfast in testing).

The appearance of Abraham and Isaac is remarkable in this context. Jdt. 8:26a reads "Remember what he did with Abraham, and how he tested Isaac." Concerning Abraham, the verse uses a rather neutral verb "to do" (ποιέω), which is specified by the previous verse "to test" (πειράζω), whereas concerning Isaac it uses the verb "to test"; however, in Genesis this verb does not refer to Isaac. The author of Judith interprets thus the *Akedah* as a test for both patriarchs, attributing an active role to Isaac, too.

The next source is 1 Maccabees, written at the end of the second century.[14] 1 Macc. 2 recounts Mattathias' deeds, testament (2:49-68),[15] and death. In the course of his final exhortation, the dying hero enumerates the example of outstanding personalities from Israel's past, among others, Abraham (1 Macc. 2:52): "Was not Abraham found faithful when tested, and it was reckoned to him as righteousness?" Similarly to what was said in Ben Sira, but in a more eloquent manner, the author of this verse interestingly combines elements of two distinct biblical sources. At the first part of the sentence, the term "testing" (ἐν πειρασμῷ) obviously refers to Genesis 22. Immediately after this, reference is made to Abraham's faith ("found faithful," εὑρέθη πιστός)—a concept absent in the *Akedah*—but, instead, it creates an allusion to another quintessential episode of the Abraham cycle, viz. Gen. 15:1-6, of which the faith of the patriarch is one of the key concepts: "and Abram believed God" (καὶ ἐπίστευσεν Αβραμ τῷ θεῷ: Gen. 15:6a). This impression is verified by the fact that the second half of the sentence contains a direct quotation of Gen. 15:6b: "and it was reckoned to him as righteousness" (καὶ ἐλογίσθη αὐτῷ εἰς δικαιοσύνην: 1 Macc. 2:52b).

This combination of separate stories from Genesis is highly creative. In Gen. 15:1-6 Abraham's problem is that he does not have a child; he labels himself "childless" (ἄτεκνος, 15:2), and complains that God did not give him descendants (ἐπειδὴ ἐμοὶ οὐκ ἔδωκας σπέρμα, 15:3). Following Abraham's doubt, a divine

14. A. Momigliano, "The Date of the 1st Book of Maccabees", in *L'Italie préromaine et la Rome républicaine. Mélanges offerts à J. Heurgon* (Rome: École Française de Rome, 1976), 657–61; J.A. Goldstein, *I Maccabees* (AB 41; New York: Doubleday, 1976), 62–89; K. Berthelot, *In Search of the Promised Land?: The Hasmonean Dynasty Between Biblical Models and Hellenistic Diplomacy* (JAJSup 24; Göttingen: Vandenhoeck & Ruprecht 2017), 67–71.

15. T. Hieke, "The Role of Scripture in the Last Words of Mattathias (1 Macc 2:49-70)", in *The Books of the Maccabees. History, Theology, Ideology*, eds. G.G. Xeravits et al. (JSJSup 118; Leiden: Brill, 2007), 61–74; F.V. Reiterer, "Die Vergangenheit als Basis für die Zukunft. Mattatias' Lehre für seine Söhne aus der Geschichte in 1 Makk 2:52-60", in *The Books of the Maccabees. History, Theology, Ideology*, eds. G.G. Xeravits et al. (JSJSup 118; Leiden: Brill, 2007), 75–100.

speech displays a promise of a child (15:5), and as an answer Abraham believes (15:6). The promised child finally is born (21:1-2), and during the test of Genesis 22 the life of this child seems to be in danger.

The third source, the book of Wisdom, is hard to date. It was very probably written in Alexandria in the decades around the turn of the era, but its dating ranges from the second century BCE to the mid-first century CE.[16] The third main part of the book, the so-called "book of History", begins with two hymns.[17] The first deals with the presence of Wisdom in the lives of the forefathers (from Adam to Joseph: Wisd. 10:1-14), while the second concentrates on the exodus of the Jews from Egypt (Wisd. 10:15-21). The first hymn mentions seven righteous figures and their antagonists, without naming them. Verse 5 apparently relates to Abraham: "She [Wisdom] also, when the nations in wicked agreement had been put to confusion/ recognized the righteous man and preserved him blameless before God/ and kept him strong in the face of his compassion for his child." The term "righteous man" (δίκαιος) is recurrent in this context: except the first man, each protagonist of the hymn is denoted as such. The third colon of this verse obviously refers to the *Akedah*, the expression "compassion for his child" (ἐπὶ τέκνου σπλάγχνοις) makes this clear. Wisdom guards (φυλάσσω) Abraham, however, in an unexpected manner; it is she, who keeps him strong *against* his *compassion* (*ἐπὶ* τέκνου *σπλάγχνοις* ἰσχυρὸν ἐφύλαξεν).[18] According to this interpretation, divine providence thus strengthens Abraham's obedience during the test. A similar view is expressed in *4 Maccabees*, which was composed somewhat later than the book of Wisdom.[19] Here the mother of the seven martyrs is told: "But sympathy for her children did not sway the mother of the young men; she was of the same mind as Abraham" (ἀλλ᾽ οὐχὶ τὴν Αβρααμ ὁμόψυχον τῶν νεανίσκων μητέρα μετεκίνησεν συμπάθεια τέκνων: 14:20). According to this tradition, paternal love was the *par excellence* characteristic of the patriarch and a trait whose emulation was thought to be desirable.

The fourth source contains a subtle, intertextual reference to Genesis 22. As Tzvi Novick demonstrated, chapter 6 of the book of Tobit—composed before the first half of the second century[20]—contains a series of allusions to the *Akedah*.[21] Here, however, the parallel between Tobiah and Isaac is much more important than the one between Azariah (Raphael) and Abraham.

16. D. Winston, *The Wisdom of Solomon* (AB 43; New York: Doubleday, 1979), 20–25.

17. On the structure of the book, see, e.g. J.M. Reese, "Plan and Structure in the Book of Wisdom", *CBQ* 27 (1965): 391–99; A.G. Wright, "The Structure of Wisdom 11–19", *CBQ* 27 (1965): 28–34; A.G. Wright, "The Structure of the Book of Wisdom", *Biblica* 48 (1967): 165–84.

18. A.T. Glicksman, *Wisdom of Solomon 10: A Jewish Hellenistic Reinterpretation of Early Israelite History through Sapiential Lenses* (DCLS 9; Berlin: de Gruyter, 2011), 117.

19. D.A. deSilva, *4 Maccabees: Introduction and Commentary on the Greek Text in Codex Sinaiticus* (SCS; Leiden: Brill, 2006), xiv–xvii.

20. On the dating of Tobit, see e.g., J.A. Fitzmyer, *Tobit* (CEJL; Berlin: de Gruyter, 2003), 50–52.

21. T. Novick, "Biblicized Narrative: On Tobit and Genesis 22", *JBL* 126 (2007): 755–64.

To sum up these sources, one might conclude that the Old Testament Apocrypha display a vivid interest in the *Akedah* story. All of them have somewhat different interpretative agendas, nevertheless common trends may also be noted. Ben Sira, Judith and 1 Maccabees are common in underlining the perspective of testing: the verb πειράζω or the noun πειρασμός appear in each context. Nevertheless, Judith differs from the two other books in referring to the patriarchs' test. When speaking about the testing of Isaac, Judith assigns, albeit tacitly, an active role to Isaac during Abraham's sacrifice. This interpretation develops in Jewish writings of the first century CE, such as the Pseudo-Philonic *Liber antiquitatum biblicarum* (32.3), Josephus (*Ant.* 1.232) or *4 Maccabees* (7.14). Similarly, when Tobit uses this story from the perspective of Isaac, it anticipates this kind of interpretation. Finally, the book of Wisdom has a completely different understanding of the original story. Here, with the help of Wisdom, Abraham proves to be victorious over his parental tenderness. Abraham serves in these stories as an example: an ideal figure who remains steadfast during his test.

The "Inheritance" Group

Abraham is continuously promised that his offspring will inherit the land (cf. Gen. 12:7; 13:15-17; 15:18-20; 17:8; etc.). This motif appears throughout in the texture of the Abraham cycle in Genesis.[22] A variant of this motif, the eschatological gathering of the Israelites into this land, is a very familiar theme in Second Temple literature.[23]

In the book of Tobit, chapter 4 relates the sapiential instructions of Tobit, before his son, Tobiah, departs to foreign lands. In course of this exhortation, Tobit admonishes against exogamous marriage (Tob. 4:12-13).[24] As a basis of the recommended marital praxis, Tobit evokes the example of the patriarchs, as follows: "Remember, my son that Noah, Abraham, Isaac, and Jacob, our ancestors of old, all took wives from among their kindred." The continuation of this sentence suggests that endogamy was the source of blessing, and the promise of the land: "and they were blessed in their children, and their posterity will inherit the land" (καὶ εὐλογήθησαν ἐν τοῖς τέκνοις αὐτῶν καὶ τὸ σπέρμα αὐτῶν κληρονομήσει γῆν,

22. Two important passages are treated in P.R. Williamson, *Abraham, Israel and the Nations: The Patriarchal Promise and its Covenantal Development in Genesis* (JSOTSup 315; Sheffield: Sheffield Academic Press, 2000). See furthermore, Levenson, *Inheriting Abraham*, 36–65; H.D. Preuss, *Old Testament Theology* (OTL; Louisville: WJK, 1995), Vol. 1, 119.

23. See e.g., M.E. Fuller, *The Restoration of Israel: Israel's Re-gathering and the Fate of the Nations in Early Jewish Literature and Luke-Acts* (BZNW 138; Berlin: de Gruyter, 2012).

24. See e.g., Fitzmyer, *Tobit*, 172–74; T. Hieke, "Endogamy in the Book of Tobit, Genesis, and Ezra-Nehemiah", in *The Book of Tobit. Text, Tradition, Theology*, eds. G.G. Xeravits et al. (JSJSup 98; Leiden: Brill 2005), 103–20. The sapiential instructions of the book are treated in F.M. Macatangay, *The Wisdom Instructions in the Book of Tobit* (DCLS 12; Berlin: de Gruyter, 2011).

Tob. 4:12c). Seeing the date of Tobit's emergence when Hellenism started to grow within Judaism, the paradigm of the patriarchs has a special strength.[25]

In the book of Tobit the theme of Abraham's inheritance reappears later, in chapter 14. This chapter contains the farewell speech of the dying Tobit, in which he exhorts his son, Tobias, once again. In his address Tobit treats, among other things, eschatological issues, including the future of just Israelites. Verse 14:7 imagines that all nations will praise God, and the Israelites will experience joyful exaltation. The *Codex Sinaiticus* manuscript version of Tobit here also contains an expanded, alternative, text.[26] This version is not interested in the gentiles; the expression "all nations" (πάντα τὰ ἔθνη) is missing. *Sinaiticus*, instead, focuses exclusively on the Israelites; these "will be gathered together; they will go to Jerusalem and live in safety forever in the land of Abraham, and it will be given over to them" (Tob. 14:7b). This clause is without parallel in the shorter version of the book; one of the fragmentary Aramaic Tobit manuscripts from Qumran, however, probably contains a similar reading (4Q196 19, 1, written between 50–25 BCE).[27] The place of the eschatological gathering is called "the land of Abraham" (ἐν τῇ γῇ Αβρααμ), which is an obvious Deuteronomic allusion,[28] and this land "will be given" (παραδοθήσεται) to the Israelites.[29] Thus, the figure of Abraham and his inheritance appears in this context as an eschatological marker.

The book of Baruch is a short and complicated early Jewish work. Its final version was composed very probably in the second half of the first century BCE, but the traditions behind its text were widely circulated in late Second Temple times.[30] Baruch 1:14–3:8 is a penitential prayer, a genre used with predilection in late biblical and extra-biblical literature.[31] The prayer's structure is tripartite: after

25. Fitzmyer, *Tobit*, 112; Hieke, "Endogamy".

26. On the textual witnesses of Tobit, see R. Hanhart, *Text und Textgeschichte des Buches Tobit* (MSU 17; Göttingen: Vandenhoeck & Ruprecht, 1984). A commentary on this version is R.J. Littman, *Tobit: The Book of Tobit in Codex Sinaiticus* (SCS; Leiden: Brill, 2008).

27. Edition of the Qumranic Tobit manuscripts: J.A. Fitzmyer, *Qumran Cave 4: XIV, Parabiblical Texts, Part 2*, eds. M. Broshi et al. (DJD 19; Oxford: Clarendon Press, 1995), 7–76.

28. A.A. Di Lella, "The Deuteronomic Background of the Farewell Discourse in Tob 14:3-11", *CBQ* 41 (1979): 382–83.

29. See Fuller, *The Restoration of Israel*, 26–32.

30. On the dating of the book, see S.A. Adams, *Baruch and the Epistle of Jeremiah: A Commentary Based on the Texts in Codex Vaticanus* (SEPT; Leiden: Brill, 2014), 4–6.

31. See the three volumes of M.J. Boda, D.K. Falk, and R.A. Werline, eds., *Seeking the Favor of God. 1: The Origins of Penitential Prayer in Second Temple Judaism* (SBLEJL 21; Atlanta, GA: SBL, 2006); M.J. Boda, D.K. Falk, and R.A. Werline, eds., *Seeking the Favor of God. 2: The Development of Penitential Prayer in Second Temple Judaism* (SBLEJL 22; Atlanta, GA: SBL, 2007); M.J. Boda, D.K. Falk, and R.A. Werline, eds., *Seeking the Favor of God. 3: The Impact of Penitential Prayer Beyond Second Temple Judaism* (SBLEJL 23; Atlanta, GA: SBL, 2008).

an admission of guilt two petitions follow.[32] The closing section of the first petition (2:27-35) is basically a complex, pseudo-Mosaic quotation of various scriptural passages.[33] The author/compiler of this passage has an eschatological vision following the Deuteronomistic sin-exile-restoration pattern. Baruch 2:34 deals with the return of the exiled Israelites; God will bring them home (ἀποστρέψω αὐτοὺς εἰς τὴν γῆν), and they will rule over the land (κυριεύσουσιν αὐτῆς). The destination of the homecoming is the patriarchs' inheritance, the land that God swore to give, among others, to Abraham (ἣν ὤμοσα τοῖς πατράσιν αὐτῶν τῷ Αβρααμ καὶ τῷ Ισαακ καὶ τῷ Ιακωβ). Again, the figure of Abraham marks the eschatological fulfilment of the divine promises.

To sum up this section, two texts in this group—Tobit 14 and Baruch 2—are common in assigning the importance of Abraham's inheritance to the eschatological future. This view is familiar in the post-exilic books of the Old Testament and in early Jewish literature,[34] beginning with the book of Ezekiel (especially chapters 38–39).[35] The labelling of the goal of Israel's eschatological regathering as the land of Abraham emphasizes the importance of the patriarch. Instead of this eschatological orientation, the interest of Tob. 4 focuses on the present, and the idea of Abraham's inheritance encourages Tobit's program of endogamous marriage. The fact that the patriarchs—including Abraham—serve as examples for this custom stresses its significance in a period when "classical" Israelite values were questioned again and again.

Passages with Various Purposes

When treating the events under the high priest Jonathan, 1 Maccabees records that he reconfirmed treaties with Rome and Sparta (1 Macc. 12:1-23; cf. *Ant.* 13.164–70).[36] In this section the author of the book inserts two official letters, creating the

32. The structure is treated in A. Kabasele Mukenge, *L'unité littéraire du livre de Baruch* (Etudes Bibliques N.S. 38; Paris: Gabalda, 1998), 111–17; Adams, *Baruch*, 60–61.

33. See S.A. Adams, "Reframing Scripture: A Fresh Look at Baruch's So-Called 'Citations'", in *Scriptural Authority in Early Judaism and Ancient Christianity*, eds. G.G. Xeravits et al. (DCLS 16; Berlin: de Gruyter, 2013), 63–83; Adams, *Baruch*, 86–87.

34. J.M. Scott, ed., *Restoration: Old Testament, Jewish, and Christian Perspectives* (JSJSup 72; Leiden: Brill, 2001) 41–221.

35. See W.A. Tooman, *Gog of Magog: Reuse of Scripture and Compositional Technique in Ezekiel 38–39* (FAT 2.52; Tübingen: Mohr Siebeck, 2011); W. Pikor, *The Land of Israel in the Book of Ezekiel* (LHBOTS 667; London: T & T Clark, 2018).

36. See V. Kókai Nagy, "Die Beziehung der Makkabäer zu fremden Nationen—die Bündnisse mit Rom und Sparta", in *The Stranger in Ancient and Mediaeval Jewish Tradition*, eds. G.G. Xeravits et al. (DCLS 4; Berlin: de Gruyter, 2010), 107–17; J. Sievers, "Josephus, First Maccabees, Sparta, the Three Haireseis—and Cicero", *JSJ* 32 (2001): 241–51.

impression that they are original, yet they seem to be pure fiction.[37] Verses 12:20-23 purport to be a letter of the Spartan king Arius to the high priest Onias. The king reports that according to their archives ("it has been found in writing," εὑρέθη ἐν γραφῇ, 12:21) Spartans and Jews are brothers (ἀδελφοὶ), because both are descendants of Abraham (ἐκ γένους Αβρααμ). The intention of the author with this passage is very probably to exalt the Jews, establishing for them a noble brotherhood among the nations. At the same time, he exalts the figure of Abraham, too, when creating the impression that an important nation acknowledges him as an ancestor. Note that for Josephus the latter detail is not important; he speaks about the relationship between Jews and Spartans ("friendship and kindred," φιλίαν καὶ συγγένειαν, *Ant.* 13.164), without, however, mentioning Abraham.[38]

2 Maccabees, written in the mid-second century BCE,[39] opens with two letters.[40] The first one, a festal letter (1:1-9), is addressed to the Egyptian Jews about the feast of the dedication of the Temple. After a salutation the letter displays a prayer for blessing (1:2-5), composed as a series of petitions. Verse 2 contains the first two petitions; of which the first is a general wish of divine benevolence, whereas the second reads: "may he remember his covenant with Abraham and Isaac and Jacob, his faithful servants." This text is heavily influenced by Pentateuchal passages.[41] The two important concepts in this clause are: the idea of the covenant ("may he remember his covenant," μνησθείη τῆς διαθήκης αὐτοῦ), and the labelling of the patriarchs as "his faithful servants" (τῶν δούλων αὐτοῦ τῶν πιστῶν). Behind these terms lies a complex exegesis of Genesis 15: Abraham believes God (καὶ ἐπίστευσεν Αβραμ τῷ θεῷ, 15:6a), and this is followed by a passage relating God's covenant with Abraham (15:7-21); 2 Maccabees extends both of these ideas to all three patriarchs. This is partly due to the influence of several Pentateuchal passages; these passages speak about the covenant established with all the three: "and God remembered his covenant with Abraham, Isaac, and Jacob," (καὶ ἐμνήσθη ὁ θεὸς τῆς διαθήκης αὐτοῦ τῆς πρὸς Αβρααμ καὶ Ισαακ καὶ Ιακωβ) Exod. 2:24; "and I will remember the covenant with Jacob and the covenant with Isaac and the covenant with Abraham," (καὶ μνησθήσομαι τῆς διαθήκης Ιακωβ καὶ τῆς διαθήκης Ισαακ καὶ τῆς διαθήκης Αβρααμ) Lev. 26:42). The plural form "faithful servants" is due to a tendency of harmonization with the first part of the sentence.

37. J.R. Bartlett, *1 Maccabees* (GAP; Sheffield: Sheffield Academic Press, 1998), 95–97.

38. Josephus' image of Abraham is treated in L.H. Feldman, *Josephus's Interpretation of the Bible* (HCS 27; Berkeley: UCLA Press, 1998), 223–89.

39. D.R. Scwartz, *2 Maccabees* (CEJL; Berlin: de Gruyter, 2008), 11–15.

40. E.J. Bickerman, "A Jewish Festal Letter of 124 B.C.E.", in *Studies in Jewish and Christian History*, ed. E.J. Bickerman (AJEC 68; Leiden: Brill, 2007), 408–31; V. Parker, "The Letters in II Maccabees: Reflexions on the Book's Composition", *ZAW* 119 (2007): 386–90; Schwartz, *2 Maccabees*, 519–29.

41. On the biblical background, see J.A. Goldstein, *II Maccabees* (AB 41A; New York: Doubleday, 1983), 142.

Finally, a passage from the book of Judith deserves attention. After the beheading of Holophernes, Judith returns to Bethulia, and relates to her compatriots the events. Then, the people bless God (Jdt. 13:17), and Ozias blesses the heroine (13:18-20). The beginning of Ozias' blessing alludes to the meeting of Abraham and Melchizedek as reported in Genesis 14.

Gen. 14:19-20
Blessed be (εὐλογημένος) Abram by God Most High (τῷ θεῷ τῷ ὑψίστῳ), who created the heaven and the earth (ὅς ἔκτισεν τὸν οὐρανὸν καὶ τὴν γῆν); and blessed be God (καὶ εὐλογητὸς ὁ θεὸς) Most High, who has delivered your enemies (ἐχθρῶν) into your hand!

Jdt. 13:18
You are blessed (εὐλογητὴ), o daughter, by the Most High God (τῷ θεῷ τῷ ὑψίστῳ) above all other women on earth; and blessed be (καὶ εὐλογημένος) the Lord God (ὁ θεός), who created the heavens and the earth (ὅς ἔκτισεν τοὺς οὐρανοὺς καὶ τὴν γῆν), who has guided you to cut off the head of the leader of our enemies (ἐχθρῶν).

One might find it strange that Judith is compared to a male hero. However, this feature characterizes the presentation of Judith throughout her book. Jan van Henten demonstrated, for example, how the figure of Judith was modelled on characteristics that remind the reader of Moses, whereas József Zsengellér detected Davidic traits in the presentation of the heroine.[42] The comparison with Abraham here is based on the fact that both passages have the same context. In both cases there is:

1. A victorious protagonist. In Genesis, this is Abraham, who defeated the coalition of great kings, and rescued his nephew, Lot. In Judith, the victorious protagonist is Judith, who defeated Holophernes and rescued the people of Bethulia.
2. The hero/ine after his/her triumphal return receives a blessing from an authoritative figure. In Genesis, this is the mysterious Melchizedek, priest-king of the city of Salem. In Judith, this is Ozias, chief leader of the city of Bethulia.

These common characteristics substantiate the correspondence between Abraham and Judith. The author nevertheless softens this unusual parallel, and strengthens the female orientation of the passage in alluding to another pretext. The beginning

42. J.W. van Henten, "Judith as a Female Moses: Judith 7–13 in the Light of Exodus 17; Numbers 20 and Deuteronomy 33:8-11", in *Reflections on Theology and Gender*, eds. A. Brenner et al. (Kampen: Kok, 1994), 33–48; J. Zsengellér, "Judith as a Female David: Beauty and Body in Religious Context", in *A Pious Seductress: Studies in the Book of Judith*, ed. G.G. Xeravits (DCLS 14; Berlin: de Gruyter, 2012), 186–210. On these characteristics, see furthermore C. Rakel, *Judit—über Schönheit, Macht und Widerstand im Krieg: Eine feministisch-intertextuelle Lektüre* (BZAW 334; Berlin: de Gruyter, 2003), 248–65.

of the verse "you are blessed . . . above all other women on earth" (εὐλογητὴ σύ . . . παρὰ πάσας τὰς γυναῖκας τὰς ἐπὶ τῆς γῆς) echoes the Song of Deborah, the praise of Jael (εὐλογηθείη ἐκ γυναικῶν Ιαηλ, Judg. 5:24). This pretext influences once more the present literary unit, in 14:7, where Achior praises Judith.[43]

Conclusion

The Old Testament Apocrypha shows an interest in the figure of Abraham; his figure appears at least once in every book of the collection. Despite the fact that the Apocrypha is a late and artificial category, and the collective books have different dates, authorship, and settings, this does not seem to have significant consequences for the reception of Abraham within the literature. At the least, the data brought together in this paper suggest the continued popularity of Abraham in the Judaism of the second/first centuries BCE.

Nevertheless, some convergent features within the corpus are noteworthy. The texts often use the same biblical passages as points of reference. The most important of them are Genesis 15 and 22, both of which have a rich history of reception within early Judaism and ancient Christianity. The Abraham figure of these pretexts is used as an example of faith, steadfastness, and trust in God. Elaboration of the *Akedah* story has a special place, for it appears in more than half of the corpus, in conformity with its popularity in the literature of the period.[44]

Another convergent feature of some of the texts is the theme of inheritance of the land. In Tobit 4, the patriarch serves, again, as an exemplary figure, whereas the eschatologically oriented passages exalt his personality. Similar tendencies occur in Sirach 44 or in 1 Maccabees 12. The first refers to Abraham by using a royal psalm, while the second exalts his figure in stating that he is a progenitor of not only the Jews, but also of such an important nation as the Spartans.

Finally, the thematic variability of these passages must be noted. Despite the converging tendencies, they display a rich and vivid exegesis of biblical sources, in which various aspects of the Abrahamic traditions are emphasized. These features establish the patriarch as one of the most important biblical figures for the communities that wrote and used these texts.

43. Gera, *Judith*, 409 and 416.

44. See chapters 4–6 of this volume.

Chapter 3

ABRAHAM IN THE OLD TESTAMENT PSEUDEPIGRAPHA: FRIEND OF GOD AND FATHER OF FATHERS

Jared W. Ludlow

Abraham is one of the most recognizable names in the Judeo-Christian tradition, where stories and allusions to him are found across canonical and non-canonical writings. The Old Testament Pseudepigrapha is one such collection of texts that makes repeated references to Abraham and his role within God's salvation history.[1] As the primary initiator of the covenant in Genesis, Abraham is often revered as the exemplar of faithfulness and righteousness. His close relationship to God is exemplified by his description as "friend of God" (2 Chron. 20:7; Isa. 41:8). His name, along with his immediate descendants, became a common title for deity: the God of Abraham, Isaac, and Jacob. This chapter will review how the Jewish and Christian authors of the Pseudepigrapha discuss Abraham or use Abrahamic imagery, both in the transmission of Abraham traditions and in the creation of new tales. The episodes and characteristics of Abraham from Genesis form the basis of some Pseudepigraphic accounts, but in the characteristic fashion of Pseudepigrapha texts, new stories are created to fill in gaps or expand on the canonical record. New accounts about his youth and afterlife status are most noteworthy, and create a type of panegyric, lauding Abraham's hospitality and righteousness which result in Abraham's immortal, heavenly status where he can serve as an intermediary for his descendants and a model for God's covenant people to aid them in receiving the same heavenly

1. A challenge when dealing with the topic of Abraham in the Pseudepigrapha is the varied nature of the texts in this collection. Some come from a Jewish origin, others are heavily Christianized, if not originally written by Christians, and they span several hundred years of time. This chapter will treat the collection as a whole and only draw distinctions between origin and chronology when there seems to be a development that can be traced from one text to another.

destination he did.[2] In such a role, Abraham becomes the definitive friend of God and father of fathers. In order to show this development of Abraham in these Pseudepigrapha texts, we will take a chronological look at Abraham references, beginning with his youth, through his prophetic ministry, and finally his post-mortal, heavenly status.

Youth

The *Apocalypse of Abraham* is one of the few Pseudepigrapha texts that focuses almost exclusively on Abraham. It is unique for telling stories from Abraham's youth, that share the problems he had with his idolatrous father and his coming to know of the true God. Various episodes unfold that show the ridiculousness of idolatry in Abraham's eyes, such as when the images break and new ones have to be made by mortal hands. Abraham wonders, "What is this inequality of activity which my father is doing? Is it not he rather who is god for his gods, because they come into being from his sculpting, his planning, and his skill? They ought to honor my father because they are his work" (*Apoc. Abr.* 3.2–4).[3] Abraham also wonders how lifeless objects are able to hear prayers and grant blessings (see 4.3–4; 6.3). In an especially comical scene, Abraham tells one of the images to watch over the fire that is cooking their meal. When he returns, the image has been burned up in the fire. Abraham laughs and later tells his father that he should give praise to this god because "he threw himself into the fire in order to cook your food" (5.14). But rather than come to understand his foolishness, Abraham's father acknowledges the power of this god and states he would make another one who could prepare his food the next day. These powerless actions by the images only strengthen Abraham's belief in their uselessness. These portrayals of idolatry and Abraham's father's growing anger provide the background and rationale for why Abraham will need to "wander from [his] father's house" as stated in Gen. 20:13. Specifically, Abraham is visited by the Lord who tells him, "You are searching for the God of gods, the creator, in the understanding of your heart. I am he. Go out from Terah, your father, and go out of the house, that you too may not be slain with the sins of your father's house" (*Apoc. Abr.* 8.3–4). As soon as Abraham departs, the house and everything in it burns to the ground (8.5–6).

2. For a helpful review of early Jewish and Christian discussions of Abraham's model example of hospitality and righteousness, see R.B. Ward, "The Works of Abraham. James 2:14-26", *Harvard Theological Review* 61 no.2 (1968): 283–90.

3. Unless noted otherwise, all quotations of texts will come from the two volumes of J.H. Charlesworth, ed., *The Old Testament Pseudepigrapha*, (Garden City, NY: Doubleday, 1983 and 1985) = *OTP*.

Prophetic Ministry

Abraham's prophetic ministry begins with his travels from Mesopotamia towards Canaan and neighboring regions. While the *Apocalypse of Abraham* gives the reason for Abraham's departure as being at odds with his father's idolatry, other Pseudepigrapha texts share likely motives for his exodus by creating new accounts about Abraham's refusal to participate in the building of the tower of Babel and the subsequent efforts by the builders to punish him in a furnace of fire.

Pseudo-Philo in the *Liber Antiquitatum Biblicarum* is unique in placing Abraham into the story of the tower of Babel and the fiery furnace (cf. Daniel 3; 2 Maccabees 7). Abraham was among those who refused to add bricks to the tower, and instead Abraham emphasized his knowledge of the one Lord whom they worshipped (*LAB* 6.3–4). Despite the threat of death, Abraham trusted in God that he could be preserved from the furnace (and if not, then he must have a serious sin worthy of fiery death: see 6.9–11). Abraham was thrown into the furnace:

> But God caused a great earthquake, and the fire gushing out of the furnace leaped forth in flames and sparks of flame. And it burned all those standing around in sight of the furnace. And all those who were burned in that day were 83,500. But there was not the least injury to Abram from the burning of the fire. And Abram came up out of the furnace, and the fiery furnace collapsed.
>
> *LAB* 6.17–18

In his honor, they named that place by the name of Abram.

As the story continues, God chooses Abram from among the people to be spared from the dividing of language. The Lord says explicitly that he will take Abraham out of their land to a special land where he will establish his covenant with him "and will bless his seed and be lord for him as God forever" (7.4). *Pseudo-Philo* thus inserts Abraham in the story of the tower of Babel, perhaps as background for why Abraham left his homeland for Canaan and why he is considered so righteous that the Lord wants to establish the covenant with him.

Some Pseudepigrapha texts (and other Second Temple Jewish texts) relate Abraham's knowledge of astrology, or the Chaldean science, he gained while in Mesopotamia, and which he then spread to other areas as part of his travels. Two brief excerpts assigned by scholars under *Pseudo-Eupolemus*,[4] and classified among Pseudepigrapha texts, show a different approach some Hellenistic Jews had towards Abraham and other early figures by making them not only spiritual leaders for themselves, but cultural leaders and pioneers for neighboring peoples.

4. Found in Eusebius' *Praeparatio Evangelica* with one quotation purportedly coming from Alexander Polyhistor. While scholars have assigned both quotations to a "Pseudo-Eupolemus," R. Doran argues that the fragment from Alexander Polyhistor should be assigned to Eupolemus, and the second anonymous fragment is likely a collection of traditions compiled by Alexander Polyhistor. See "Pseudo-Eupolemus," in *OTP*, 873–78.

In the case of Abraham, he was born in Mesopotamia and "excelled all in nobility and wisdom; he sought and obtained the knowledge of astrology and the Chaldean craft, and pleased God because he eagerly sought to be reverent" (*Ps.-Eupol.* 9.17.3). Abraham departed from the land of Chaldeans with knowledge about astrology and went to Phoenicia where he shared it.[5] When famine hit, Abraham went to Egypt where he "lived in Heliopolis with the Egyptian priests and taught them much: He explained astrology and the other sciences to them" (9.17.8), though Abraham claims that the initial discovery of this knowledge goes back to Enoch. The second excerpt gives a much briefer summary of these events: "After Abraham had learned astrology, he first went to Phoenicia and taught it to the Phoenicians; later he went to Egypt" (9.18.2). Another citation in Eusebius' *Praeparatio Evangelica*, from an earlier source, shares a similar tradition. Artapanus in his *Judaica* relates that Abraham "came to Egypt with all his household to the Egyptian king Pharethothes, and taught him astrology, that he remained there twenty years and then departed again for the regions of Syria" (*Art.* 9.18.1).

The tradition of Abraham learning astrology himself and then teaching this science to others, particularly to the Egyptians, becomes commonplace in other Second Temple Jewish texts. *Jubilees* and Josephus' *Antiquities* both share accounts of Abraham coming to learn knowledge about the stars, and Josephus goes on to explain how Abraham passed on the science of astronomy to the Egyptians (*Ant.* 1.8.2). Philo, in *De cherubim*, said that Abram "delighted in the lofty philosophy which investigates the events which take place in the air, and the sublime nature of the beings which exist in heaven" (*Cher.* 1:4). But, unlike his Chaldean neighbors, Abraham properly understood their relation to the true God so he was not merely an astronomer, but a wise man who perceived the heavens. "The man [Abraham] who had been bred up in this doctrine, and who for a long time had studied the philosophy of the Chaldaeans, as if suddenly awakening from a deep slumber and opening the eye of the soul, and beginning to perceive a pure ray of light instead of profound darkness, followed the light, and saw what he had never seen before, a certain governor and director of the world standing above it, and guiding his own work in a salutary manner, and exerting his care and power in behalf of all those parts of it which are worthy of divine superintendence" (*Abr.* 70).

The elevation of cultural figures over non-Jewish communities is not exclusive to Abraham. For example, Eupolemus claims Moses was the first wise man, and that he taught the alphabet to the Jews, and from the Jews it was disseminated to the Phoenicians who in turn passed it on to the Greeks (*Fr.* 1.26). Enoch, Abraham claims in another likely text from Eupolemus, first discovered astrology.[6] But Abraham becomes a favorite target in this promotion of Jewish ethnic pride

5. The text relates various events from Genesis (capture of Lot: 14:12-14, Abraham refusing gifts: 14:21-24, and Melchizedek blessing Abraham: 14:18-20), but alters the location and order of some events.

6. Eusebius, *Praep. Ev.* 9.17.8.

because of his dramatic spiritual experiences and his travels throughout the region where he could transfer knowledge and influence others. This phenomenon has been explored by Erich Gruen and others as examples of Jews elevating their kings and religious figures to impact neighboring peoples and to reinforce a sense of cultural superiority.[7] It is also indicative of what became a major motif in Jewish folklore and rabbinic literature: Abraham's mastery of Chaldean science.[8]

Besides teaching other peoples, Abraham is known as a teacher within his own extended family. In the *Testaments of the Twelve Patriarchs*, Abraham was an important teacher about God, the covenant, and other practices. In the *Testament of Levi* (*T. Levi* 9.12), Levi recounts how he and Judah visited their grandfather Isaac who taught them things he had learned from his father, Abraham, related to the law of Moses and other ways to worship the Lord.[9]

The key event in Abraham's prophetic ministry is the establishment of the Abrahamic covenant as recorded in Genesis 12, 15, and 17. Various Pseudepigrapha texts extend the discussion of this vital covenant.[10] The *Psalms of Solomon*, while focusing primarily on the Davidic covenant, makes a couple of references to the Abrahamic covenant: "For you chose the descendants of Abraham above all the nations, and you put your name upon us, Lord, and it will not cease forever. You made a covenant with our ancestors concerning us, and we hope in you when we turn our souls toward you" (*Pss. Sol.* 9.9–10); "Your compassionate judgments (are) over the whole world, and your love is for the descendants of Abraham" (18.3). These passages highlight Abraham as the origin of this covenant along with the eternal efficacy this covenant has on his descendants.

Pseudo-Philo (*LAB* 8) follows the storyline of Genesis by making allusions to Abraham dwelling in Canaan with Lot, his nephew, and Sarai, his wife. The story of Lot in the city of Sodom is briefly alluded to while Abraham remained in the land of Canaan where, through a theophany, the covenant was restated. "And God appeared to Abram, saying, 'To your seed I will give this land, and your name will

7. See E.S. Gruen, *Heritage and Hellenism: The Reinvention of Jewish Tradition* (Berkeley: University of California Press, 1998), 146–53.

8. See B.Z. Wacholder, "Pseudo-Eupolemus' Two Greek Fragments on the Life of Abraham", *Hebrew Union College Annual* 34 (1963): 83–113, here 103.

9. According to H.C. Kee, "Isaac's instructions to Levi are a briefer version of those given by Abraham to Isaac in *Jub.* 21:1-25": H.C. Kee, "Testaments of the Twelve Patriarchs", in *OTP*, 791, n. 9c.

10. This new covenant ushers in a new stage of relationship with God. The beginning of a new age with Abraham is the theme of a passage in *2 Baruch*. In this text, Adam's fall led to a period of darkness upon the world represented by black waters. But for the first time Abraham is able to counteract the effects and darkness of the fall. "And after these you saw the bright waters; that is the fountain of Abraham and his generation, and the coming of his son, and the son of his son, and of those who are like them. . . . the hope of the world which will be renewed was built at that time, and the promise of the life that will come later was planted. Those are the bright waters which you have seen" (*2 Bar.* 57:1-3).

be called Abraham, and Sarai, your wife, will be called Sarah. And I will give to you from her an everlasting seed, and I will establish my covenant with you.' And Abraham knew Sarah, his wife, and she conceived and bore Isaac" (*LAB* 8.3). The covenant and promises extended to Abraham are repeated a few more times in the text as reminders of God fulfilling his prophecies. "And there will be fulfilled the covenant that God established with Abraham when he said, 'Indeed your sons will dwell in a land not their own and will be brought into bondage and afflicted 400 years.' And behold from the time when the word of God that he spoke to Abraham was spoken, there are 350 years" (9.3). God also tells Balaam that the promise of Abraham's descendants becoming as numerous as the stars in the heaven is being fulfilled, a promise God told Abraham when he "lifted him above the firmament and showed him the arrangements of all the stars" (18.5).

In *Pseudo-Philo*'s version of Joshua reestablishing the covenant with the Israelites in the newly-entered land, the story of Abraham is recounted to encourage righteousness in the face of adversity. "When all those inhabiting the land were being led astray after their own devices, Abraham believed in me and was not led astray with them. And I rescued him from the flame and took him and brought him over all the land of Canaan and said to him in a vision, 'To your seed I will give this land'" (*Ps.-Philo* 23.5). When Abraham inquired how he would have posterity from his barren wife, the Lord commanded him to bring a sacrifice and then placed him in a deep sleep where he saw the afterlife and the place of judgment.[11] Then God promised him that he would have offspring "from one who is closed up" (23.7), which, according to *Pseudo-Philo*, was fulfilled in Sarah's seventh month of pregnancy.

Within *4 Ezra*, Ezra is being told that as the father of a new nation—because the old Judah has been scattered and destroyed because of wickedness—he will have Abraham, Isaac, Jacob, and the twelve Minor Prophets as leaders for his people (*4 Ezra* 1.38–9). These covenant people hearken back to the initial covenant established with Abraham in Gen. 17:1-8. In reflecting back on the establishment of this covenant, *4 Ezra* discusses how God chose Abraham "and you loved him and to him only you revealed the end of the times, secretly by night. You made with him an everlasting covenant, and promised him that you would never forsake his descendants; and you gave to him Isaac" (*4 Ezra* 3.13–15).

Another Ezra text, the *Greek Apocalypse of Ezra*, has a dialogue between Ezra and God debating over theological principles, with Ezra turning to the example of Abraham for support of his perspective. In this episode, Ezra wonders why God created his children if he was only going to wipe them out. How then would he receive glory from his creations? God responded that he would be glorified by his angels. So Ezra pressed further, "Lord, if this was your calculation, why did you form man? You said to Abraham our father, 'I will surely multiply your seed as the stars of the heaven and as the sand along the shore of the sea.' And where is your

11. An experience of Abraham seeing the afterlife and the place of judgment is recounted in the *Testament of Abraham*.

promise?" (*Gk. Apoc. Ezra* 3.9–10). The Lord never directly responds to this point, but it is another example of a Pseudepigrapha text focusing on the Abrahamic covenant and its blessings for Abraham's posterity.

The second, much longer part of the *Apocalypse of Abraham* (chapters 9–32) recounts the actual apocalypse experience Abraham has, wherein we learn a little more about his character and the special covenant relationship he developed with God. In the first place, he is selected by God to receive this vision after he has fulfilled God's requested sacrifices (as outlined in Genesis 15). It reiterates that the covenant will come through him. At the start, Abraham is overcome with spiritual power and collapses to the ground like a stone. An angel is sent to strengthen him and guide him. The angel, Iaoel, greets Abraham as "friend of God who has loved you" (*Apoc. Abr.* 10.5). The angel encourages Abraham to proceed because "a venerable honor has been prepared for you by the Eternal One. Go, complete the sacrifice of the command. Behold, I am assigned (to be) with you and with the generation which is predestined (to be born) from you. And with me Michael blesses you forever. Be bold, go!" (10.15–17).

As part of his experience, Abraham sees Azazel, but refuses to worship him. Iaoel commands Azazel to depart because "you cannot deceive him [Abraham], because he is the enemy of you and of those who follow you and who love what you wish. For behold, the garment which in heaven was formerly yours has been set aside for him, and the corruption which was on him has gone over to you" (13.13–14). Iaoel then turns to Abraham and encourages him, "Know from this that the Eternal One whom you have loved has chosen you. Be bold and do through your authority whatever I order you against him who reviles justice [i.e., Azazel]" (14.2–3).

Abraham then has a direct worship experience with God wherein he recites grand praises culminating in seeing the throne of God. Abraham ends with the plea, "Receive me favorably, teach me, show me, and make known to your servant what you have promised me" (17.21). Abraham is then given a vision of all the firmaments and God's many creations. God's voice commands, "Look at the expanses which are under the firmament to which you have now been directed and see that on no single expanse is there any other but the one whom you have searched for or who has loved you" (19.3). Then, like in Genesis 15 and 18, Abraham is told to look at the stars and is promised, "As the number of the stars and their power so shall I place for your seed the nations and men" (20.5).

The apocalypse experience of Abraham briefly connects back to the earlier part of the story that discussed Abraham's father's idolatry, when Abraham sees someone worshipping an idol, "like a carpenter's figure such as my father used to make" (25:1). God later asks Abraham why his father, Terah, did not obey Abraham's voice and "abandon the demonic worship of idols until he perished, and all his house with him?" (26:3). Abraham responded that "it did not please him to obey me, nor did I follow his works" (26:4). The *Apocalypse of Abraham* ends with another connection to Genesis, with an allusion to the prophecy in Gen. 15:13 that Abraham's descendants would be enslaved in an alien land for a season (see 32:2-3).

Throughout the *Apocalypse of Abraham* we see some of Abraham's characteristics common to other texts that resulted in such a strong covenant relationship. He is exactly obedient to God's commands especially in his sacrifices, which lead to his revelatory experience.[12] He becomes worthy to enter the presence of God's throne and praises him while earlier rejecting Azazel. Abraham is inquisitive, always seeking to learn, such as in the *Testament of Abraham* when he asks to see the entire created world before his death (*T. Abr.* A9.6) or all the faces of Death (A19.5–6). Like other apocalypses, he has an *angelus interpres*, but the *Apocalypse of Abraham* goes beyond this by also having the Lord directly interpreting things for Abraham. This divine dynamic puts Abraham on a higher level than a typical prophet and affords him special privileges. Abraham's status as friend of God is solidified, and God reiterates his promise that Abraham will be the father of many nations.

An interesting text about Melchizedek includes interactions between him and Abraham, some of which correspond to the Genesis account, but parts of which expand upon their experiences there. In the *Story of Melchizedek* attributed (most likely falsely) to Athanasius,[13] Melchizedek has to escape from his father who was trying to sacrifice him. He went up on Mount Tabor and hid in the forest. After a seven-year span of time there, during which his hair and fingernails grew out to great lengths, God ordered Abraham to go up on Mount Tabor. Abraham's first order of business was to shave Melchizedek, cut his nails, clothe him, and then be blessed by him.

> And Abraham did as the Lord had commanded him: he went up to Mount Tabor, stood by the depths of the forest, and cried out three times, "Man of God!" And Melchizedek rose up. Abraham saw him and was afraid. Melchizedek said to him, "Do not be afraid, but tell me who you are and what you are seeking." And Abraham replied, "The Lord commanded me to shave you, cut your nails, clothe you, and be blessed by you." And Melchizedek said to him, "Do as the Lord has commanded you." And Abraham did as the Lord had commanded him.
>
> *The Story of Melchizedek*, 11.1–7

Three days later Melchizedek came down with a horn of oil and blessed Abraham, saying, "Blessed are you by the Most High God, and henceforth your name will be perfected: your name will no longer be Abram, but your name will be perfect, (i.e.) Abraham" (12.1–2). Even later, as Abraham was returning from defeating the kings who had kidnapped Lot, Melchizedek gave him a cup of pure wine in which he had put a piece of bread (see 13.1) an apparent retelling of their encounter in Gen. 17:18-20, where Melchizedek brought forth bread and wine and blessed Abram. While the *Story of Melchizedek* primarily focuses on Melchizedek

12. See *Apoc. Abr.* 9.5–10 for the commandment and promise, and 12.1–10 and 13.1 for Abraham's execution of the commandment.

13. See P. Piovanelli, "The Story of Melchizedek with the Melchizedek Legend from the *Chronicon Paschale*. A New Translation and Introduction", in *Old Testament Pseudepigrapha. More Noncanonical Scriptures*, Vol. 1, eds. R. Bauckham, J.R. Davila, and A. Panayotov (Grand Rapids, MI: William B. Eerdmans Publishing Company, 2013), 64–81.

and attempts to explain some aspects of his story in Genesis and the New Testament (how he knows Abraham and why he has no family), it reiterates Abraham's status as a messenger of God and shares his blessing under the hands of Melchizedek. In addition, it gives a different meaning to Abraham's name change, from one of being the father of nations (see Gen. 17:4-5), to being perfect.

Another aspect of Abraham's covenant relationship with God is the test to offer his son Isaac to the Lord, the *Akedah*. A few Pseudepigrapha texts allude to this formidable experience, but it is not a central focus and, with one exception discussed below, is usually brought up as evidence of Abraham's unfaltering faithfulness, which further solidified the covenant. *Philo the Epic Poet*, whose brief fragments are usually listed alongside Pseudepigrapha texts due to his unknown origin, refers to the *Akedah* of Isaac when discussing Abraham. In the midst of Eusebius' discussion of Abraham in *Praeparatio Evangelica*, Eusebius cites some words from Philo praising the greatness of Abraham:

> O far-famed Abraham, resplendently did your God-beloved prayers abound in wondrous counsels. For when you left the beauteous garden of dread plants [possible reference to the wood for the sacrifice], the praiseworthy thunderer quenched the pyre and made his promise immortal. From that time forth the offspring of that awesome born one have won far-hymned praise . . . as mortal hand readied the sword with resolve, and crackling (wood) was gathered at the side, he brought into his hands a horned ram.
>
> *Praep. Ev.* 9.20.1

In *Pseudo-Philo*'s work, the *Liber Antiquitatum Biblicarum*, God recounts his request for Abraham to offer his son, Isaac, as a burnt offering. "And he brought him to be placed on the altar, but I gave him back to his father and, because he did not refuse, his offering was acceptable before me" (*LAB* 18.5). Later in the *Liber Antiquitatum Biblicarum*, following the defeat of Sisera, Deborah and the people sang a hymn which included several elements from Abraham's story.[14] The first

14. Another reference which connects singing with Abraham, but more directly, is an early Christian excerpt (from Niceta of Remesiana [*De Psalmodiae Bono* 3]) which debates the origin of singing to God, and quotes from a text called "The Inquiry of Abraham" (or "The Interrogation of Abraham") which claims Abraham as the first singer. In this brief reference, Abraham sang alongside the animals, springs of water, and the elements. The author quoting this text, however, refutes the notion that Abraham was the first singer and instead claims it was Moses, as seen in Exodus 15, the Song at the Sea. The origin of the episode about Abraham is unknown, although it is possible that it is an allusion to the *Apocalypse of Abraham* where Abraham learns a song to sing in the heavenly throne-room alongside heavenly fiery creatures (*Apoc. Abr.* 18.1–3). See R. Bauckham, "The Inquiry of Abraham (A Possible Allusion to the *Apocalypse of Abraham*). A New Translation and Introduction", in *Old Testament Pseudepigrapha. More Noncanonical Scriptures*, eds. Bauckham, Davila, and Panayotov, Vol. 1, 60–61.

element was his deliverance from the furnace after refusing to help build the tower of Babel. "And he [God] chose our nation and took Abraham our father out of the fire and chose him over all his brothers and kept him from the fire and freed him from the bricks destined for building the tower" (32.1). The second element was the miraculous birth of Isaac to the formerly-barren Sarah. For some unexplained reason, this miracle led to the angels being jealous of him, "and the worshiping hosts envied him" (32.1).[15] Perhaps the angels' jealousy gives the reason behind the third element unique to this text: God's request of Abraham to sacrifice his new son, Isaac. "And since they were jealous of him, God said to him, 'Kill the fruit of your body for me, and offer for me as a sacrifice what has been given to you by me.' And Abraham did not argue, but set out immediately" (32.2). The ensuing dialogue between Abraham and Isaac explores the motivation and perspective of each participant in the sacrifice, which is repeated later in the story of Jephthah's daughter who stated, "Do you not remember what happened in the days of our fathers when the father placed the son as a [burnt offering], and he did not refuse him but gladly gave consent to him, and the one being offered was ready and the one who was offering was rejoicing" (40.2). Yet before Abraham carried out the task to kill him,

> the Most Powerful hastened and sent forth his voice from on high saying, "You shall not slay your son, nor shall you destroy the fruit of your body. For now I have appeared so as to reveal you to those who do not know you and have shut the mouths of those who are always speaking evil against you. Now your memory will be before me always, and your name and his will remain from one generation to another."[16]
>
> 32.4

15. The notion of angels being jealous of Abraham is also found in *Genesis Rabbah* 55.4, where they accuse Abraham before God.

16. The angel who stayed Abraham's hand from sacrificing Isaac is likely also referred to in the *Testament of Joseph*. Although Abraham is not mentioned in Gen. 39:1-20 (the original story of Joseph and Potiphar's wife), the *Testament of Joseph* adds an Abrahamic twist. As Joseph is fighting to withstand Potiphar's wife's advances, he prays aloud in front of her for not only God's help, but assistance from the "angel of Abraham" (*T. Jos.* 6.8). This angel seems to be a reference to the angel who visited Abraham in Genesis 22:15-18, however there it is usually seen as a circumlocution for Yahweh while here it is an actual intermediary. For a brief review of the possible relationship and development between "angel of YHWH" and YHWH, see G. von Rad, *Genesis. A Commentary*, revised edn. (Philadelphia: The Westminster Press, 1972), 193–94, where he argues that the original understanding of this title was that "the angel of the Lord is therefore a form in which Yahweh appears (*eine Erscheinungsform Jahwes*). He is God himself in human form" (193). For another review of the ambiguity of these terms, see V. Hirth, *Gottes Boten im Alten Testament* (Theologische Arbeiten 32; Berlin: Evangelische Verlagsanstalt, 1975), 13–23. C. Newsom argues that this ambiguity is the narrator's effort to maintain the paradox of mortals encountering Yahweh's authority in close encounters, yet maintaining the impossibility of humans having unmediated access to God's presence. See "Angels" in *ABD*, Vol. 1, 250.

Abraham's willingness is thus lauded and the covenant relationship is solidified from one generation to another.

One "gap" that is missing in Genesis at the end of Abraham's life is Abraham giving a final blessing to his son, Isaac, like Isaac will give to Jacob (Genesis 27–28), and Jacob to his twelve sons (Genesis 49). One Pseudepigrapha text exploits this opportunity to create a unique depiction of the character Abraham. The *Testament of Abraham* is one of the most interesting depictions of Abraham among the Pseudepigrapha texts because, while it hearkens back to some characteristics and episodes from the Genesis account, it also modifies, even reverses them, resulting in quite a different Abraham.[17] The beginning of the story, for example, recounts Abraham's characteristic hospitality to any who may visit him, but it also puts his age just before death at 995 years, far beyond Genesis's 175 years (cf. *T. Abr.* 1.1 with Gen. 25:7). Abraham's status as God's friend is repeated several times in the text (*T. Abr.* 1.6; 4.7; 8.2) as his obedience and faithfulness is lauded; however, Abraham is anything but obedient in the *Testament of Abraham*. He constantly refuses God's messengers and will not bless Isaac and make a disposition of his goods so that he can properly die (9.4–6). Even after promising to follow Michael to heaven, after a requested journey above the earth, he reverses course and continues his stubbornness (15.1–10). This duplicitous characterization seems to have made ancient copyists uneasy to the point that they "corrected" these flaws and created a shorter version, known today as Recension B, which keeps many elements of the story of Recension A, but without the same negative traits of Abraham.[18] Since these two recensions or versions have significant differences, we will treat each separately with comparisons drawn between them.

Recension A shows God's favor upon Abraham as God's friend, but puts some distance between Abraham and God since God always speaks to Abraham through an intermediary, and Abraham's requests to God are relayed through an intermediary (a significant difference from the *Apocalypse of Abraham* seen above). When it is time for Abraham to die, God wants to afford him the opportunity to properly pass on his possessions and a last blessing to his son Isaac before dying. God's desire is transmitted through the archangel Michael and sets up the perfect testamentary opportunity for Abraham, a setting which occurs several times in the story, but in the end no testament is given because of Abraham's repeated refusals (Recension A 20.1–11). Abraham is seen as the beneficiary of God's blessings in

17. For an in-depth discussion on the possible dating of this text, which is commonly dated to the first century CE before the revolt between 115 and 117 CE, which decimated Egyptian Jewry in Alexandria and after which Egyptian Jewish literature dried up: see D.C. Allison, Jr., *Testament of Abraham* (Berlin: de Gruyter, 2003), 34–40.

18. There has been much scholarly debate on the relationship between the two recensions, especially whether one is derivative of the other. The scholarly consensus today seems to favor Recension A as earlier with Recension B reacting to it. See J. Ludlow, *Abraham Meets Death: Narrative Humor in the Testament of Abraham* (Sheffield: Sheffield Academic Press, 2002), 152–80. See also Allison, *Testament of Abraham*, 12–15.

fulfillment of God's promises to bless Abraham "as the stars of heaven and as the sand by the seashore, and he lives in abundance, (having) a large livelihood and many possessions, and he is very rich. But above all others he is righteous in all goodness, (having been) hospitable and loving until the end of his life" (1:5; cf. Gen. 22:17 where the promise is posterity, but here it is prosperity).

The dialogue between Abraham and Michael leaves it unclear whether Abraham knows who Michael is, as Abraham experiences things and hides them from others until confronted by the truth from Sarah and Isaac, whereupon Abraham claims he knew all along (6:6-7). With everything out in the open, Abraham is given the opportunity to share a last testament with his family and follow Michael to heaven (to die). Abraham hesitates. He says he will follow Michael but only if and after he is given a tour above the earth. Michael secures permission from God for such an experience, but has to be commanded to stop it shortly thereafter because Abraham begins killing some sinners he sees committing sins (far different from his merciful concern for the inhabitants of Sodom in Genesis) (10:12-15). God worries that Abraham will destroy everything that exists because he lacks mercy since he has not sinned. Instead, Abraham is taken to the place of judgment where he can learn mercy, which is accomplished as the whole process of judgment is described and interpreted. Abraham now asks to restore to life those sinners he earlier destroyed, and his request is granted (14:10-15).

At this point of the story, one would think Abraham would willingly follow Michael and proceed to his death, but despite his earlier promise to follow Michael after the heavenly journey, he still refuses. God turns to plan B and sends the actual character Death (Thanatos) to secure Abraham's soul, but only after beautifying himself in appearance and smell (16:1-6). Abraham continues his stubbornness, but is physically affected by Thanatos's presence. Still, he requests to see Death's many faces and learn more about him. When Death reveals his many faces, thousands of Abraham's servants instantly die (17:18). Abraham castigates Death for killing his servants and then requests that they pray together to restore them to life. So, in one of the most ironic scenes in ancient literature, Death prays with Abraham to bring people back to life (18:8-11). Eventually Death convinces Abraham to grasp or kiss his hand whereupon Abraham's soul leaves his body and angels escort his precious soul to heaven.[19]

19. Angels escorting Abraham's soul can be found in some short excerpts from missing Abrahamic texts mentioned in early Christian sources. One, labeled "The Dispute over Abraham," discusses how "the angel of righteousness and the angel of wickedness disputed over the salvation or perdition of Abraham, each of the bands claiming him for their own company." Quotation from Origen, *Hom. Luc.* 35.3 as found in R. Bauckham, "The Dispute over Abraham. A New Translation and Introduction", in *Old Testament Pseudepigrapha: More Noncanonical Scriptures*, Vol. 1, eds. Bauckham, Davila, and Panayotov, 58. The wider context of this excerpt discusses a phenomenon shared in several Pseudepigrapha texts, most notably about Moses in the *Testament of Moses* (cf. Jude 9), how angels contest over the souls of the dead and how those who are righteous will be taken up to heaven saved from

As mentioned above, some ancient Jewish and Christian interpreters and copyists felt uncomfortable with this unusual depiction of Abraham which seems to reverse many of Abraham's characteristics that are lauded and set forth as models for others to follow in other texts, so they altered the story in an effort to reform this duplicitous characterization.[20] The resulting story in Recension B still maintains some of the narrative elements of Recension A, but they no longer make sense without the surrounding context or narrative development. Instead, Recension B foregrounds Abraham's thoughts and intentions, thereby changing and giving explanations for some of Abraham's unusual, stubborn actions, and it ties the story much closer to the biblical account.

One question that naturally arises about this text is why it presents Abraham in this surprising manner. It never denigrates Abraham to the point where his status or salvation is endangered, but it feels comfortable to use him in an entertaining fashion. It seems to be a function of creating "historical fictions" under Greek novelistic influence in order to attract readers' attention to see these characters in a new light.[21] Thus, entertainment seems to be behind this text like other Hellenistic Jewish texts (e.g., Tobit, Judith) that appear to signal their playfulness with obvious historical inaccuracies, but are still didactic in promoting faithfulness in a diaspora setting where they felt comfortable enough to poke fun at their heroes.[22]

the clutches of evil spirits. While the text specifically mentions one angel from each side, it also alludes to each having a "band" which is similar to these other texts where groups of angels show up. There is some question whether the events surrounding Abraham occur near the time of his death or earlier as a contest of discipleship, but its correlation with other similar texts seems to point towards being near the time of death because it is disputing over his salvation or perdition. For more Christian sources with this theme, see the *Homily of John of Thessalonica on the Dormition of Mary*, chapter 5 (Brian E. Daley, trans., *On the Dormition of Mary: Early Patristic Homilies* (Popular Patristics Series 18; Crestwood, NY: St. Vladimir's Press, 1998), recension 1, pp. 47–70, introduction, pp. 12–13) and the Syriac *Apocalypse of Paul* (J. Perkins, "The revelation of the blessed apostle", *JAOS* 8 (1864): 183–212). A possible comparable example is found among the Dead Sea Scrolls in 4Q544 [VisAmr^{b} ar] 1 9–12 where Amram, father of Moses and Aaron, sees two angels disputing over him, either for his allegiance in life or at the time of his death.

20. For more on Recension B's reformation of Recension A's more humorous narrative, see J. Ludlow, "Humor and Paradox in the Characterization of Abraham in the Testament of Abraham", in *Ancient Fiction: The Matrix of Early Christian and Jewish Narrative*, eds. J.A. Brant, C.W. Hedrick, and C. Shea (SBL Symposium Series 32; Atlanta, GA: SBL, 2005), 199–214. See also Allison, *Testament of Abraham*, 23, discussing negative marginal notes from manuscripts of Recension A.

21. For some discussion of this phenomenon, see L.M. Wills, "Jewish Novellas in a Greek and Roman Age: Fiction and Identity", *JSJ* 42 (2011): 141–65.

22. For more on the topic of humor in Hellenistic Jewish texts, see E.S. Gruen, *Diaspora. Jews Amidst Greeks and Romans* (Boston: Harvard University Press, 2004), 135–212, for Abraham specifically, see pp. 183–93, 202–3.

Heavenly Status

Many Pseudepigrapha texts go beyond Genesis' Abrahamic account and focus on Abraham's post-mortal status as a heavenly figure, one who, because of his righteousness, sits eternally as God's friend, and who continues to watch over, and even in some cases intercede on behalf of, his posterity. His heavenly station is frequently tied up with his son and grandson, as the three—Abraham, Isaac, and Jacob—stand together as beneficiaries of the covenant blessings and are the eternal possessives in the common title for the deity, i.e., the God of Abraham, Isaac, and Jacob. In the midst of a grand eschatological vision for Levi in the *Testament of Levi*, Abraham is elevated to a brief comparison with the divine. "The heavens will be opened, and from the temple of glory sanctification will come upon him, with a fatherly voice, as from Abraham to Isaac" (*T. Levi* 18.6). Abraham's status as father of fathers is here symbolized by his fatherly voice and is compared to the temple, sanctification, and the glory of the Most High. At the end of the eschatological events, the righteous will trample on the wicked spirits "and the Lord will rejoice in his children; he will be well pleased by his beloved ones forever. Then Abraham, Isaac, and Jacob will rejoice, and I [Levi] shall be glad, and all the saints shall be clothed in righteousness" (18.12–14). Here we see Abraham listed with his son and grandson, emphasizing not only their continued existence, but their continuing care over their covenant children.

In a similar eschatological vein of combining the three patriarchs and their immortality, the *Testament of Judah* shares another passage about Abraham and the great things that will happen to his descendants. After being promised future leadership and judgment over the nations, Judah is promised that Abraham, Isaac, and Jacob will be resurrected to life and that he and his brothers will be chiefs (wielding) scepters in Israel (*T. Jud.* 25.1).

The *Testament of Benjamin* has a brief reference to Abraham as part of its ending exhortation to righteousness. In this case, not only are Abraham's descendants mentioned, but Abraham's progenitors as well. Abraham stands in the middle of a righteous line of patriarchs who will be glorified and rejoice at the righteousness of their posterity. "'Keep God's commandments until the Lord reveals his salvation to all the nations.' And then you will see Enoch and Seth and Abraham and Isaac and Jacob being raised up at the right hand in great joy" (*T. Benj.* 10.5–6).

Abraham's elevated status in the heavenly realm can be seen in a few other texts as well. In the *Sibylline Oracles* (*Sib. Or.* 2.245–49), Abraham is listed with Isaac, Jacob, and others as ones who will be resurrected in the last days. Specifically, Abraham is called "Great Abraham," the only one with an adjectival title. In another list of "righteous ones" residing in Paradise, found in the *Apocalypse of Zephaniah*, Abraham is mentioned along with Isaac and Jacob and others, where an angel converses with them "as friend to friend speaking with one another" (*Apoc. Zeph.* 9.4–5). Later in this text, Abraham, Isaac, and Jacob are seen interceding for the saints in torment. "Then at a certain hour daily they come forth with the great angel. He sounds a trumpet up to heaven and another sound upon the earth. All the righteous hear the sound. They come running, praying to the Lord Almighty daily on behalf of these who are in all these torments" (11.4–6). *3 Enoch* relates a vision of the righteous souls in heaven which includes Abraham: "I saw the souls of the fathers of the world, Abraham, Isaac, and Jacob, and the rest of the righteous, who had been raised from their graves and had ascended into heaven. They were praying before the Holy One, [asking him to redeem his children on the earth] . . ." (*3 En.* 44.7). After God explains and details their many sins which prevent him from delivering them, "at once Abraham, Isaac, and Jacob began to weep. Then the Holy One, blessed be he, said to them: '*Abraham, my friend*, Isaac, my chosen one, Jacob, my firstborn, how can I save them at this time from among the nations of the world?" (44.10, my emphasis).

As Ezra proceeds in *4 Ezra* through his visionary experience, he begins asking many questions of the Lord including whether the righteous may intercede for the ungodly. The Lord responds that they will not because "everyone will bear his own righteousness or unrighteousness" (*4 Ezra* 7.105). Ezra disputes the Lord's answer because there are examples from the past of the righteous successfully praying for the wicked such as Abraham praying for the people of Sodom (7.106). "If therefore the righteous have prayed for the ungodly now, when corruption has increased and unrighteousness has multiplied, why will it not be so then as well?" (7.111). The Lord acknowledges Abraham's intermediary role as an example of the strong praying for the weak, but stated that it is only effective in this present world and once the immortal age begins, "no one will then be able to have mercy on him who has been condemned in the judgment, or to harm him who is victorious" (7.115). This perspective may contradict some of the other Pseudepigrapha texts about Abraham that emphasize Abraham's continued function in overseeing the spiritual welfare of his descendants (e.g., *Apoc. Zeph.* 11.4–6; *T. Levi* 15.4), or it may imply that there will come a time when even that assistance from Abraham will no longer be possible (but until the final Day of Judgment, he can still intercede).[23]

The "bosom of Abraham" shows up in the New Testament parable of Lazarus and the rich man (see Lk. 16:22). One Pseudepigrapha text, the *Apocalypse of Sedrach*, which is heavily Christianized and whose Jewish origin is increasingly doubted, similarly reports that the righteous will be received in the bosom of Abraham.[24] This phrase seems to be dependent upon the New Testament rather

23. For a general overview of Abraham's role as intermediary in early Jewish and Christian tradition (as seer, priestly figure, and prophetic judge), see J.S. Siker, *Disinheriting the Jews: Abraham in Early Christian Controversy* (Louisville, KY: Westminster/John Knox Press, 1991), 24–27.

24. J.H. Charlesworth and G.S. Oegema, *The Pseudepigrapha and Christian Origins: Essays From the Studiorum Novi Testamenti Societas* (New York: T&T Clark International, 2008), 10–11.

than on Jewish sources, but regardless it reemphasizes Abraham's heavenly location and his eternal destiny as the locus for the righteous.[25]

The *Testament of Isaac* is a derivative work of the *Testament of Abraham* and often shows up alongside it and the *Testament of Jacob* as the *Testaments of the Three Patriarchs*, and thus not surprisingly makes some connections to that text. Near the beginning of the testament, the archangel Michael is sent to Isaac to prepare him for his death just as he had done with Abraham (*T. Isaac* 2.1). When the angel first meets Isaac, Isaac notes that he resembles his father Abraham (2.3).[26] In the ensuing dialogue, Michael explains that he has been sent to take Isaac up to heaven to be with his father. "For your father Abraham is awaiting you; he himself is about to come for you, but now he is resting. There has been prepared for you the throne beside your father Abraham" (2.6–7). Isaac is promised that he, Abraham, and Jacob would be above everyone else in the kingdom of heaven. "You shall be entrusted with this name for all future generations: The Patriarchs. Thus you shall be fathers to all the world . . ." (2.8–9). The patriarchal triumvirate is thus declared in heaven for all the future generations as further testimony of their everlasting existence as well as in their formative roles as fathers ruling on thrones through the eternities.[27] Even the chief of the angels, Michael, ministers to Abraham in the heavens (see 2.11).

Later in the text, Isaac meets Abraham in heaven and they proceed to the throne of God to worship him (*Testament of Isaac* 6). Abraham is identified as one of the "godly ones" and Isaac joins Abraham and the saints in prostrating themselves and praising God before the curtain and the throne of God. The Lord pronounces a blessing and singles out Abraham: "Excellent is your coming, O Abraham, faithful one; excellent is your lineage, and excellent is the presence here of this blessed lineage. So now, everything which you ask in the name of your beloved son Isaac you shall have today as a covenant forever" (6.7–8). Abraham then begins bargaining with the Lord—similar to his petitions on behalf of the wicked inhabitants of Sodom—on what would be required for salvation. Rather than have a strict rule that required multiple acts, Abraham inquires about exceptions and barters down to the bare minimum needed to achieve salvation (see 6.9–23). Within this dialogue, God mentions that those that do some of the required acts will be given to Abraham "as a son in my kingdom" (6.18), reiterating Abraham's location and status in heaven.

25. This notion is also seen in *4 Macc.* 13:17 but extended to include Isaac and Jacob: "After our death in this fashion Abraham and Isaac and Jacob will receive us, and all our forefathers will praise us."

26. Later Isaac needed further clarification that Michael was not his father, Abraham, because he resembled him so much, see *T. Isaac* 2.10–11. Perhaps this is similar to Death disguising himself in beauty before visiting Abraham in the *Testament of Abraham*; now it is Michael who comes "in disguise."

27. Another brief allusion to Abraham's continued existence after death is his granting his "amen" to Isaac's blessing of Jacob in the heavens alongside the Trinity (see *T. Isaac* 2.20).

In the final testament scene, Jacob heavily weeps over his dying father Isaac. Witnessing this scene of great distress, Abraham petitions the Lord to remember also his [grand]son Jacob (see 6.31). From Abraham's petitions and actions in this chapter, we see Abraham's role as a watchful ancestor over his descendants.

The text ends with the exhortation to observe the memorial of Isaac's death, which seems to have fallen on the same date as Abraham's death. They were also to memorialize Abraham's offering of Isaac for on that day,

> when Abraham, the father of fathers, offered him as a sacrifice to God, the perfume of his sacrifice ascended to the veil of the curtain of the one who controls everything. Blessed is everyone who manifests mercy on the memorial day of the father of fathers, our father Abraham and our father Isaac, for each of them shall have a dwelling in the kingdom of heaven, because our Lord has made with them his true covenant forever.
>
> 8.4–5

Another reference to Abraham is found in the *Testament of Jacob* where his "guardian angel" comforts Jacob before his death and blesses the name of "your father Abraham, for he has become the friend of God" because of his generosity and love of strangers (*T. Jac.* 2.12). Acceptance of strangers is a principle that Jacob says the patriarchs taught, and following their examples would allow the patriarchs to intercede on their behalf and would be the way to enter into heaven where they reside. "These are the ones whom the Arabs have designated as the holy fathers" (7.12). "Be generous to strangers and you will be given exactly what was given to the great Abraham, the father of fathers" (7.22).

Conclusion

The Genesis episodes about Abraham are frequently passed down in the Jewish and Christian reception history of Abraham traditions. The Pseudepigrapha texts sometimes follow this pattern, but in the characteristic fashion of Pseudepigrapha texts, new stories are created to fill in gaps or expand on the canonical record. New accounts about Abraham's youth and afterlife status, lacking from Genesis, are most noteworthy, and create a type of panegyric lauding Abraham's hospitality and righteousness. This results in Abraham's immortal, heavenly status where he can serve as an intermediary for his descendants and a model for God's covenant people to aid them in receiving the same heavenly destination he did.

His youth was dominated by contests with his father over idolatry, which eventually led him to leave his homeland for a new promised land. This is one of the various explanations given for why Abraham left Mesopotamia, along with fleeing the Tower of Babel and sharing knowledge with others. Thus, some Abrahamic Pseudepigrapha texts point out that Abraham is not only for the Jewish people; they raise him to a universal status among the neighboring peoples as well. Abraham thus becomes a cultural pioneer who shares knowledge with others, like the Phoenicians and Egyptians. His travels throughout the region provide the opportunity for dissemination of this scientific knowledge, but even more importantly its relationship to the knowledge of the one true God.

Some texts try to explain the rationale for the *Akedah* as well as the subsequent blessings that resulted from it. *Pseudo-Philo*, for example, proposed an explanation for why Abraham would offer his son Isaac in sacrifice: to soothe the jealousy of the angels.

The lack of a testament for Abraham before his death in Genesis is exploited by the *Testament of Abraham* which plays with this notion by providing several ideal testamentary settings, only to have Abraham die before giving one, thus staying true to the original account but in a radically unexpected way.

Throughout the variety of texts about Abraham in the Pseudepigrapha, one can see great honor and reverence bestowed upon this venerable patriarch. Abraham's hospitality and righteousness are frequently modeled as the ideal for God's covenant people. Abraham's ministry denotes a new age or time which pushes God's children into new spiritual experiences after the Fall of Adam and the Flood of Noah. He is viewed as the father not only of the covenant, but of the people themselves. As such, his fatherly voice and teachings are heeded. He is usually closely connected with his posterity by the frequent reference to the patriarchal triumvirate: Abraham, Isaac, and Jacob. It highlights the fulfillment of God's covenant promises of numberless seed and a line through which the covenant could be passed down.

Many Pseudepigrapha texts go beyond Genesis's mortal Abrahamic account and focus on Abraham's post-mortal status as a heavenly figure, one who, because of his righteousness, sits eternally as God's friend, and who continues to watch over, and even in some cases intercede on behalf of, his posterity. These texts highlight Abraham's immortal existence (usually through resurrection), and his continued role among his posterity as "father of fathers" manifested by his care, intercession, and rejoicing for his children. In fact, Abraham's heavenly elevation becomes the locus for the righteous, to dwell eternally with him in his bosom. Abraham is thus consistently found among the righteous ones, usually as one of the preeminent ones noted by the exceptional, and eternally earned title, "friend of God."

Chapter 4

ABRAHAM IN REWRITTEN SCRIPTURE

Susan Docherty

Introduction: "Rewritten Scripture"

The extant literature of the Second Temple period attests to widespread and ongoing reflection on the significance of Israel's founding ancestor Abraham. The scriptural narratives about his life are frequently re-shaped by later authors in order to express their theological convictions, and respond to the challenges of changing social and historical contexts. This chapter will explore the treatment of Abraham within a small sub-set of this corpus, a group of texts traditionally categorized as "rewritten bible".[1] These offer a continuous retelling of large sections of the scriptures, following their broad outline, but re-presenting them through a combination of expansion, abridgement, omission, and reordering of their material. This designation has become contested in recent decades, partly because of a concern that it may give the misleading impression that a fixed or canonical "bible" existed in the early centuries BCE, so the term "rewritten scripture" has increasingly come to be preferred within scholarship.

These texts form part of a broad spectrum of reworking older authoritative sources, ranging from minor scribal revisions to the composition of new "parabiblical" writings anchored only loosely in the scriptural narratives, like the *Life of Adam and Eve*, for example.[2] The boundaries of the genre are somewhat imprecise, then, and continue to be debated. Nevertheless, definite examples of this form of interpretation can be identified, so this investigation will focus on three works which are widely accepted as major representatives of it: the book of *Jubilees*,

1. See G. Vermes, *Scripture and Tradition in Israel* (SPB, 4; Leiden: Brill, 1961), 95; for further description of the literary form and its characteristics, see P.S. Alexander, "Retelling the Old Testament", in *It Is Written: Scripture Citing Scripture. Essays in Honour of Barnabas Lindars*, eds. D.A. Carson et al. (Cambridge: Cambridge University Press, 1988), 99–118.

2. For a discussion of this exegetical process and the scope of the terms "rewritten scripture" and "parabiblical", see S. White Crawford, *Rewriting Scripture in Second Temple Times* (Grand Rapids: Eerdmans, 2008), 2–15.

the Qumran *Genesis Apocryphon* and the *Biblical Antiquities* of *Pseudo-Philo*.[3] The primary aim of the chapter is to sketch out the main features of the presentation of Abraham within these rewritten scriptures, highlighting especially any shared themes or common exegetical techniques. It will also consider how the treatment of the patriarch relates to the wider theological emphases and historical setting of each author.

Book of Jubilees

The starting point for this study is the book of *Jubilees*, which provides a particularly comprehensive treatment of the figure of Abraham. This work presents itself as a record of divine revelation made to Moses through an angel on Mount Sinai (see e.g., *Jub.* 1:1, 26; 2:1), and retells in detail, and with considerable amplification, the narratives of Genesis 1 through to Exodus 14. Many of the author's supplements emphasize the theme of God's covenant with Israel, and the need to maintain this relationship by careful observance of the traditional laws and separation from other nations.[4] Some connections between *Jubilees* and the Enochic literature are evident, including advocacy of a 364-day solar calendrical system (e.g., *Jub.* 6:32; see also *Jub.* 4:15-25 for other shared traditions).[5] *Jubilees* is generally dated to around the middle of the second century BCE.[6] Originally composed in Hebrew, it survived mainly in an Ethiopic translation.[7] At least fifteen fragmentary manuscripts of a Hebrew text were also discovered at Qumran,[8] demonstrating its influence in some sections of early Judaism.

3. Josephus, *Ant.* 1–11 is also generally included within the category of rewritten scripture, but will not be considered here as his writings are treated in full elsewhere in this volume.

4. For further detail on the key themes of *Jubilees*, see J.C. Vanderkam, *The Book of Jubilees* (Sheffield: Sheffield Academic Press, 2001); and S.E. Docherty, *The Jewish Pseudepigrapha* (London: SPCK, 2014), 14–23.

5. These parallels are explored more fully in J.C. Vanderkam, "Enoch Traditions in *Jubilees* and Other Second Century Sources", in *SBL Seminar Papers 13*, ed. P.J. Achtemeier (Missoula: Scholars Press, 1987), Vol. 1, 229–51.

6. For further detail, see Vanderkam, *Jubilees*, 17–21.

7. As well as this Ge'ez version, a partial Latin translation and some quotations in Greek are extant. Further discussion of textual transmission and translations can be found in J.C. Vanderkam, *The Book of Jubilees* (2 vols.; Corpus Scriptorum Christianorum Orientalium, 510–11/Scriptores Aethiopici, 87–8; Leuven: Peeters, 1989), 1:ix; 2:xi–xiv; and O.S. Wintermute, "Jubilees: A New Translation and Introduction", in *OTP*, Vol. 2, 41–3.

8. 4Q216, or 4QJub[a], is the most extensive of these, on which see J.C. Vanderkam and J.T. Milik, "The First *Jubilees* Manuscript From Qumran Cave 4: A Preliminary Publication", *JBL* 110 (1991): 243–70.

Approximately one quarter of the book is devoted to the life of Abraham. This section follows closely both the sequence and content of the Pentateuchal sources (Genesis 12–25), covering in full key episodes, such as Abraham's call to journey to the land of Canaan (Gen. 12:1-10; *Jub.* 12:22–13:9); the two accounts of the making of the covenant (Gen. 15:1-21; 17:1-14; *Jub.* 14:1-20; 15:1-34); and the aborted sacrifice of Isaac (Gen. 22:1-19; *Jub.* 17:15–18:19). Heavily summarized versions are also included of the break with Lot (Gen. 13:5-13; *Jub.* 13:17-18); the battle with the kings (Gen. 14:1-12; *Jub.* 13:22-24); and the visit of three messengers to Abraham at the Oaks of Mamre, and his subsequent dialogue with God about the destruction of Sodom (Gen. 18:1-33; *Jub.* 16:1-6). His second attempt to pass off his wife as his sister to a king outside Canaan (Gen. 20:1-18) is omitted entirely. There is a lacuna in the surviving texts at the point of Abraham's encounter with Melchizedek (*Jub.* 13:25; see Gen. 14:14-20), so it is not clear exactly how that meeting was originally treated; but, in line with a wider interest in ritual and priestly matters,[9] the incident is used to stress the enduring nature of the commandments about tithing (*Jub.* 13:25; cf. Gen. 14:20).

Within this extensive and largely faithful rewriting of the Abraham Cycle, however, the figure of the patriarch is subtly re-shaped to serve as a model of law-abiding piety.[10] A range of exegetical methods characteristic of rewritten scripture are employed to achieve this end of creating a wholly positive picture of him. First, the use of selective omission and abridgement enables the author to eliminate content that is less central to his overall aims, or to deal with passages perceived as problematic. Perhaps the best-known case of this in *Jubilees* comes in the retelling of the visit to Egypt by Abraham and Sarah during a time of famine in Canaan. Abraham's morally dubious plan to save his own skin by sending his wife into Pharaoh's harem is passed over with only the brief notice that Sarah "was taken from him" (*Jub.* 13:12-13; cf. Gen. 12:10-20; *Gen. Apoc.* 20.14).[11]

Second, small but nonetheless telling divergences from the scriptural narratives are introduced. In the account in *Jubilees* of the divine announcement that the elderly Sarah would soon conceive a son, for instance, rather than *laughing* at this news, Abraham is said to have responded far more appropriately by *rejoicing* at it (*Jub.* 15:17; cf. Gen. 17:17). Since the text is now available only in Ethiopic translation, it is not possible to be certain whether the author chose to use a different, but closely-related, Hebrew verb from the one found in Genesis (צחק), or

9. A priestly background is suggested for the author by several commentators because of these concerns; see, for example, Vanderkam, *Jubilees*, pp. 56, 141–2.

10. For a detailed exploration of the relationship between the presentation of Abraham in *Jubilees* and the Genesis source, see J.T.A.G.M. Van Ruiten, *Abraham in the Book of Jubilees: The Rewriting of Genesis 11:26–25:10 in the Book of* Jubilees *11:14–23:8* (Leiden: Brill, 2012); and J.C. Endres, *Biblical Interpretation in the Book of Jubilees* (CBQMS, 18; Washington: Catholic Biblical Association of America, 1987), 18–50.

11. The English translation used throughout is that provided in Wintermute, "Jubilees".

else interpreted that verb in a particular or extended sense.[12] The latter move is possible, however, given that צחק is translated with a form of συγχαίρω ("rejoice with") in the Septuagint of Genesis 21:6. In another example of a minor difference added in order to aggrandize Abraham, the whole of his life is presented as a series of ten trials, which he successfully negotiates (*Jub.* 17:17-18; 19:8; cf. *M.Aboth* 5.3). This motif is evidently an extension of the scriptural account of the divine "testing" of his faith and obedience in the command to sacrifice Isaac (Gen. 22:1).

Third, since the rewritten scriptures are not constrained by the need to follow the order of the source text in the same way as other forms of interpretation, such as lemmatized commentary, elements within the underlying narrative can be rearranged. In *Jubilees*, for example, Abraham and Jacob are depicted as interacting closely with each other over five chapters, even though the death of Abraham is recounted before the birth of his twin grandsons in Genesis. In this section, Abraham is shown bestowing special blessings on Jacob, and confirming him as the one true heir to the divine promises (*Jub.* 19:16-29; 22:10-30). This helps to smooth over some of the more questionable aspects of the Pentateuchal accounts, justifying Rebecca's favoritism of Jacob over Esau (*Jub.* 19:15-31; cf. Gen. 25:28), for instance, and clarifying that Jacob's acquisition of the right of primogeniture was not a result of underhand trickery, but was rather a fulfilment of what God had always intended, approved in advance by Abraham (*Jub.* 19:17-25; 22:10-15; cf. *Jub.* 2:20; 15:30; 26:24; *LAB* 18.6; Gen. 25:29-34). The effect on the overall narrative of *Jubilees*, however, is to minimize the significance of Isaac, as Abraham's role extends further into the patriarchal history, and Jacob becomes active earlier in it.[13]

This reordering of events may serve a particular theological agenda, as argued especially by Halpern-Amaru, in underlining the transmission of Israel's covenant inheritance through a single, pure, and divinely-chosen patriarchal line centering on Jacob.[14] It is important to recognize, however, that this theme is not simply an ideological import, but has deep scriptural roots. The question of Abraham's rightful heir is raised in the Pentateuch itself (e.g., Gen. 15:2-5; 17:19-21), for example, and the expectation that the covenant made with him will be fulfilled only through his descendants is frequently reaffirmed there (e.g. Gen. 12:7; 15:18; 17:7-8; 22:17-18; Exod. 32:13; Deut. 1:8). Furthermore, the chronology of the book of Genesis does allow for the interpretation that Abraham and Jacob overlapped

12. Extending or narrowing the range of meaning of a word has been identified as a rabbinic exegetical technique, so arguably is rooted in earlier interpretative practice; see A. Samely, *Rabbinic Interpretation of Scripture in the Mishnah* (Oxford: Oxford University Press, 2002), 359–76.

13. This is noted by several commentators; Endres, for example, concludes that "Jacob clearly emerges as the central and pre-eminent character in Jubilees" (Endres, *Biblical Interpretation*, 18; see also pp. 19, 25–7, 43–7); cf. Vanderkam, *Jubilees*, 45, 54–6.

14. B. Halpern-Amaru, *Rewriting the Bible: Land and Covenant in Postbiblical Jewish Literature* (Valley Forge: Trinity Press International, 1994), 25–54.

for fifteen years (see Gen. 21:5; 25:7, 26; cf. Heb. 11:9 which may reflect such an understanding), and the connection between them is also highlighted in the application of the words of the divine blessing of Abraham to Jacob in his prayer for deliverance from Esau (*Jub.* 19:21-24; Gen. 32:9-12; cf. Gen. 12:2-3; 13:16).

The inclusion of supplementary material is the main tool employed in *Jubilees* to reshape the presentation of the patriarch and to fill in perceived gaps in the underlying scriptural accounts. Apart from his relationship with Jacob, the author demonstrates a particular interest in two periods of Abraham's life about which the book of Genesis provides very little information: his early years, before his call to journey to the promised land, and his last days and death. In extensive additions inserted at these points in his narrative, the author embellishes the character of Abraham in a number of ways, emphasizing especially his learning, prayerfulness, and opposition to idolatry. Abraham is said, therefore, to have possessed various kinds of knowledge, including of writing, astrology, and the Hebrew language (*Jub.* 11:8, 16; 12:25-27), and also to have been able, at a remarkably tender age, to teach the Chaldeans how to make more effective farming implements (*Jub.* 11:23). This motif of Abraham's exceptional wisdom is shared with other examples of rewritten scripture (see e.g. *Gen. Apoc.* 19.25; *Ant.* 1.167).

He is also depicted throughout *Jubilees* as a man of constant prayer. He is shown asking for divine guidance about whether to leave Haran, for instance (*Jub.* 12:19-21); regularly offering sacrifices (*Jub.* 13.4, 8-9; 14:11; cf. Gen. 12:8; 13:18); like Noah before him (*Jub.* 6:17-19; cf. 14:20), keeping the major festivals even before their prescription in the Mosaic Law (*Jub.* 15:1-2; 16:20-31; 18:18; 22:1); and praying in thanksgiving to God for the blessings of his life as he approaches his death (*Jub.* 22:6-9). The efficacy of Abraham's prayer is widely celebrated within early Jewish literature (see e.g. *T. Abr.* 14.5-15; *Gen. Apoc.* 20.12-23), in a development of the scriptural reports of his intercession on behalf of the people of Sodom (Gen. 18:22-33) and frequent direct converse with God (Gen. 12:1-3; 13:14-17; 15:1-21; 17:1-21; 21:12-13; 22:1-2, 11-12).

The principal theme in these expansions, though, is Abraham's strong rejection of idolatry. According to *Jubilees*, he even separates from his own father in his youth in order to avoid its futility (*Jub.* 11:16-17; 12:1-8). His hostility to idol-worship eventually culminates in his decision to burn a local temple, an event which causes his brother to lose his life and prompts the family's departure from Chaldea, a move which is unexplained in scripture (*Jub.* 12:12-15; cf. *Apoc. Abr.* 1–6; cf. Gen. 11:31-32). This passage reflects an interpretative connection between the place name "Ur" (Gen 11:28, 31) and the similar-sounding Hebrew word for "flame" אור (cf. *LAB* 6.1–18), thereby demonstrating the close attention paid by early Jewish interpreters to the individual words of scripture. The older Abraham continues to accentuate the dangers of both idolatry and close contact with gentiles in his ethical exhortations (e.g. *Jub.* 21.3-4; 22.16-22), so the importance of this message for the author is evident. This may be an indication of the *Sitz im Leben* of *Jubilees*; Vanderkam, for instance, argues that it was composed in the Maccabean period to oppose any accommodation to the Hellenizing reforms of Antiochus IV

Epiphanes.[15] However, since the claim that Abraham's monotheism was the initial cause of his migration is not unique to *Jubilees* (see e.g. *Ant.* 1.155–57) and may reflect traditional exegesis, these passages do not provide decisive evidence about the work's historical setting. Indeed, this narrative may well have been created primarily to deal with the potentially problematic implication of a particular verse in the book of Joshua that Abraham himself participated in the worship of foreign gods: "Thus says the Lord, the God of Israel, 'Your fathers lived of old beyond the Euphrates, Terah, the father of Abraham and of Nahor; and they served other gods . . .'" (Josh. 24:2).[16]

Many of the supplementary passages included in *Jubilees* are written in the form of monologues or dialogues, and so increase the amount of direct speech present within a narrative that is already rich in direct speech, following the scriptural sources. This feature adds both vividness and a sense of authenticity to the retelling. Abraham's life ends in *Jubilees*, for example, with him giving a series of blessings and lengthy farewell speeches to his descendants (*Jub.* 19:26–22:30). In these, the author is able to express directly, and with apparent patriarchal authority, teaching that he wants his contemporary audience to hear.[17] He is clearly drawing on the examples of the death-bed speeches of figures like Jacob (Gen. 49:1-27) and Moses (Deut. 31:30–33:29), perhaps on the basis of a hermeneutical assumption that if one of Israel's ancestors gave such a final testament, so, too, must others have done.

This axiom about the coherence of scripture prompts the author to draw out further correspondences between Abraham and other characters. His accounts of Abraham's early monotheism, for instance, reflect traditions about the destruction of a temple housing idols by Job (*T. Job* 2.1–5.3). An association between Abraham and the righteous-but-Satan-tested Job is also exploited in the development of the *Akedah* narrative in *Jubilees*, in which responsibility for initiating this trial is attributed to Mastema, chief of the evil spirits (*Jub.* 17.15-18; cf. Job 1:1-12), thereby absolving God of any implication of cruelty (cf. 4Q225 2.i.9–10; *LAB* 32.1–2; *b. Sanh.* 89b; *Gen. Rab.* 55.4).[18] In another non-scriptural expansion about Abraham's

15. Vanderkam, *Jubilees*, 139–41.

16. For similar attempts to distance Abraham from the paganism of his ancestors, see also e.g. *LAB* 23.5; Judg. 5:6-9. All biblical quotations in English in this chapter follow the RSV.

17. This use of the testamentary form to put forward theological or ethical teaching is exemplified particularly clearly in the *Testaments of the Twelve Patriarchs*. Abraham's testaments in *Jubilees* are treated at length in Van Ruiten, *Abraham in the Book of Jubilees*, 253–329.

18. Parallels between Job and the Abraham of *Jubilees* are suggested by a number of commentators; see e.g. J.C. Vanderkam, "The *Aqedah*, *Jubilees and Pseudojubilees*", in *The Quest for Context and Meaning: Studies in Biblical Intertextuality in Honor of James A. Sanders*, eds. C.A. Evans et al. (Biblical Interpretation Series, 28; Leiden: Brill, 1987), 241–62; and M. Kister, "Observations on Aspects of Exegesis, Tradition, and Theology in Midrash,

early life, he is described as saving the populace of Chaldea from starvation by turning away flocks of crows sent by Mastema at sowing time to eat all the seed before it had taken root (*Jub.* 11:11-13, 18-24). Here, Abraham takes on some of the attributes of Joseph, an Israelite who was likewise able to provide the inhabitants of a foreign land with sufficient food (Gen. 37:56-57).[19] This story also echoes the first account in Genesis of the sealing of the covenant, in which Abraham prevents birds of prey from landing on the animal carcasses being offered (Gen. 15:11), so that his actions on one occasion are assumed to be capable of repeating at another.

The Abraham of *Jubilees* is, then, a very recognizable version of his scriptural counterpart, the founder of the people of Israel and the vehicle of God's covenant with them. He comes across, however, as a clearer model of virtue and proper behavior. His more questionable actions, like offering his wife to Pharaoh's harem in order to save his own skin, or laughing at a divine message, are smoothed over, and his wisdom, righteousness, and steadfast monotheism are enhanced. In important supplements to the Genesis narratives, which depend on a close engagement with the scriptures as a whole, correspondences between Abraham and other key biblical figures, such as Noah, Jacob, Joseph, and Job, are highlighted.

The Genesis Apocryphon

The Qumran discoveries raise fresh questions about the scope and form of rewritten scripture, such as whether the category should be expanded to include revised and expanded biblical manuscripts like the *Reworked Pentateuch* (4Q158 or 4QRP), or works like the *Temple Scroll* (11QT), which re-presents legal rather than narrative material.[20] Only the *Genesis Apocryphon* however (1Q20 or

Pseudepigrapha, and Other Jewish Writings", in *Tracing the Threads: Studies in the Vitality of the Jewish Pseudepigrapha*, ed. J. Reeves (SBLEJL, 6; Atlanta: Society of Biblical Literature, 1994), 1–34. Van Ruiten, however, stresses rather important differences between Job and Abraham in his "Abraham, Job and the *Book of Jubilees*: The Intertextual Relationship of Genesis 22:1-19, Job 1:1–2:13 and *Jubilees* 17:15–18:19", in *The Sacrifice of Isaac: The Aqedah (Genesis 22) and its Interpretations*, eds. E. Noort et al. (TBN, 4; Leiden: Brill, 2001), 58–85.

19. This episode is discussed in some detail in Van Ruiten, *Abraham in the Book of Jubilees*, 27–30. Similar traditions in Syriac sources are highlighted in S. Brock, "Abraham and the Ravens: A Syriac Counterpart to *Jubilees* 11–12 and its Implications", *JSJ* 9 (1978): 132–52. Some commentators see this tale involving literal seed as a metaphor for the future establishment of Abraham's "seed" or descendants in the land; see e.g. C.D. Crawford, "On the Exegetical Function of the Abraham/Ravens Tradition in *Jubilees* 11", *HTR* 97, no. 1 (2004): 91–7 (93–4).

20. For a helpful overview of this debate, see M. Bernstein, "'Rewritten Bible': A Generic Category Which Has Outlived its Usefulness?", *Textus* 22 (2005): 169–96.

1QapGen)—found in Cave 1 in a single, though incomplete, copy—has so far achieved wide (albeit not universal) acceptance as an example of the genre. Doubts have been expressed about this classification, because it is written in Aramaic, prompting suggestions that it is closer to an interpretative translation like the targumim.[21] In addition, large parts of the narrative are presented as first-person speech, and often differ markedly from the Pentateuchal sources. Nevertheless, given that the rewritten scriptures characteristically include substantial supplements, and were not all composed in Hebrew (cf. Josephus's *Jewish Antiquities*), this term remains the best description for the *Genesis Apocryphon*. The text appears to draw on a number of sources, and shares some exegetical, chronological, and geographical traditions with the Enochic literature and with *Jubilees*. There is, however, no settled consensus as to whether it was written after and in dependence on *Jubilees*, or vice versa, or if both authors made independent use of common material.[22] Its composition is usually dated to the second century BCE,[23] and the language and handwriting of the scroll itself to the first century BCE.[24]

The extant text covers Genesis 5:18–15:4, approximately, but the original work was almost certainly more extensive. The first seventeen, often-fragmentary columns, focus on the antediluvian patriarchs, primarily Noah, demonstrating a particular interest in his unusual conception and his visionary powers. An evident emphasis on the legitimacy of Noah's parentage may reflect a concern similar to that present in *Jubilees* to defend the purity of Israel's ancestral line (*Gen. Apoc.* 4.14–16; cf. e.g. *Jub.* 19.16-29). This section illustrates several of the exegetical techniques commonly employed within rewritten scripture, including the creation of new narratives about the early lives of scriptural characters, and the insertion of additional dialogue (see e.g., *Gen. Apoc.* 2.3–18; 19.17–21).

The retelling of the Abraham Cycle is found in columns 19 to 22, although it probably began in the now badly damaged column 18. This part of the scroll is reasonably intact, and the scriptural source is followed more closely than is the case in the earlier treatment of Noah. The surviving narrative opens just before Abraham's excursion into Egypt at the time of the famine, goes on to cover his

21. See e.g., M.R. Lehmann, "1Q Genesis Apocryphon in the Light of the Targumim and Midrashim", *RevQ* 1 (1958–59): 249–63.

22. See e.g., J.L. Kugel, "Which is Older, Jubilees or the *Genesis Apocryphon*? An Exegetical Approach", in *The Dead Sea Scrolls and Contemporary Culture: Proceedings of the International Conference held at the Israel Museum, Jerusalem (July 6–8, 2008)*, eds. A.D. Roitman et al. (STDJ, 93; Leiden: Brill, 2010), 257–94.

23. For further detail on dating, see e.g., D.A. Machiela, *The Dead Sea Genesis Apocryphon: A New Text and Translation with Introduction and Special Treatment of Columns 13–17* (STDJ, 79; Leiden: Brill, 2009), 8–17, 141.

24. See e.g., the early detailed study by E.Y. Kutscher, "Dating the Language of the *Genesis Apocryphon*", *JBL* 76 (1957): 288–92.

separation from Lot and his involvement in the battle with the kings, and then ends abruptly mid-way through his discussion with God about whether Eliezer would be his heir (see Gen. 12:7–15:4). There is no way of knowing how much more of the book of Genesis was originally rewritten, nor whether extra information about Abraham's life before his call was provided, as is the case in both *Jubilees* and the *Biblical Antiquities*.

It is the account of Abraham's time in Egypt which receives the greatest elaboration in the *Genesis Apocryphon*. Abraham is presented here as speaking in the first person, perhaps to add vividness and dramatic effect to the narrative, or to enhance its authority, creating the impression that the audience are now privy to what the patriarch really said and thought. He is, for instance, shown weeping with distress at Sarah's removal into Pharaoh's harem (*Gen. Apoc.* 20.10, 16; cf. the sadness he later feels at parting from his nephew Lot, *Gen. Apoc.* 21.7). The author's main concern, however, appears to be to justify Abraham's rather questionable behavior on this occasion. He thus includes a description of a warning dream he experiences on the night he crosses over the Egyptian border, in which he sees a palm tree saving a cedar tree from being destroyed by people. In discussion of this dream with his wife, they realize that its message is that, as they travel on, he (the cedar) must ask Sarah (the palm tree) to pretend to be his sister in order to save his life (*Gen. Apoc.* 19.14–22). This supplementary passage makes clear, then, that Abraham's deception is approved in advance by both God and his wife. It also helps to fill in some of the gaps in the scriptural version of this episode, explaining, for instance, how Abraham knew that he would be in danger in Egypt (cf. Gen. 12:11-13), and later how Pharaoh eventually learned from Lot of the real relationship between Abraham and Sarah (*Gen. Apoc.* 20.22–23). The order of events is also slightly rearranged, so that Abraham receives gifts from Pharaoh only after he has healed him and Sarah has been returned to him. This is a less problematic sequence than that recorded in Genesis, where Abraham is rewarded as soon as Sarah is taken away from him (*Gen. Apoc.* 20.27–33; Gen. 12:15-16); this difficulty is already addressed in the second scriptural narrative of his journeys abroad to escape famine (Gen. 20:14-16). Abraham's virtue and special status are thus enhanced, and his superior learning is highlighted, as in other rewritten scriptures: the Egyptians look to him for wisdom and truth, for example, and he is able to read and so pass on the ancient teaching of Enoch (*Gen. Apoc.* 19.25).

The motif of the efficacy of Abraham's prayer, present in the parallel Genesis narrative of his dealings with Abimelech, is also heightened here (*Gen. Apoc.* 20.21–29; Gen. 20:17), and elsewhere in the text, where, as in *Jubilees*, he is shown repeatedly building altars and offering thanksgiving sacrifices (*Gen. Apoc.* 21.1–4). This rewriting of Abraham's time in Egypt may be partly intended to harmonize Genesis chapters 12 and 20, then, since it also details the physical afflictions visited on the Pharaoh which prevent him from defiling Sarah (*Gen. Apoc.* 20.16–29; Gen. 20:3-7, 17-18).

As is frequently the case in the rewritten scriptures, this narrative brings out underlying correspondences between biblical characters and events. Abraham's symbolic dream, for instance, links him to Joseph and Daniel, who are both saved from harm at the hands of foreign rulers through their ability to interpret dreams (Gen. 40:9-19; 41:17-36; Dan. 2:1-49; 4:4-27). Joseph's location in Egypt activates this connection, and Abraham's dream shares with Nebuchadnezzar's the specific image of a tree threatened with destruction (*Gen. Apoc.* 19.14–17; Dan. 4:10-14). Earlier in the text, Noah also receives a vision about the cutting down of some trees and his own establishment as a great cedar (*Gen. Apoc.* 13.9–14.7). The author's intention to present Noah and Abraham as parallel figures is clear, then, especially as Noah is also addressed with words reminiscent of those spoken in scripture to Abraham: "Do not be afraid, Noah, I am with you and with your sons ..." (*Gen. Apoc.* 11.15; cf. Gen. 15:1).[25]

Abraham's actions also appear to be interpreted here in the light of analogies with the Exodus narratives, which depict another Egyptian ruler suffering plagues as part of God's plan to save the Israelites, and show Moses as more powerful than all of the Pharaoh's magicians (*Gen. Apoc.* 20.18–21; cf. e.g., Exod. 7:8-12).[26] The lengthy, poetic expansion in the *Genesis Apocryphon* of the brief notice about Sarah's beauty (Gen. 12:15) is also influenced in both form and content by scriptural models, drawn especially from the wisdom literature (*Gen. Apoc.* 20.1–8; cf. Song 4:1-5; 6:4-7; 7:1-9; Prov. 31:10-31).

The retelling of the subsequent Abraham narratives closely follows the scriptural sequence and content, without much supplementation. The separation with Lot is summarized and arguably minimized, with care being taken to ensure that no blame for it should be attached to Abraham (*Gen. Apoc.* 21.6–7). His righteousness and virtue are intensified in this account of the aftermath of the battle with the kings, as, in addition to refusing any of the spoils of war, he also frees all those who were taken prisoner (*Gen. Apoc.* 22.24–26; Gen. 14:22-24). Although the covenant narratives themselves are not discussed in the surviving fragments, the divine promises of descendants and land, repeated to Abraham after his parting from Lot in Genesis, are included here (*Gen. Apoc.* 21.12–14; Gen. 13:14-17). The precise descriptions given of the extent of this promised land may indicate a concern with proving the ownership and occupancy rights to it of contemporary Israelites (*Gen. Apoc.* 19.12–13; cf. 16.9–17.19; 21.8–22).

The presentation of Abraham in the *Genesis Apocryphon* is more limited than that of *Jubilees*, partly as a result of its fragmentary extant state, and there are no clues about the way in which this author may have treated those events of the patriarch's life which generated most interest among other early Jewish interpreters, such as his call, the covenant, and the aborted sacrifice of Isaac. This work does,

25. All translations of the *Genesis Apocryphon* in this chapter are taken from F. Garcia Martinez and E.J.C. Tigchelaar, *The Dead Sea Scrolls Study Edition* (Leiden: Brill/Grand Rapids: Eerdmans, 1997), Vol. 1, 28–49.

26. The use of intertextuality in this section of the text is explored particularly in M.J. Bernstein, "The *Genesis Apocryphon*: Compositional and Interpretive Perspectives", in *A Companion to Biblical Interpretation in Early Judaism*, ed. M. Henze (Grand Rapids/Cambridge, UK: Eerdmans, 2012), 157–79 (173–4).

however, resemble other examples of rewritten scripture in offering a version of Abraham who is even more righteous and prayerful than his scriptural counterpart, who expresses his thoughts and emotions more fully, and whose connections with other significant figures, such as Noah, Joseph, Moses, and Daniel are highlighted.

Biblical Antiquities

The final example of rewritten scripture to be included in this study is the *Biblical Antiquities*, also known as *LAB* (from the initials of its Latin title, *Liber Antiquitatum Biblicarum*). Its author is unnamed, but is often referred to as *Pseudo-Philo*, because the text was transmitted together with Latin versions of the writings of Philo of Alexandria. He provides an often free re-telling of the scriptural narratives from the time of Adam to the death of Saul, substantially summarizing some sections, whilst greatly embellishing others. Now extant only in Latin, *LAB* was almost certainly composed originally in Hebrew, then translated into Greek, and from Greek into Latin. It is generally dated towards the end of the first century CE, although there have been occasional attempts to place it later.[27] The Abraham Cycle is not retold fully in it, nor presented in straightforward chronological order, but many of its central episodes are at least alluded to. This rewriting shares with *Jubilees* a particular interest in Abraham's early life, and an emphasis on the centrality of the covenant made with him.

Pseudo-Philo's treatment of the patriarch exemplifies several of his most characteristic exegetical techniques. First, he introduces Abraham early in his narrative, in two "flashforwards" in which his birth and future role in the establishment of the covenant are predicted, initially by one of his ancestors, and then by God himself (*LAB* 4.11; 7.4). These establish both the significance and the righteousness of Abraham from the outset, and also subtly point to correspondences between him and Noah, the first recipient of God's covenant, and an equally "blameless" figure (*LAB* 3.4; 4.11).

Second, the author includes additional material which fills in perceived gaps in the scriptural accounts, removes any suggestion that Israel's founding ancestor was

27. There is no clear indication of date or provenance within the text, so inferences have to be drawn from, for example, the form of the biblical quotations, or any references to the Temple (e.g. *LAB* 13.1; 19.7; 22.8; 26.15). For arguments for a date post-70 CE, see H. Jacobson, *A Commentary on Pseudo-Philo's* Liber Antiquitatum Biblicarum *with Latin Text and English Translation* (2 vols.; AGAJU, 31; Leiden: Brill, 1996), Vol. 1, 195–212. A slightly earlier date in the first century CE is preferred by a number of other commentators, however: see D.J. Harrington, "Pseudo-Philo", in *OTP*, Vol. 2, 297–377 (299); and C. Perrot and P.-M. Bogaert, *Les antiquités bibliques. Tome 2: introduction littéraire, commentaire et index* (SC, 230; Paris: Editions du Cerf, 1976), 67–70. For a more recent argument that it was produced by a Latin-speaking Jewish community in Rome in the third or fourth century CE, see T. Ilan, "The Torah of the Jews of Ancient Rome", *JSQ* 16 (2009): 363–95.

an idolater, and generally highlights his virtues. In an important expansion describing Abraham's life prior to his call, for instance, he inserts him into the Tower of Babel episode (*LAB* 6.3–18; cf. 23.5; 32.1; Gen. 11:1-9). In this narrative, Abraham and eleven others, including his kinsmen Nahor and Lot, are shown refusing to join the rest of the population of Babylon in making the bricks for the tower's construction—an activity possibly understood as carrying magical overtones (*LAB* 6.2)[28] even when threatened with death by fire. Abraham alone resists an offer of help to escape the country from a well-disposed chief, Joktan, confident in God's power to protect and save him (*LAB* 6.4–11). As a consequence, he is thrown into a furnace by his adversaries, but remains completely unharmed, while 83,500 (a typically exaggerated figure, see e.g. *LAB* 43.8; 46.2–3) of those who gather to watch his killing are themselves burned alive (*LAB* 6.17). Abraham is presented here, then, as an exceptional character who stands out from all others,[29] and his bravery, righteousness, and trust in the one true God are all emphasized. This serves both to explain his election as the recipient of the covenant, and to enhance his suitability as a role model for later generations, who may face similar dilemmas about how far to participate in the idolatrous practices of their gentile neighbors, a subject on which it appears that *Pseudo-Philo* takes a particularly uncompromising stance.

This supplementary narrative may have been created partly to interpret an otherwise unexplained scriptural reference to Abraham having been "redeemed" (presumably from some dangerous situation) by God (Isa. 29:22). It is an important illustration of the author's exegetical method, however, as it deliberately links two events (the building of the Tower of Babel and the call of Abraham) which are adjacent to one another, but not explicitly related, in the book of Genesis.[30] This is part of the wider hermeneutical approach underpinning the rewritten scriptures, in which connections between originally discrete texts and characters are consistently drawn out. This passage, for instance, is clearly inspired by the early chapters of the book of Daniel, in which another scriptural hero, together with his companions, remains steadfast in his rejection of the idolatry of the Chaldeans despite the threat of death by fire, and whose faith brings about his deliverance (Dan. 1:1–3:30; cf. Daniel 6).[31] Specific parallels between Abraham and Daniel

28. This is suggested by Bogaert, but is rejected by Jacobson: see P.-M. Bogaert, *Abraham dans la Bible et dans la tradition Juive* (Brussels: Institutum Iudaicum, 1977), 48; and Jacobson, *Commentary*, Vol. 1, 355–6.

29. The extent to which Abraham is strongly contrasted with all his contemporaries in *LAB* chapters 6–8 is drawn out particularly in P.-M. Bogaert, *Abraham dans la Bible*, 51.

30. See also e.g., the definite causal link made between the pronouncement of the law about tasseled garments and Korah's rebellion against Moses (*LAB* 16.1; cf. Num. 15:37–16:3).

31. Compare the use of scriptural models to develop the character of Kenaz in *LAB* chapters 25–28.

include the details that all those who accuse them suffer the very fate intended for them (Dan. 3:22; 6:24; *LAB* 6.17); that both are addressed by a gentile ruler as servants of God (Dan. 3:26; *LAB* 6.11); and that Joktan is as reluctant to punish Abraham as King Darius is to throw Daniel into the lions' den (Dan. 6:14; *LAB* 6.6).

After this rather dramatic introduction to Abraham, the main events of his life are summarized in just a few lines, including his journey to Canaan, his parting from Lot, the birth of Ishmael from his concubine Hagar, the making of the covenant, and the conception of Isaac (*LAB* 8.1–4). The whole patriarchal history is retold very succinctly at this point in the *Biblical Antiquities*, and without the kind of elaboration with which the later period of the Judges is treated.[32] Such selectivity enables the authors of rewritten scripture to emphasize those parts of their source which they consider particularly important or relevant for their audiences. Despite this economical coverage of the Abraham Cycle here, however, the actual covenant promises made to him are stated: "And God appeared to Abram, saying, 'To your seed I will give this land, and your name will be called Abraham, and Sarai, your wife, will be called Sarah. And I will give to you from her an everlasting seed, and I will establish my covenant with you'" (*LAB* 8.3).[33] This is not a verbatim reproduction of any one Genesis text, but unmistakably draws from several passages, especially the second account of the establishment of the covenant (Gen. 17:2-8, 15-21). The frequent use of direct speech and divine announcements (see e.g., *LAB* 7.4; 10.2; 12.4; 14.2; 18.5; 23.5–7; cf. 49.6) to encapsulate particularly important information within summary passages, is a striking feature of the *Biblical Antiquities*.[34]

As in the other rewritten scriptural texts, a large amount of new dialogue and direct speech is also added into the narrative, thereby heightening the authority, immediacy, and ongoing relevance of the teaching presented. For instance, *Pseudo-Philo* creates a number of lengthy speeches in which major characters review Israel's history. Within these, he frequently employs the device of retelling scriptural

32. Some commentators argue that *Pseudo-Philo*'s evident interest in this era indicates that he perceived a need for a new kind of leadership for the people of his own time, inspired by the bold, decisive and law-observant judges of the past; see especially G.W.E. Nickelsburg, "Good and Bad Leaders in Pseudo-Philo's *Liber Antiquitatum Biblicarum*", in *Ideal Figures in Ancient Judaism: Profiles and Paradigms*, eds. G.W.E Nickelsburg et al. (Ann Arbor: Scholars Press, 1980), 49–65.

33. The English translation of *LAB* used throughout is that provided in Harrington, "Pseudo-Philo".

34. A similar tendency to retain direct speech within speeches and reviews of history, is also in evidence in sections of the New Testament, such as Stephen's speech before his stoning (Acts 7:3, 7). For a fuller examination of this feature, see S.E. Docherty, "Why So Much Talk? Direct Speech as a Literary and Exegetical Device in Rewritten Bible with Special Reference to Pseudo-Philo's *Biblical Antiquities*", *Svensk Exegetisk Årsbok* 82 (2017): 52–75.

events out of sequential order by means of "flashbacks". The events of Abraham's life thus receive further interpretation in speeches attributed to Balaam, Joshua, and Deborah (*LAB* 18.5–6; 23.4–8; 32.1–4). In two of these passages, the offering of Isaac, omitted from the initial summary of the Abraham Cycle (*LAB* 8.1–4), is recalled (*LAB* 18.5; 32.2–4; cf. the further allusion to the *Akedah* in the context of the sacrificial death of Jephthah's daughter in 40.2).[35] This episode is sketched only in outline in these speeches, but with important interpretative amplifications, some of which also appear elsewhere in early Jewish tradition. As in *Jubilees*, for example, this incident is said to have been prompted by the jealousy of the angels towards Abraham (*LAB* 32.3; *Jub.* 17:15-16; cf. *Gen. Rab.* 55.4), and, as in Josephus, Isaac is presented as accepting his fate joyfully (*LAB* 18.5; *Ant.* 1.232). These developments are doubtless partly a response to concerns that the *Akedah* narrative, as it is recorded in scripture, presents neither God nor Abraham in an especially favorable light, and they may also have been prompted by questions about what "words" or "things" (Hebrew דברים) immediately preceded God's request that Abraham sacrifice his son according to Genesis 22:1.

Pseudo-Philo's retelling of the *Akedah* is shaped above all, however, by his ability to discover and exploit intertextual connections from right across the scriptures. In emphasizing the voluntary nature of Isaac's offering within Deborah's speech (*LAB* 32.3), for instance, he is subtly interacting with the motif present in the scriptural song of Deborah, that the Israelites and their leaders offered themselves willingly in battle on behalf of the people (Judg. 5:2, 9).[36] Balaam's address also highlights correspondences between God's promises of blessings to Abraham, the blessing of Jacob after he wrestles with God, and Balaam's words to Balak in the book of Numbers about blessing and cursing: "And do you propose to go forth with them to curse whom I have chosen? But if you curse them, who will there be to bless you?" (*LAB* 18.6; cf. Gen. 12:2-3; 32:28-29; Num. 22:6, 12; 23:8, 11; 24:9). These connections are implicit in the scriptural Balaam narrative itself, and are recognized by other early Jewish interpreters, such as Josephus (*Ant.* 4.116).[37]

Similarly, *Pseudo-Philo*'s version of Joshua's covenant renewal speech (*LAB* 23.4–8) enriches this base-text (Josh. 24:2-3) by bringing together several other scriptural references to Abraham, including the Genesis narratives (Gen. 12:1-2; 15:1-21; cf. 11:29) and the description in Isaiah of Abraham as the "rock" from

35. A number of studies treat in detail the presentation of the *Akedah* in *LAB* and its possible influence on early Christian understanding of the death of Jesus; see e.g., Vermes, *Scripture and Tradition*, 193–227; R.J. Daly, "The Soteriological Significance of the Sacrifice of Isaac", *CBQ* 39, no. 1 (1977): 45–75; and J. Swetnam, *Jesus and Isaac: A Study of the Epistle to the Hebrews in the Light of the Aqedah* (AB, 94; Rome: Biblical Institute Press, 1981).

36. This connection is discussed in B.N. Fisk, "Offering Isaac Again and Again: Pseudo-Philo's Use of the Aqedah as Intertext", *CBQ* 62, no. 3 (2000): 481–507 (493). For a full discussion of the structure and content of this speech, see A. Livneh, "Deborah's New Song: The Historical Résumé in *LAB* 32:1-11 in Context", *JSJ* 48 (2017): 203–45.

37. See further Fisk, "Offering Isaac Again and Again", 483–4.

which the people of Israel are quarried (Isa. 51:1-2). In a final interesting allusion to the Abraham Cycle within this passage, the nations are envisaged acknowledging the faithfulness of the people of Israel in a clear echo of the statement in Genesis that Abraham's faith was reckoned to him as righteousness: "Behold a faithful people! Because they believed in the Lord, therefore the Lord freed them and planted them" (*LAB* 23.12; cf. Gen. 15:6). This scriptural verse is re-applied to Abraham's descendants, then, and so made directly relevant to the author's own audience, who can hope in God's constant protection from their enemies as long as they remain faithful.

The treatment of Abraham in the *Biblical Antiquities* may be briefer than that found in either *Jubilees* or the *Genesis Apocryphon*, then, but it nevertheless demonstrates the author's convictions about the patriarch's righteousness, faith in the one God of Israel, and enduring significance as the chosen vehicle of the eternal covenant. His depiction of Abraham is enhanced by the employment of several exegetical techniques characteristic of the rewritten scripture genre, particularly the inclusion of extra-scriptural material and the underscoring of his connections with other characters, such as Noah, Jacob, and Daniel.

Conclusions

The Abraham who emerges from the pages of these works of rewritten scripture is recognizably related to the patriarch of Genesis, but is both a smoothed-out and a fuller figure. Perceived gaps in the underlying scriptural accounts, such as the lack of information about his life before his move to Canaan, are filled in; potential problems, including his pagan origins, are addressed; his more dubious actions, like sending his wife into Pharaoh's harem to protect himself, are toned down or omitted; and he can give voice to his innermost thoughts and emotions. Almost all the main events of the Abraham Cycle are retold in detail or alluded to in these texts, but their authors go beyond their source in various ways in order to embellish his righteousness, piety, learning, and suitability as a model for emulation. Both *Jubilees* and the *Biblical Antiquities* pay particular attention to the period before his call, his role in the covenant, and the offering of Isaac. The treatment of Abraham in the extant text of the *Genesis Apocryphon* is only partial, but this author shares a similar concern to exonerate him from any hint of wrongdoing and to enhance his virtues.

The re-presentation of Abraham in these three texts does not provide any definite information about their historical setting or theological purposes, since motifs such as his opposition to idolatry and his prayerfulness are similarly accented within early Jewish literature more broadly. Other emphases detected in them, such as the Israelites' ancient claim to their land, or the importance of covenant faithfulness even under threat, would suit a range of time periods and social contexts equally well.

This investigation does highlight, however, some exegetical techniques employed prominently across this genre. First, it is above all by means of the inclusion of additional material that the figure of Abraham is reshaped, rather than through other kinds of alteration of the Genesis accounts. The scriptural narratives can certainly be adapted, through re-ordering, summary, and omission, for example, but outside of the major expansions such changes are often minor and limited in scope. The example of the reading "rejoice" for "laugh" in the description of Abraham's response to the suggestion that his elderly wife would bear a son, is an illustration of this tendency to remain close to the Pentateuchal sources where possible (*Jub.* 15:17; Gen. 17:17). Second, these supplements often take the form of direct speech—monologues, dialogues, prayers, dream reports, and so on—a feature which adds vividness, immediacy, and authority to the presentation of Abraham's life. Since a considerable amount of the original direct speech is retained even when an episode is being summarized (e.g. *LAB* 8.1–3), or else is re-applied to other characters (e.g. *Gen. Apoc.* 11.15; *LAB* 23.12), scriptural speech may have been accorded a special status by these interpreters, who therefore sought to preserve and accurately reproduce these divine words.

Third, these texts are all characterized by a deep awareness of the intertextuality of the scriptures. The "flashback" method employed by *Pseudo-Philo* exemplifies particularly clearly this interpretative aim of highlighting the implicit connections between events and characters. However, such correspondences are drawn out in *Jubilees* and the *Genesis Apocryphon* too, and all three re-presentations of Abraham are influenced by perceived correlations between him and a range of other major figures in Israel's story, most notably the first recipient of the covenant, Noah, but also Jacob, Joseph, Daniel, Moses, and Job. These authors therefore approached the scriptural narratives expecting to find in them recurring patterns and analogies, and they appear to have extended this hermeneutical axiom to the entire lives of their characters: thus, what Abraham does once (for example, pass a divine test, or drive away circling birds), he can do again; what one person does (such as escape from a furnace, or make a final testament), others can do; and if individuals share one thing in common (birth outside of Israel, for instance, like Abraham and Job, or time spent in Egypt, like Abraham and Joseph), other points of connection between them can be assumed. This form of exegesis depends on a detailed engagement with the scriptures as a whole, but also on a close reading of their individual words, as illustrated, for instance, in the link made between the place name "Ur" and the Hebrew word for "flame" (*Jub.* 12:14; *LAB* 6.1–18). The rewritten scriptures are primarily exegetical rather than ideological in their motivation, then, and share with other forms of early Jewish interpretation a commitment to the internal coherence, truth, and ongoing relevance of the scriptures.

Chapter 5

ABRAHAM IN PHILO OF ALEXANDRIA

Sean A. Adams

Abraham is a major figure in Philo's writings with numerous treatises dedicated to his narrative in Genesis. An article-length treatment, therefore, will naturally not be able to cover all or even most of what could be discussed. Indeed, Samuel Sandmel expresses his difficulty in covering the breadth and depth of Philo's discussion of Abraham, and he had a full book with which to work.[1] Not wishing to duplicate previous scholarship unnecessarily, this chapter, in addition to providing an overview of how Abraham features in Philo's corpus, will highlight a less-discussed feature, namely how Philo constructs Abraham through his relationships to others.

Before commencing with the chapter, a brief reflection on methodology is in order. Although Philo dedicates specific treatises to Abraham, such as *De Abrahamo*, and those that have Abraham as the focus of the lemma in his allegorical commentaries,[2] Philo does not provide a singular reading of Abraham's narrative, nor does he treat the Genesis account in strict biblical order. Rather, as per his usual method, Philo forges links between characters, ideas, and terms that allow

1. S. Sandmel, *Philo's Place in Judaism: A Study of Conceptions of Abraham in Jewish Literature* (New York: Ktav, 1971).

2. Five allegorical treatises interpret part of the story of Abraham: *De migratione Abrahami* (Gen. 12:1-6), *Quis rerum divinarum heres sit* (Gen. 15:2-18), *De congressu eruditionis gratia* (Gen. 16:1-6), *De fuga et inventione* (Gen. 16:6-12), and *De mutatione nominum* (Gen. 17:1-5, 15-22). Although *Quaestiones in Genesin* and *Quaestiones in Exodum* are fragmentary, surviving mainly in an Armenian translation, a majority of Abraham's narrative (Gen. 15:7–25:8) is preserved in Philo's *Quaest. in Gen.* 3.1–4.153. On the state of *Quaestiones in Genesin*, see J.R. Royse, "The Works of Philo", in *The Cambridge Companion to Philo*, ed. A. Kamesar (Cambridge: Cambridge University Press, 2009), 32–64 (34–8). The poorly named *De Deo* also provides a commentary on the Abraham narrative, citing Gen. 18:2 as a primary lemma. See, A. Terian, "*Philonis De vision trium angelorum ad Abraham*: A New Translation of the Mistitled *De Deo*", *SPhA* 28 (2016): 77–107.

him to reference Abraham when desired. As a result, it is often necessary to cull statements from different places in order to provide a fuller picture of how Abraham is employed and interpreted by Philo. This approach is not without problems as Philo's exegesis of a passage or character is contextually dependent, resulting in some distinct interpretations.[3] Nevertheless, the nature of Philo's writings and the limitations of this chapter require such actions to be taken.

Abraham in Philo

Scriptural characters are important for Philo, not only in how he structures his works, but also in how he discusses and explains his theological perspective. Characters, in addition to being historical persons, also symbolize ideas, and can be read allegorically as representatives of specific virtues, vices, inclinations, etc. Although Abraham is the focus of this chapter, he is by no means unique in his treatment by Philo, who provides allegorical interpretations for most biblical characters. Abraham is read in two ways by Philo: literally and allegorically.[4] The literal Abraham is taken from the text of Genesis and represents an historic figure who lived, married, travelled to and from specific geographical locations, encountered God, produced offspring, died, and was buried. The allegorical Abraham, as the metaphor of the soul, abandoned polytheism, saw God, learned wisdom, and advanced in virtue.[5] Both are integral to Philo's understanding of Abraham, and any attempt to tease these two Abrahams apart too discretely will result in a flawed reading of Philo.[6]

Philo begins his presentation of Abraham, both in his allegorical commentaries and *De Abrahamo*, by closely interpreting Gen. 12:1-3, in which God calls Abram to leave his land, family, and father's house, and to go to a land that will be shown to him, promising that in doing so he will be blessed. This passage forms the

3. For example, in *De migratione Abrahami*, Joseph is presented positively as one who "lives" in Egypt (*Migr. Abr.* 21), but elsewhere in Philo's corpus Philo treats Joseph's governing of Egypt negatively. Cf. M. Niehoff, *The Figure of Joseph in Post-Biblical Jewish Literature* (AGJU 16; Leiden: Brill, 1992), 54–83.

4. The language of two Abrahams occasionally used by Sandmel gives the wrong impression of separation between the literal and allegorical readings of Abraham, something that neither Philo nor Sandmel would endorse. Sandmel, *Philo's Place*, 96.

5. Cf. T. Tobin, "The Beginning of Philo's *Legum allegoriae* I", *SPhA* 12 (2000): 29–43.

6. For a study of characters (including Abraham, Sarah, Lot, etc.) and how they are presented in the different corpora of Philo (i.e., *Exposition*, *Allegorical Commentary*, *Questions*), see M. Bohm, *Rezeption und Funktion der Vatererzahlungen bei Philo von Alexandria: Zum Zusammenhang von Kontext, Hermeneutik und Exegese im fruhen Judentum* (BZNW 128; Berlin: De Gruyter, 2005). Bohm rightly argues that the differences between these groups are not because of inconsistencies, but are due to Philo's intended purpose.

primary lemma for the *De migratione Abrahami* and provides a framework for Philo of how to progress in virtue. This schema is outworked through his reading of Genesis and his interpretation of specific locations as stops along his spiritual journey.[7] The events at each location, especially Abraham's interaction with others and his willingness to relocate, are allegorically understood as revealing Abraham's spiritual character, showing him to be a person who loves God and one who outworks his piety through beneficial actions to his fellow humans (e.g., *Abr.* 208).

One of the prominent representations of this journey is the change in Abraham's name. For Philo, following Plato,[8] the name of a person or place provides insight into the character of the individual, item, or location (*Cher.* 56).[9] Name changes, therefore, signal to Philo that a change has occurred within the individual and that s/he has a new nature or has reached a new stage in their development.[10] The change of name from Abram ("uplifted father") to Abraham ("the chosen father of sound") signifies a transition from his preoccupation with lower elements to his contemplation of higher issues (*Gig.* 62–4; *Mut. Nom.* 69–76), specifically his move from the study of nature to ethical philosophy (ἀπὸ φυσιολογίας πρὸς τὴν ἠθικὴν φιλοσοφίαν, *Mut. Nom.* 76) and from specific to generic virtue (*Cher.* 5–7). The acquisition of virtue allows Abraham to become a philosopher king, one who is appointed, not by humans, but by Nature, a reality acknowledged by those around him (*Mut. Nom.* 151–2, citing Gen. 23:6). Abram is an astronomer, but Abraham is the Sage.[11]

That the Genesis narrative is the foundation and starting point of Philo's interpretation of Abraham is clear. However, this is not to say that the Genesis narrative is complete or without need of interpretation. Unlike some of his predecessors, who attempt to fill gaps in the biblical story with additional narrative

7. On Philo's use of place and movement in *De migratione Abrahami*, see S.A. Adams, "Movement and Travel in Philo's *Migration of Abraham*: The Adaptation of Genesis and the Introduction of Metaphor", *SPhA* 30 (2018): 47–70.

8. Plato develops this idea in *Cratylus*, especially 397c1–2 for the giving of divine names.

9. Cf. L.L. Grabbe, *Etymology in Early Jewish Interpretation: The Hebrew Names in Philo* (Brown Judaic Studies 115; Atlanta: Scholars Press, 1988).

10. In *Cher.* 5, 7; *Mut. Nom.* 77 and *Quaest. in Gen.* 3.53, Philo makes it clear that the change in Sarah's name from Σάρα to Σάρρα indicates a fundamental change in her nature; no longer is she specific and perishable, but she has become generic and imperishable (cf. *Congr.* 2).

11. The rejection of Abraham's association with astrology stands in sharp contrast to how Abraham was perceived by Greek and Latin authors. Cf. Berossos, *FGrH* 680 Fr. 6 (=Josephus, *Ant.* 1.158, although not mentioned by name); Vettius Valens, *Anth.* 2.28; Firmicus Maternus, *Math.* 4.*prooemium*.5; Julian, *Con. Gal.* 356C; cf. J.S. Siker, "Abraham in Graeco-Roman Paganism", *JSJ* 18 (1987): 188–208 (195–7). See now the chapter by Margaret Williams in this volume.

material,[12] Philo predominately resists this practice, but does extrapolate meaning by adding certain elements, most prominently, speeches attributed to Abraham (and others).[13] This practice allows Philo to have Abraham say exactly what he thinks he should say and to articulate a previously cloaked idea more explicitly.[14] In particular, created speech allows Philo to present his vision of the character's inner thought world, something that is said to be lacking in the biblical accounts.[15]

Philo's primary method of interpretation is to allow the richness of Scripture to illuminate obscure and opaque passages.[16] Accordingly, Philo draws broadly from Scripture as a means to provide internal interpretation, allowing Scripture to interpret Scripture.[17] Abraham's narrative, therefore, is not read in isolation, and many elements of Abraham's story are read in conjunction with other accounts from the Pentateuch, especially Genesis and Exodus.[18] For example, Philo's biography of Abraham does not open with standard biographical topoi (e.g., *Vit. Mos.* 1.1–4), but with a triad of lives (Enos, Enoch, and Noah), each representing a

12. Some rewritings of the Genesis narrative have slightly different accounts of the travels of Abraham. For example, 1Q20, also known as the *Genesis Apocryphon*, has Abraham dwelling in Hebron for two years prior to his travels to Egypt because of the famine (1Q20 XIX, 9). After a much-expanded Egyptian narrative, Abraham travelled to Bethel (1Q20 XXI, 1). Following his separation from Lot, Abraham toured his promised land, surveying the different areas, before settling in the oaks of Mamre (1Q20 XXI, 15–19; cf. *Jub.* 13:21). The text of 1Q20 breaks off after the rescue of Lot. *Jubilees* also expands on the Abrahamic narrative, particularly with regard to the theme of circumcision (15:25-34), the near-sacrifice of Isaac (17:15–18:19), and his farewell discourses (20:1–22:30). So too does Josephus (e.g., *Ant.* 1.166–8). Conversely, Pseudo-Philo, in *LAB* 8.1–3, omits substantial portions of Abraham's narrative (e.g., Egypt, the sacrifice of Isaac, death, etc.), only retaining the most elementary details.

13. E.g., *Rer. Div. Her.* 27, 29; *Congr.* 151–2, 156; *Abr.* 71. *Abr.* 248–52 provides a speech in character by Sarah regarding giving Hagar to Abraham. This practice is not limited to Philo (e.g., *Jub.* 19:26–22:30).

14. On the ancient practice of creating speech for characters, see Thucydides, *Hist.* 1.22.1–4; Theon, *Prog.* 115–18.

15. Cf. R. Alter, *The Art of Biblical Narrative* (New York: Basic Books, 1981), 114.

16. Cf. J. Cazeaux, *La Trame et la Chaine: Ou les Structures littéraires et l'Exégèse dans cinq des Traités de Philon d'Alexandrie* (ALGHJ 15; Leiden: Brill, 1983), 5–7, who argues that the biblical narrative moves slowly between events in order to leave "spaces" and "distances" for the interpreter to explore the deeper meanings of the text.

17. Cf. Porphyry, *Hom. Quaes.* 2.297.16–17, "Considering it right to explain Homer with Homer, I have shown that Homer interprets himself sometimes in passages which are nearby, sometimes in other passages." Cf. Galen, *Dig. Puls. iv* 8.958.6 (Kühn); Plutarch, *Adol. poet. aud.* 4 [=*Mor.* 20d-e].

18. For Philo's use of Exodus, see G.E. Sterling, "The People of the Covenant or the People of God: Exodus in Philo of Alexandria", in *The Book of Exodus: Composition, Reception, and Interpretation*, eds. T.B. Dozeman et al. (VTSup 164; Leiden: Brill, 2014), 404–39.

different aspect of virtue (hope, repentance, and perfection, respectively; *Abr.* 7–47; *Praem. Poen.* 13–23).[19] To the life of Abraham, Philo appends the (now lost) lives of Isaac and Jacob as symbols of virtue (*Abr.* 52–54), which encourages the reader to view this trio of works as a collected biography in three volumes.[20] In localized discussions, Philo creates links through shared characters, names, places, terms, concepts, etc., creating unified interpretations from multiple passages.[21]

Although the text of Genesis is foundational for Philo's understanding and interpretation of Abraham, he is not slavishly beholden to it. This is not to say that Philo changes the text, but that his unified view of the Pentateuch, including the Abraham narrative, allows him to present elements of the text as they are appropriate. For example, in *Abr.* 72–76, Philo recounts how Abraham turned away from polytheism and abandoned the study of the material universe to examine himself as a microcosm. These events are said to take place at Haran (i.e., "sense perception") with the result that God is said to have been seen immediately by Abraham (εὐθὺς…ὤφθη δὲ ὁ θεὸς τῷ Ἀβραάμ, *Abr.* 77, citing Gen. 12:7).[22] However, in the *De migratione Abrahami*, Philo shows that Abraham is only able to truly see God after a lengthy process of toil. This is why the lover of learning (i.e., Abraham) needed to take possession of Shechem, which is metaphorically understood as "shouldering" (ὠμίασις, *Migr. Abr.* 221; cf. *Leg. All.* 3.25), because much labor is required to achieve perfection in virtue. Such differences in Philo's depiction of Abraham result from tailoring his reading to fit the context of his treatise.

19. For a detailed outline of *De Abrahamo*, its structure and use of Scripture, see D.T. Runia, "The Place of *De Abrahamo* in Philo's Œuvre", *SPhilo* 20 (2008): 133–50 (138–9).

20. Borgen suggests that *De Abrahamo*, the works on Isaac and Jacob, and *De Josepho* could be considered a "rewritten Bible", or a "history of the lives of virtuous persons and of evil persons": P. Borgen, *Philo of Alexandria: An Exegete For His Time* (NovTSup 86; Leiden: Brill, 1997), 71.

21. For example, in *De migratione Abrahamo*, Abraham's time in Haran is dependent on Jacob's narrative and the inclusion of "beastly" (θρεμμάτων, *Migr. Abr.* 212; cf. *Cher.* 70; *Somn.* 1.42–60). Similarly, Abraham's experience in Egypt is read through Joseph and Moses' narrative (*Migr. Abr.* 17–25). On the importance of this structure for interpreting Philo, see D.T. Runia, "The Structure of Philo's Allegorical Treatises: A Review of Two Recent Studies and Some Additional Comments", *Vigiliae Christianae* 38 (1984): 209–56 (236–41).

22. F.H. Colson and G.H. Whitaker, *Philo, with an English Translation*, 12 volumes (Loeb; Cambridge, MA: Harvard University Press, 1929–53), 6.42. Colson rightly notes that, according to Gen. 12:7, God's revelation to Abraham took place in Canaan (Gen. 12:5-6). However, I am not convinced that this was a "mistake" by Philo, but a compression of the journey. At a later point in *De Abrahamo*, Philo omits a number of details from the binding of Isaac, which he includes in other treatises (e.g., *Deus Imm.* 4; *Fug.* 132; *Leg. All.* 3.203). Although they could have fit within his schema, they were likely thought not to be necessary for his current point.

Philo's high view of Abraham leads him to minimize passages that the uninitiated might wrongly interpret.[23] For instance, in Abraham's interaction with Pharaoh (Gen. 12:10-20), Philo assures his reader that Abraham acted innocently; although he concedes that the story is liable to misinterpretation by those who have not tasted virtue (*Abr.* 89).[24] Here, Philo recasts the narrative to place Abraham in a better light, omitting his request for Sarah to be called his sister (Gen. 12:13), and framing the incident as the Egyptians' violation of hospitality norms (*Abr.* 94). This retold narrative is then allegorically interpreted, pitting Abraham (the good mind) against Pharaoh (the body-loving mind) for access to Sarah (generic virtue, *Abr.* 99–106).[25] This positive depiction of Abraham fits with Philo's understanding of him as a "man of God" (*Gig.* 64) and a prophet through whom God speaks (*Rer. Div. Her.* 258–66, citing Gen. 20:7). Even more than this, Abraham is one who fully followed the natural law and so became a model for the written law penned by Moses (*Abr.* 3–4).

Abraham's Relationships

For the remainder of this chapter I will evaluate Philo's depiction of Abraham through the lens of character relationships, highlighting the interconnectedness of Abraham with other individuals. In what follows, I argue that Philo presents Abraham as part of a network of characters and that, far from being on the periphery, Abraham is a primary node by which other characters are connected and defined, and is in turn also understood in light of these points of contact. This understanding of characterization is modern and is not explicitly adopted or discussed in antiquity.[26] Nevertheless, this interconnected view of individuals, I

23. E.g., Philo felt the need to defend Abraham against envious and bitter detractors who critique his plan to sacrifice his son (*Abr.* 184–99). Cf. D.M. Hay "Philo's References to Other Allegorists", *SPhilo* 6 (1979–80): 41–75.

24. Philo omits the parallel story of Abraham and Sarah in Gerar (Gen. 20:1-18) when discussing Pharaoh, only quoting Abraham's explanation (20:12) in *Ebr.* 61, which is allegorized in *Rer. Div. Her.* 62.

25. In the Sodom narrative, Philo omits any mention of Lot and his family in *De Abrahamo*. Lot might be implied by the preservation of one city (*Abr.* 141), presumably the one that he fled to (Gen. 19:20-23), but the five cities of the area are allegorized as the five senses, the best of which is sight (*Abr.* 151–4).

26. For example, Aristotle's discussion of "character" (ἦθος) is not that of a fictional person, but that which reveals moral choice (*Poet.* 1450a5; 1450b7). For types of characters based on a characteristic range of behaviors, see Theophrastus, *Characters* and the fragments of Ariston of Keos. For character *topoi*, see Quintilian, *Inst.* 3.7.10–22; 5.10.23–31; Theon, *Prog.* 109–110. For other ancient discussions of characterization, especially with regard to rhetoric and *progymnasmata*, see A.C. Myers, *Characterizing Jesus: A Rhetorical Analysis of the Fourth Gospel's Use of Scripture in its Presentation of Jesus* (LNTS 458; London: T&T

think, provides interpretive insight into the way that Philo contrasts Abraham with other biblical characters, and so needs to be taken into account when reading Philo's treatises.

The study of character has been important for literary theorists in the last century, and has become prominent in classical and biblical studies.[27] Scholars who have adopted a literary or narrative-critical approach have explored the ways that authors, both modern and ancient, have presented characters by means of a variety of models, evaluating character depth, symbology, narrative purpose, etc.[28] Although these approaches have made varying contributions to the study of character, they are not ideal for this study as we are not interpreting a narrative, but a work of scholarship. Accordingly, an additional layer of complexity is introduced in our discussion of Philo because he is not the author of the biblical narrative, but its interpreter. Philo does not have complete say over character relationships, but is constrained (to some degree) by the associations established in the Pentateuch. On the other hand, Philo has almost complete freedom to assign specific meaning(s) to individuals and to craft original interpretations and interpersonal connections. It is this freedom that Philo exploits frequently throughout his works, affording him the space to make unique readings and creative explanations regarding character relationships.

This chapter's specific focus on character relationships obviates the adoption of a singular literary model. Rather, certain elements of character discussion seem

Clark, 2012), 42–61. For a good introduction to characterization in antiquity, see K. De Temmerman and E. van Emde Boas, eds., *Characterization in Ancient Greek Literature: Studies in Ancient Greek Narrative, Volume Four* (MneSup 411; Leiden: Brill, 2018), esp. 6–11; R. Nünlist, *The Ancient Critic at Work: Terms and Concepts of Literary Criticism in Greek Scholia* (Cambridge: Cambridge University Press, 2009), 238–56.

27. E.g., V. Propp, *Morphology of the Folktale* (2nd edn.; trans. Laurence Scott; Austin: University of Texas Press, 1968); J. Frow, *Character and Person* (Oxford: Oxford University Press, 2014), ch. 3; C.B.R. Pelling, ed., *Characterization and Individuality in Greek Literature* (Oxford: Clarendon Press, 1990); C. Bennema, *A Theory of Character in New Testament Narrative* (Minneapolis: Fortress Press, 2014).

28. For example, scholars have used Forster's flat/round categories, Harvey's character categories (protagonists, cards, ficelles), Chatman's open theory of character, Wolfgang Müller's "interfigural" view of character (i.e., interrelations that exist between characters of different texts), etc. Cf. E.M. Forster, *Aspects of the Novel* (New York: Harcourt, 1927), 69–81; B. Hochman, *Character in Literature* (Ithaca: Cornell University Press, 1985); W.J. Harvey, *Character and the Novel* (Ithaca: Cornell University Press, 1965), 52–73; S. Chatman, *Story and Discourse: Narrative Structure in Fiction and Film* (Ithaca: Cornell University Press, 1978), 108–27; W.G. Müller, "Interfigurality: A Study of the Interdependence of Literary Figures", in *Intertextuality*, ed. H.F. Plett (Berlin: De Gruyter, 1991), 101–21.

pertinent.[29] For example, the recognition that character that is revealed by actions is vague—requiring the reader to infer the meaning of the action in order to understand the character—is important for our study of Philo, who imputes meaning to specific actions taken by characters. Even direct speech (either by the individual or those around them) and narrator declarations require interpretation, and Philo attempts to eliminate ambiguity by providing a specific understanding(s) to the biblical text. Abraham and other characters, when presented by Philo, are not neutral, but have been integrated within a larger interpretive framework.

Second, characters are not isolated, but integrated within a larger work in which other characters exist. As a result, a character is defined by and is a function of his or her relationships to the other characters introduced over the course of a story.[30] One of the consistent elements of Philo's depiction of Abraham is that he is not a solitary figure, but interacts with others on his journeys and in the locations where his travels take him.[31] Abraham's interactions with other individuals provide concrete examples of his piety and journey towards perfection, and his actions are often contrasted with the negative actions of others.[32] This understanding of intersecting space and contrasting definition will be of central importance for this chapter as the other characters, through their interactions with Abraham, shape Philo's allegorical interpretation and his reading of the text.[33]

Third, interfigural theory—the idea that authors and readers create a network of relationships, especially, but not exclusively, between characters in different texts—helps us understand Philo as a reader of texts and how he made connections

29. Many of these points were identified by J.A. Darr, *On Character Building: The Reading and the Rhetoric of Characterization in Luke-Acts* (LCBI; Louisville: Westminster/John Knox Press, 1992), 38–49.

30. For example, in Greek literature, a disciple is almost always defined by his/her relationship with his/her master. Cf. S.A. Adams, "The Characterization of Disciples in Acts: Genre, Method, and Quality", in *Characters and Characterization in Luke-Acts*, eds. F. Dicken et al. (LNTS 548; Bloomsbury, 2016), 155–68.

31. In some instances, Philo downplays the role of Abraham's travelling companions, wishing to focus on the spiritual meaning of the biblical text. For example, in *De Abrahamo*, when Abraham leaves Haran (Gen. 12:1), Philo interprets his journey as that of the soul (τῇ ψυχῇ), not of the body, and, as this journey is by nature solitary, Philo needs to minimize his companions' presence, stating that he departed with "few, or even alone" (μετ᾽ ὀλίγων δὲ οὗτος ἢ καὶ μόνος, *Abr.* 66). Cf. *Virt.* 218.

32. E.g., Abraham's piety and Pharaoh's *hybris* (*Abr.* 98). Cf. A-C. Geljon, "Abraham in Egypt: Philo's Interpretation of Gen 12:10-20", *SPhA* 28 (2016): 297–319 (306–9).

33. On "intersecting space" as a means by which to evaluate character, specifically the protagonist and minor characters, see A. Woloch, *The One vs. the Many: Minor Characters and the Space of the Protagonist in the Novel* (Princeton: Princeton University Press, 2003).

between Abraham and other characters.[34] Philo views the Pentateuch as a unified work, composed of five treatises, and penned by a single author (i.e., Moses). The Pentateuch is primary for Philo's reading and analysis of Abraham and other Genesis characters, but it is clear that Philo also draws from other texts as part of his explicit reading strategy.[35] These links evidence a complex web of connections identified by Philo, and show the wider structure of Philo's mental map.[36]

Fourth, proponents of social-cognitive theory argue that individuals understand and define themselves in contrast to others, and that an individual's identity is embedded in a larger group or community.[37] Philo's reading of Scripture is within a specific geographic, temporal, and cultural setting, and this profoundly influences his interpretation. In particular, his theological perspective of the narrative, that it is divinely inspired, not only shapes how the text is read, but also how it is to be used. In the case of Abraham and others, the biblical text provides both models to emulate and actions to avoid as one attempts to walk the path of virtue. The view of text as authoritative leads Philo to read the text in a very different way, forging specific links between the characters presented in the text and himself and his community.

Abraham and His Relationships

In the biblical narrative, Abraham is introduced through family relationships, specifically his father, Terah.[38] However, there is no discussion of his early life prior

34. E.g., I.R. Kitzberger, "Synoptic Women in John: Interfigural Readings", in *Transformative Encounters: Jesus and Women Re-viewed*, ed. I.R. Kitzberger (BIS 43; Leiden: Brill, 2000), 77–111 (108–9).

35. This is evidenced by the sizable number of references to other, non-Pentateuchal biblical books, as well as to Greek literature more broadly (esp. Plato and Homer). Cf. D. Lincicum, "A Preliminary Index to Philo's Non-Biblical Citations and Allusions", *SPhA* 25 (2013): 139–67; D.T. Runia, *Philo of Alexandria and the Timaeus of Plato* (PhilASup 44; Leiden: Brill, 1986). Cf. G.E. Sterling, "When the Beginning Is the End: The Place of Genesis in the Commentaries of Philo", in *The Book of Genesis: Composition, Reception, and Interpretation*, eds. C.A. Evans et al. (VTSup 152; Leiden: Brill, 2012), 427–46.

36. One of the benefits and challenges of interfigural reading is that connections are not static or fixed, but change over time as the reader's knowledge of literature expands and as different ideas grow or fade in importance/relevance. As a result, a systematic reconstruction of Philo's (or anyone's) connections is not possible, nor should difference in connections with a single character be seen as a detriment.

37. E.g., S.M. Andersen and S. Chen, "The Relational Self: An Interpersonal Social-Cognitive Theory", *Psychological Review* 109 (2002), 619–45; B.J. Malina, *The New Testament World: Insights from Cultural Anthropology* (3rd edn.; Louisville: Westminster John Knox, 2001), 60–7.

38. For Abraham's genealogical relationships, both in Philo and in other second temple authors, see F. Siegert, "'Und er hob seine Augen auf, und siehe': Abrahams Gottesvision

to his call in Genesis 12, implying that Abraham was in alignment with his father, sharing the same theological outlook and astronomical knowledge (*Mut. Nom.* 71).[39] This view is adopted by Philo and is part of his argument that good individuals can come from poor parental stock (*Virt.* 211–12).[40] However, although Terah did not establish Abraham in good theological principles, he was not completely devoid of insight, having taken up residence in Haran.[41] This is best seen in Philo's attribution of the saying "know yourself" (γνῶθι σαυτόν) to Terah, who is contrasted, but not equated with Socrates; Socrates is a human, but Terah was the principle itself (Θάρρα δ᾽ αὐτὸς ὁ λόγος).[42] Ultimately, the seed of self-knowledge comes to maturity in Abraham and bears good fruit. Terah, therefore, represents an intermediate position on the soul's progression to virtue. By leaving Chaldea, Terah embraces the secondary virtue of sense perception, and so provides an individual through whom Philo could contrast Abraham.

Nahor, although also fathered by Terah (Gen. 11:26), is not defined by his relationship with his father; rather, his kinship with Abraham is most important for Philo. Interpreted as "rest of light" through a Hebrew etymology (*Congr.* 45;

(Gen:18) im hellenistischen Judentum", in *"Abraham, unser Vater": die gemeinsamen Wurzeln von Judentum, Christentum und Islam*, eds. R.G. Kratz et al. (Göttingen: Wallstein Verlag, 2003), 67–85.

39. Terah recognizes the fundamental unity of the world, but wrongly attributes causality to non-material entities by assimilating God with the world, believing that God is contained in it (as the soul of the universe, so *Migr. Abr.* 179; cf. *Abr.* 78. On this stoic perspective, see *SVF* 1.157, 532; Diogenes Laertius, 7.148). On the contrary, God created the universe and so is not limited by it (*Migr. Abr.* 192–3). This was not the only reading of the silence. For example, *Jub.* 11:1–12:21 presents Abraham in conflict with the local inhabitants over idol worship from an early age, and is the reason that Terah and his family needed to move. This begs the question as to when Abraham had his revelation about God and the true nature of the universe, which, for Philo, was when Abraham was in Haran (*Virt.* 214; *Abr.* 70).

40. Here, Philo compares Abraham with Cain, who is an example of evil being born from good (*Virt.* 198–200, 211). Cain's ignobility, evident in his evil action, is contrasted with Abraham's nobility evident in his epistemology and his knowledge of the Existent (γνῶναι τὸν ὄν). This is another example of Philo creating connections between characters for which none is found in the original.

41. Cf. *Somn.* 1.45. According to *Congr.* 49, Abraham is called to leave Chaldea, but not to abandon the study of astrology, because he rightly knows the heavens are not God, but created by him. In contrast, the science of ἀστρονομία is praised as one of the intellectual disciplines worthy of study (e.g., *Congr.* 11). For a recent study on Philo and astronomy/astrology in Alexandria, see J.E. Taylor and D. Hay, "Astrology in Philo of Alexandria's *De Vita Contemplativa*", *ARAM Periodical* 24 (2012): 56–74.

42. Cf. *Somn.* 1.42–58, esp. 1.58. This interfigural reading of Terah goes beyond the Genesis narrative and shows Philo's reading of the Genesis narrative in conversation with the character of Socrates.

Quaest. in Gen. 4.93), Nahor is granted this name because he is Abraham's brother and so has access to wisdom's light because of him (although exactly how this is the case is not explained). However, his settlement in Chaldea and his refusal to travel with Abraham, result in the arresting of his understanding (*Congr.* 48–49).[43] Accordingly, Nahor provides a counter example to Abraham's pursuit of virtue and his willingness to move beyond astrological science and the study of the physical world.

Lot, the son of Abraham's brother Haran (Gen. 11:26, who is said to have died in Ur, Gen. 11:28),[44] has an important role in the Genesis narrative. Although he is discussed apart from Abraham,[45] it is primarily by this relationship that he is defined. In the Genesis narrative, Lot travels with Abraham from Chaldea, through Haran, Egypt, and the Negev, until they reach Bethel (Gen. 13:3), where they separate due to conflict amongst their servants.[46] Lot moves to Sodom where he is captured by foreign kings, liberated by Abraham, and subsequently preserved from destruction by an angel.[47]

Foundational for Lot's narrative is his travel with Abraham, which is allegorically interpreted through the metaphor of the path (*Migr. Abr.* 13). Here the migration styles of Abraham and Lot are contrasted. The former, as a lover of the incorporeal, is not like the latter, a lover of sense perceptions, who is defined as one who "turns away" (ἀπόκλισις) and is not able to stay the course (*Migr. Abr.* 148). According to Philo's interpretation of the Genesis narrative, Lot is one who turns away, not only from bad, but also from good, wavering back and forth. What might originally appear as positive actions, namely Lot's willingness to follow Abraham out of Chaldea or his departure from Sodom (Gen. 19:1-23; *Somn.* 1.85–6), are actually

43. Pseudo-Eupolemus (Fr. 1.3–4, 8; Fr. 2) and Artapanus (Fr. 1) present a positive view of "Chaldean science", but more often it is portrayed negatively. E.g., *Abr.* 68–72; *Jub.* 12:16-18; *1 En.* 8; *Sib. Or.* 3.218–30; Josephus, *Ant.* 1.168; Gen. Rab. 44:12.

44. The character of Haran is not mentioned by Philo.

45. Lot and his wife, who is defined as "custom", and is also afflicted with ἀπόκλισις (*Somn.* 1.246–8), were unable to produce any male offspring, but only two daughters ("council" and "consent", *Ebr.* 162–6). With the detrimental influence of alcohol, the mind assents to pleasurable suggestions and attempts to "raise up" offspring for itself. This is a poor idea and the outcome is that Lot's children by his daughters, Moab and Ammon, are excluded from the congregation of the Lord (*Poster. C.* 175–7, citing Deut. 23:3).

46. According to Philo, it was good that Lot and Abraham separated, as Lot's servants, which took after their master, were in regular conflict with Abraham and so, not wishing to war and ultimately defeat Lot, Abraham withdrew, offering Lot his choice of dwelling place (*Abr.* 212–16).

47. For the pleading of Abraham for Sodom (not bargaining), see L.H. Feldman, "The Destruction of Sodom and Gomorrah according to Philo, Pseudo-Philo and Josephus", *Henoch* 23 (2001): 185–98.

not creditable, as they, along with his turning towards vice, are not deliberate actions.[48]

More problematic for Philo is the fact that Lot becomes a hindrance to Abraham. Lot's inability to unlearn (ἀπομαθεῖν) his natural tendencies leads him into trouble, forcing Abraham to leave temporally the safety of the middle path and to risk battle with the senses and passions in order to come to his nephew's rescue (Gen. 14:1-22). The issue is that, at this time, Abraham is still a novice in divine matters and so these detours retard Abraham's progress in virtue (*Migr. Abr.* 150) and put him in a position to become entrapped by the senses.[49] Philo's retelling of the Genesis narrative highlights the unequal relationship between Abraham and Lot. This imbalance is not unintentional, but is symbolic of the disparity between the one pursuing virtue and the one who lacks that goal. Lot, therefore, provides a dark foil by which Abraham shines brightly.

By far the most important relationship for Abraham is that of his wife and half-sister, Sarah. Philo's discussion of Abraham's relationship with Sarah is unequally distributed across his treatises. For example, discussion of Sarah as a travelling companion is absent in the *De migratione Abrahami* despite her being part of the primary lemma (Gen. 12:1-6). One possible explanation is that Sarah and Abraham's relationship led to actions in which Abraham appears to behave deceitfully (e.g., Gen. 12:10-20; 20:1-18).[50] Although positing a rationale for this omission is speculative, I would suggest that Philo did not want to complicate his positive portrayal and metaphor of Abraham, and to include actions that might be thought by others to be morally ambiguous (e.g., *Quaest. in Gen.* 4.60).[51] In contrast, the eulogy for Sarah in *Abr.* 245–54 speaks of her steadfastness and how she accompanied her husband in all aspects of his travels: his departure from his homeland, his unceasing wanderings, his privation in famine, and on his military campaigns (*Abr.* 245).[52] Sarah's outstanding qualities become an opportunity for Philo to praise Abraham, who, after her death, did not give way to unrestrained

48. A similar understanding is ascribed to Adam, who is not by nature good or bad, but adopts either virtue or vice based on the people around him (*Leg. All.* 3.246).

49. On the importance of choosing correct traveling companions, see Epictetus, *Dis.* 4.5.17–18. For dangers of people who are migrating, see P. Van Nuffelen, "*De migratione Abrahami* und die antike Exilliteratur", in *Abrahams Aufbruch: Philon von Alexandria: De migratione Abraham*, eds. M. Niehoff et al. (SAPERE 30; Tübingen: Mohr Siebeck, 2017), 203–18 (216–17).

50. As far as we know, neither passage was used as a lemma in Philo's *Allegorical Commentary*, although he does mention Sarah as sister in *Ebr.* 61 and *Rer. Div. Her.* 62 (cf. *Rer. Div. Her.* 258; *Abr.* 89–98).

51. For Rabbinic interpretation, see Meg. 14a; Sanh. 58b.

52. The final element is not found explicitly in Genesis, and may be an allusion to Gen. 14:13-16. This positive emphasis is not found in the corresponding verses in *Quaestiones in Genesin*.

grief, but mourned in moderation (*Abr.* 256–7), earning the admiration of those around him (*Abr.* 260–1).[53]

Abraham's statement that Sarah and he shared a father (Gen. 20:12), but not a mother, is important for Philo, and he uses this declaration to define Sarah's allegorical nature.[54] In particular, Sarah, or generic virtue, does not have maternal parentage, but, being born of the father and cause of all things (ἐκ τοῦ πάντων αἰτίου καὶ πατρός), she has no relation to material substance (*Ebr.* 61; *Rer. Div. Her.* 62; *Quaest. in Gen.* 4.68). This interpretation fits with Philo's larger argument that Sarah is generic virtue, but is grounded in a specific statement from Abraham.

In addition to being Abraham's sister, Sarah is also his wife, therefore drawing two major identity markers from her relationship with Abraham. Their marriage is a partnership, not of bodies, but between thoughts (*Abr.* 100) and here Sarah acts as the generative male, sowing good council and noble words to the receptive and fertile Abraham (*Abr.* 101). Abraham's childlessness is not only on the physical level, but also relates to his need to produce heirs of virtue (*Rer. Div. Her.* 35–38). Philo's attribution of childlessness to Abraham, and not to Sarah or to them as a couple, is distinct. Here it is Abraham and his lack of education that is the problem, and Sarah is fully exonerated (*Congr.* 3–4, 9).[55]

Abraham's relationship with Sarah is also influenced by their relationship with Hagar, and the triad of Abram, Sarah, and Hagar forms the basis of Philo's discussion

53. Abraham's superiority in virtue led those among whom he settled to regard him as a king (*Virt.* 216, Gen. 23:6) and to treat him with awe and respect. This respect was not won by force or by weapons, but because of his election by God who rewards those who love piety with imperial powers (αὐτοκρατέσιν ἐξουσίαις, *Virt.* 218). As a result, those within the vicinity of Abraham acknowledge the philosophical doctrine that the Sage alone is king (*Migr. Abr.* 197; *Mut. Nom.* 152; *Somn.* 2.244; cf. *SVF* 3.169). Philo highlights the contrast between Abraham and his neighbors, emphasizing the superiority of the virtuous life and the respect that should be given to those who pursue it. This support of Abraham is emphasized in his interaction with Melchizedek (Gen. 14:18-20). Although he has a small role in the Genesis narrative, the importance of Melchizedek in subsequent Jewish thought is substantial (11QMelch [11Q13]; Heb. 7:1-28; *2 En.* 71.1–72.11). For Philo, Abraham's interaction with Melchizedek is also significant as both are examples of God's graciousness in giving original endowments (*Leg. All.* 3.79–103). Melchizedek provides an example of a character who accurately recognizes Abraham for who/what he is and blesses him (*Abr.* 235). In turn, Abraham gives him a tenth of all he had in recognition of his divinely given priesthood (*Congr.* 99, citing Gen. 14:20).

54. For Philo's explanation and exoneration of Abraham's actions in Gerar, see *Quaest. in Gen.* 4.60–70.

55. Cf. D. Sly, *Philo's Perception of Women* (BJS 209; Atlanta: Scholars Press, 1990), 147–54. For a negative discussion of Philo's depiction of women that places too much emphasis on the Greek-Jewish divide, see J.R. Wegner, "Philo's Portrayal of Women: Hebraic or Hellenic?", in *"Women Like This": New Perspectives on Jewish Women in the Greco-Roman World*, ed. A.-J. Levine (SEJL 1; Atlanta: Scholars Press, 1991), 41–66.

in *De congressu eruditionis gratia* (*Mating with Preliminary Studies*).[56] The relationship between Sarah and Hagar is foundational, not only in the Genesis text, in which Hagar is Sarah's handmaid (Gen. 16:1-16),[57] but also in their allegorical symbolism, in which Hagar represents lower knowledge and Sarah higher (*Leg. All.* 3.244; *Congr.* 11).[58] The dichotomies of slave/mistress, encyclopedic study/wisdom, concubine/lawful wife permeate all aspects of the Hagar-Sarah relationship, including how their children are interpreted. In this relationship, Abram is represented as an outsider and a partaker of aspects embodied by each woman. The biblical hierarchy of Abraham as the head of the house is absent, being replaced by Sarah's prominence and wisdom's authority. Abraham's growth from lower to higher reasoning and attainment of virtue is allegorized through his interactions with Sarah and Hagar; however, once his educational training is complete and he receives his new name, Abraham no longer has need of Hagar and she is cast away (*Cher.* 7–8).

The most important outcome of Abraham's relationship with Sarah is the birth of Isaac, Abraham's joy (*Abr.* 201–4; Gen. 21:6). Isaac is the lawful offspring, coming from Sarah, his citizen wife, and represents the fulfilment of God's promise and the one with whom the covenant will continue (Gen. 17:19).[59] As a result, it was

56. In contrast, Keturah, Abraham's third wife (Gen. 25:1-6), is only mentioned in *Sacr.* 43–44 and *Quaest. in Gen.* 4.147. According to Philo, her name is interpreted as "incense burning", and she represents the sense of smell, the third most virtuous and middling of the senses, and one that is clearly inferior to that of sight (Sarah) and hearing (Hagar). She is a very minor character in Philo's corpus, and her children are only alluded to in reference to Isaac. In Keturah's case, her relationship to Abraham is minimized by Philo, who instead contrasts her with Abraham's other wives, a comparison that is not prominent in Genesis.

57. The Sarah-Hagar relationship can fruitfully be read through the Platonic allegories of Penelope and her handmaidens in Homer's *Odyssey* (cf. Ps.-Plutarch, *Lib. ed.* 10 = *Mor.* 7d), recently argued for by M. Cover, "Philo's *De mutatione nominum*: Sample Commentary, Exegetical Structure, and its Place in the 'Abrahamic Cycle' of the Allegorical Commentary", paper presented at SBL Annual Meeting, San Antonio, November 2016 (http://torreys.org/philo_seminar_papers/).

58. In *Congr.* 23 Abraham is presented as the mind, with Sarah as virtue, and Hagar as education. However, at the end of the treatise, Philo claims that Sarah and Hagar are not women in this discussion, but minds (*Congr.* 180). For a recent study, see A.P. Bos, "Abraham and the *Enkyklios Paideia* in Philo of Alexandria", in *Abraham, the Nations, and the Hagarites: Jewish, Christian, and Islamic Perspectives on Kinship with Abraham*, eds. M. Goodman et al. (Leiden: Brill, 2010), 163–75.

59. Abraham is also said to have borne a number of children (Gen. 25:2), but all were faulty and needed to be sent away, save Isaac, to whom he gave all he had (*Sacr.* 43; *Praem. Poen.* 58; *Quaest. in Gen.* 4.148). Of his other children, only one is named: Ishmael. Ishmael is the progeny of Hagar ("preliminary education"), and so is by nature a sophist (*Cher.* 8–10). Primarily contrasted with self-taught Isaac (*Congr.* 129; *Mut. Nom.* 255; *Quaest. in Gen.* 3.33), Philo does not pair Ishmael and Abraham often. The notable exception is *Mut. Nom.* 201–2, where Abraham prays that Ishmael might "live".

right for Abraham to offer back to God Isaac as a sacrifice, not as a person, but as one who represents the fruit of a rich and fertile soil (*Leg. All.* 3.209; *Migr. Abr.* 139–42; cf. *Abr.* 167–207). Drawing on the statement in Gen. 22:8-9 that "both journeyed and came together to the place which God had told him," Philo claims that by travelling together the διδακτικὴ ἀρετή and the αὐτομαθὴς ἀρετή reached their full potential (*Migr. Abr.* 166–7).[60] These allegorical significations are not mutually exclusive or competing, but specific aspects are expressed according to the literary context and Philo's argument, even within the same treatise. This malleability of characterization is not part of literary theory, but represents Philo's appropriation of a narrative and his reading of it through his interpretive framework.

The literal patriarchs, Abraham, Isaac, and Jacob come from one house and represent three generations: father, son, and grandson. However, for Philo, paternal relations are not always linearly fixed. For example, Abraham is thought to be Jacob's father because he is the practicer (commenting on Gen. 28:13), but if he fully attains the name of Israel, Isaac would become his father (*Somn.* 1.166–71).[61] Based on their shared view of God, they are grouped together as partners in God's eternal name: the God of Abraham, the God of Isaac, and the God of Jacob (*Abr.* 49–51, citing Exod. 3:15, cf. *Mut. Nom.* 12). According to Philo, the trio is also a metaphor, representing the threefold division of time: past, present, and future (*Migr. Abr.* 125).[62]

These three patriarchs allegorically represent the natural endowments attributed to the soul or mind that empower it to achieve perfection in virtue; Abraham embodies the ability to be taught, Isaac the natural virtue, and Jacob the perfection attained through practice.[63] Each of the (literal) patriarchs, according to Philo, possesses all three qualities, as they are interconnected and interdependent (*Abr.* 53). These abilities, rightly paired with the Graces, are either gifts from God

60. This is reinforced by additional lemmata taken from Exodus, recounting Moses' supportive companions: Aaron, Nadab, and Abihu (*Migr. Abr.* 168–70; cf. Exod. 24:1).

61. Jacob's new name, given by an angel unlike Abraham, and the fact that Jacob is still called by his original name, signifies that the transformation was not complete (*Mut. Nom.* 83–7).

62. This is a distinctive interpretation in Philo's corpus and is not explicitly employed by him in other sections. Colson and Whitaker, *Philo*, 5.563 suggest that this interpretation might be more fully understood from the contents of *Migr. Abr.* 154 and Exod. 3:15. The latter suggestion is not particularly helpful for this interpretation; although *Migr. Abr.* 154 does have more potential.

63. E.g., *Congr.* 34–38; *Mut. Nom.* 12, 88; *Abr.* 52–55; *Praem. Poen.* 24–7. This trio is also read in contrast with another trio, Enos, Enoch, and Noah: *Abr.* 7–47. See E. Birnbaum, "Exegetical Building Blocks in Philo's Interpretation of the Patriarchs", in *From Judaism to Christianity: Tradition and Transition: A Festschrift for Tomas H. Tobin, S.J., on the Occasion of His Sixty-fifth Birthday*, ed. P. Walters (Leiden: Brill, 2010), 69–92 (74–88); E. Birnbaum, "What in the Name of God Led Philo to Interpret Abraham, Isaac, and Jacob as Leaning, Nature, and Practice?", *SPhA* 28 (2016): 273–96.

or a gift to the reasonable soul from itself (*Abr.* 54), but either way all are necessary for virtuous living. Nevertheless, they are not equal. Rather, natural virtue is superior to that acquired by learning or practice, because the self-taught one receives his virtue directly from God.[64] Accordingly, Isaac, as a γένος, is superior to Abraham and Jacob, who are classified among the λαοί.[65] Thus, Philo creates a specific hierarchy among them, identifying Isaac as a genus and the generic, and Abraham and Jacob as the species and specific.[66] This understanding places the son above his father, inverting the expected hierarchy between Abraham and Isaac. The reason for Isaac's priory is his origin, being given as a promise from God and born from Sarah (generic virtue).[67] This example shows not only how Philo interprets Abraham as an integral member of a group, but also how specific relationships are created through the logical implementation of his allegorical reading.

In addition to earthly relationships, Philo also depicts Abraham's relationship with God (esp. *Abr.* 62–207).[68] Unlike the majority of humanity, who attempt to hide themselves from God (*Leg. All.* 3.6), Abraham is said to have desired intimacy with God, allowing God to come close to him (*Cher.* 18–19; *Somn.* 2.226, citing Gen. 18:22-3). Ultimately, God reveals himself to Abraham, allowing Abraham to see him as much as he is able to bear (*Abr.* 77–80).[69] These visions allow Philo to identify Abraham as a "friend of God"[70] and, as God's companion (*Gig.* 64), Abraham travels the "king's road" to attain the summit of virtue (*Migr. Abr.* 170–1; cf. Num. 20:17) with the assistance of angels who escort him on his way (*Migr. Abr.* 173–5; *Quaest. in Gen.* 4.20; cf. Gen. 18:16; Exod. 33:15). Abraham's trust in God (*Abr.* 262, citing Gen. 15:6; cf. *Quaest. in Gen.* 4.17) freed him from deep-seated doubt, but still permitted him to ask questions as to how God will achieve his

64. E.g., *Sacr.* 6–7; *Somn.* 1.160–2. God taught Abraham but begat Isaac (*Leg. All.* 3.219; *Somn.* 1.173).

65. This explains why Isaac only has one wife, but Abraham and Jacob have many wives and concubines (*Congr.* 34–38) and why Isaac did not have need of a name change, but Abraham and Jacob did (*Mut. Nom.* 83–8).

66. Cf. E. Birnbaum, *The Place of Judaism in Philo's Thought: Israel, Jews, and Proselytes* (BJS 290; SPM 2; Atlanta: Scholars Press, 1996), 56–8, who discusses how Philo differentiates between λαός and γένος in his reading of Gen. 25:8; 35:29; 49:33.

67. Isaac is given priority in other books/passages (e.g., in Tobit; Jdt. 8:26). Cf. T. Novick, "Biblicized Narrative: On Tobit and Genesis 22", *JBL* 126 (2007): 755–64.

68. For Philo's piety, see G.E. Sterling, "'The Queen of the Virtues': Piety in Philo of Alexandria", *SPhA* 18 (2006): 103–23.

69. For Philo's discussion of a human's ability to see God, either in one or in three parts, see *Abr.* 119–32; *Deo* 12. Cf. J. Ryu, *Knowledge of God in Philo of Alexandria* (WUNT 2.405; Tübingen: Mohr Siebeck, 2015), 112–17.

70. Cf. φιλόθεος, *Abr.* 89; *Deo* 3; *Somn.* 1.193–5; *Sobr.* 55–57; *Quaest. in Gen.* 4.21. A similar epithet is found in *Jub.* 19:9. This is not part of Gen. 18:17. In *Sobr.* 56, Philo adds "friend of God" and in *Leg. All.* 3.27 it is "servant of God". Sandmel, *Philo's Place*, 177 n.347 argues that "friend of God" is equivalent to "prophet".

promise. The fact that doubt passed through Abraham's mind momentarily, distinguishes his faith from divine faith (*Mut. Nom.* 177–8, referencing Gen. 15:8; cf. *Quaest. in Gen.* 3.2). This difference is important for Philo as it differentiates the human from divine, creating a clear hierarchy between the two.

Abraham's relationship with God is one of the defining elements of who Abraham is. Not only does God bless Abraham and give him gifts,[71] but his call in Genesis 12 is the catalyst for Abraham's physical and spiritual migration. This relationship also differentiates Abraham from all of the other individuals whom he meets in his travels; Abraham is defined by this relationship and it becomes the determinative feature of Philo's evaluation of him. At the same time, God defines himself in light of his relationship with Abraham; disclosing to Moses that he is the God of Abraham, Isaac, and Jacob (Exod. 3:6; cf. 2:24; Lev. 26:42; 2 Macc 1:2). This mutually-defining relationship is central for Philo's interpretation of Abraham and his place within Scripture (*Abr.* 49–51; *Mut. Nom.* 12).

Finally, Abraham not only is interpreted in relationship to other, biblical characters, but, as part of Scripture, Abraham also has an important role in shaping the life of Philo and his reading community. Scripture, for Philo, records the historical actions of Abraham, his experiences, life events, and relationships. However, such an historical reading would not adequately represent how Abraham was understood by Philo and his readers.[72] Philo sees in Scripture the varied experiences of humanity, and holds the position that the text is therefore relevant for him. Accordingly, Abraham is not only an historical figure, but one that speaks to aspects of contemporary life. For example, Philo moves beyond the narrative world by applying the allegory of Abraham, Sarah, and Hagar to his own person. Here, in *Congr.* 6–7, Philo assigns himself the role of Abraham, one who has produced too many offspring from Hagar and now needs to focus on true virtue in order to produce legal offspring. This passage, along with others (cf. *Congr.* 88; *Somn.* 1.164–165; *Abr.* 3–5), provides a good example of how Philo read the life of Abraham and applied it to his personal experience.[73]

71. The five gifts are: 1) land (*Migr. Abr.* 36–52), 2) great nation (*Migr. Abr.* 53–69), 3) God's blessing (*Migr. Abr.* 70–85), 4) magnification of Abraham's name (*Migr. Abr.* 86–105), and 5) Abraham will be blessed, being in actually what is reported of him (*Migr. Abr.* 106–8). Cf. *Abr.* 98.

72. Philo does recognize the inherent difficulty of leaving one's family and living as a stranger in a foreign land, thus reading Abraham through personal or shared experiences (*Abr.* 63–7).

73. On the topic of exemplars and models, particularly with regard to Abraham, see the insightful article by A.Y. Reed, "The Construction of Subversion of Patriarchal Perfection: Abraham and Exemplarity in Philo, Josephus, and the Testament of Abraham", *JSJ* 40 (2009): 185–212. Cf. A. Mendelson, *Secular Education in Philo of Alexandria* (Cincinnati: HUC Press, 1982), 62–5.

Conclusions

Although character theory is typically limited to narrative texts, we have seen how certain aspects can be fruitfully applied to interpretive works. Here, theoretical frameworks provide insight into Philo's analysis of Genesis, and how one ancient reader interpreted standard literary features and the inherent ambiguity of character construction. Philo's interpretation of Genesis takes advantage of the interpretive space within the Genesis narrative, allowing him to define characters and relationships in unique ways. Regarding Abraham's narrative, Philo regularly interprets specific actions as meaningful and/or symbolic. The high ambiguity of actions for understanding character affords Philo the space to portray Abraham and others in ways that align with his philosophical perspective. The same practice is also applied to dialogue and narration, with Philo interpreting speech in specific ways and/or attributing new statements to biblical characters in order for them to fully articulate ideas that Philo wishes to make clear. As a result, even though Philo is commenting on the text, he is not constrained by it nor does it limit what he can say.

The most important aspect for understanding Abraham is how Philo refuses to view him in isolation, choosing instead to define him through his relationships with other characters. How Abraham is characterized is not static. Rather, Philo adapts his interpretation of him based on the immediate interpretive context. In certain situations, Abraham is presented as being part of a specific group, intricately tied to other characters (e.g., Abraham, Isaac, and Jacob; Abram, Sarah, and Hagar). At other times, Philo's interpretation is based on contrast, often with the other character acting as a foil in order for Abraham to shine more brightly (e.g., Lot, Pharaoh, Nahor). Abraham is not always presented as the dominant member in a relationship; Philo subordinates him to his son Isaac, whose natural endowment is superior to Abraham's learning. Similarly, both Sarah, his wife, and Hagar, his concubine, are presented as Abraham's teachers and he in the position of pupil.[74]

74. Thank you to Michael Cover who gave some helpful comments on a draft of this chapter.

Chapter 6

ABRAHAM IN JOSEPHUS' WRITINGS

Michael Avioz

The figure of Abraham played a prominent role in Abrahamic religions. Every generation has its own image of Abraham, but in all cases the departure point was the biblical narrative. One of the early platforms of the reception history of Abraham is found in the works of the first century Jewish historian Flavius Josephus.

Abraham's narrative cycle[1] begins in Genesis 11 and ends in Genesis 25. The approximate sequence of events runs thus: Abram and Sarai journey through Canaan and descend to Egypt (Genesis 12); Abram parts ways with Lot (13); the war of the four kings (14); God makes a covenant with Abram (15); the flight of Hagar (16), the circumcision (17); the angels visit Abraham (18); the destruction of Sodom (19); Abraham and Sarah in Gerar (20); the birth of Isaac and expulsion of Ishmael (21); Abraham and Abimelech's covenant (21); the binding of Isaac (22); Sarah's burial (23); finding a wife for Isaac in Haran (24); Abraham's death (25).[2] Josephus retells this narrative cycle in *Ant.* 1.149–256.[3]

1. I will use the forms "Abram" or "Abraham" throughout this paper according to their appearance in the MT. I will use "Abraham" for general reference.

2. See J. Grossman, *Abram to Abraham: A Literary Analysis of the Abraham Narrative* (Bern: Peter Lang, 2016).

3. Translations of Josephus are based upon L.H. Feldman, *Judean Antiquities Books 1–4* (Flavius Josephus: Translation and Commentary 3; Leiden: Brill, 2000). Josephus calls Abraham "Habramos"; he does not distinguish between Abram and Abraham. The LXX calls him Ἀβραμ. Sarai is always Σάρρα in Josephus. Begg explains these omissions in Josephus' wish to spare "such readers elements of Genesis that they would find boring". See C.T. Begg, "Genesis in Josephus", in *The Book of Genesis: Composition, Reception, and Interpretation*, eds. C.E. Evans et al. (Leiden: Brill, 2012), 303–29, here 316. For the appellations of Abraham in Josephus' writings, see P. Spilsbury, *The Image of the Jew in Flavius Josephus' Paraphrase of the Bible* (Tübingen: Mohr Siebeck, 1998), 55–6. Josephus does not mention Abraham in *Against Apion*. Bar Kochva deduces that this may prove that Josephus did not have at his disposal the work of Hecataeus of Abdera, named "On Abraham". Had Josephus access to this work, he would have undoubtedly made use of it in his apologetic work and would have mentioned Abraham as well. See B. Bar Kochva, "On Abraham and the Egyptians:

Josephus was not the first Hellenistic Jew to write about Abraham; he was preceded by Demetrius the Chronographer, Cleodemus Malchus, Artapanus, and Philo.[4] Also, Josephus cites Berosus, Hecataeus, and Nicolaus of Damascus (*Ant.* 1.158–9) as historians who mention Abraham.[5]

Walter Hansen begins his brief review of Abraham in Josephus' writings thus: "The apologetic goals of Josephus are quite obvious in his introduction of Abraham."[6] Carol Bakhos' review of Abraham's family in Josephus opens similarly: "Though by most accounts the ancient Jewish historian Josephus (37–*c.* 100 CE) *was not an exegete*, his history of the Jewish people from the biblical period in his Jewish Antiquities is part of the long trajectory of Jewish scriptural interpretation."[7]

Louis Feldman, a leading Josephus scholar, wrote a comprehensive chapter on Abraham in Josephus' writings. He summarizes Josephus' portrayal of Abraham as follows: "[Josephus aggrandizes] Abraham the philosopher and scientist, the general, the perfect host and guest, and the man of virtue generally."[8] However, the

A Hellenistic-Greek or a Hellenistic-Jewish Composition", *Tarbiz* 70 (2011): 327–52 (Hebrew). Abraham is briefly referred to in Josephus' *War* 4.531; 5.379–81.

4. See J. S. Siker, "Abraham in Greco-Roman Paganism", *JSJ* 18 (1988): 188–208; B. Bar Kochva, "On Abraham".

5. Louis Ginzberg interweaves rabbinic, Hellenistic, early Christian, kabbalistic, and other textual sources that deal with Abraham. See L. Ginzberg, *The Legends of the Jews*, 7 vols. (Philadelphia: Jewish Publication Society, 1909–38). A second edition was published in 2003 in two volumes (Philadelphia: JPS, 2003). For a comprehensive review of other Jewish compositions rewriting the Abraham narrative, see A. Mühling, *Blickt auf Abraham, euren Vater': Abraham als Identifikationsfigur des Judentums in der Zeit des Exils und des Zweiten Tempels* (FRLANT 236; Göttingen: Vandenhoeck & Ruprecht, 2011). She mentions *Judith*, *Tobit*, Maccabees, *Jubilees*, *Ben Sira*, the Dead Sea Scrolls, Philo, *Pseudo-Philo*, Josephus, the *Testament of Abraham*, the *Apocalypse of Abraham* and the NT. For Abraham in the Midrash, see the section "Rabbinic Judaism", in *Abraham, the Nations, and the Hagarites: Jewish, Christian, and Islamic Perspectives on Kinship with Abraham*, eds. M. Goodman et al. (Leiden: Brill, 2010) [203–275]. See also J.L. Kugel, *Traditions of the Bible* (Cambridge, MA: Harvard University Press, 1998); N. Calvert-Koyzis, *Paul, Monotheism and the People of God: The Significance of Abraham Traditions for Early Judaism and Christianity* (JSNTSupp 273; London: T&T Clark, 2004), 6–84; A.D. Roitman, "The Traditions about Abraham's Early Life in the Book of Judith (5:6-9)", in *Things Revealed: Studies in Early Jewish and Christian Literature in Honor of Michael E. Stone*, eds. E. Chazon et al. (Leiden: Brill, 2004), 73–87; R.J. Foster, *The Significance of Exemplars for the Interpretation of the Letter of James* (WUNT II, 376; Tübingen: Mohr Siebeck, 2014), 59–103.

6. G.W. Hansen, *Abraham in Galatians: Epistolary and Rhetorical Contexts* (JSNTSup 29; Sheffield: JSOT, 1989), 193.

7. C. Bakhos, *The Family of Abraham: Jewish, Christian, and Muslim Interpretations* (Cambridge, MA: Harvard University Press, 2014), 26. My emphasis.

8. L.H. Feldman, *Josephus's Interpretation of the Bible* (Berkeley: University of California Press, 1998), 249. The chapter on Abraham in Josephus' writings is from pages 223–89.

question is whether Josephus' main objective in *Antiquities of the Jews* is apologetic. In my book on Josephus' interpretation of Samuel,[9] I argue that Josephus' central aim is not apologetic but interpretative and that his *Antiquities of the Jews* are classified as "rewritten Scripture", focusing mainly on the interpretive aspects of the biblical text.[10]

Philip Alexander has described the characteristics of texts labeled as "rewritten Bible". He defines them as:

1. Narratives that follow a sequential and chronological order.
2. Freestanding works that follow the form of the biblical texts on which they are based.
3. Works not intended to replace the Bible (their authors typically rewrite a significant portion of Scripture while making use of additional legendary material, integrating it within the biblical narrative).
4. Texts which follow the general order of biblical accounts but are selective in what they include.
5. Texts whose intention is to produce an interpretative reading of Scripture by offering "a fuller, smoother and doctrinally more advanced form of the sacred narrative."
6. Texts whose narrative form only allows them to reflect a single interpretation of the original.
7. Whose narrative form also renders it implausible for the writers to offer their exegetical reasoning.
8. Texts which use extra-biblical tradition and non-biblical sources (oral and written), and utilize legendary material by fusing it with the biblical narrative, thereby creating a synthesis of the whole tradition (biblical and non-biblical).[11]

Moshe Bernstein defines the same approach as "simple sense exegesis" (פשט).[12] It deals with "difficulties in language, grammar, context, issues which could confront

9. M. Avioz, *Josephus' Interpretation of the Books of Samuel* (Library of Second Temple Studies 86; London: Bloomsbury, 2015).

10. See Avioz, *Josephus' Interpretation*, with earlier literature. See also L. Novakovic, *Raised from the Dead According to Scripture: The Role of Israel's Scripture in the Early Christian Interpretations of Jesus' Resurrection* (London/New York: Bloomsbury T&T Clark, 2012), esp. 28–34. The label "Scripture" was added since there is no "Bible" in Josephus' age.

11. P.S. Alexander, "Retelling the Old Testament", in *It Is Written—Scripture Citing Scripture: Essays in Honour of Barnabas Lindars*, eds. D.A. Carson et al. (Cambridge: Cambridge University Press, 1988), 99–121, esp. 116–18. Other compositions that are labeled "rewritten Scripture" are: the Palestinian Targums, *Pseudo- Philo, Liber Antiquitatum Biblicarum*, *Jubilees*, and the *Genesis Apocryphon* and some Qumranic compositions.

12. M.J. Bernstein, "4Q252: From Re-Written Bible to Biblical Commentary", *JJS* 45 (1994): 1–27, here 1.

any (rationalist) reader of a given text (as opposed to those which would affect only an ideologically oriented reader) and then attempts to solve them more or less within the parameters and boundaries of the biblical text alone." The second kind of exegesis, "applied exegesis", tries to answer non-biblical questions by searching for implicit general principles in the biblical text which can be applied to new situations and problems.[13]

One cannot deny the presence of the apologetic in Josephus' writings, but it should not be perceived as the main objective of his biblical rewriting. To do so reduces his biblical characterizations to two dimensional symbols of virtue, and drains his writing of its essence; as we shall see below, Josephus has much to offer with regard to biblical exegesis. I will analyze Josephus' additions, omissions, and changes to the biblical text, and attempt to explain them, arguing that, when Josephus retold the biblical narrative of Abraham, he worked more as an interpreter rather than an apologist. He had in mind Graeco-Roman readers, both Jewish and non-Jewish,[14] not able to read or comprehend the biblical narrative, thus taking the role of a mediator between the reader and the text.

Josephus as an Exegete

Several scholars have discussed Josephus' exegetical abilities. The biblical exegete's tasks are, among others[15]:

1. To translate the biblical text into a language familiar to its readers.
2. To explain and clarify complicated halakhic issues (issues of Jewish law).
3. To reconcile contradictions in the Hebrew Bible.
4. To address problematic ethical issues that arise in the biblical narrative.
5. To emphasize the relevance of the Hebrew Bible for the contemporary reader.

I will try to show that Josephus makes great efforts to accomplish at least some of these tasks and will focus mainly on points one, three, and four. Josephus had to offer his Greek translation of the Hebrew text, albeit not in full. His work is more than a mere translation, as was already done by the Septuagint. He tried to reconcile contradictions as well as explaining other difficulties arising from the biblical texts. In the following, I will give some examples of Josephus' methods of interpretation when retelling the biblical narrative of Abraham.

13. See also the literature cited in Avioz, *Josephus' Interpretation*, 6–7.

14. See the discussion in Avioz, *Josephus' Interpretation*, 191–5.

15. J.L. Kugel, "Early Interpretation: The Common Background of Late Forms of Biblical Exegesis", in *Early Biblical Interpretation*, eds. J.L. Kugel and R.A. Greer (Library of Early Christianity, 3; Philadelphia: Westminster Press, 1986), 9–106.

The reason for Terah's relocation in Genesis 11:31-2 is not given in the biblical narrative,[16] but Josephus (*Ant.* 1.152) fills this gap: "Because Therros came to hate Chaldaia owing to his grief for Aranes, they all emigrated to Charran in Mesopotamia."[17] Similarly, in Gen. 12:1, God mandates Abraham's departure from Ur to Canaan, but there is no allusion to God's word in 11:31, and the decision to move is apparently initiated by Terah and Abraham. In order to solve this tension, Josephus provides two different reasons for Abraham's departure from Ur: "Therros also died and was buried after living 205 years. For already the life expectancy was being shortened and was becoming briefer until the birth of Moyses, after whom God set a limit of life at 120 years, the number that Moyses also happened to live" (*Ant.* 1.152). In this passage, Josephus does not mention God, yet a few lines later he mentions God explicitly: "Since, for these reasons, the Chaldeans and the other Mesopotamians fell into discord against him, he, having decided to emigrate in accordance *with the will and assistance of God*, settled in the land of Chananaia. And having settled there he built an altar and offered a sacrifice to God" (*Ant.* 1.157; my emphasis).

This combination of earthly and divine causes also appears in Josephus' retelling of the Jacob narrative: "For, indeed, an abundant presence of great blessings in every respect will await you [Jacob] by virtue of my assistance. For I led Habramos hither from Mesopotamia when he was being driven out by his kinsmen, and made your father prosperous. I shall allot to you a destiny not less than theirs" (*Ant.* 1.281).[18]

As a rule, Josephus emphasizes in his *Antiquities of the Jews* the role of providence in the course of history. However, in *The Jewish War* there is more stress on "human foresight or will."[19] In the above example, we have a rare case of a combination of both aspects.

One of the new elements that Josephus introduces in his rewriting of Lot and Abram's relationship, is Abram's adoption of Lot. Genesis 12:4 reads: "and Lot went with him", but earlier, in Genesis 11:31, we are told that "Terah took his son Abram and his grandson Lot son of Haran." Josephus explains that Lot joins Abram because Abram adopted Lot as his son (*Ant.* 1.154). This claim is not paralleled in the rabbinic literature, moreover, there is no scholarly consensus as to whether adoption was customary in the Hebrew Bible.[20] However, there is no disputing the

16. J. Grossman, *Abram to Abraham: A Literary Analysis of the Abraham Narrative* (Bern: Peter Lang, 2016).

17. Mühling, *Blickt auf Abraham*, 297.

18. Cf. Spilsbury, *Image of the Jew*, 62.

19. See J.T. Squires, *The Plan of God in Luke-Acts* (SNTS Monograph Series 76; Cambridge: Cambridge University Press, 1993), 47. See also D.R. Schwartz, "Josephus, Catullus, Divine Providence, and the Date of the Judean War", in *Flavius Josephus: Interpretation and History*, eds. J. Pastor et al. (Leiden: Brill, 2011), 331–52.

20. See M. Avioz, "Josephus's Portrayal of Lot and His Family", *JSP* 16 (2006): 3–13.

fact that this was common practice in the ancient Near East.[21] According to Sterling, Josephus' intended audience was Eastern Mediterranean Greek Jews and Romans,[22] and if so, then his readers were presumably familiar with the practice of adoption.

Genesis 12:10-20, 23 describes Abram and Sarai's[24] descent into Egypt. Various questions arise from the story: how can we explain Abram's departure from Canaan to Egypt due to famine when God promised him the land only a few verses earlier? Was Sarai Abram's real sister, or did he lie? What exactly happened between Sarai and Pharaoh? Why was Pharaoh punished? How does Pharaoh learn that Sarai is Abram's wife?[25] These questions have been dealt with by scholars in various ways,[26] but I shall now examine which questions were dealt with by Josephus.

According to Josephus, Abraham goes to Egypt not only because famine strikes Canaan, but also in order to become acquainted with Egyptian science and religion and to engage in discussions with Egyptian wise men. Josephus characterizes Abraham as the wise man and sage par excellence who taught the Egyptians astronomy, the science for which they eventually became famous (*Ant.* 1.167–8).[27] This addition is undoubtedly apologetic, it calculated to promote Judaism as playing a major part in developing the art of astronomy.

Josephus explains that Abram claims that Sarai is his sister because he "fear[s] the frenzy of the Egyptians" (*Ant.* 1.162). This addition is not Josephus' invention, it is supported by Ezek. 23:21: "Thus you longed for the lewdness of your youth, when the Egyptians fondled your bosom and caressed your young breasts."[28] Josephus commends Abram's ploy (τέχνην ἐπενόησε τοιαύτην, *Ant.* 1.162), so does

21. F.W. Knoblock, "Adoption in the Old Testament and ANE", in *ABD*, Vol. 1, 76–79; H.M. Wahl, "Ester, das adoptierte Waisenkind. Zur Adoption im Alten Testament", *Bib* 80 (1999): 78–99.

22. G.E. Sterling, *Historiography and Self Definition, Josephus, Luke-Acts and Apologetic Historiography* (Leiden: Brill, 1992), 298–308.

23. For a thorough analysis of the reception of this story in early biblical interpretation, see A. Shinan and Y. Zakovitch, *Abram and Sarai in Egypt, Gen. 12.10–20 in the Bible, the Old Versions and the Ancient Jewish Literature* (Hebrew; Jerusalem: The Hebrew University, 1983).

24. For a full analysis of Sarah in Josephus, see J. McDonald, *Searching for Sarah in the Second Temple Era: Portraits in the Hebrew Bible and Second Temple Narratives* (PhD diss; Brite Divinity School, 2015), 300–67. I would like to thank Dr. McDonald for providing me with a copy of his dissertation.

25. Cf. G. Vermes, *Post-Biblical Jewish Studies* (Leiden: Brill, 1975), 67.

26. See e.g., Shinan and Zakovitch, *Abram and Sarai in Egypt*; Kugel, *Traditions of the Bible*, 244–73; Y. Peleg, "Was the Ancestress of Israel in Danger? Did Pharaoh Touch (נגע) Sarai?", *ZAW* 118 (2006): 197–208.

27. See A.Y. Reed, "Abraham as Chaldean Scientist and Father of the Jews: Josephus, Ant. 1.154–168, and the Greco-Roman Discourse about Astronomy/Astrology", *JSJ* 35 (2004): 119–58.

28. For Ezekiel's view of Egypt, see S. Marzouk, *Egypt as a Monster in the Book of Ezekiel* (Tübingen: Mohr Siebeck, 2015).

not present him as a liar, but rather as a clever man taking legitimate action to defend himself.[29]

Feldman argues that Josephus introduces erotic traits into the biblical narrative by writing that Pharaothes "seized with zeal to behold her, was on the point of laying hands on Sarra" (*Ant.* 1.163). However, it seems to me that Josephus was simply trying to solve a difficult verse: Genesis 20:17 relates that great plagues were inflicted upon Egypt "because of Sarai, Abram's wife" (על דבר שרי). Erotic depictions are found in the *Genesis Apocryphon* (1Q20 20.2–8), while Josephus was merely trying to make the biblical narrative clearer.[30] According to Josephus, Pharaoh's priests inform him that Sarai is Abram's wife (*Ant.* 1.164). This addition is probably part of an exegetical tradition, and we find it in *Pseudo-Eupolemus* (Eusebius, *Praep. Ev.* 9.17.7) and the *Genesis Apocryphon* (col. 20).[31]

Also, Josephus provides a more elaborate description of Abram's military skills than the biblical narrative in Genesis 14,[32] portraying Abraham as military leader as well as philosopher and astronomer. Josephus' exegesis continues in the story of Sodom and Gomorrah. In his retelling of this narrative (MT Genesis 18–19),[33] Josephus solves an exegetical question: why were these cities destroyed? Josephus writes that the Sodomites were: "overweeningly proud of their populousness and greatness of wealth, were insolent toward men and irreverent toward the Divinity, so that they no longer remembered the advantages that they had received from Him and hated strangers and shunned relations with others" (*Ant.* 1.194). Denouncing the Sodomites of having pride, hating strangers, and arrogance helps readers find the proportionality between their sin and their punishment in a clearer way than is stated in the MT. Josephus may have taken his cue from Ezek. 16:49: "she and her daughters had pride, excess of food, and prosperous ease, but did not aid the poor and needy."[34]

29. For Josephus' treatment of lies, see Avioz, *Josephus' Interpretation*, 76, with earlier literature.

30. Cf. Spilsbury, *Image of the Jew*, 63, n. 48.

31. Feldman, *Judean Antiquities*, 61, n.523. For the *Genesis Apocryphon*, see D.A. Machiela, *The Dead Sea Genesis Apocryphon: A New Text and Translation with Introduction and Special Treatment of Columns 13–17* (Leiden: Brill, 2009).

32. See Y. Muffs, "Abraham the Noble Warrior. Patriarchal Politics and Laws of War in Ancient Israel", in idem, *Love and Joy: Law, Language and Religion in Ancient Israel* (New York: Jewish Theological Seminary, 1992), 67–95.

33. On this story see J.A. Loader, *A Tale of Two Cities: Sodom and Gomorrah in the Old Testament, Early Jewish and Early Christian Traditions* (CBET, 1; Kampen: Kok Publishing House, 1990); M. Carden, *Sodomy: A History of a Christian Biblical Myth* (London: Equinox, 2004); E. Noort and E. Tigchelaar, eds., *Sodom's Sins: Genesis 18–19 and its Interpretations* (Leiden: Brill, 2004). See also Kugel, *Traditions*, 333–4.

34. See Kugel, *Traditions*, 333. Josephus mentions Ezekiel in *Ant.* 10.79. See C.T. Begg, "The 'Classical Prophets' in Josephus' 'Antiquities'", *LS* 13 (1988): 341–57 (Repr. in "'*The Place is too Small for Us*': *The Israelite Prophets in Recent Scholarship*, ed. R.P. Gordon [Winona Lake: Eisenbrauns, 1995], 547–62).

In retelling Genesis 20 (*Ant.* 1.207–12), Josephus writes that God struck Abimelech with a painful disease (*Ant.* 1.208). Though this is not explicitly stated in the biblical narrative, it is a reasonable inference based on Gen. 20:17; if God cured Abimelech, this implies that he had a disease.[35] As in other occurrences, Josephus fills a gap in the biblical narrative.[36] Sometimes this gap-filling contributes to a better understanding of these narratives and at other times it is a midrashic-like expansion. In this particular case, his addition is useful.

The Abraham narrative reaches its peak with the binding of Isaac (Genesis 22). This narrative raises many questions. Verse 1 opens: "After these things God tested Abraham": after which things? How can God command Abraham to sacrifice his son? Why does Abraham not question the divine command, or ask how it is consistent with God's earlier promises? Does Sarah ever learn of this command? Does Isaac remain passive, and how old is he? Why does Abraham bind Isaac? Is this story a model of behavior for future generations?

Josephus views Abraham as a true believer in God and lauds his piety, but avoids answering the question of why Isaac was bound. Instead, he writes that Isakos "rushed to the altar and the slaughter" (*Ant.* 1.232): Isaac's response precludes the need for binding. According to Josephus, Abraham willingly agrees to sacrifice Isaac, and he does not conceal this command from him. Intriguingly, Josephus is bothered by Sarah's absence from the narrative, and to this effect, he adds that Abraham concealed God's command from her (*Ant.* 1.225). This fact went unnoticed by many Second Temple sources,[37] and Josephus should be applauded for raising the question while others disregarded it. In Josephus' retelling, Isaac remains passive; though he does state his willingness to be sacrificed, his role is not emphasized any more than it is in the MT.[38] Josephus provides Isaac's age, a detail missing in the MT; he writes that Isaac "was in his twenty-fifth year" (*Ant.* 1.227). The source of this number is unclear. Feldman

35. Feldman (*Judean Antiquities*, 79, n.640) states that Josephus "used this account with that of Pharaoh (Gen. 12:17), who was beset with great plagues because he had taken Sarah." See also A-C. Geljon, "Abraham in Egypt: Philo's Interpretation of Gen 12:10-20", *Studia Philonica Annual* 28 (2016): 297–319, here 317. In light of my explanation, Feldman and Geljon's explanation is unnecessary.

36. See e.g., C.T. Begg, "Josephus' Retelling of 1 Kings 1 for a Graeco-Roman Audience", *TynBull* 57 (2006): 85–108.

37. See S.P. Brock, "Creating Women's Voices: Sarah and Tamar in Some Syriac Narrative Poems", in *The Exegetical Encounter between Jews and Christians in Late Antiquity*, eds. E. Grypeou et al. (Leiden: Brill, 2009), 125–41, at 130.

38. L.A. Huizenga, *The New Isaac: Tradition and Intertextuality in the Gospel of Matthew* (NovTSup 131; Leiden: Brill, 2009), 123–6. For a different view, see E. Kessler, *Bound by the Bible: Jews, Christians and the Sacrifice of Isaac* (Cambridge: Cambridge University Press, 2004), 120–1.

explains that Josephus aims to show that in this scene Isaac is not a young boy, but a grown man.[39]

The location of Abram's meeting with Melchizedek, and the events of the *Akedah* are not precisely clear in the MT of Genesis 14 and 22, but Josephus specifies that these events took place in Jerusalem. In *Ant.* 1.224 he writes that the *Akedah* took place upon Mount Moriah (εἰς τὸ Μώριον), "the mountain, upon that King David later built the Temple" (*Ant.* 1.226). This description concurs with several Second Temple traditions.[40]

These examples from Genesis 11–22 clearly show that Josephus had an exegetical interest in the Abraham narrative. He is a careful reader, paying attention to small nuances and trying to intrigue his readers with them; he invites them to do the same when reading these narratives in Greek. Yet his interpretation is far from being exhaustive, and he does not answer other questions and difficulties that were raised by other interpreters.

Juxtaposition

The vague biblical text does not always clarify connections between narratives, psalms, or oracles that initially seem unrelated.[41] Yet, the biblical authors and redactors did employ various devices to connect certain scenes or compositions, using association, key words, and others methods.

The narratives in Genesis 14 and 15 are loosely connected through the formula ויהי אחרי כן ("After these things"),[42] but Josephus offers a more meaningful connection: "And God, extolling his virtue, said, 'But you shall not lose the rewards that it is worthy for you to receive for such good deeds'" (*Ant.* 1.181). He also connects the narratives in chs 15 and 16. His retelling of Genesis 15 ends with the following:

39. Feldman, *Josephus's Interpretation*, 275–6. In *Jubilees* 17:15, Isaac is said to be 23 years old in this scene. Feldman rightly dismisses the view that Josephus was trying to depict Isaac as a voluntary martyr facing death with joy like an adult warrior, since the age of 25 was the minimum for active military service (pp. 276–7, n. 122).

40. See Kugel, *Traditions*, 320–2.

41. See, most recently, R. Gilmour, *Juxtaposition and the Elisha Cycle* (LHBOTS, 594; London: Bloomsbury T&T Clark, 2014). See also A. Shinan, and Y. Zakovitch, "Why is 'A' Placed Next to 'B'? Juxtaposition in the Bible and Beyond", in *Tradition, Transmission, and Transformation from Second Temple Literature through Judaism and Christianity in Late Antiquity*, eds. M. Kister et al. (STDJ 113; Leiden: Brill, 2015), 322–42; Y. Zakovitch, "Juxtaposition in the Abraham Cycle", in *Pomegranates and Golden Bells: Studies in Biblical, Jewish, and Near Eastern Ritual, Law, and Literature in Honor of Jacob Milgrom*, eds. D.P. Wright et al. (Winona Lake, IN: Eisenbrauns, 1995), 509–24.

42. On this formula, see B.L. Harmelink, *Exploring the Syntactic, Semantic, and Pragmatic Uses of* ויהי *in Biblical Hebrew* (PhD diss., Westminster Theological Seminary, 2004).

> Habramos was dwelling near the oak called Ogyges[43] (it is a place in Chananaia not far from the city of the Hebronites), and being distressed at his wife's not becoming pregnant, he besought God to grant him offspring of a male child.
>
> *Ant.* 1.186

This paragraph is an addition to Genesis 15, based on the MT to Gen. 15:3: "And Abram said, 'You have given me no offspring, and so a slave born in my house is to be my heir'". Moving the verse from its original place helps Josephus connect chs 15 and 16, while in the opening of his retelling of Genesis 16, Josephus writes: "When God encouraged him to be confident, as in all other things he had been led from Mesopotamia for his wellbeing, so also he would have children, Sarra, at God's command, caused him to lie down with one of her handmaidens, Agare by name, who was an Egyptian by race, so that he might procreate children by her" (*Ant.* 1.187).

These chapters are thus connected through the theme of anxiety regarding Abram' and Sarai's heir. Another advantage of this change is that it places emphasis on Abram: it is he who prayed to the Lord, not Sarai.[44] In his retelling of Genesis 21, Josephus adds that "Not long afterwards a son was born to Habramos from Sarra" (*Ant.* 1.213); this is a way of connecting ch. 20 to ch. 21, a connection that is lacking in the biblical narrative.

We are largely familiar with juxtaposition from rabbinic literature and in the later Jewish medieval commentary of the Bible. Yet, in the aforementioned examples we have seen that Josephus preceded them, and was aware of the exegetical problem of the connections between adjacent narratives, a riddle that still puzzles modern scholars and commentators.

Omissions

Omissions may be the result of several factors. Shaye Cohen[45] writes that Josephus freely omits whatever he does not need. This includes long lists of Semitic names and embarrassing incidents, such as Reuben and Bilhah; Judah and Tamar; the golden calf; and the complaint of Aaron and Miriam against Moses' wife. Josephus also condenses technical material (the laws and rituals of the Pentateuch) and uninteresting details (the complications of the apportionment of Canaan among the tribes).

43. For this addition, see Feldman, *Judean Antiquities Books 1–4*, 70, n. 584; A.D. Tropper, *Rewriting Ancient Jewish History: The History of the Jews in Roman Times and the New Historical Method* (London/New York: Routledge, 2016), 66.

44. Tropper, *Rewriting*, 67.

45. S.J.D. Cohen, *Josephus in Galilee and Rome: His Vita and Development as a Historian* (Leiden: Brill, 2002), 37.

When it comes to the Abraham narrative, Josephus omits several portions from Genesis 15, 17, 18, 21, 22, 23, and 24, including any reference to the dreams described in Gen. 13:14-17 and Genesis 15.[46] Josephus also significantly abridges God and Abraham's extensive dialogue about Sodom's fate in Gen. 18:16-33 (*Ant.* 1.199–200), which may be due to his reservations about anthropomorphic language.[47]

Josephus, in addition, omits the scene with Abraham and Abimelech in Gen. 21:22-33 and the genealogical list in Gen. 22:20-24. He also omits Abraham's negotiations with Ephron for the Machpela cave (Genesis 23), possibly because he does not consider it important. In this, he misses the narrative's great significance, as summarized by Sarna: "Machpelah is the first piece of real estate in the promised land secured by the founding father of the nation; its acquisition presages the future possession of the entire land; all three patriarchs and three matriarchs were interred in the cave."[48]

Various scholars have argued that Josephus deliberately omits the idea of God's covenant regarding the possession of Canaan in his rewriting of the Pentateuch. Elsewhere, I have refuted this claim, however, arguing that there is no meaningful difference between Josephus and the Bible in this regard.[49]

In another omission, Josephus fails to mention that Abraham serves the angels both meat and dairy products (Gen. 18:8). In contrast to Begg,[50] I do not think that this exclusion was calculated to prevent his readers' being scandalized, given that the prohibition of mixing milk and meat was not necessarily widespread in the Second Temple era. This restriction does appear in the Talmudic literature, but not in Philo (*Virt.*, 143–44), Josephus, or Qumran.[51]

46. Th.W. Franxman, *Genesis and the Jewish Antiquities of Flavius Josephus* (Rome: Pontifical Biblical Institute, 1979), 137, adds also 26:2-5, 24; 31:3, 11-13; 35:9-12. See also R. Gnuse, *Dreams and Dream Reports in the Writings of Josephus: A Traditio-Historical Analysis* (Leiden: Brill, 1996), 145.

47. See Loader, *Sodom*, 102.

48. N.M. Sarna, "Genesis Chapter 23: The Cave of Machpelah", *HS* 23 (1982): 17–21, here 17.

49. See M. Avioz, "Josephus' Land Theology: A Reappraisal", in *The Gift of the Land and the Fate of the Canaanites in Jewish Thought*, eds. K. Berthelot et al. (New York: Oxford University Press, 2014), 36–49.

50. Begg, "Genesis in Josephus", 316; Cf. Feldman, *Josephus's Interpretation*, 286, n.150.

51. See D. Kraemer, *Jewish Eating and Identity through the Ages* (London: Routledge, 2007), 37: "In all probability, observant Jews did not cook young animals in the milk of their own mothers. But they ate meat prepared with dairy without compunction." Cf. C. Werman and A. Shemesh, "The Halakha in the Dead Sea Scrolls", in *The Dead Sea Scrolls*, eds. M. Kister et al. (Jerusalem: Yad ben Zvi, 2009), 423–4; P.W. van der Horst, *Studies in Ancient Judaism and Early Christianity* (Leiden: Brill, 2014), 21–9.

Thus, the nature of omitted narratives in Josephus is not meaningful; the reader can still get a good idea of who Abraham was, and what were his great deeds.

Doublets

One of the most well-known features of Genesis relates to its repetition of narratives with a similar plotline. Nicol summarizes this issue as follows:

> Best known, perhaps, are the doublets where one of the patriarchs travelling abroad pretends that his wife is his sister, thereby coming into conflict (whether actual or potential) with the ruler of the land in which he finds himself (12:10-20; 20; 26:7-11), the stories which tell of the meeting of a traveler with a woman beside a well (24:10-14; 29:1-14 and Exod. 2:15-21), and the stories concerning the expulsion of Hagar.[52]
>
> 16 and 21:8-21

When confronting doublets, Josephus generally takes one of three different exegetical approaches:

1. Synthesizing the multiple versions into one: in both Genesis 17–18 Abraham is promised a son, but the parents are sceptical (Gen. 17:15-21; 18:10-14). In *Ant.* 1.191–3, Josephus condenses the narratives in Genesis 17–18: Abraham was not sceptical, but rather inquired (πυνθάνομαι) about Ishmael. He refers to Sarah's "smiling" in *Ant.* 1.198 and again in *Ant.* 1.213, and does not repeat the announcement of Isaac's impending birth. Thus Genesis 18 is not redundant, but rather focuses on Sarah's forthcoming pregnancy and her reaction to it.
2. Omitting one of the repeating stories: in such a case, Josephus chooses which one to omit, thus avoiding repetition. Wife-sister stories appear in Genesis 12, 20, and 26, but he does not retell the episode in Genesis 26.[53] It may be that Josephus considers it strange for the same event to occur three times.
3. Considering the stories as separate and different: in his retelling of the Hagar stories in Genesis 16 and 21, Josephus describes both (*Ant.* 1.186–90, 215–19), presumably because they are sufficiently different. For example, in Genesis 16 Hagar chooses to flee, while in Genesis 21 it is Sarah who demands Hagar's expulsion.[54]

52. G.G. Nicol, "Story-patterning in Genesis", in *Text as Pretext: Essays in Honour of Robert Davidson*, ed. R.P. Carroll (Sheffield: JSOT Press), 215–33, here 223. On doublets in general, see the literature cited in M. Avioz, *Josephus' Interpretation*, 167–75.

53. See Franxman, *Genesis*, 177–8.

54. For further differences between the two stories, see T. Desmond Alexander, *Abraham in the Negev: A Source Critical Investigation of Genesis 20:1–22:19* (Carlisle: Paternoster, 1997), 52–69.

Contradictions

One of the exegetical problems in Genesis 15 relates to chronology. Gen. 15:13 states that the Israelites will stay 400 years in Egypt, while in Exod. 12:40, the number is 430. In his rewriting of Exod. 12:40, Josephus writes that Israel "left Egypt in the month of Xanthikos on the fifteenth according to the lunar reckoning, 430 years after our forefather Habramos came to Chananaia, Iakobos' departure to Egypt having occurred 215 years later".[55] In his rewriting of Genesis 15, however, he mentions 400 years, as in the MT. He apparently felt unable to reconcile these verses.

Another contradiction is found in Gen. 16:11, where the angel tells Hagar to call her child Ishmael, while 16:15 assigns the name giving to Abram. Instead Josephus credits neither the angel nor Abram with naming Ishmael, but rather states that "she [Agare, Hagar] gave birth to Ismaelos; someone might render it 'heard by God', because God had listened to her entreaty" (*Ant.* 1.189).

In Gen. 18:20-21 the order of events is problematic: God determines to punish Sodom and Gomorrah in v. 20, but v. 21 then implies that God will descend to investigate the cities before making a decree. Josephus avoids any contradiction by simply writing: "Therefore, indignant at this behavior, God decided to punish them for their overweening contempt and to raze their city" (*Ant.* 1.195); moreover, this phrasing helps Josephus avoid anthropomorphism.[56]

Modern readers may not be persuaded by Josephus' solutions to the contradictions inherent in the Abraham narrative, but even so, one is impressed by his sensitivity to the subtleties of biblical narrative. He offers harmonistic solutions, thus presenting smoother versions of the narratives.

Josephus' Changes as the Product of His Cultural Background

Since Josephus lived in a Graeco-Roman milieu, it is to be expected that he will have been influenced by these circumstances, and change, add, or omit details that reflect this when retelling the biblical narratives. Louis Feldman devotes in each of his dealings with Josephus' retelling of the Bible, a section on Hellenization.[57]

Feldman deems Josephus' retelling of the *Akedah* "a supreme example of Hellenization."[58] Josephus psychologized (Abraham "loved exceedingly" Isaac,

55. B.Z. Wacholder, "How Long Did Abram Stay in Egypt? A Study in Hellenistic, Qumran, and Rabbinic Chronology", *HUCA* 35 (1964): 43–56.

56. See C.H. Von Heijne, *The Messenger of the Lord in Early Jewish Interpretations of Genesis* (BZAW, 412; Berlin: de Gruyter, 2010). She emphasizes also the omission of the role of the angel in the story of Hagar.

57. See e.g., Feldman, *Josephus's Interpretation*, 171–214.

58. Ibid, 266.

Ant. 1.222) and rationalized the biblical story, and added both drama and human emotions.[59] Feldman notes that:

> There are several striking parallels between Isaac and Iphigenia, notably in the enthusiasm with which they both approach the sacrifice and, in particular, in Isaac's statement that he could not even consider rejecting God's decision (*Ant.* 1.232) and Iphigenia's observation, that she, a mortal woman, cannot stand in the way of the goddess (Euripides, *Iphigenia at Aulis* 396). There is pathetic irony in the fact that Abraham seeks happiness only through his son, who, paradoxically, is about to be sacrificed, just as there is irony in the Chorus's ode (*Iphigenia at Aulis* 590–91) that begins, "Oh! oh! great happiness of the great!" One may also note the remarkable addition to the biblical narrative in which G-d declares that He gave His order to Abraham "from no craving for human blood" (*Ant.* 1.233), which is clearly in contrast to the statement of Artemis, who is said to rejoice in human sacrifices.
>
> *Iphigenia at Aulis* 1524–25[60]

While I concur with Feldman that the retelling of the *Akedah* has some Hellenistic traits,[61] to call it a "supreme example" of such is an exaggeration,[62] after all, the midrashic treatment of the story extends far beyond Josephus' elaboration. Feldman's argument that the midrashim focus solely on theodicy and analogies with the book of Job is unconvincing;[63] more accurately, they deal with a wide range of exegetical issues, some of which are also discussed by Josephus.

However, the most problematic issue is the parallels that Feldman cites. He cannot, apparently, prove that Josephus created these parallels, and one is inclined

59. See F. Mirguet, *An Early History of Compassion: Emotion and Imagination in Hellenistic Judaism* (New York: Cambridge University Press, 2017), 38; Begg, "Genesis in Josephus", 311.

60. Feldman, *Josephus's Interpretation*, 176.

61. Such as emphasizing emotions: Josephus knows how Abraham felt after God's decree. He dramatizes the biblical scene, emphasizing Abraham's love for his son; he also adds logic to the dialogues between Abraham and Isaac. All of these may be deemed Hellenistic traits.

62. Another example relates to Feldman's argument (*Josephus's Interpretation*, 257) that Josephus made great efforts to indicate that "the place was mount Moriah, since in Greek μωρίαν means 'folly', and 'mountain of folly' might evoke mocking from Greek readers." This is an extremely complex explanation; a more likely, straightforward, one is that it is an exegetical tradition that the *Akedah* took place in Jerusalem. In general, one may find echoes of the Hellenistic world, but sometimes Feldman seems to push the case too far. It is doubtful whether Josephus makes any allusions to specific Greek tragedies or Homeric literature. Cf. Spilsbury, *Image of the Jew*, 32, 186–7.

63. See Kugel, *Traditions*, 300–26.

to view them as artificial and forced. Josephus may have known Greek authors, but that is simply not enough to prove that he shaped his retelling in a way that the Greek or Roman reader would be aware of such parallels.[64]

The exemplary character of Abraham might raise the impression that Josephus had a missionary goal, namely to attract potential proselytes among his pagan readers. This issue is much debated and goes beyond the scope of my inquiry, but we need to differentiate between *Ant.* 1–11 and Josephus' other writings. While in *Against Apion* and in *Ant.* 12–20 we may find a favorable attitude towards converts, this is not the case in the first half of *Antiquities of the Jews*, specifically when the Abraham narrative is concerned.[65]

Finally, a point to note is that Josephus' characterization of Abraham as an astronomer[66] and monotheist is a product of his times and environment. According to Josephus (*Ant.* 1.157), Abraham leaves Ur because his countrymen are angered by his independent monotheistic beliefs, which he reaches after careful astronomical and astrological consideration. In Josephus' (*Ant.* 1.155) retelling, Abraham "was the first who dared to declare that God was the one craftsman of the universe." Throughout his writing, Josephus emphasizes the topic of monotheism in Judaism in contrast with polytheistic beliefs.[67] To be the first to develop an idea, or achieve in an area, was considered significant in the Roman world, and this explains Josephus' emphasis on Abraham being the first. Emphasizing astronomy as a wisdom transferred by Abraham helps Josephus in presenting Judaism as contributing to world culture;[68] Josephus argues that it is the Chaldeans rather than the Egyptians who invented astronomy and astrology. This addition is not based on the biblical text, and seems calculated to present Abraham as a universal hero and the Jews as the source of celebrated sciences.[69]

64. Spilsbury, *The Image of the Jew*, 186–7 criticized Feldman who claimed that there are parallels between Solomon and Sophocles in Josephus' retelling: "Feldman can point to no substantial verbal similarities between the two accounts, and there are clearly no striking narrative similarities. The character quality similarities he cites are all common-places and hardly cause for speculative schemes" (p. 187).

65. See S. Mason, "The "Contra Apionem" in Social and Literary Context: An Invitation to Judean Philosophy", in *Josephus' "Contra Apionem": Studies in Its Character and Context with a Latin Concordance to the Portion Missing in Greek*, eds. L.H. Feldman et al. (Leiden: Brill, 1996), 187–228.

66. Bar Kochva, "On Abraham and the Egyptians", 349, n.90 points out that Josephus does not state explicitly that Abraham invented astronomy but that he was an intermediator: Abraham received this wisdom from Babylon and brought it to Egypt (*Ant.* 1.168).

67. See Spilsbury, *The Image of the Jew*, 59; R. Liong-Seng Phua, *Idolatry and Authority. A Study of Corinthians 8.1–11.1 in the Light of the Jewish Diaspora* (London/New York: T. & T. Clark, 2005), 69–76.

68. See Reed, "Abraham as Chaldean Scientist", 127.

69. Reed, "Abraham as Chaldean Scientist".

Conclusion

In *Antiquities of the Jews*, Josephus depicts Abraham as a wise man, an obedient worshipper, and a philosopher, astronomer, and military commander. Josephus did not invent these traits, as such qualities are mentioned in the Bible, for example: obedience, righteousness, peacefulness (Genesis 13); hospitability (Gen. 18:1-8); and faith in God (Gen. 15, 22). In his rewriting of the Abraham narrative, Josephus simply emphasized and developed these traits. In his encomium, Josephus writes that Abraham was a "man outstanding in every virtue who had been deservedly honored by God because of his zeal in His service" (*Ant.* 1.256).

According to Martin Goodman, Josephus missed the opportunity to emphasize the idea that Abraham was "the source of blessings to the whole world to be known to his Gentile readers."[70] However, even though this was not his purpose, then Josephus' project should still be considered a success. As an exegetical project, his retelling can be considered an achievement because it clarifies the text for his readers.

The existence of the apologetic in Josephus' retelling cannot be denied, but what I have tried to show is that his exegetical motivation is more inherent than some scholars assume. Though there are some imprints of Graeco-Roman influence upon Josephus' writing, most of his retelling of the Abraham cycle is motivated by exegetical concerns. He omitted unimportant details, settled contradictions, and made efforts to make the biblical narrative of Abraham more readable and smooth. Josephus was not writing a biography of, or an apology on, Abraham.

70. M. Goodman, "Josephus on Abraham and the Nations", in *Abraham, the Nations, and the Hagarites: Jewish, Christian, and Islamic Perspectives on Kinship with Abraham*, eds. M. Goodman et al. (Leiden: Brill, 2010), 177–83, here 183. Cf. J.R. Wisdom, *Blessing for the Nations and the Curse of the Law: Paul's Citation of Genesis and Deuteronomy in Gal 3.8–10* (Tübingen: Mohr Siebeck, 2001), 82–6.

Chapter 7

ABRAHAM IN THE SYNOPTIC GOSPELS AND THE ACTS OF THE APOSTLES

Joshua W. Jipp

Within the canonical Gospels and the Acts of the Apostles, the biblical patriarch Abraham plays a significant, if not primary, role in determining the identity of the people of God, establishing continuity between God's covenantal dealings with Israel *and* Jesus of Nazareth and his followers. This ensures a connection between the Abrahamic promise for seed and God's promise to David to raise up seed for him, and in setting forth a paradigm for the ethical behavior demanded by the God of Israel. In what follows, I will examine the role of Abraham within the canonical Gospels and the book of Acts. While I will attend on occasion to important traditions which may have influenced these writings, my primary interest and emphasis is on the literary nature of the compositions, and the role that Abraham plays within their broader narrative worlds.

The Gospel of Matthew

Matthew begins his Gospel by describing Jesus Christ with two titles: "son of David" and "son of Abraham" (Mt. 1:1). While Matthew's primary interest is in portraying Jesus as Israel's Davidic Messiah (e.g., 2:5-6; 21:9-15),[1] his royal-messianic identity only makes sense in light of the way in which Israel's Davidic traditions presuppose and expand upon the Abrahamic traditions (cf. Gal. 3:16). The seed of David is, then, the heir of the promises made to Abraham. This can be seen immediately in the way Matthew structures his genealogy as neatly moving from three periods of fourteen generations, moving from Abraham (1:2-6), to

1. The centrality of Jesus as Davidic Messiah for Matthew is argued for in a variety of important works. See, for example, N.G. Piotrowksi, *Matthew's New David at the End of Exile: A Socio-Rhetorical Study of Scriptural Quotations* (NovTSup 170; Leiden: Brill, 2016); A. LeDonne, *The Historiographical Jesus: Memory, Typology, and the Son of David* (Waco, TX: Baylor University Press, 2009).

David (1:6-11), to the Babylonian exile (1:12-16) and culminating with the birth of Jesus the Messiah (1:16-17). We will have to attend to Matthew's narrative to discern the precise meaning and significance of Jesus' identity as "son of Abraham," but already it would seem justifiable to claim that Matthew is presenting Jesus Christ as the goal of God's election of Israel. Matthew's reference to Jesus as "the son of Abraham" draws, then, the identity of Jesus together with God's election and origins of Israel as his people. Anders Runesson rightly notes that one cannot "understand Matthew's story and focus on Israel without also acknowledging the notion of Israel's election as implied."[2] Matthew's genealogy thereby demands that his Gospel be interpreted in such a way that there is deep continuity between Matthew's story and God's election of Israel.[3]

Matthew is adamant that Abrahamic descent does not provide a safeguard against divine judgment. John the Baptist, forerunner of Jesus' proclamation of repentance for the forgiveness of sins (3:2; 4:17), preaches that Abrahamic descent and election does not translate into salvation. John's call for repentance is situated within the warning directed toward "the Pharisees and Sadducees" (3:7) that only "fruit worthy of repentance" rather than confidence that one has "Abraham as our father" (3:8-9) will enable one to escape "the coming wrath" (3:7). God has the power, in fact, to create "children for Abraham" (τέκνα τῷ Ἀβραάμ) out of the stones and rocks at the Jordan river (3:9). As Jon Levenson has noted, the election of Abraham and genealogical descent from his family is quite simply irrelevant as it pertains to salvation and the avoidance of God's wrath.[4] Nothing that the Baptist states here is necessarily in conflict with the assertion of God's election of Abraham and his family in Matthew 1:1-17, nor *should* his statement be seen as implying God's rejection of his election of Israel. John's warning, however, does preview Matthew's ongoing polemic against Israel's religious leaders who, Matthew warns, must not presume that their descent from Abraham provides them with an excuse to refuse John's and Jesus' proclamation of the kingdom of heaven and the need for repentance. This is the beginning of Matthew's narration of the conflict with the Pharisees and Sadducees and the pronouncement of judgment for their refusal to repent.[5] John's message previews Jesus' parable of the owner of the vineyard (Mt. 21:33-45), an owner who in response to the tenants' failure to procure fruit "takes away the kingdom of God [from Israel's authorities] and gives it to a people

2. A. Runesson, *Divine Wrath and Salvation in Matthew: The Narrative World of the First Gospel* (Minneapolis: Fortress Press, 2016), 182.

3. R.B. Hays, *Echoes of Scripture in the Gospels* (Waco, TX: Baylor University Press, 2016), 110.

4. J.D. Levenson, *Abraham Between Torah and Gospel* (The Pere Marquette Lecture in Theology; Milwaukee: Marquette University Press, 2011), 34.

5. On this theme, and the way in which the warning is directed *primarily* to the authorities of Israel (rather than the people as a whole), see M. Konradt, *Israel, Church, and the Gentiles in the Gospel of Matthew* (trans. K. Ess; Baylor-Mohr Siebeck Studies in Early Christianity; Waco, TX: Baylor University Press, 2014), 167–264.

(ἔθνει) producing its fruit" (21:43). That this is directed against Israel's authorities (rather than the people of Israel) is made explicit in 21:45 where the chief priests and Pharisees understand that Jesus directs the parable against them (21:45).[6] John's demand that only the fruits of repentance will enable one to avoid God's wrath is consistent with the narrative's broader portrayal of entrance into the kingdom of God as contingent upon repentance, obedience, and doing what Jesus teaches (e.g., Matt. 7:13-23; 16:27).

Finally, Jesus declares that sharing in the eschatological banquet with Abraham and the patriarchs is contingent upon a faithful response to his person and teaching. In Jesus' encounter with the Roman centurion (8:5-13), Jesus responds to the man's understanding of and submission to Jesus' authority with the pronouncement: "Truly I tell you, I have not found anyone in Israel with so great a faith" (8:10). Jesus portrays this non-Jewish man as an exemplar of "the many" when he declares that "many will come from the east and west and will recline with Abraham, Isaac, and Jacob in the kingdom of heaven, but the sons of the kingdom will be cast out into the outer darkness where there is weeping and the gnashing of teeth" (8:11-12). God's election of Abraham and the patriarchs and his affirmation of the divinely created origins of Israel are upheld, and yet Jesus' pronouncement again engages in a surprising definition of who will experience the hospitality of the kingdom and who will be excluded. In Hays' words: "In the Matthean narrative context, this can only mean that the centurion exemplifies 'many' *non-Israelites* who will ultimately be included in salvation and the great final eschatological feast. . . ."[7] Again, it would be too simplistic and wrong-headed to interpret this as a contrast between Gentiles who are welcomed and Jews who are excluded. Jesus' exaltation of the centurion's faith is spoken to those Jews "who are following" him (8:10), namely "the large crowds" (8:1; cf. 4:25) listening to his proclamation of the Sermon on the Mount. The commendation of the centurion's faith thereby functions as an exhortation to the crowds who are listening to his teaching (7:28-29). Entrance into the eschatological banquet with Abraham is mediated through one's response to Jesus, and therefore a faithless or hostile response will result in a situation where even "the sons of the kingdom" are excluded (8:11).

While many have seen here a reference to Israel's exclusion, it may make better sense to understand the warning to "the sons of the kingdom" as referring to those who have heard and responded to Jesus' teaching but are in need of further exhortations to follow. This makes good sense of the fact that the parallel phrase "sons of the kingdom" in Matthew 13:38 refers to "the good seed" in Jesus' parable of the wheat and the tares (13:36-43) as well as the literary context of 8:5-13, which seems much more concerned with exhortations and warnings to followers of Jesus

6. For a further defense of interpreting this parable in a non-supersessionist manner, see Konradt, *Israel, Church, and the Gentiles in the Gospel of Matthew*, 173–93.

7. Hays, *Echoes of Scripture in the Gospels*, 181.

to continue to listen and respond to his teaching (cf. 7:21-9).[8] However, Jesus' note that "many will come from east and west" (8:11) almost certainly previews the fulfillment of the Abrahamic promises that the nations will be blessed through the seed of Abraham (Gen. 12:1-4; 15:1-6; et al.). Just as Isa. 25:6-8 envisioned a banquet that is for "all the peoples" and "all the nations," (Isa. 25:7), so Mt. 8:5-13 portrays participating in the eschatological banquet as for both Jews and Gentiles who respond positively to Jesus.

Thus, Matthew's initial statement that Jesus is "the son of Abraham" (1:1) would seem to have universalistic connotations, and this possibility may be further strengthened by the fact that, as is often noted, Matthew's genealogy includes four non-Jewish women in Jesus' family lineage (Tamar, Ruth, Rahab, and Bathsheba).[9] As the climax of God's dealings with his people Israel, the Messiah thereby opens up salvation to the nations; for this reason, one finds within Matthew a variety of texts speaking of the extension of salvation to Jews *and Gentiles* as fulfilling scriptural texts which signal God's faithfulness to his promise to Abraham that *through him* he would bless the nations (e.g., Mt. 2:1-12 and Isa. 60:1-6; 4:15-16 and Isa. 9:1-2; 12:15-21 and Isa. 42:6-7; 28:16-20, and Dan. 7:13-14).[10]

The Gospel of Mark

Abraham is only mentioned by name in one place in the Gospel of Mark as part of Jesus's response in 12:18-27 (cf. Mt. 22:23-33; Lk. 20:27-38) to some Sadducees who challenge Jesus by asking him about a woman married (consecutively) to seven different men: "whose wife will she be in the resurrection? For the seven men had her as a wife" (12:23).[11] Their question is intended, it would seem, to trip up Jesus by mocking the belief in the resurrection from the dead. Jesus rebukes them, however, for failing to understand both "the Scriptures and the power of God" (12:24b). Jesus argues that their own Scriptures testify to the doctrine of the resurrection for the dead, and he appeals to Exod. 3:6: "I am the God of Abraham, Isaac, and Jacob. He is the God of the living, not the dead. You are greatly deceived"

8. More typical, however, are interpretations that follow Siker's conclusion that "Jews who do not demonstrate faith will be cut off from the kingdom, while the Gentiles who do exhibit faith will find themselves included in the kingdom and will sit at table with Abraham." See J.S. Siker, *Disinheriting the Jews: Abraham in Early Christian Controversy* (Louisville: Westminster John Knox Press, 1991), 84

9. See, for example, U. Luz, *Matthew 1—7: A Commentary* (trans. W. C. Linss; Minneapolis: Augsburg, 1985), 107–11; J.B. Hood, *The Messiah, His Brothers, and the Nations: Matthew 1.1—17* (LNTS 441; New York: T&T Clark, 2011).

10. Whether Matthew envisions the nations as saved *qua* the nations *or* as proselytes cannot be entered into here. See, for example, Runesson, *Divine Wrath and Salvation in Matthew*, 364–73.

11. Their question presumes the practice of levirate marriage (e.g., Gen. 38:8).

(12:26b-27; cf. Acts 3:13; 7:32). Joel Marcus notes that this is "hardly the sense that the formula 'the God of Abraham, of Isaac, and of Jacob' had in the original . . . [and that it] means that just as he delivered those patriarchs from their distress, so will he now liberate and succor their enslaved descendants."[12] And yet if God is the God of life who continues to demonstrate his power and covenant faithfulness to his people, then it is not too far removed to suggest that the recipients of his faithfulness "will ultimately be crowned by their liberation from the power of death itself."[13] Jesus' response is congruent with Luke's parable which will depict Abraham and those in his bosom as participants in some form of blessed postmortem existence (Luke 16:22-23).

The Gospel of Luke

In the Gospel of Luke and the Acts of the Apostles, the author draws upon Abraham in order to establish "a connection and continuity between the history of Abraham and the events of which he himself is writing."[14] Abraham is the father of Israel, the recipient of God's promises, the father of the repentant, the outcasts, and marginalized within Israel, and the one through whom God will bless all the families of the earth.

Unlike Matthew, however, who draws a more obvious or explicit connection through his fulfillment citations, Luke accomplishes a similar end through subtle hints that his story is a continuation of God's covenantal promises made to Abraham. The miraculous conceptions of John and Jesus resonate powerfully with the stories of the barren women in Israel's Scriptures, not least that of Sarah (Genesis 12–21) and Hannah (1 Samuel 1–2). Joel Green has set forth an impressive list of the parallels between God's powerful mercy to the barren Sarah and God's opening of the wombs of Elizabeth and Mary in Luke 1–2.[15] To give just a few examples: Sarai and Elizabeth are barren (Gen. 11:30; Luke 1:7); promises are made which share the common language of greatness, blessing, and seed (Gen. 12:2-7; 13:14-17; Luke 1:15, 32, 55, 73); the recipients of the promise are advanced in age (Gen. 17:1; Gen. 18:11-13; Luke 1:7, 11, 18); both are recipients of divine/angelic visitations (Gen. 17:22; Luke 1:38). Many more parallels could be adduced, but enough have been invoked to indicate Luke's intention to portray to the reader that God's merciful kindness to Abraham has not been forgotten, and

12. J. Marcus, *Mark 8–16* (AYBC 27A; New Haven: Yale University Press, 2009), 835.

13. Ibid, 835. See further the argument of J.D. Levenson, *Resurrection and the Restoration of Israel: The Ultimate Victory of the God of Life* (New Haven, CT: Yale University Press, 2006).

14. N.A. Dahl, "The Story of Abraham in Luke-Acts", in *Studies in Luke-Acts*, eds. L.E. Keck and J. Louis Martyn (Mifflintown, PA: Sigler Press, 1966), 139–58, here, 140.

15. J.B. Green, "The Problem of a Beginning: Israel's Scriptures in Luke 1–2", *BBR* 4 (1994): 61–86, here, 68–71.

that in the event Luke is narrating in his Gospel (and the second volume as well), God is continuing the story and promises he had initiated with Abraham in Genesis. Both the speeches of Mary and Zechariah interpret God's act to open the wombs of Mary and Elizabeth in relationship to the promises made to Abraham. Thus, Mary: "[God] has helped his servant Israel, to remember mercy (μνησθῆναι ἐλέους), just as he spoke to our ancestors, to Abraham and to his seed forever" (Luke 1:54-55). Similarly, Zechariah declares that God has "shown mercy (ἔλεος) with our fathers and remembered (μνησθῆναι) his holy covenant, the oath which he swore to Abraham our father" (Luke 1:72-73). For Luke, then, Abraham functions as the initial and primary recipient of God's promises, and thus God's opening of the wombs of Elizabeth and Mary function as the concrete display of God's merciful remembrance of these promises.[16] Despite lacking the literary adornment of Matthew, Luke's genealogy does not surprise the reader when it lists Abraham and the patriarchs as the ancestors of Jesus (3:34).

Yet, even within Luke's infancy narrative, the reader is alerted to the expectation that God's merciful remembrance of his promises to Abraham will not take place without conflict and division. Thus, Simeon prophesies to Mary that her son has been "appointed for the fall and rising of many in Israel and a sign to be spoken against and that even a sword will pierce your soul" (2:34b-35a). Mary's hymn has interpreted God's actions to be good news for the poor, the hungry, and humiliated and judgment for the proud, powerful, and rich (1:51-53). John the Baptist's primary task is to lead Israel to turn back to God so that there will be a "people made ready, prepared for the Lord" (1:17, 76; 3:1-6). Not unlike what we have seen in Matthew's Gospel, the Baptist functions as a sign that God's election of Abraham does not translate into salvation *apart* from a believing response to John and Jesus.[17] Thus, just as in Matthew's Gospel, John warns them that their descent from Abraham is irrelevant apart from producing fruit that is worthy of repentance (3:8a). Non-fruit bearing trees will be "cut off and cast into the fire" (3:9). John describes this repentant, fruit-bearing response in embodied and tangible terms of sharing one's possessions and refusing to engage in exploitation of the vulnerable (3:10-14).[18]

Luke's remaining explicit references to Abraham serve to highlight the surprising recipients of God's merciful kindness and the response of right behavior or the fruits of repentance. Thus, in Jesus' healing of the woman "bent over," who is "unable to stand up straight," and is plagued by an unclean spirit for fourteen years (13:11, 16), Jesus heals her and publicly declares her to be "a daughter of Abraham"

16. Dahl, "The Story of Abraham in Luke-Acts", 142.

17. Siker, *Disinheriting the Jews*, 108: "Luke rules out completely the notion that mere physical descent from Abraham gives one a special claim on God's mercy. Only repentance and ethical behavior that demonstrates this repentance counts before God."

18. Dahl, "The Story of Abraham in Luke-Acts", 140 may overstate the point when he denies that Luke portrays Abraham as a model or prototype for behavior.

(13:16a).[19] Luke describes her as coming to the synagogue on the Sabbath (13:10) and responding by "giving glory to God" in response for her healing. She is one of Israel's poor but pious worshippers of the God of Israel described by Mary in Luke 1:51-53. Her identity as a daughter of Abraham reveals that she and others like her, those considered to be excluded from or on the margins of the society of Israel, are in fact the target of Jesus' mercy (e.g., Luke 4:18-29).[20] Jesus' healing releases her from the bondage of Satan and vindicates her as Abraham's daughter (13:16), and functions as a surprising literary fulfillment of Zechariah's hymn, which linked God's remembrance of his covenant to Abraham with the promise of deliverance from God's enemies.[21] A similar designation of Zacchaeus, the rich but short-in-stature tax collector (19:1-3), occurs in Luke 19:9 when Jesus declares him to be "a son of Abraham." As Zacchaeus engages his quest to *see Jesus* (19:3a), Jesus makes eye contact with the tax-collector in the tree (19:5) and demands that Zacchaeus receive Jesus hospitably in his own home: "Hurry up and come down, for I must receive welcome in your home today" (19:5).[22] The shared hospitality between Jesus and Zacchaeus creates the context whereby Zacchaeus is able to engage in repentant practices of sharing possessions and making restitution for his former exploitative practices.[23] As a result of the shared hospitality and Zacchaeus' repentance, Jesus grants salvation to the former outcast and refers to him as a son of Abraham (19:9, 10). Just as Abraham was remembered as hosting the divine strangers in his dwelling and thereby received the promise of Isaac as a gift in return, so Zacchaeus welcomes the travelling Lord in his home and receives salvation. His sharing of his possessions for the poor demonstrates that he is one who will do the deeds of the hospitable Abraham (cf. Gen. 18:14).[24]

There are two further significant texts from Luke's Gospel which portray Abraham as granting, or alternatively excluding, individuals from eschatological fellowship/hospitality. We have already examined the parallel pericope of Luke

19. On Jesus's overturning the prevalent and negative stereotyping based upon bodily attributes and appearance, see M. Parsons, *Body and Character in Luke-Acts: The Subversion of Physiognomy in Early Christianity* (Grand Rapids: Baker Academic, 2006).

20. See further, J.B. Green, "Jesus and a Daughter of Abraham (Luke 13:10-17): Test Case for a Lucan Perspective on Jesus' Miracles", *CBQ* 51 (1989): 643–54, esp., 651–3.

21. This point is made clearly by Siker, *Disinheriting the Jews*, 111–12.

22. I have discussed the relationship of Lk. 19:1-10 to the broader theme of hospitality in Luke-Acts in my *Divine Visitations and Hospitality to Strangers in Luke-Acts: An Interpretation of the Malta Episode in Acts 28:1-10* (NovTSup 153; Leiden: Brill, 2013), 228–9.

23. I remain convinced of the traditional interpretation of this episode as a story of salvation. See, for example, the important parallels with Lk. 5:27-32. For further defense, see D. Hamm, "Luke 19:8 Once Again: Does Zacchaeus Defend or Resolve?", *JBL* 107 (1988): 431–7.

24. Some of these parallels are set forth by A.E. Arterbury, "Zacchaeus: 'A Son of Abraham'?", in *Biblical Interpretation in Early Christian Gospels*, Vol. 3, *The Gospel of Luke*, ed. T. Hatina (LNTS 376; London/New York: T&T Clark, 2010), 18–31, here, 26–7.

13:23-30 in our discussion of Matthew's Gospel (8:5-13). In response to someone's question whether only a few will be saved (Luke 13:23), Jesus declares that some will seek entrance to the eschatological banquet and will demand "Open up for us" (13:25) and even declare to him "we ate and drank together with you" (13:26). But Jesus will respond: "I never knew you, depart from me all of you workers of injustice" (13:27; cf. LXX Ps. 6:9). Jesus warns that they will experience torment "when you see Abraham, Isaac, Jacob, and all the prophets in the kingdom of God, and you are cast outside and they will come from east and west and from north and south and will recline in the kingdom of God" (13:29). The parable contributes to Luke's reversal motif, for Jesus concludes the parable with the words: "behold, the last will be first and the first will be last" (13:30; cf. 14:11). This warning of impending eschatological inhospitality within the context of Luke's reversal motif is directed precisely against those who, within Luke's narrative, grumble and complain about Jesus extending salvation and welcome to those "sinners" and outcasts on the margins of society. They are warned not to presume their election will act as a safeguard for them, all the while continuing to act as "workers of injustice" (13:27; cf. 3:8). Just as John had stated, Jesus declares that they will be cut down like trees and cast into the fire if they remain unrepentant (13:6-9). More precisely, Jesus' parabolic warning is directed to those Pharisees who, in the very next chapter, eat and drink with Jesus but as a means of testing him (14:1; cf. 7:36-39; 11:37-44) and who refuse to receive the invitation to the master's "great feast" (14:16-24). Their grumbling at Jesus' extension of hospitality and table-fellowship with tax collectors and sinners (15:1-2) shows them to be like the elder brother who, in the parable of the prodigal son (15:1-32), refuses to join in with the joyous celebration of the father who has received back his son (15:28-29). Thus, Luke portrays eschatological salvation through the imagery of food, hospitality, and fellowship with Abraham and the patriarchs.[25]

A similar image of feasting or reclining with Abraham can be found in Jesus' parable of the Rich Man and Lazarus in 16:19-31. The parable functions as a critique of the greed of the wealthy who fail to show hospitality and perform acts of mercy to the poor.[26] The Rich Man "clothed in purple and fine linen joyously-feasts in luxury every day" (16:19b) while Lazarus suffers "having been tossed outside his [i.e., the rich man's] gate" (16:20). At the very least, the Rich Man was obligated to show hospitality to the stranger "lying at his gate", an obligation that is obvious to those familiar with Torah (e.g., Deuteronomy 14:28-29; 15:1-8). Poor Lazarus, covered in sores, longs "to be filled with some food falling from the table

25. There are a variety of Jewish and early Christian texts which speak of eschatological salvation in relationship to Abraham and the patriarchs. See, for example, P-B. Smit, *Fellowship and Food in the Kingdom: Eschatological Meals and Scenes of Utopian Abundance in the New Testament* (WUNT 2.234; Tübingen: Mohr-Siebeck, 2008), 151–2.

26. I have written in more detail about this episode in my *Saved by Faith and Hospitality* (Grand Rapids: Eerdmans, 2017).

of the rich man" (16:21; cf. 15:16), but even table-scraps are denied him. When the two men die, Lazarus is accompanied "by the angels" (16:22; cf. 15:10) into "Abraham's bosom," while the rich man descends to Hades (16:22b-23) where "he sees Abraham at a distance and Lazarus in his bosom" (16:23b). Contributing to the ironic reversal throughout the parable is the likelihood that "Abraham's bosom" (16:22-23) functions as the heavenly and eschatological counterpart to the earthly banqueting of the rich man. The reason for the rich man's punishment is obvious; his punishment is not the result of his wealth but is in his luxurious consumption and refusal to share with the poor stranger at his gate. Not unlike Jesus' warning to "workers of injustice" in 13:27, so here the man's unjust use of possessions and lack of deeds of mercy result in his being barred from fellowship with Abraham in paradise.

Jesus' use of "Abraham" as character and "Abraham's bosom" as image of the messianic feast is not accidental given Abraham's reputation as a paragon of hospitality. Had the rich man been a son of Abraham he would have bestowed hospitality upon the stranger at his gate. It is fitting, then, that the inhospitable rich man is denied access to the feast with the hospitable Abraham, for the rich man is not of the same lineage or heritage (cf. Luke 3:8; 13:26-29). Those who do not extend hospitality to those to whom the Messiah bestows welcome will not share in the Messiah's feast.[27] Further, in response to the rich man's request to send Lazarus back to warn his household, Abraham twice tells him "they have Moses and the Prophets, let them listen to them" (16:29; cf. 16:31). According to Jesus, the rich man is a Torah-breaker and Prophet-rejecter, for these Scriptures teach hospitality to the poor, love of neighbor, and the extension of one's possessions to those in need (cf. 11:37-54).[28]

The Acts of the Apostles

In the Acts of the Apostles, Abraham is invoked in the speeches of Peter (Acts 3:13, 25), Stephen (7:2-8, 16-17, 32) and Paul (13:26) primarily to demonstrate continuity between God's election of Israel *and* the life, death, and resurrection of Jesus of Nazareth. After the healing of the lame man at the temple (3:1-10), Peter engages in a lengthy speech which has the primary purpose of arguing that this healing has taken place as an example of the restoration blessings proceeding from the resurrected and enthroned Jesus of Nazareth (3:11-26). Robert Brawley rightly

27. On the conceptual blending and background of the image of "Abraham's bosom," see A. Somov and V. Voinov, "'Abraham's Bosom' (Luke 16:22-23) as a Key Metaphor in the Overall Composition of the Parable of the Rich Man and Lazarus", *CBQ* 79 (2017): 615–33.

28. E.g., Isa. 61:1 and 58:6 in Lk. 4:18-19; Lev. 19:16-18, 33-34 in Lk. 10:26-29; Deut. 15:7-11 in Acts 4:32-35.

notes that the "healing of the lame man at the Temple gate is a concrete case of God's bestowal of Abrahamic blessings. . . ."[29] The man functions as an instance of how God's Abrahamic blessings are reaching all peoples.

The theme of continuity between God's election of Israel and his resurrection of Jesus is set forth clearly in 3:13: "the God of Abraham, Isaac, Jacob, the God of our fathers, has glorified his servant Jesus (ἐδόξασεν τὸν παῖδα αὐτοῦ Ἰησοῦν)." The rhetorical force of this statement is brought forth in Peter's depiction of Jesus as one that Israel's leaders handed over to Pilate to be crucified but "God raised him from the dead" (3:15b). God has ironically used their ignorance and rejection of the Messiah as a means of fulfilling his scriptural promises (3:17-18). But God has resurrected Jesus from the dead, and thus Peter exhorts the people to repent so that they might experience "times of refreshment from the face of the Lord" (3:19-20). The God of Abraham who has resurrected Jesus from the dead enables the glorified Messiah to send forth times of refreshment (3:21). Therefore, Peter exhorts them to turn to God and to pay attention to what God has done. They are "the sons of the prophets and of the covenant which God established with your fathers *saying to Abraham*, 'In your seed (ἐν τῷ σπέρματί) all the peoples of the earth will be blessed'" (3:25). Peter quotes the Abrahamic promise from Genesis (here Gen. 12:3; 22:18) that Abraham would be the means whereby God would bless all the peoples of the earth.[30] But here the emphasis is upon Peter's call to Israel to embrace their Messiah, for "to you first, God has raised up his servant and has sent him to you *in order to bless you* (εὐλογοῦντα ὑμᾶς) in order that each one of you might turn away from your evil deeds" (3:26). Luke creates a connection here between God's promise to bless all the families of the earth "in his seed" (3:25b) *and* Jesus who blesses Israel (3:26).[31] God's fulfillment of his promises to Abraham is universal in scope and will reach to all the nations, but Peter is emphatic that the order is first Israel *and then* the nations (cf. Luke 2:30-32).

In Paul's sermon in Pisidian Antioch (Acts 13:16-41), he too seeks to establish continuity between God's election of Israel (13:16-23) and God's resurrection of Jesus the Davidic Messiah (13:23-37). Though Abraham is not invoked directly, Paul's beginning statement that "the God of this people Israel has chosen our father and the people" is a simple affirmation of God's election of Abraham and Israel as his covenant people. Paul's selective retelling of Israel's history is quite clearly geared toward David as the historical retelling of Israel's history drives toward

29. R.E. Brawley, "Abrahamic Covenant Traditions and the Characterization of God in Luke-Acts", in *The Unity of Luke-Acts*, ed. J. Verheyden (BETL 142; Leuven: Leuven University Press, 1999), 109–32, here, 125.

30. On the inclusion of the Gentiles through the fulfillment of the Abrahamic promises, see J. Jervell, *Luke and the People of God* (Minneapolis: Augsburg Pub. House, 1972), 58–61.

31. A good case can be made for understanding "seed" in Acts 3:26 as referring to both Israel and the Messiah from the line of David. See further the helpful comments by S. Wendel, *Scriptural Interpretation and Community Self-Definition in Luke-Acts and the Writings of Justin Martyr* (NovTSup 139; Leiden: Brill, 2011), 223–4.

God's fulfillment of promises made to David in 2 Sam. 7:12-14: "God has, from [David's] seed, and according to his promise, brought forth for Israel the Savior Jesus" (Acts 13:23). Just as in Peter's speech, so here Paul situates the basic Christological kerygma within Israel's history and then exhorts his contemporary audience: "Men, brothers, children of the people of Abraham, and those among you who fear God, this word of salvation has been sent to us" (13:26). Just as Peter exhorts his audience as "the sons of the covenant" to pay attention to what the God of Abraham and the patriarchs (3:13) have done in raising Jesus for their benefit (3:25-26), so Paul now exhorts the audience to recognize that the meaning of Israel's history and the election of Abraham are now discerned only in God's act of raising Jesus from the dead (13:30-37). Both Peter and Paul's speeches are more directly concerned with God's promises to David, but Nils Dahl is right that Luke understands that "all messianic prophecies reiterate and unfold the one promise to the fathers, first given to Abraham."[32]

Stephen engages in some sustained reflection upon the patriarch Abraham in his lengthy defense speech (7:2-53). Stephen's emphasis upon Abraham centers upon his relation to the land and minimizes the covenant of circumcision.[33] Unsurprisingly, Stephen begins his speech with God's calling and election of Abraham in Mesopotamia (7:2). Thus, Stephen's argument, like Peter's in Acts 3 and Paul's in Acts 13, situates God's actions in Jesus of Nazareth (albeit here in an analogous or typological rather than kerygmatic form) within the context of God's election of Abraham and the people of Israel. This is all rather typical to the form of Luke-Acts, but Stephen surprisingly emphasizes Abraham as an immigrant and sojourner who encounters God outside of the land of Israel.[34] Thus, "the God of glory appeared to our father Abraham while he was in Mesopotamia" (7:2); God called him to leave his land and his family to a new place (7:3); Abraham dwelt in Haran (7:4); God brought him into Canaan but gave him none of the land as his own possession (7:5).[35] David Moessner rightly notes that "movement to the 'land' is the dynamic pivot of the plot" in Stephen's speech.[36] Later, Stephen makes the surprising comment that Jacob and his sons were buried "in the tomb

32. Dahl, "The Story of Abraham in Luke-Acts", 148. On the relationship between God's promises to Abraham and David, see Brawley, "Abrahamic Covenant Traditions", 111–15.

33. See further J. Jeska, *Die Geschicte Israels in der Sicht des Lukas: Apg 7,2b–53 und 13,17–25 im Kontext antic-jüdischer Summarien der Geschichte Israels* (Göttingen: Vandenhoeck and Ruprecht, 2001), 155–61.

34. See throughout C.S. Keener, *Acts: An Exegetical Commentary: 3:1–14:28*, Vol. 2 (Grand Rapids: Baker Academic, 2013), 1351–62.

35. Siker, *Disinheriting the Jews*, 121: "Luke highlights in particular the relationship between Abraham and the land, but he does so in such a way that he actually undercuts the significance of the promise of the land per se."

36. D.P. Moessner, "'The Christ Must Suffer': New Light on the Jesus—Peter, Stephen, Paul Parallels in Luke-Acts", in *Luke the Historian of Israel's Legacy, Theologian of Israel's "Christ": A New Reading of the "Gospel Acts" of Luke* (BZNW 182; Berlin: de Gruyter, 2016), 246.

that Abraham purchased for some silver from the sons of Hamor in Shechem" (7:15-16). This is in tension with the LXX which indicates that Jacob was buried in Hebron (LXX Genesis 49:29-32). However, to explain the incongruity, Stephen notes that Jacob and his sons were buried outside of Judea, which fits the portrait of Abraham who encountered God outside the land of Israel and who spent his life as a sojourner without a homeland. This fits with one important theme of Stephen's speech, namely, the common theme that Israel's patriarchs and heroes encountered the God of Israel outside of the land of Israel and beyond the Jerusalem Temple.[37]

Worthy of note is Stephen's quotation of Genesis 15:13-14 in Acts 7:6-7, to the effect that God had foretold that Abraham's offspring would be sojourners in a strange land, would be enslaved for 400 years, and after these things would then "worship me in this place" (7:7b). Luke here has actually conflated Genesis 15:13-14 and Exodus 3:12. Whereas the former indicates that after God's judgment upon Egypt, "they shall come out with great possessions" (Gen. 15:14), the latter text notes that "you will serve God upon this mountain" (Exod. 3:12). As numerous commentators have noted, the effect of this change or conflation is to center the promise to Abraham upon worshipping God in the land. And this aspect of Stephen's speech makes an important connection with Zechariah's hymn in Luke 1:68-79, which linked God's covenantal mercies to Abraham with the promise of deliverance from one's enemies and worshipping God (1:72-75).[38] One of the effects of Stephen's linkage of the land with worship, then, is to declare that those who commit idolatry and do not worship the God of Abraham cut themselves off from the Abrahamic promises and blessings (cf. 3:22-26).[39]

The majority of the rest of Stephen's speech expands upon the events predicted in Acts 7:2-8. Thus, the Joseph story shows how Abraham's offspring find their way to Egypt (7:9-16) and the Moses story depicts how God leads them out of slavery and judges the Egyptians (7:18-36). Stephen portrays God as one who fulfills the promises made to Abraham as he had described them in Acts 7:2-8. Perhaps this is seen most clearly when Stephen portrays the initial fulfillment of God's promise to Abraham in 7:17, which hearkens back to God's prediction in 7:6, namely, the events of the Exodus.[40] Sadly, however, the fulfillment of 7:17 is frustrated by means of the rejection of God's chosen deliverers (Moses) and through worshipping false gods (esp. 7:39-43). Instead of securing the Abrahamic promises and blessings

37. See here the very helpful and illuminating essay by G.E. Sterling, "'Opening the Scriptures': The Legitimation of the Jewish Diaspora and the Early Christian Mission", in *Jesus and the Heritage of Israel: Luke's Narrative Claim upon Israel's Legacy*, ed. D.P. Moessner (Harrisburg, PA: Trinity Press International, 1999), 199–217.

38. Helpful here is R.L. Brawley, *Luke-Acts and the Jews: Conflict, Apology, and Conciliation* (SBLDS 33; Atlanta: Scholars Press, 1987), 118–32.

39. Wendel, *Scriptural Interpretation*, 218.

40. See further, Dahl, "The Story of Abraham in Luke-Acts", 144.

through worshipping God in the land, the people's idolatry blocks the longed-for and promised fulfillment of the Abrahamic blessings.[41]

The Gospel of John

Abraham only appears in the Fourth Gospel in one passage, and yet the entire back-and-forth dialogue between Jesus and his conversation partners centers upon the meaning of Abrahamic paternity (Jn 8:31-59), initiated by Jesus' audience retort to his teaching that "we are the seed of Abraham" (8:33a). This stretch of text is notoriously difficult and it, in particular the reference to "your father the devil" (8:44), has had a deplorable reception history.[42] I intend here, however, to primarily focus upon the major themes and exegetical questions raised by the references to Abraham in John 8.

First, I suggest that Jesus' audience should not be understood as "the Jewish people" but rather that Jesus is addressing "those Jews who had believed in him" (τοὺς πεπιστευκότας αὐτῷ Ἰουδαίους, 8:31). I suggest that the perfect participle should be taken as a reference to those Jews who had professed belief in Jesus but who were no longer following him (cf. also Jn 11:44).[43] This group is distinguished, then, from the group referred to in 8:30: "the many who believed in him." This is further justified by means of contextual observations. For example, it is difficult to imagine that within the span of a few verses a group comes to believe in Jesus and then seeks to stone him, referring to him as a Samaritan with a demon (8:48). The audience is, after all, referred to as *not believing* Jesus twice in 8:45-46. Further, given that Jn 7:1–8:30 focused upon Jesus' discourses articulating the meaning of the Feast of Tabernacles, it is likely that 8:31-59 should be connected with the immediately preceding discourse in 6:60-71. Here, John describes many of Jesus' disciples who chafe and grumble at Jesus' difficult bread of life discourse (6:60-61). These disciples are "scandalized" by Jesus' teaching (6:61b), and as a result, many "of his disciples" stopped following Jesus (6:66). This fits more broadly within

41. Wendel, *Scriptural Interpretation*, 221.

42. There is a host of literature devoted to John and Judaism. Good starting points both broadly and with respect to John 8 are, respectively: C.W. Skinner, *Reading John* (Cascade Companions; Eugene, OR: Cascade, 2015), 47–67; A. Reinhartz, "John 8:31-59 From a Jewish Perspective", in *Remembering for the Future 2000: The Holocaust in an Age of Genocides*, 2 vols, eds. J.K. Roth and E. Maxwell-Meynard (London: Palgrave, 2001), 787–97.

43. On the perfect participle as having the possibility of indicating a state that no longer holds for the action of the main verb, see especially T. Griffith, "'The Jews who had Believed in Him' (John 8:31) and the Motif of Apostasy in the Gospel of John", in *The Gospel of John and Christian Theology*, eds. R. Bauckham et al. (Grand Rapids: Eerdmans, 2008), 183–92, here, 183–4. See further J. Swetnam, "The Meaning of πεπιστευκότας in John 8,31", *Biblica* 61 (1980): 106–9.

John's anthropological pessimism and his depiction of faith in Jesus as often lacking or insufficient (see especially Jn 2:23-25).[44]

Second, it is important to note that within this context, and within the broader narrative of John's Gospel, the devil functions as one who motivates people to commit apostasy. Thus, within the context of disciples who had once believed but are now turning away from Jesus, Jesus refers to Judas as a "devil" (6:70). Later John notes that "the devil" had put it into Judas' heart to betray Jesus (13:2; cf. 13:27).[45] Thus, Jesus' statement in 8:44 that "you are of the father your devil" should not be taken to refer to polemic against the Jewish people *in toto* but is, rather, a still remarkably harsh reference to those fellow Jews who had at one time believed in Jesus but now, having committed apostasy, are seeking to murder Jesus. Griffith notes, then, that "it would be wrong to conclude from 8:44 that John regarded all Jews as children of the devil. The language of *diabolization* is restricted to those who had once been followers of Jesus and is appropriate to them alone."[46]

Third, the debate between Jesus and his audience as to who belongs to their father Abraham, centers not upon biological genealogical descent but, rather, upon who does "the deeds of Abraham" (8:39). Jesus shifts the conversation from "seed/offspring" of Abraham to "children of Abraham" and "seems to define Abrahamic "paternity [as] strictly a matter of behavior" so that Abraham's children are those who do what Abraham did.[47] Abraham is held up as a model for emulation.[48] I think a strong case can be made here that Jesus' reference to "the deeds of Abraham" (τὰ ἔργα τοῦ Ἀβραάμ, 8:39b) should be understood as a reference to Abraham's extension of hospitality to the divine visitors in Genesis 18. It is well known that Abraham was understood within Jewish tradition as an exemplar of hospitality to strangers, and this portrait of hospitable Abraham was also carried on by early Christian texts as well, for example in James (Jas 2:20-26) who also refers to Abraham's deeds.[49]

44. See E. Clement Hoskyns, *The Fourth Gospel* (London: Faber and Faber, 1947), 338, who notes that this discourse is addressed to "the Jews who believed when they saw His miracles, and to whom Jesus did not trust Himself (ii.23, 24, cf. vii. 31, xi. 45, xii. 11, 42, 43."

45. Griffith, "'The Jews who had Believed in Him'", 186–7.

46. Ibid, 186–91 (emphasis original). Griffith further notes that this conclusion fits well with 1 Jn 3:14-15. See T. Griffith, *Keep Yourselves from Idols: A New Look at 1 John* (JSNTSup 233; London: Sheffield Academic Press, 2002).

47. Levenson, *Abraham between Torah and Gospel*, 36.

48. C.H. Williams, "Patriarchs and Prophets Remembered: Framing Israel's Past in the Gospel of John", in *Abiding Words: The Use of Scripture in the Gospel of John*, eds. A.D. Myers et al. (Atlanta: SBL Press, 2015), 187–212, here, 202.

49. There are a host of texts one could set forth here. I have examined them in more detail in my *Divine Visitations and Hospitality to Strangers in Luke-Acts*, 131–55. On Abraham's deeds in James 2 as inclusive of his mercy and hospitality to strangers, see R. Bowen Ward, "The Works of Abraham: James 2:14-26", *HTR* 61 (1968): 283–90.

But hospitality and inhospitality to Jesus and his word also plays a significant theological role within John's Gospel as well. Thus, the prologue notes: "he came to his own and his own did not receive (οὐ παρέλαβον) him, but to as many as did receive him (ἔλαβον αὐτόν), he gave them the right to become children of God (τέκνα θεοῦ), to those who believe (τοῖς πιστεύουσιν) in his name" (Jn 1:11-12). John's prologue thus characterizes divine paternity in terms of whether or not one provides a welcoming or believing response to Jesus, the divine Word. I have argued that hospitality has a significant theological role in terms of humans welcoming the stranger from heaven who himself extends "redemptive hospitality" (bread, water, wine, foot washing, and entrance into his Father's home).[50] Steven Hunt has also noted that the language of hospitality is "a major motif in the narrative, as the author uses a cluster of words to talk about reception, favoring the word λαμβάνω which gets employed mostly with the sense of receiving Jesus (Jn 1:12; 5:43; 6:21; 13:20) or his word (see, e.g., 3:11, 32-33; 17:8)."[51] But instead of doing Abraham's deeds and receiving Jesus the divine stranger with hospitality, they persist in inhospitality to Jesus and his teaching. Thus, they do not continue in Jesus' word (8:31); they seek to kill Jesus because their word does not remain in them (8:37, 45, 46); they have heard divine truth but are trying to kill him (8:40); they do not accept Jesus' word (8:43). They extend inhospitality to Jesus and his word, and thereby they demonstrate that God is not their father (8:42, 47). One belongs to Abraham, then, if one provides a hospitable response to the heavenly messenger Jesus and his word who, for the author of the Fourth Gospel, has been sent by God. It would seem, then, that for John's Gospel, Jesus' audience is the "offspring of Abraham" (8:33, 37) but not "children of Abraham" (8:39).[52] Both Isaac and Ishmael are the offspring of Abraham, but only Isaac is construed as one of Abraham's children; those who receive Jesus are construed as Abraham's free children who remain in his house forever (8:34-36). Hunt nicely re-paraphrases Jesus' argument: "'If you were Abraham's children, you would be showing the hospitality that Abraham showed when he welcomed me and received my word. In trying to kill me, you are doing the opposite of what Abraham did.'"[53]

Fourth, Abraham was understood in a variety of Jewish traditions as one who saw the glory of God in visions (e.g., Genesis 15; *Testament of Abraham*; *4 Ezra* 3.14).[54] But Jesus makes the audacious assertion that "Your father Abraham rejoiced

50. Jipp, *Saved by Faith and Hospitality*, ch. 3.

51. S.A. Hunt, "And the Word Became Flesh—Again? Jesus and Abraham in John 8:31-59", in *Perspectives on Our Father Abraham: Essays in Honor of Marvin R. Wilson*, ed. S.A. Hunt (Grand Rapids: Eerdmans, 2012), 81–109, here, 88. Similarly, see Williams, "Patriarchs and Prophets Remembered," 202–5.

52. Hunt, "And the Word Became Flesh—Again?", 94.

53. Ibid, 97.

54. See here, J. Ashton, *Understanding the Fourth Gospel* (2nd edn.; Oxford: Oxford University Press, 2007), 300–1.

that *he saw my day*, and he saw it and rejoiced" (8:56). In response to the audience's outrage, Jesus declares "before Abraham came into being, I am" (8:58), and they seek to stone him for blasphemy (8:59). Jesus' claim declares that Abraham is subordinate to him and that he is divine alongside God the Father. If "the works of Abraham" in John 8:39 refer to Abraham's hospitality to the divine visitors in Genesis 18, then the mutual seeing of Jesus and Abraham may further allude to Abraham's seeing the pre-incarnate Word as the divine visitor and extending hospitality to him in his tent. Thus, Abraham is made to conform to John's larger theological vision of Jesus as the focal point of Israel's Scriptures, institutions, and visionary experiences of Israel's heroes.[55]

Conclusion

My study of Abraham demonstrates that each composition draws upon the figure of Abraham for diverse purposes. Surprisingly, Mark's Gospel shows no serious interest at all in Abraham, as even the singular pericope which refers to Abraham does not actually center upon him in any meaningful way. While it is difficult to make an argument from silence, it may be that Mark's Gospel, as an apocalyptic drama, is simply less interested in making the kinds of salvation-historical claims for continuity between Israel and Jesus as are other NT compositions. Unlike Mark's Gospel, Abraham rises to a consistent theme and even a character within the narrative world of Luke-Acts. Further, the Gospel of Luke is the only text which takes up Abraham into its broader theme of 'reversal' in order to show that outcasts, the sick, and the poor are not excluded from the people of God. The Gospel of Matthew draws upon Abraham to make claims of salvation-historical continuity, but the narrative shows little, if any, interest in the moral character of Abraham, whereas in Luke and John one finds allusions to Abraham's hospitality to strangers, his believing response to God, and forefather of the repentant. And John's Gospel seems to be the only text examined which holds up Abraham as one who saw the glory of the pre-incarnate Christ. It is surprising, at least to me, that Abraham's near sacrifice of Isaac (the *Akedah*) in Genesis 22, does not play a more direct role (at least beyond echoes and allusions) in the NT texts examined above, as it does, for example, in Jas 2:20-26.[56]

There are, however, significant commonalities across the NT compositions in the way in which they draw upon Abraham. Let me conclude by simply noting four of them. First, except for the Gospel of Mark, every text draws upon Abraham to establish continuity between God's election of Israel *and* the person of Jesus and those believing in him as Israel's Messiah. And this claim of continuity is one that would appear to be deeply contested as Jewish believers in Jesus are defining

55. See Williams, "Patriarchs and Prophets Remembered", 205–6.

56. See, however, L.A. Huizenga, *The New Isaac: Tradition and Intertextuality in the Gospel of Matthew* (NovTSup 131; Leiden: Brill, 2009).

Abrahamic descent through Jesus of Nazareth. This is most obvious in Luke-Acts where, within Luke, the births of John and Jesus are interpreted within the framework of the stories of Abraham and Sarah, and in Acts where the basic kerygma is situated within God's election of Abraham and Israel. But one sees a similar dynamic in John 8 where "children of Abraham" are defined not *only* by genealogical descent but also through doing the deeds of Abraham.

For these texts, while God may be doing something surprising in the person of Jesus, these events are to be understood within the framework of God's prior promises to, and election of, Israel as his people. But the continuity is also readily apparent in Matthew's genealogy, which refers to Jesus as within the line of Abraham and as Abraham's son. Second, God's covenant with Abraham and his later covenantal promises to David are inextricably bound together in both Matthew's Gospel and Luke-Acts. Thus, they portray the seed of David as the only one who can inherit and bring to fulfillment God's promises to Abraham. Third, Abraham is a model for appropriate behavior. Children of Abraham demonstrate their identity through repentance, hospitality, and the sharing of possessions in Matthew, Luke, and John. Finally, both Mark and Luke portray Abraham as one who already experiences a blessed afterlife and who receives his children into this eschatological fellowship and banquet.

Chapter 8

ABRAHAM IN NEW TESTAMENT LETTERS

Chris Tilling

Introduction

Abraham remains at the center of complex debates in Pauline scholarship. An analysis of Abraham in the New Testament letters must focus upon two chapters in particular: Romans 4 and Galatians 3. But before exegetical comment is made on these texts, it will be important to examine scholarly taxonomies for understanding the relationship between Abraham and Paul. These will be analyzed and found wanting. Instead, alternative distinctions will be suggested, which will facilitate engagement with the data, particularly Romans 4 and Galatians 3. Finally, similarities and differences between the deployment of Abraham in Paul's letters and Hebrews will be presented.

Searching for a Taxonomy

Given the centrality of Abraham traditions in certain construals of Paul, it is important to analyze critically common scholarly taxonomies relating to Paul's deployment of Abraham. This will facilitate a more nuanced engagement with the primary material.

N.T. Wright, in his more rhetorical moments, juxtaposes two basic approaches to Abraham in Paul, namely those that present Abraham as an *illustration* of "justification by faith," on the one hand, and those which speak of Abraham in terms of the "*scope and the nature of [his] family*", on the other.[1] This allows the debate between two interpretive paradigms to drive the agenda in scholarly analysis of Paul's use of Abraham. It is a distinction that is pressed through interpretations of Romans 4, the most extensive Pauline engagement with

1. N.T. Wright, "The Letter to the Romans. Introduction, Commentary, and Reflections", in *The New Interpreter's Bible*, ed. L.E. Keck et al. (Nashville: Abington, 2002), 489, emphasis is mine.

Abraham. Hence, "old perspective" accounts, on the one hand, are supposed to emphasize "justification by faith" and focus more on Rom. 4:1-8, with its language of "boasting," being "credited," "righteousness," "works," "faith," and "wages." "New perspective" concerns, on the other, will emphasize the social nature of "justification" and the scope of the Abrahamic family.[2] For this reason, they tend to focus more on Rom. 4:9-17. In Wright's hands the "new perspective" takes a particular narrative twist. The upshot is that, although he can make more of 4:9-17, it is based upon his wider construal of Paul. So, his argument goes, Abraham is mentioned at this point in Romans because God's covenant faithfulness is revealed in the faithfulness of the Messiah. This is to say that God's promise to Abraham, to bless the families of the world by means of this covenant family, can now come about despite Israel's unfaithfulness (Rom. 3:3), because the Messiah of Israel, her representative, is faithful (Rom. 3:21-31). This is why Paul mentions Abraham in Romans 4, because, now the covenant righteousness of God has been revealed, Paul returns to its basis, the promise to Abraham to create a family of faith.[3]

This awareness of commitments to either "old" or "new" perspectives can illuminate readings of Romans 4. For this reason, the twofold (old or new perspective) taxonomy is used to structure John Barclay's recent engagement with Romans 4, in such a way that simultaneously seeks to drive a course between these two reading paradigms. It will serve both this section, and the following (for reasons that will become clear), briefly to overview Barclay's approach to Romans 4.

Barclay proposes, with Douglas Campbell (see below), that Rom. 3:27-31 begins the argument which continues in Romans 4,[4] and he endorses the broad twofold taxonomy, which we have used Wright to exemplify. Hence, he argues that Romans 4 is concerned with "the scope [or goal: the inclusion of Gentiles with Jews] and the means of justification," namely justification by faith. Here "scope" is taken to refer to "new perspectives," while "means" refers to "old." But rather than accepting this either/or, Barclay's reading will unite what others have sundered. Hence, he argues, reference to Abraham "encapsulates both the means (through faith, 4:1-8) and this goal (Jew and Gentile alike, 4:9-12)."[5] The social goal, the inclusion of Gentiles with Jews, follows elaboration on the *means* of justification as this is the way the goal will be obtained, in "faith dependence upon a divine decision irrespective of inherent human worth."[6] Barclay thus draws his wider thesis

2. Introductory summaries of "old" and "new" perspectives can be found in many places, including S. Westerholm, *Perspectives Old and New on Paul: The "Lutheran" Paul and His Critics* (Grand Rapids: Eerdmans, 2004); K.L. Yinger, *The New Perspective on Paul: An Introduction* (Eugene, OR: Cascade Books, 2011).

3. For this in deliberate debate with "justification by faith alone" approaches, see Wright, "Romans", 464–505. See now also N.T. Wright, *Paul and the Faithfulness of God* (Minneapolis: Fortress Press, 2013), 774–850.

4. Although this does not make too much of a difference for his exegesis of Romans 4.

5. J.M. Barclay, *Paul and the Gift* (Grand Rapids: Eerdmans, 2015), 482.

6. Ibid, 483.

relating to incongruous grace in Paul into Romans 4. So incongruous grace, namely a gift given "without regard to the worth of the recipient,"[7] grounds Paul's social goals. The emphasis on faith thus makes sense as the means by which the goal is obtained. For "faith," as he defines it in exegeting Galatians 2, is not an "alternative human achievement nor a refined human spirituality, but a *declaration of bankruptcy*, a radical and shattering recognition that the only capital in God's economy is the gift of Christ crucified and risen."[8] Because of this emphasis on the means of salvation, the playing field is levelled, so to speak, which establishes the stated social goal (the inclusion of all without regard for any symbolic capital).

To explicate this in a little more detail, let us first outline Barclay's account of the first half of Romans 4. Given that Abraham discovered that nothing he "did made him worthy of the favor of God,"[9] this lack of congruity is repeatedly underscored in 4:4-8, by contrasting "pay" and "gift." Hence, Abraham's faith makes sense, registering "a state of bankruptcy by every measure of symbolic capital," a point underscored by citation of David (4:6-8). God's gift incongruously given and acknowledged in faith dependence, is then developed in 4:9-12 with reference to Abraham's chronology, which emphasizes the circumcision that "took place *after* the blessing of Genesis 15:6," thereby becoming merely a sign of the "righteousness of faith."[10]

Turning to 4:9-12, then, Barclay explains that the goal or scope of salvation comes into purview, namely the inclusion of Gentiles with Jews in God's blessing. The final section, 4:13-22, then joins these themes by "interpreting the promise to Abraham and his offspring as the impossible creation of a multiethnic family."[11] Rom. 4:13-15 explains that this happens "not through law," while 4:16-18 makes clear that Abraham is father of many nations "from faith." Rom. 4:19-22 further elaborate the narratives that speak of Abraham's faith in God (4:17). The logic throughout, once again, is the incongruity of grace, such that faith apart from works (4:5-6) mirrors hoping against hope (4:18). Both come, as it were, with empty hands, with no means to obtain the promised child (for they were "as good as dead," 4:19) or the righteousness, apart from works (4:6). It follows that Abraham's faith is about grasping the incongruous gift. And just as Abraham believed God would create life *ex nihilo*, as it were, so Christ-followers believe in God who has raised Jesus from the dead. So, 4:23-25 applies this (limited) parallel to Christ-believers.

The upshot is that Barclay claims to bring together two competing readings of the significance of Abraham in Romans 4. For "old perspective" accounts, the heart of Romans 4 is the opening eight verses, emphasizing the justification of the ungodly over and against a legalistic soteriology of works. "New perspective" readings, on the other hand, focus on 4:9-17 and the way in which Abraham is presented not as

7. See, e.g., Ibid, 73.

8. Ibid, 383–4, emphasis mine.

9. Ibid, 484. This involves a particular (and problematic) construal of the grammar of 4:1, to which we will return below.

10. See Ibid, 486–7, emphasis his.

11. Ibid, 488.

scriptural proof of a theological principle (the justification of the ungodly by faith alone, or some such), but as the father of a family, including both Jew and Gentile.[12] Barclay thus claims that his reading brings together these themes, highlighting the significance of Abraham as both believer and father of a multi-ethnic family. A twofold taxonomy, therefore, drives Barclay's constructive work.

But the extent to which this account of Abraham (in Romans 4) accurately represents scholarly variations must be disputed. "Old" and "new" perspectives tend to be more nuanced and carefully construed than such sharp distinctions would suggest. Moo's learned commentary on Romans, for example, offers a good example of a so-called "old perspective" reading. Although we would now expect to see Abraham presented as an example of "justification by faith alone," this is not what one reads Rather, his account is more complicated, such that Abraham is not reducible to "exemplar." Rather, Abraham is also deployed, according to Moo, for polemical reasons. So Paul undermines his "Jewish and Jewish-Christian opponents" who "undoubtedly cited [Abraham texts] against his teaching."[13] What is more, because Paul's gospel is the "gospel of God" (Rom. 1:1), Paul needs to integrate Abraham into his theological scheme; hence such extended exegesis is found in Romans 4. Related to this, Paul deploys Abraham because he is an expositor of Scripture. Finally, Paul elaborates on Abraham also to draw out the *implications* of *sola fide*. And this is the treatment of Abraham by a self-confessed "old perspective" scholar.[14] It is questionable, then, to insist that "old perspective" approaches present Abraham as an example, or scriptural proof text of a theological argument, namely, "justification by faith alone," and that they do so by relying more on 4:1-8.[15]

But it can also be questioned if the "new perspective" is correctly portrayed. After all, Wright, who is deployed as Barclay's evidence for a "new perspective" reading that focuses on the latter half of Romans 4, doesn't fit as neatly as one would expect. As Barclay himself acknowledges, Wright's own account of 4:1-8 has been strengthened more recently (even if he still fails, in Barclay's eyes, to account for 4:4).[16] But as we shall explore next, Wright has more recently adjusted his taxonomy for understanding readings of Abraham in relation to Paul, moving decisively beyond the twofold approach evidenced in Barclay and the early Wright.

12. See Ibid, 479–80.

13. D.J. Moo, *The Epistle to the Romans* (Grand Rapids: Eerdmans, 1996), 256.

14. Moo, *Romans*, 255.

15. Though reference to Longenecker's recent commentary could be made, where Abraham is *exemplum* (cf. R.N. Longenecker, *The Epistle to the Romans* (NIGTC; Grand Rapids: Eerdmans, 2016), 475–537.

16. See Barclay, *Paul and the Gift*, 481 n.84, and reference to Wright's essay, "Paul and the Patriarch", now reprinted in N.T. Wright, *Pauline Perspectives: Essays on Paul, 1978–2013* (Minneapolis, MN: Fortress Press, 2013), 554–92. Indeed, Wright is well aware of the dangers involved here, and insists that "[n]othing that I have said means that (as some have suggested) I have allowed ecclesiology (the single worldwide family) to elbow soteriology (how people are rescued from sin and its consequences) out of the picture" (587).

Be that as it may, Barclay still presents an elegant, as well as economic, exegetical case relating to Romans 4 and Abraham, and we will lean on some of his exegetical insights in our own constructive case below.

Wright's aforementioned recent work clarifies matters considerably, and offers the following six-fold taxonomy for understanding the ways scholars imagine Paul's relationship with Abraham in his arguments:

(a) Paul only refers to Abraham because his opponents have done so and he must defeat them on their own ground, but left to himself he would not have mentioned the patriarch.
(b) Paul is happy to introduce reference to Abraham, but only because this provides him with a convenient but random scriptural proof-text for a doctrine, in this case "justification by faith," whose real ground is elsewhere.
(c) Abraham is a kind of "test case" for Paul's doctrine, not just a proof-text; Paul needs to be able to show some continuity with Israel's founding fathers.
(d) Abraham is the "narrative prototype" whose faith prefigures the faithfulness of the Messiah.
(e) Paul is expounding the covenant-making chapter (Genesis 15) in order to show that the revelation of God's righteousness in the gospel is (however shocking and paradoxical it may be) the fulfilment of this ancient promise.
(f) Paul envisages a smooth, continuous, salvation history in a crescendo all the way from Abraham to Jesus.[17]

My proposal is that this taxonomy, though considerably more helpful than the twofold account enumerated above, is constructed on the basis of an unnamed commitment to the controlling force of a particular account of *necessity*, which will ultimately distort matters. That is to say it constructs these six options (a–f) in relation to the extent to which these categories assume Paul's engagement with Abraham to be necessary in the mind of the Apostle. The taxonomy is, then, about degrees of Abraham's importance construed in a very particular manner. In the following, I will parse and examine Wright's proposal bearing in mind my claim that much hangs on Wright's conception of necessity.

To take Wright's (a), then, the key phrase is that "left to himself" Paul "would not have mentioned the patriarch." In other words, Paul's reference to Abraham is based *entirely* on contingent factors, here related to the presence of Paul's (usually Jewish-Christian) opponents.[18] He puts it even more sharply elsewhere, claiming

17. Wright, *Pauline Perspectives*, 555–6.

18. These characters are variously named. "Teachers," "Judaizers," "opponents," "counter-missionaries," and so on. It is not necessary to canvass these differences now. It is enough simply to state that I propose "counter-missionaries" captures best their activity and role. Ultimately, however, not too much hangs on this. A summary of various positions can be found in J.J. Gunther, *Saint Paul's Opponents and Their Background* (Leiden: Brill, 1973). See also S.E. Porter, ed., *Paul and His Opponents*, Vol. 2 (Pauline Studies; Leiden: Brill, 2005).

that "the suggestion that Paul would not otherwise have brought Abraham into the argument strikes me as the thin edge of the Marcionite wedge."[19] Paul's recourse to Abraham would thus be entirely contingent, and as far away from "necessary" for Paul as it could be. In Galatians, so the argument goes, Paul is *forced* to engage with the figure of Abraham precisely because the troublesome counter-missionaries were deploying Abraham as the perfect example for why Gentile believers in Jesus should be circumcised.[20] Abraham is thus only important to Paul in so far as the issue is put upon him by others.

It should be obvious that this first category is directed at "apocalyptic" readings of Paul, which foreground the historical particularity of Galatians (and sometimes Romans) as responses to the activity and preaching of certain Jewish-Christian counter-missionaries. But it should immediately be noted that Wright's category is somewhat forced given the fact that even Martinus de Boer does not argue that Paul's only reason for alighting upon Abraham is the activity of the "new preachers in Galatia." De Boer, to the contrary, argues as follows: "*One probable reason* [for citing Abraham] is that the Galatians have been hearing much about Abraham from the new preachers in Galatia."[21] Not even J. Louis Martyn, who famously foregrounds the interpretive significance of the "Teachers", can be read as suggesting that Paul wouldn't speak of Abraham unless it were not raised by his (exegetical) opponents. After all, as Martyn himself points out, Paul "gladly accepts" the theme of descent from Abraham, "affirming without ambivalence that 'children of Abraham' is one of the ways of naming the church of God."[22] It is important for Martyn, however, that the terms on which Paul engages with the patriarch are determined primarily by the "Christ-event." Furthermore, Douglas Campbell spends a good deal of space in his most recent book outlining the various reasons why Paul engaged with Scripture—and scriptural characters, including Abraham—even if he would agree with Martyn and de Boer that the most pointed reason for deploying Abraham in Romans 4 and Galatians 3–4 was due to the argumentation of the counter-missionaries, and the claims they were making about Abraham.[23]

There were many reasons why Paul might make recourse to Abraham, yet it made sense, in Galatians in particular, to discourse on Abraham in a certain manner due to the argumentation of Paul's opponents. For these reasons, then, it is doubtful that apocalyptic readings are an example of the claim that if "left to himself" Paul would "not have mentioned the patriarch." If contingent factors determined Paul's particular use of Abraham in Galatians and Romans, it does not follow that Abraham is important to Paul only in so far as the issue was forced

19. Wright, "Romans", 488.

20. This is admittedly not an undisputed position, but most Pauline scholars affirm it.

21. M.C. de Boer, *Galatians: A Commentary* (The New Testament Library; Louisville, KY: Westminster John Knox Press, 2011), 186, emphasis mine.

22. J. Louis Martyn, *Galatians: A New Translation with Introduction and Commentary*, AB (London: Doubleday, 1997), 306.

23. D.A. Campbell, *Paul: An Apostle's Journey* (Grand Rapids: Eerdmans, 2018), 153–60.

upon him by others. But, if not apocalyptic readers, to whom does Wright's first category refer? I submit that his category is a rhetorical construct, created by the demands of a scale of necessity.

Moving up the necessity scale, we turn to Wright's (b). Paul is now "happy" to introduce Abraham, "but only because" it is convenient. Abraham can illustrate the doctrine of "justification by faith," but this relationship is *not necessary*. The real ground of this doctrine "is elsewhere." It should become more obvious, now, that Wright's rhetoric is designed to create a taxonomy based on an evaluation of Paul's intentions, or mental landscape, in terms of necessity. For, now moving up the necessity scale even further, Wright turns to (c), in which Abraham is deployed as a "test case." So, in contrast to (b), Abraham isn't referred to merely as a *random* proof text, but because there is a measure of necessity. Wright refers to Simon Gathercole's claim as representative of this (third) category, that Abraham "is not *an* illustration from the Old Testament . . . he is *the* example. If Paul's theology cannot accommodate him, it *must* be false."[24]

This all leads to Wright's final three categories, which interestingly turn to narrative as representing what must be the most fundamental level for understanding Paul's relationship to Abraham in terms of necessity. Now Abraham is internal to the core framework of Paul's narrative thought-world, and for this reason it would be unthinkable for Paul not to mention the patriarch. So from (d), where Abraham is "the 'narrative prototype'" of the faith of the Messiah, Wright promotes (e), which presents Paul's argument about Abraham as the (paradoxical) unfolding of Paul's central narrative commitments, such that Christ is seen as "the fulfilment of this ancient promise" to Abraham. His final category, (f), adjusts (e) in obvious debate with his own critics, whom he opines take issue with his narrative argument due to its emphasis on narrative continuity or "smoothness". This suggests that Wright imagines that the highest degree of necessity would be in a presentation of Abraham, in relation to Paul's gospel, as the smooth and obvious continuation of the narrative of Abraham.[25]

This suggests that Abraham is seen as most important or necessary, for Paul, if he is construed as an internal and non-negotiable element of Paul's theological narrative, which explains the nature of Wright's exegesis of Romans 4 in light of Romans 1–4, outlined above. This is, Wright argues, the furthest point one can get from apocalyptic readings which "would not have mentioned the patriarch" if it were not for Paul's opponents, establishing the logical coherence of his taxonomy.

However, a few further critical points should now be mentioned. Not only are some of these categories straw-men, as we have already noted, they also construct

24. See S.J. Gathercole, *Where is Boasting? Early Jewish Soteriology and Paul's Response in Romans 1–5* (Grand Rapids: Eerdmans, 2002), 233, emphasis original, cited in Wright, *Pauline Perspectives*, 555.

25. Wright imagines that "apocalyptic" readers are concerned about continuity as opposed to discontinuity, but the matter actually hinges on the *terms* of continuity, which all agree are part and parcel of understanding Paul.

falsely contrasting positions. That is to say, it is entirely feasible to maintain that Paul's occasion to make reference to Abraham was conditioned by the needs of a particular community, in light of the activity of certain "counter-missionaries." But this need not be taken as a reason for thinking Abraham is thus purely incidental to Paul's theological landscape, as argued above. An "apocalyptic" approach, for example, may suggest that the most obvious reason why Paul made reference to Abraham in, say, Galatians 3–4 or Romans 4, was the content of the teaching of the counter-missionaries. But the fact that Paul engaged in this discussion implies shared commitments with the Galatians and counter-missionaries. After all, it can be agreed by all in these debates, that Paul speaks of Abraham due to a shared commitment to the Scriptures of Israel, even if the precise extent of Paul's "canon"—as well as the different ways "canon" would likely have been understood—are accepted.[26]

Abraham was a fundamental part of Paul's shared scriptural resource. Framing the matter in this way, however, is not to commit Paul to a particular account of a supposed wider scriptural-narrative imagination, and to muscle this "controlling story" into Paul by means of "intertextual maximalism."[27] Narrative matters can be alternatively handled.[28] Paul's recourse to Abraham need not be attached to narrative in precisely the way Wright imagines for Abraham to remain a necessary part of Paul's theological "symbolic universe,"[29] "cultural encyclopedia,"[30] and so on. Indeed, Foster has argued that Abraham, for Paul, should be understood as constituting a "mythomoteur," which is defined as a community's "driving political myth."[31] Abraham, as such, provides "shared meanings that unite otherwise disparate subgroups, factions, or parties";[32] hence he speaks of the "Abrahamic mythomoteur" in Paul's letters.[33] The point is both that necessity need not be

26. On these often neglected issues, see H. Lichtenberger, "Das Tora-Verständnis im Judentum zur Zeit des Paulus", in *Paul and the Mosaic Law*, ed. J.D.G. Dunn (Tübingen: Mohr Siebeck, 1996), 7–24; F. Crüsemann, *Das Alte Testament als Wahrheitsraum des Neuen: die neue Sicht der christlichen Bibel* (Gütersloh: Gütersloher Verlagshaus, 2011); T.M. Law, *When God Spoke Greek: The Septuagint and the Making of the Christian Bible* (Oxford: Oxford University Press, 2013), 85–98.

27. C. Tilling, "*Paul and the Faithfulness of God*. A Review Essay (Part 2)", *Anvil* 31, no. 1 (March 2015): 57–69.

28. See C. Tilling, "Paul, Christ, and Narrative Time", in *Christ and the Created Order: Perspectives from Theology, Philosophy, and Science*, eds. A.B. Torrance and T.H. McCall (Grand Rapids: Zondervan, 2018), 151–66.

29. P.L. Berger and T. Luckmann, *The Social Construction of Reality: A Treatise in the Sociology of Knowledge* (Garden City, NY: Doubleday, Anchor, 1967).

30. U. Eco, *A Theory of Semiotics* (Bloomington: Indiana University Press, 1976).

31. R.B. Foster, *Renaming Abraham's Children: Election, Ethnicity, and the Interpretation of Scripture in Romans 9*, WUNT II (Tübingen: Mohr Siebeck, 2016), 43–4.

32. Ibid, 44.

33. Ibid, 43–83.

construed in terms of a particular narrative, and that one could accept Foster's position *at the same time* as affirming the contingency of occasion driving Paul's particular references to Abraham in Romans 4 and Galatians 3.

Furthermore, it seems that Wright's categories are based on levels of necessity of intention in Paul's mind which are frankly difficult to assess. It sounds as though Wright has succumbed to an "intentional fallacy," at least if intention is understood in terms of mental states as it was in pre-Wittgensteinian linguistics.[34] Certainly, "intentionality" need not be so understood, nor do I wish here to endorse "the death of the author,"[35] so Thiselton's turn to Searle and speech-act theory, to address this challenge is helpful.[36] But Wright's taxonomy does not align with Thiselton's adjustments, namely that "[i]ntention is better understood adverbially: to write with an intention is to write in a way that is directed towards a goal."[37] Rather, Wright's taxonomy is based upon consideration of an alleged scale of necessity in Paul's mind, from "must do so because of his opponents" through to "Abraham is a fundamental aspect of his mental (narrative) furniture," so to speak, and thus is of necessity referred to irrespective of contingent factors. Hence, the arguments of Wimsatt-Beardsley's critique of the "intentional fallacy" may cast a shadow over Wright's categories.

Another way of phrasing this critique of Wright's taxonomy is to suggest that he has muddled together two separate (but of course related) questions about Paul's deployment of Abraham. Namely, Wright has collated two questions that need to be treated—to a certain extent and at least procedurally—separately: "*why* does Paul refer to Abraham in such and such a context?" and "*what* is Paul doing in referring to Abraham in these verses?" This allows for certain categories, which Wright divides, to be brought back into play together, thus avoiding false either-or statements.

Asking why Paul mentions Abraham is an important question, of course, but is one best assessed according to the nature of Paul's deployment, namely with recourse to the *what* question. In order to establish what Paul is doing in referring to Abraham, numerous factors come into play. Namely, one needs to consider the following two issues.

First, one must negotiate wider theological construals of Paul's theology which are taken to frame given pericopes, and thus determine rhetorical strategy, emphases, etc. This will take account of specific traditions, such as "old perspectives," front-loading "salvation-history," "social scientific" readings, "apocalyptic" approaches, "Paul within Judaism," and so on. What Paul is doing with Abraham will, to a certain extent, hang on the way the textual data is framed by such

34. See e.g., the famous essay W.K. Wimsatt and M.C. Beardsley, "The Intentional Fallacy", in *20th Century Criticism*, ed. D. Lodge (London: Longman, 1972), 334–45.

35. R. Barthes, *Image-Music-Text*, ed. and trans. S. Heath (New York: Farrar, Straus and Giroux, Hill and Wang, 1977).

36. See A.C. Thiselton, *New Horizons in Hermeneutics: The Theory and Practice of Transforming Biblical Reading* (Grand Rapids: Zondervan, 1992), 558–62.

37. Ibid., 560.

paradigms.[38] It was shown above that these issues have dominated the two taxonomies already summarized. The first, twofold account, divided portrayals of Abraham between old and new perspectives. Wright's more elaborate taxonomy is a little bit more difficult to clarify in such terms, but it is possible. So (a) represents "apocalyptic" approaches, (b) "old perspectives," and (c) to (f), "new perspectives," particularly those which deploy a narrative framework, namely Wright's own. This is all largely unspoken in Wright's taxonomy, and a focus on the primacy of the *what* question allows greater nuance and flexibility, simultaneously avoiding straw-men.

Second, foregrounding the *what* question means to assess the way Paul's actual argumentation and concrete Pauline textual data coordinates Abraham with other Pauline themes. A danger associated with Wright's taxonomy is that classifications of accounts of Paul's deployment of Abraham are categorized according to structures and construals that are not explicitly named or detailed in Paul's letters.[39] This is not to suggest that a "thick description" of Paul's letters,[40] and the work of foregrounding the historical particularity of Paul's letters, should be ignored. On the contrary.[41] The issue, rather, is a matter of methodological prioritizing, and we will insist that Paul's letters must remain center-stage in this task. To do this, Paul's language about Abraham needs to be coordinated and understood in terms of the proximate themes in play. So, in Galatians 3, this will mean assessing Paul's Abraham-language (3:6-9, 14, 16, 18, 22) in terms of: the experience of the Spirit (3:1-5); the Christ-language which shapes the whole chapter (3:13-14, 16, 22–29); the various references to πίστις (3:2, 5, 7–9, 11–12, 14, 22–26); and so on. This leads to a portrayal of Paul's Abrahamic language that can be more realistically plotted.

There are a variety of ways to graphically represent data, but the radar chart might be a useful analogy for the method suggested here, for it allows one to coordinate specific information (here, the Abraham-language) in light of multivariate data.[42] As we shall see, these decisions are of no small importance, and

38. On the terminology of "paradigm", see T.S. Kuhn, *The Structure of Scientific Revolutions*, Vol. 2, no. 2, *Foundations of the Unity of Science*, 2nd edn., reprint 1967, International Encyclopedia of Unified Science (Chicago: University of Chicago Press, 1962), and Hacking's introduction in the 50th anniversary edition: T.S. Kuhn and I. Hacking, *The Structure of Scientific Revolutions: 50th Anniversary Edition*, (Chicago: University of Chicago Press, 2012), xvii–xxv.

39. For a critical review of the way this plays out in Wright's account of Pauline theology in general, see Tilling, "*Paul and the Faithfulness of God*", 67–9.

40. See C. Geertz, *The Interpretation of Cultures; Selected Essays* (New York: Basic, 1973), *passim*, often referred to by Wright in the volumes constituting his Christian Origins and the Question of God.

41. As I have begun to argue elsewhere. See Tilling, "Paul, Christ, and Narrative Time", 164–6.

42. For the application of this method to Paul's Christ-language in terms of the divine-Christology debates, see C. Tilling, *Paul's Divine Christology* (2nd edn.; Grand Rapids: Eerdmans, 2015), *passim*.

means that Paul's deployment of Abraham is undertaken in terms of a robust Christological dynamic.

It is more flexible and exegetically engaged, then, to allow the *what* question procedural priority before imputing degrees of necessity to Paul's intentions in referring to Abraham. It facilitates direct engagement with Paul's actual usage of Abraham in particular pericopes, and resists the imposition of categories that might otherwise obfuscate. Our thesis is that greater light can be shed on the way Paul deploys Abraham if these points and distinctions are granted, and so we turn to overview some important textual data in the following.

The Pauline Textual Data

Scattered references to Abraham are found in Rom. 9:7, 11:1, 2 Cor. 11:22, and Gal. 4:22. Most of these brief references are concerned with Abrahamic descent, including Paul's (Rom.11:1; 2 Cor. 11:22), or to establishing the extent of Abraham's fatherhood (Rom. 9:7).[43] Gal. 4:22 introduces an allegorical argument (in 4:22-31) based upon Abraham's two sons who are birthed by two women. The women are taken to represent two covenants. Hagar, the slave woman (παιδίσκη), is associated with Mount Sinai, the "present Jerusalem" (τῇ νῦν Ἰερουσαλήμ), who gives birth "according to the flesh," and to slavery. Sarah, the free woman, on the other hand, is associated with giving birth "through a promise," the "Jerusalem above," freedom, and the motherhood of the children of the promise, like Isaac and the Galatians. Often unnoticed, in overviews of Paul's use of Abraham,[44] is Rom. 8:32, in which Paul quotes a part of Genesis 22, thereby alluding to Abraham's "binding of Isaac." Paul appears to emphasize in particular the love of God in making this allusion.[45]

However, by far the most important and extensive engagements with Abraham come in Romans 4 and Galatians 3. To begin with Romans 4, we immediately confront a famous debate relating to the correct translation of 4:1, which has ramifications for the construal of the chapter as a whole. Indeed, already we observe the force of framing paradigms, as noted above. Is Paul citing Abraham in 4:1 to establish his own argument ("What then shall we say that Abraham, our forefather according to the flesh, has discovered?"), or is this Paul's interlocutor

43. "[N]ot all of Abraham's children are his [true] descendants" (Rom. 9:7). On this chapter, see now Foster, *Renaming Abraham's Children*.

44. See e.g., S. Moyise, *Paul and Scripture* (London: SPCK, 2010), whose chapter "Paul and Abraham" (pp. 31–45) does not reference this passage. See also N.L. Calvert, "Abraham", in *Dictionary of Paul and His Letters*, ed. G. F. Hawthorne et al. (Leicester: IVP, 1993), 1–8.

45. See D.A. Campbell, "The Story of Jesus in Romans and Galatians", in *Narrative Dynamics in Paul: A Critical Assessment*, ed. B.W. Longenecker (Louisville, KY: Westminster John Knox, 2002), 97–124.

who asks "What then shall we say that we have found out in relation to Abraham, 'our forefather according to the flesh?'" Richard Hays has famously argued that the sentence be rendered "What then shall we say? Have we found Abraham (to be) our forefather according to the flesh?"[46] Crucially, the subject of the verb εὑρίσκω is now the first person plural personal pronoun, not Abraham. This has more recently been adjusted,[47] by Campbell, to read "What then shall we say that we have found out in relation to Abraham, 'our forefather according to the flesh?'"[48]

Barclay proposes that Hays' reading is "fatally flawed" due to the presence of the definite article (*τὸν προπάτορα*), which, he opines, means that "forefather" cannot be read as a predicate,[49] and so reads the verse in the traditional sense.[50] But Barclay's argument is itself flawed. After all, Paul's letters evidence use of the definite article with the predicate: see e.g., within Rom. 11:11 (and the predicate τοῖς ἔθνεσιν); 11:27 (and the predicate ἡ παρ' ἐμοῦ διαθήκη); and multiple references in 1 Corinthians, including 6:13; 10:26; 15:39, 56; and so on.[51] So we endorse Hays' translation, which has the force of foregrounding the diatribal nature of Paul's argument, which begins in 3:27.

For these insights we turn to an alternative construal of the data as presented by Douglas Campbell, whose lengthy monograph, *The Deliverance of God*, is often overlooked for its account of exegetical details beyond Romans 1–3. A brief introduction to his proposals will begin our more constructive task, to be completed via analysis of Galatians 3. Not only will we lean on some of Barclay's insights, summarized above, we will also acknowledge the diatribal nature of Paul's argument (Stowers). The result will be to adopt a modified version of Campbell's account of the structure of Romans 4 and its link to 3:27–4:2, all of which will demonstrate the contours of Paul's engagement with Abraham in such a way that honors the demands of the historical-critical task by foregrounding proximate themes (note our discussion above relating to taxonomies), thus presenting a controlled reading of the significance of Abraham in this important chapter.

Campbell's account of the deployment of Abraham in Romans 4 is folded into his portrayal of the purpose of Romans. That purpose, Campbell opines, involves

46. R.B. Hays, "'Have We Found Abraham to Be Our Forefather According to the Flesh?' A Reconsideration of Romans 4:1", *NovT* 27 (1985): 76–98, 81.

47. The adjustments take into account a rendering of the accusative "Abraham" as an accusative of respect.

48. D.A. Campbell, *The Deliverance of God: An Apocalyptic Rereading of Justification in Paul* (Grand Rapids: Eerdmans, 2009), 724.

49. For this and other points, including reference to Engberg-Pedersen's complaints, see Barclay, *Paul and the Gift*, 483 n.88.

50. "What then shall we say that Abraham, our forefather according to the flesh, has discovered?"

51. "Predicate nouns as a rule are anarthrous. Nevertheless, the article is inserted if the predicate noun is presented as something well known or as that which alone merits the designation (the only thing to be considered)": BDF §273.

negating the influence of hostile "Jewish-Christian" counter-missionaries.[52] As Stowers earlier argued, "Paul's resumed dialogue with the teacher in 3:27–4:2 establishes the issues for the discussion of Abraham."[53] Campbell builds on and extends this claim by maintaining that the terms set in this "resumed dialogue" structure Romans 4.[54] With a degree of tentativeness, he suggests the following construal. Rom. 3:27 begins the diatribe, which continues until 4:2a. Rom. 3:27-28 is a diatribe against "boasting," and the basis of its refutation (namely by "the teaching of πίστις"); 3:29-30 is a refutation of the claim that salvation is limited to the Jews alone, while 3:31–4:1 pertains to the claim that Paul negates Torah due to the gospel of πίστις, to which Paul responds with a μὴ γένοιτο (by no means!), claiming instead that "on the contrary, we uphold the law." This, then leads into a debate about Abraham who, in the hands of the counter-missionaries, is the pagan convert to Judaism *par excellence*,[55] which would affirm the first point in this diatribe, namely about Abraham having something to boast about (4:2).

So Paul's specific task is determined by a particular occasion: how is Abraham to be understood in this light, and how to wrestle him out of the hands of the counter-missionaries? Paul's response, now dropping into direct discourse,[56] begins in 4:2, counter-claiming that any boasting on Abraham's part would not count "before God." In 4:3 Paul then turns to engage in extended exegesis, and does so in a way that corresponds to the three issues raised in 3:27–4:1. These three sub-units are 4:2-8, 9-12, 13-22.[57]

Rom. 4:2-8, then, concerns boasting (4:2), the meaning of "works" (4:2, 4, 6), and includes regular references to Scripture, all of which corresponds with 3:27-28. What is involved here, as Barclay argues, is the incongruity of God's grace, which involves crediting Abraham with δικαιοσύνη,[58] therefore not according

52. The use of the terms in the inverted commas is, of course, problematically anachronistic, but other options remain cumbersome.

53. S.K. Stowers, *A Rereading of Romans: Justice, Jews, and Gentiles* (New Haven: Yale University Press, 1994), 227. That there is a dialogue, a to-and-fro of debate, is not controversial. But how this is to be understood remains disputed. See some early comments in Hays, "Have We Found Abraham", 78–9.

54. Indeed, the verbal parallels are strong. See Campbell, *Deliverance*, 725–7.

55. This is indeed how Abraham was understood by Paul's contemporary Jewish exegetes: see F. Watson, *Paul and the Hermeneutics of Faith* (London: T&T Clark, 2004), 172–82.

56. A reading first suggested by S.E. Porter, as documented in Campbell, *Deliverance*, 724, 1122 n.20.

57. In Campbell, *Deliverance*, 728–9, Campbell argues that Romans 4 contains a fourth section, 4:16b-22, which means the third section was 4:13-16a. In recent email correspondence with Campbell, however, it emerges that he now thinks the fourth section should be folded into the third. We have discovered reasons to substantiate this change of mind, as we shall explore below.

58. On this translation, together with associated exegetical decisions relating to the verb λογίζομαι, and the preposition, εἰς (in 4:9), see Campbell, *Deliverance*, 731–2.

to merit.[59] This indeed defines the nature of the faith involved, at this point. This without-works trusting (μὴ ἐργαζομένῳ) has an object, namely God, as one who "justifies the ungodly." Such faith is credited as δικαιοσύνη. Referencing David (4:7) underscores the point: boasting is excluded by the Torah (focused on πίστις); grace is incongruous.

Abraham must, of course, remain the focal point for considering circumcision (Gen. 17). Given this link between Abraham and circumcision, the counter-missionary's particular distinction between Jew and pagan seems vindicated (3:29). So Paul, in 4:9-12 (corresponding to 3:29-30), shifts from considering an accumulation of works, negated by incongruous grace in the previous verses, to making a temporal point: the time at which Abraham was promised or credited δικαιοσύνη. In agreement with Barclay (see above), this enables Paul to redefine the sign of circumcision (see Gen. 17:11) as a confirmatory seal (σφραγίς), using a term best understood, here, as something which confirms or attests to something created, negotiated or undertaken earlier.[60] This is precisely why Abraham is able to be the father of those who trust without being circumcised, because a seal is only a confirmation; it is not concurrent to that which it confirms, and therefore not as fundamental. But Abraham is just as much father of all those who are circumcised and who trust. In this way Abraham is the father of all those who trust: Jews and pagans.[61] All ethnically based "symbolic capital," as Barclay calls it,[62] are thus excluded by this argument. In these verses, then, Paul extends his initial overture relating to the negation of the accumulation of merit.

In the third, and final, section of Romans 4, Paul begins, in 4:13-15 by contrasting the "law of works" with the "law of πίστις" (now picking up the theme starting in 3:31). Then, having reaffirmed the nature of God's gratuitous grace in 4:16 and the corresponding dependency on faith, Paul outlines the nature of Abraham's "heroic" trust, in 4:17-21.[63] Wright has argued that the language deployed here directly contrasts with language in 1:20-27.[64] Abraham's trust is, here, the reversal of all that went wrong in "the fall." It is also reasonable to suggest that the message of the counter-missionaries was to promote a Torah of works on fundamentally

59. Barclay, *Paul and the Gift*, *passim*.

60. See M. Wolter, *Der Brief am die Römer. Teilband 1: Röm 1–8* (EKK; Neukirchen-Vluyn: Neukirchener Verlagsgesellschaft, 2014), 290.

61. Campbell points out how this corresponds now to 3:29-30, and the distinction between Jews and pagans.

62. Barclay, *Paul and the Gift*, *passim*.

63. "Heroic" is Campbell's description (see, e.g., Campbell, *Deliverance*, 330), but Paul's account of Abraham may also have influenced Paul's choice of words in 5:3, particularly ὑπομονή, which Jewett translates as "fortitude" because it "conveys the quality of 'manly courage'", which his analysis suggests should not be repressed by a chosen English gloss (R. Jewett, *Romans: A Commentary* [Minneapolis: Fortress, 2007], 354). The reason why Abraham's faith should be so described at all will be offered below.

64. See, e.g., Wright, "Romans", 500.

meritocratic grounds, that obedience to Torah would lead to life. This is why Paul's earlier argumentation in this chapter, emphasizing the logic of incongruous grace, was so potent and pointed for Paul's purposes.[65] But Paul's case, anticipating a fuller account of ethics in the chapters to come, is that the law of faith nullifies the supposed benefit of works. It is fulfilled in trust, as Abraham's heroic faith shows, such that he "was strengthened in faith as he gave glory to God" (4:20).[66]

It is, consequently, much more difficult to extend Barclay's account of faith as "a declaration of bankruptcy" into these verses, for Abraham's trust is spoken of as "hoping against hope," as "not weakening" when he considered his own good-as-dead body and Sarah's barren womb. Instead, Paul repeatedly emphasizes Abraham's positive agency, here, such that "no distrust made him waver ... but he grew strong in his faith ... being fully convinced."[67] Paul concludes from this account of Abraham's "extraordinary fidelity" in 4:22, using the inferential conjunction διό.[68] *Therefore*, it was credited to Abraham (or "to his advantage" [αὐτῷ][69]) with δικαιοσύνη.[70] But this raises interpretive problems that only a Christological dynamic can solve, one which emerges in these verses.

Barclay opines that to speak of Christological dynamics at work towards the end of Romans 4 "is to foist something extraneous onto the text."[71] But this leaves a problem unresolved. Abraham's faith in 4:17-21, after all, might strike the auditors as frankly intimidating, and perhaps more demanding than the message of the counter-missionaries. Let's be clear: the rhetorical emphasis on Abraham's faith in 4:17-21 is not to establish its own bankruptcy.

Of course, this would be to miss Paul's rhetorical point, which is not simply to "have faith like Abraham." Rather, the chapter finishes (4:24-25) with Christological language that picks up on hints in the preceding verses (e.g., 4:17, "giving life to the dead" [θεοῦ τοῦ ζῳοποιοῦντος τοὺς νεκροὺς], cf. with 4:24). Furthermore, 16b is a likely parallel to 3:26, and hence to the faithfulness of Christ.[72] Likewise, Paul

65. Cf. D.A. Campbell, *Deliverance*, 506–11; D.A. Campbell, *The Quest for Paul's Gospel: A Suggested Strategy* (London: T&T Clark, 2005), 248–53.

66. This is why, it should be noted, 4:16a does not end the third section of Romans 4, as Campbell initially outlined in *Deliverance*, as referenced above.

67. To be noted is Paul's refusal to speak of circumcision at this point, which would undermine his rhetoric somewhat.

68. Campbell, *Deliverance*, 744.

69. As, for example, Wallace argues, the dative is "the case of personal interest": D.B. Wallace, *Greek Grammar Beyond the Basics* (Grand Rapids: Zondervan, 1996), 139.

70. This important Pauline inference from the nature of Abraham's positive and heroic trust, is adequately accounted for by Barclay. Cf. Barclay, *Paul and the Gift*, 489–90.

71. Ibid, 490 n.110.

72. This involves a particular reading of ἐκ πίστεως Ἰησοῦ. For a balanced account of the debates, see D. Heliso, *Pistis and the Righteous One: A Study of Romans 1:17 Against the Background of Scripture and Second Temple Jewish Literature* (WUNT II; Tübingen: Mohr Siebeck, 2007).

explains that Christ is given over to death for the sake of our trespasses and raised for the sake of our δικαίωσις (καὶ ἠγέρθη διὰ τὴν δικαίωσιν ἡμῶν), language which associates resurrection and δικαίωσις, and hence language in 4:2, 5–6, with Christ. If Abraham's faith is presented as the opposite of what went wrong, as described in 1:20-27 (Wright), Paul's forthcoming ethical argument, in Rom. 6:2-13, 16-18, 23, will be enumerated in terms of dying and rising with Christ, liberating those in Christ from what is wrong, namely the power of Sin, and so on. The good news for Paul's auditors is not simply the faith of Abraham, but "peace with God through our Lord Jesus Christ" (Rom. 5:1),[73] through whom we hope in sharing the glory of God (cf. 5:2 with 4:20). All of this suggests that no one is "foisting" Christology into these verses: it is important for the cogency of Paul's argument.

This all shows not only that Christology is involved in Paul's argument, but how it solves problems. As Joshua Jipp has argued, "Paul's portrait of the faith of Abraham is generated by his commitment to the revelation of God's saving act through the faithful Jesus who trusted God for his own resurrection in the face of death."[74] So those in Christ participate, in trust, in Christ's life. This faithfulness, which is part of that ambiguous and difficult life of Christ-followers, together with hope, character, and so on (5:3-5), and which was evidenced in Abraham, is now revealed in the faithfulness of Christ. Paul's argument, then, points to the identity of God as the grounds of his good news. Indeed, Paul's argument has consistently foregrounded the object of faith (4:5, 20–21). Faith is central to these concerns, but Paul's use of Abraham causes us to ask: whose?; and what role does that faith play? Paul's use of Abraham traditions points to the news of God in Jesus Christ. The incongruous nature of the gospel (Barclay), and Paul's confidence in the kindness and grace of God, is based on the activity of God in the life of Christ. As he puts it a few verses later in Rom. 5:8: "God demonstrates his love for us in that while we still were sinners Christ died for us." So Christ-followers trust, to draw on themes in the immediate frame, by Spirit-participation in the faithfulness of the Messiah (5:1-8). The Christological logic emerging in the final verses of Romans 4 is thus central to the coherence of Paul's argument concerning Abraham's faith.

There is not enough space in this essay to canvas Abraham in Galatians 3 in similar depth, but the outline of Romans 4 above leaves further questions hanging that a careful reader of Genesis will notice: not only does the everlasting nature of this covenant "in the flesh" (Gen. 17:13) pose continued problems, so do the continuing narratives relating to Abraham, Isaac, and circumcision. As Joshua Jipp argues, Rom. 4:22 (διὸ ἐλογίσθη αὐτῷ εἰς δικαιοσύνην), "must refer to God's granting of the birth of Isaac as the means whereby Abraham is made the father of many nations (cf. Rom. 9:7-9)." But this (rightly) brings together what Paul's argument has sought to keep apart, namely Abraham's faith and circumcision, as it

73. This translation assumes ἔχομεν is original, which is disputed. The major commentaries canvas this issue extensively, and the majority accept the reading used here.

74. J.W. Jipp, "Rereading the Story of Abraham, Isaac, and 'Us' in Romans 4", *JSNT* 32 (2010): 217–42, 237.

extends his biography to his children. Hence Jipp notes that "Paul's argument will, it should be clear, only prove convincing to those who share the christological kerygma that Paul sets forth in 4:24b-25."[75] There is, in other words, an issue of establishing the veracity of Paul's reading, which, as Jipp explains, is grounded upon a Christological hermeneutic. Such matters are foregrounded in Galatians 3, to which we now briefly turn.[76]

The claim that Paul, in Galatians, engages in exegetical debate with (Jewish-Jesus Christ-following) counter-missionaries is not as controversial as it is for readers of Romans.[77] But the way in which Paul deploys Abraham in these verses reflects wider hermeneutical forces that begun to emerge in relation to Romans 4 above. Namely, in Galatians 3 we see Paul establishing the grounds for his own (correct) engagement with Scripture, in debate with wrongheaded scriptural exegesis.

This is to say that Paul seeks to show the way in which the true gospel and its reading of Scripture is established by the reality and impact of Jesus Christ in the lives of these Christ-followers (and his own). Much of Galatians 1–2 was concerned with establishing the revelatory priority of Jesus Christ in Paul's own story, in explicit contrast with the counter-missionaries and their theology and its impact (Gal. 1:1, 6-16; 2:4, 11-15, 16, 19-21). At the start of Galatians 3 Paul re-emphasizes the reality of the presence of the Spirit in their lives, a life-changing actuality which accompanied the proclamation of Christ's fidelity (Gal. 3:1, 2, 5),[78] something also spoken of in Christological terms in Galatians (4:6).[79] This is not unrelated to what follows, an impression one might obtain, to a certain extent, from the major commentaries. Rather, along with the first two chapters of

75. J.W. Jipp, "What Are the Implications of the Ethnic Identity of Paul's Interlocutor? Continuing the Conversation", in *The So-Called Jew in Paul's Letter to Romans*, ed. R. Rodriguez et al. (Minneapolis: Fortress Press, 2016), 183–203, 190.

76. All of this does suggest, to honor Wright's own taxonomy, that Paul speaks about Abraham because of the counter-missionaries. This doesn't make Abraham unnecessary to Paul's own theology, but Paul is aware of misunderstandings that could be engendered and seeks to avoid them.

77. See n.18, above.

78. Das writes that Paul's language, here, means he "preached the message of Christ crucified so vividly in his words and life that they could envision it": A.A. Das, *Galatians* (Concordia Commentary; Saint Louis, MO: Concordia Publishing House, 2014), 287. The offered translation of ἐξ ἀκοῆς πίστεως (3:2, 5) corresponds best with 3:1, so understood, for it foregrounds the centrality of Jesus Christ in Paul's missionary proclamation. See also de Boer, *Galatians: A Commentary*, 174–6; Campbell, *Deliverance*, 853–6. It remains, however, a debated translation.

79. On the relationship between God-language, Christ-language and the Spirit in Paul, see M. Fatehi, *The Spirit's Relation to the Risen Lord in Paul: An Examination of its Christological Implications* (Tübingen: Mohr Siebeck, 2000), and now Tilling, "Paul the Trinitarian", in *Essays on the Trinity*, ed. L. Harvey (Eugene, OR: Cascade, 2018), 36–62.

Galatians, Gal. 3:1-5 frames Paul's reality-of-Christ-by-the-Spirit reading of Scripture, and particularly Abraham (mentioned eight times in Galatians 3 alone).

This is why Paul begins 3:6 with a comparative coordinating conjunction (καθώς), for what he is about to detail with respect to Abraham (and his faith) relates the message of πίστις, namely the content of the gospel proclamation about Jesus.[80] The reality of Jesus constrains his reading of the Scriptures in a particular way, and this is his point. Hence Paul assumes the links he does between Abraham, faith, the Galatians, and Christ (Gal. 3:6-9). Hence Paul presents Scripture as an active witness in understanding what God has done in Jesus Christ (3:8. See also 3:22; 4:30).[81] This is also why Paul does not seem phased by the obvious counter-argument that the descendants of Abraham are established through Isaac, and thus involves circumcision (see above), for that would simply be problematic exegesis, i.e. Scripture reading not in tune with the reality of God in Christ. This is why Paul understands the promise to Abraham (see 3:15-18) to be about Abraham and the one offspring, namely the *one* person, Christ (ὡς ἐφ' ἑνός· καὶ τῷ σπέρματί σου, ὅς ἐστιν Χριστός, 3:16). This is why his exegesis flows straight into language which emphasizes the relation between Christ and his followers ("in Christ Jesus you are all children of God . . . baptized into Christ . . . clothed [. . .] with Christ . . . one in Christ . . . belong to Christ," 3:26-29). The counter-missionaries are using the Scriptures incorrectly due to an exegesis that does not sufficiently allow Christ to shape it.[82] The reality of the God of Scripture is bound up with the presence of Jesus Christ and God in their midst by the Spirit. Paul's engagement with Abraham, in other words, is established by the need to demonstrate the insufficiently Christological exegesis of his opponents, not because of abstract or academic distinctions, but because the alternative undermines their own experience of Christ and the Spirit of God (3:1-5).

This raises further questions relating to the veracity of Paul's engagement with Abraham, which would likely leave his interlocutors unimpressed. But there is only space to mention two in passing. It can be argued that the basis for Paul's truth claims, as we have argued was especially clear in Galatians 3, is the reality of God by the Spirit, in the career of Jesus Christ. Certainly, this could be understood as a Pauline "dogmatic imposition." But for Paul, this reading of Scripture in general, and the Abraham traditions in particular, represents his understanding of the reality of God in Christ, in whom God reveals his love (Rom. 5:8), and in

80. Cf. H. Balz and G. Schneider, eds., *The Exegetical Dictionary of the New Testament* (Grand Rapids: Eerdmans, 1993), 226. Das correctly argues that καθώς, here, "refers backward to 3:1-5", but his exegesis of what follows does not sufficiently demonstrate the import of this insight for Paul's following exegesis, and is, instead, content to make superficial points about the correspondence of πίστις language throughout (Das, *Galatians*, 300).

81. See B.R. Gaventa, "The Singularity of the Gospel: A Reading of Galatians", in *Pauline Theology*, Vol. 1, *Thessalonians, Philippians, Galatians, Philemon*, ed. J.M. Bassler (Minneapolis: Fortress, 1991), 147–59.

82. "[T]hey view God's Christ in the light of God's Law, rather than the Law in the light of Christ": L. Martyn, *Galatians*, 124.

whom are hidden "all the treasures of wisdom and knowledge" (Col. 2:3).[83] This leads Karl Barth, with Overbeck, to claim that the OT "did not, in the ordinary sense of the word, 'precede' Christ. Rather it lived in him."[84] Precisely "[*t*]*his* is the claim we make for Abraham".[85]

An alternative approach to the veracity of Paul's exegesis is presented in Matthew Thiessen's important work, *Paul and the Gentile Problem*, in which he outlines a case for understanding the logic of Paul's appeal to Abraham. Beginning with Paul's commitment that Gentiles must indeed become sons of Abraham, Thiessen asks the important question as to why this is the case. The solution, he maintains, is in the link between faith, which makes one a son of Abraham, and the reception of Christ's πνεῦμα, but not in the sense outlined above. Rather, as he argues, when "God had promised the *pneuma* to Abraham and his seed (Gal. 3:14-16), Paul intends his readers to recognize that Gen. 15:5 and 22:16-18, in promising that Abraham's seed would be like the stars of the heaven, contained the implicit promise of the *pneuma*, the stuff of the stars/angels."[86] Gentiles who receive Christ's πνεῦμα thus become Abraham's seed. Paul's argument is thus a sophisticated exegetical argument that does not hang on Christological realities in the same way.

While these issues need further analysis, it is possible, from the vantage point obtained from the exegesis above, to now ask the *why* question, namely why does Paul make recourse to Abraham. Given that the terms of the debate have been set by the counter-missionaries, it appears Paul's particular deployment of Abraham in Romans 4 and Galatians 3 is defensively orientated, anxious to avoid mis-interpretation. In other words, his particular deployment of Abraham in these passages is bound to very particular contingencies. But this is not to say that Abraham is therefore dispensable for Paul. One could certainly make the case that Abraham is necessary for Paul's gospel, given the centrality of Abraham in Paul's Scriptures. And it is obvious that Paul draws lines of continuity between Christ, Christ-followers, and Abraham, especially in Romans 4.[87] But these lines of

83. For the language in this sentence, see S.V. Adams, *The Reality of God and Historical Method: Apocalyptic Theology in Conversation with N. T. Wright* (Downers Grove, IL: IVP Academic, 2015), and a critical appraisal in C. Tilling, "From Adams's Critique of Wright's Historiography to Barth's Critique of Religion: A Review Essay of Sam Adams's The Reality of God and Historical Method", *Theology Today* 73, no. 2 (2016): 168–77.

84. K. Barth, *The Epistle to the Romans* (trans. Edwyn C. Hoskyns; Oxford: Oxford University Press, 1968), 118.

85. Ibid, 118, emphasis mine.

86. M. Thiessen, *Paul and the Gentile Problem* (Oxford: Oxford University Press, 2016), 159.

87. Cf. "Abraham, of course, plays a foundational role in the unfolding drama of redemption in the OT, so it is not unexpected for Paul to make significant reference to him in his attempt to persuade the Galatians to accept his view of redemptive history": D.J. Moo, *Galatians* (Baker Exegetical Commentary on the New Testament; Grand Rapids: Baker Academic, 2013), 192; though the last two words may not specify precisely enough what is at stake.

continuity are understood in light of the career of Christ, which means that the terms of Paul's engagement are thereby negotiated by a Christological-hermeneutical disruption. No doubt given different circumstances and more time, Paul could outline the way in which this key scriptural figure relates to Christ and Christ-followers in a whole host of ways that do not emerge in his letters. But the relevant material in Paul's letters is primarily addressing questions raised by his opponents.

Abraham in Hebrews

Space does not permit a similar treatment of Abraham in Hebrews, nor does the scholarly literature demand the same attention, hence this final section is best used to point out the similarities and differences between the use of Abraham in Hebrews and Paul.

The similarities are striking. First, if one accepts the addresses include pagans,[88] Heb. 2:16 suggests that the seed of Abraham's is likewise divorced from ethnic mores and applied to a mixed "Christian community."[89] Lane also argues that the σπέρματος Ἀβραάμ is taken as a description of "the community of faith,"[90] Similarly for Paul, those who are of Christ are Ἀβραὰμ σπέρμα (Gal. 3:29). But to be noted is that both Paul and Hebrews continue to speak of the seed of Abraham in more ethnic terms as well (cf. Rom. 9:7; 11:1; 2 Cor. 11:22; Heb. 7:5; 11:18), even if these moments remain in the shadow of the reframing undertaken in light of Christ.

Second, this reframing of seed-language in Paul is driven by Christological motifs, as was established earlier. So too for Hebrews. Hence, Johnson argues that the author of Hebrews' "understanding of Jesus shapes the way he reads the story of the people."[91] But we can be more specific. I have argued elsewhere that Paul's Christology, in ways that correspond to Paul's relational epistemology, is consistently spoken of in relational terms, such that an important facet of Paul's Christology is what I have called the Christ-relation. Crucially, this Christ-relation corresponds to Israel's God-relation, which is thus Christological data of great significance.[92] Likewise Hebrews, according to deSilva, speaks of the reframing of seed-language, in such a way that generates the following effect, namely "to ascribe to the relationship between Jesus and the many sons and daughters the relationship celebrated between God and Israel."[93] Furthermore, the extended engagement with

88. For discussion on these matters, see D.A. deSilva, *Perseverance in Gratitude: A Socio-Rhetorical Commentary on the Epistle "to the Hebrews"* (Grand Rapids: Eerdmans, 2000), 2–8.

89. deSilva, *Hebrews*, 119.

90. W.L. Lane, *Hebrews 1–8* (Word Biblical Commentary; Dallas: Word, 1998), 63.

91. L.T. Johnson, *Hebrews: A Commentary* (Louisville, KY: Westminster John Knox, 2012), 169.

92. On all this, see Tilling, *Paul's Divine Christology*.

93. deSilva, *Hebrews*, 119.

Abraham traditions in Hebrews 7 is undertaken in the service of a Christological argument about Jesus as High Priest, which arguably corresponds to Paul's "in Christ" language, at least in so far as it serves to encourage these communities that Christ's agency, or Christ's career, present the faithful before God in terms established by Christ (cf. e.g., Rom. 8:1, 33-34; Phil. 3:9; and compare with Heb. 4:16; 7:24-27; 9:11-15, etc.).[94] As Macaskill has argued "The author to the Hebrews ... may have nothing that resembles the "in Christ" language found in Paul. What he does have, however, is a thoroughgoing concept of access to the divine presence in the heavenly temple that is grounded in the ontology and history of the Incarnate Son, the heavenly High Priest."[95]

Third, Hebrews associates Abraham with the promise in such a way that avoids discussing circumcision (6:13, 15), which relates to Paul's rhetoric in Galatians 3 and Romans 4, even if their reasons for this distancing of the promise and circumcision are different.

Finally, the depiction of Abraham's faithfulness in Rom. 4:18-22, which leads to the advantage of being crediting with δικαιοσύνη, can be compared with the way Heb. 6:15 presents Abraham as one who, "having patiently endured, obtained the promise." The heroic nature of Abraham's faith, in Rom. 4:18-21, likewise resonates with language in Heb. 11:8, 17.

The differences between Paul and Hebrews must also be noted. First, the particular Christological rhetoric in Hebrews is undertaken in the service of establishing the high priesthood of Christ, which does not interest Paul. Second, what could be called the "divine conditions" relating to the promise to Abraham are, in Hebrews, elucidated in exegetical comment on Gen. 22:16. So the author explains that "God made a promise to Abraham, [and] because he had no one greater by whom to swear, he swore by himself" (Heb. 6:13). Finally, the relationship between πίστις and obedience is elaborated in a different way in Hebrews, such that the focus becomes Abraham's *journey*. So deSilva writes, in comment on Heb. 11:8-16, that the "... portrayal of Abraham's faith emphasizes not, as in Paul, the firm conviction that God would fulfill his promise to give Abraham offspring

94. Some of the "pastoral" dynamics, associated with high priesthood, which correspond to Paul's "in Christ" terminology, are elaborated in A.J. Torrance, "Reclaiming the Continuing Priesthood of Christ: Implications and Challenges", in *Christology Ancient and Modern: Explorations in Constructive Dogmatics*, eds. O. D. Crisp et al. (Grand Rapids: Zondervan, 2013), 184–204. One need only compare, say, the definition of union with Christ offered in C.R. Campbell, *Paul and Union with Christ: An Exegetical and Theological Study* (Grand Rapids: Zondervan, 2012), 412–14, to see conceptual overlap here. As T. Bertolet pointed out to me, μέτοχοι γὰρ τοῦ Χριστοῦ γεγόναμεν (Heb. 3:14) might deepen these comparisons. See also G.W. Grogan, "The Old Testament Concept of Solidarity in Hebrews", *TynBull* 49, no. 1 (1998): 159–73.

95. G. Macaskill, *Union with Christ in the New Testament* (Oxford: Oxford University Press, 2018), 186.

(cf. Gal. 3:15-18; 18; Rom. 4:13-21). Rather, it is his departure from his native land in obedience to God's call (11:8-10) that the author highlights in 11:8-10, 13-16."[96]

To circle back to the discussion above relating to Wright's taxonomy, this is further reason to establish the procedural priority of the *what* question before the *why*, given the very different ways Abraham could be deployed by Hebrews and Paul. The first task must be to establish the various contingencies and concrete arguments of selected texts, before second-guessing the *why* question.

Conclusion

The deployment of Abraham in Paul's letters is best understood, at least in the key texts, as a pastoral response to questions set in motion by hostile counter-missionaries. Paul's exegetical arguments relating to Abraham are to be seen in this light, but that is not to suggest that Paul would not have otherwise made reference to Abraham. Rather, the reality of what God has done in Jesus Christ controls the way Paul understands the exegetical task, and thus the way he makes reference to Abraham, in debate with his opponents. Although Hebrews faces a different set of problems, the upshot of the author's Christological focus means that there are numerous similarities between the letters of Paul and Hebrews in how they engage with Abraham. The differences relate to the historical contingency of each of these texts, which shows how fertile and important the Abraham traditions are for the authors of the New Testament letters.

96. deSilva, *Hebrews*, 393.

Chapter 9

ABRAHAM IN THE APOSTOLIC FATHERS

Seth M. Ehorn

Introduction

The Abraham story is pliable and there is, perhaps, no better corpus for observing this than the Apostolic Fathers.[1] Many of these authors were engaged in extensive identity formation, and, because family relations are among the most important identities, Abraham's lineage (either literal or spiritual) proved to be a topic of interest among many early Christian writers. As we will see in the corpus of the Apostolic Fathers, different authors evoked and modified the narrative in order to support their own aims and interests.[2] Specifically, *1 Clement*, Ignatius of Antioch, and *Barnabas* each evoke Abraham in order to provide moral examples and spiritual ancestry for Gentile readers.

Abraham in 1 Clement

The early Christian text we know as *1 Clement* is typically dated to 95 or 96 CE and was written as a letter to "the church of God that sojourns in Corinth" (τῇ ἐκκλησίᾳ τοῦ θεοῦ τῇ παροικούσῃ Κόρινθον, 1.0).[3] The figure of Abraham is evoked three

1. For ease of reading, I refer to "Abraham" throughout this chapter, acknowledging that prior to Genesis 17 he is called "Abram" in the biblical text.

2. Although scholars remain keenly interested in the reception of the Abraham story in early Judaism and Christianity, very few studies consider the significance of Abraham in the Apostolic Fathers. E.g., there is no chapter on the Apostolic Fathers in M. Goodman, G.H. van Kooten, and J.T.A.G.M. van Ruiten, eds., *Abraham, the Nations, and the Hagarites: Jewish, Christian, and Islamic Perspectives on Kinship with Abraham* (TBN, 13; Leiden: Brill, 2010).

3. For a general orientation to the letter, including issues of authorship and dating, see A.F. Gregory, "*1 Clement*: An Introduction", in *The Writings of the Apostolic Fathers*, ed. P. Foster (London: Bloomsbury T&T Clark, 2007), 21–31; cf. H.E. Lona, *Der Erste Clemensbrief* (KAV, 2; Göttingen: Vandenhoeck & Ruprecht, 1998), 75–8. Some scholars believe the letter dates earlier: K. Erlemann, "Die Datierung des ersten Klemensbriefes—Anfragen an eine Communis Opinio", *NTS* 44 (1998): 591–607.

times in *1 Clement* (10.1–7; 17.2; 31.2), each time as an example of how his readers should behave as Christians.

1 Clement *10.1–7*

The author of *1 Clement* first evokes Abraham when he is encouraging readers to "fix our eyes on those who perfectly served [God's] magnificent glory" (ἀτενίσωμεν εἰς τοὺς τελείως λειτουργήσαντας τῇ μεγαλοπρεπεῖ δόξῃ αὐτοῦ, 9.2). Following brief references to Enoch (9.3) and Noah (9.4), the author introduces Abraham in an extended discussion of his works and deeds (10.1–7). In addition to the Genesis narrative, this sequence follows Hebrews (11:5, 7, 8-12, 17-19, etc.) and is probably dependent upon it.[4]

The bulk of Abraham material in *1 Clement* 10 is presented as direct, essentially verbatim quotations of LXX Gen. 12:1-3 (*1 Clem.* 10.3), Gen. 13:14-16 (*1 Clem.* 10.4–5), and Gen. 15:5-6 (*1 Clem.* 10.6).[5] The quotations function as proof of *1 Clement*'s claims from 10.1–2 that Abraham obeyed God. But here, *1 Clement* sets up the theme of Abraham's obedience in a paradoxical way. Although ostensibly commenting on his obedience (cf. ὑπήκοος, *1 Clem.* 10.1; ὑπακοῆς, *1 Clem.* 10.2), the author, at the same time, downplays this dynamic[6]: "Abraham, who was called 'the friend,' was found faithful when he became obedient to the words of God. He obediently went forth from his country, from his people, and from his father's house, leaving a small country, a weak people, and an insignificant house in order that he might inherit the promises of God" (10.1–2). Abraham departs from 'a *small* country' (γῆν *ὀλίγην*), 'a *weak* people' (συγγένειαν *ἀσθενῆ*), and 'an *insignificant* house' (οἶκον *μικρόν*). These adjectival modifiers are not part of the source text from Gen. 12:1[7]: '"Εξελθε ἐκ τῆς γῆς σου καὶ ἐκ τῆς συγγενείας σου καὶ ἐκ τοῦ οἴκου τοῦ πατρός σου εἰς τὴν γῆν, ἣν ἄν σοι δείξω' (Go forth from your country and from your kindred and from your father's house to the land that I will show you). These added descriptions in *1 Clem.* 10.2 downplay the significance of Abraham's obedience. The purpose, it seems, is not to diminish Abraham's commitment to God but to align with the author's emphasis on 'humility' (e.g., ταπεινοφρονέω in 2.1 and esp. 31.4) and to help create space for another theme: hospitality.

4. See A.F. Gregory, "*1 Clement* and the Writings that Later Formed the New Testament", in *The Reception of the New Testament in the Apostolic Fathers*, eds. A.F. Gregory et al. (Oxford: Oxford University Press, 2007), 129–57; cf. D.A. Hagner, *The Use of the Old and New Testaments in Clement of Rome* (NovTSup, 34; Leiden: Brill, 1973), 184.

5. On the text of the quotations, see esp. Hagner, *Use of the Old and New Testaments*, 185.

6. For the Greek and English texts of the Apostolic Fathers, I follow M.W. Holmes, *The Apostolic Fathers: Greek Texts and English Translations* (Grand Rapids: Baker, 3rd edn., 2007), 33–9. At times, I emend the English translations myself.

7. I note that the Göttingen edition of Genesis does not present any variant readings that correspond to *1 Clement* here.

The theme of Abraham's hospitality (φιλοξενία) emerges overtly in 10.7: "because of his faith and hospitality a son was given to him in his old age" (διὰ πίστιν καὶ φιλοξενίαν ἐδόθη αὐτῷ υἱὸς ἐν γήρᾳ). Although this is a common theme in early Jewish and Christian interpretations of Abraham (and others, like Lot and Rahab),[8] the argument that faith and hospitality result in Abraham's blessing is based upon a reading of the Abraham story itself. Following God's promises to Abraham in Gen. 15:1-6 and 17:1-14, Abraham shows hospitality to three visitors (Gen. 18:1-15).[9]

Abraham's righteousness, then, is demonstrated both by his faith and hospitality. *1 Clement* further develops this theme by appealing to Lot's (11.1) and Rahab's hospitality (12.1) as a (partial) ground for being saved (σῴζω in 11.1; 12.1). In *1 Clem.* 10.1–7 Abraham is one of several examples presented to motivate Christian behavior in light of the fact that believers at Corinth have "assumed that attitude of unrighteous and ungodly jealousy through which death entered into the world" (ζῆλον ἄδικον καὶ ἀσεβῆ ἀνειληφότας, δι᾽ οὗ καὶ θάνατος εἰσῆλθεν εἰς τὸν κόσμον, 3.4).

1 Clement *17.2*

In *1 Clem.* 17.2 Abraham is presented as one (of many) example(s) of humility. The author refers to Abraham as "friend of God" (cf. *1 Clem.* 10.1), and sets this in parallel with Abraham's claim that "I am only dust and ashes" (Ἐγὼ δέ εἰμι γῆ καὶ σποδός, 17.2).[10] The title "friend" (φίλος) ultimately derives from two passages in the Hebrew Bible that refer to Abraham as אהב (Isa. 41:8; 2 Chron. 20:7).[11] But, in light of numismatic evidence, the claim to be "friend" in the Greek tradition, including *1 Clement*, may well include not simply a personal notion of "friendship", but also the dimension of allegiance.[12] This sense comes through clearly in 10.1, where "Abraham, who was called 'the friend,' was found faithful when he became

8. See esp. H. Chadwick, "Justification by Faith and Hospitality", in *Studia Patristica*, vol. 4, ed. F.L. Cross (TU, 79; Berlin: Akademie-Verlag, 1961), 281–5; C.D. Pohl, *Making Room: Recovering Hospitality as a Christian Tradition* (Grand Rapids: Eerdmans, 1999); J. Jipp, *Saved by Faith and Hospitality* (Grand Rapids: Baker, 2017).

9. On this passage, see S.M. Ehorn, "Galatians 1:8 and Paul's Reading of Abraham's Story", *JTS* 64, no.2 (2013): 439–44.

10. Here I depart from Holmes's translation: "Abraham was greatly renowned and was called 'the friend of God'; *yet* [καί] …"

11. D.J.A. Clines (ed.), *Dictionary of Classical Hebrew.* 9 vols. (Sheffield: Sheffield Phoenix Press, 1993–2014), Vol. 1, 140: "friend, lover," cf. CD 3.2–3; 4QpGen[a] 2.8; 4Q372 1.21. The sense I argue for in what follows may also be suggested by the parallel between אהבי ("my friend") and עבדי ("my servant") in Isa. 41:8.

12. See M.P. Theophilos, "John 15.14 and the ΦΙΛ- Lexeme in Light of Numismatic Evidence: Friendship or Obedience?", *NTS* 64 (2018): 33–43.

obedient to the words of God" (Ἀβραάμ, ὁ φίλος προσαγορευθείς, πιστὸς εὑρέθη ἐν τῷ αὐτὸν ὑπήκοον γενέσθαι τοῖς ῥήμασιν τοῦ θεοῦ).

The claim to be "dust and ashes" is a verbatim quotation of LXX Gen. 18:27b, which comes from an OT context where Abraham dialogues with God about the fate of Sodom and Gomorrah. Specifically, Abraham discusses God's justice and righteousness, presuming to think that God would not destroy an entire city if it contained even a few righteous people. As the negotiation begins, Abraham admits his inferiority by claiming to be "dust and ashes." This rhetorical posturing sets him up to make the bold request that God should act mercifully toward the city. Abraham serves as a model of humility and as an example of someone who "fixed their eyes upon [God]" (ἀτενίζω). In every other use of this significant term in *1 Clement*, the author uses the first-person plural to motivate his readers and describe their actions: ἀτενίσωμεν ("let us fix our eyes", 7.4; 9.2; 19.2) and ἀτενίσομεν ("we look steadily," 36.2). In *1 Clement* only Abraham is an example of someone who fixed his gaze upon God and, thus, he is a model for how believers might do this and make requests of God.

1 Clement *31.2 and 32.2*

Abraham emerges briefly again in *1 Clem.* 31.2, where the author notes that Abraham's blessing is attained "through faith" (διὰ πίστεως). The blessing is related specifically in *1 Clem.* 32.2, which conflates Gen. 15:5 and 22:17, referring to both as the promise.[13] In all tables, I utilize underlining to indicate verbatim agreement between columns 1 and 2 and **bold** to indicate verbatim agreement between columns 2 and 3. *Italics* are added to indicate non-verbatim agreement (e.g., same lexeme inflected in a different case).

Gen. 15:5	***1 Clem.* 32.2**	**Gen. 22:17**
ἐξήγαγεν δὲ αὐτὸν ἔξω καὶ εἶπεν αὐτῷ Ἀνάβλεψον δὴ εἰς τὸν οὐρανὸν καὶ ἀρίθμησον τοὺς ἀστέρας, εἰ δυνήσῃ ἐξαριθμῆσαι αὐτούς. καὶ εἶπεν Οὕτως ἔσται τὸ σπέρμα σου.	. . . ὡς ἐπαγγειλαμένου τοῦ θεοῦ ὅτι ἔσται **τὸ σπέρμα σου ὡς *οἱ ἀστέρες* τοῦ οὐρανοῦ**.	ἦ μὴν εὐλογῶν εὐλογήσω σε καὶ πληθύνων πληθυνῶ **τὸ σπέρμα σου ὡς *τοὺς ἀστέρας* τοῦ οὐρανοῦ** καὶ ὡς τὴν ἄμμον τὴν παρὰ τὸ χεῖλος τῆς θαλάσσης, καὶ κληρονομήσει τὸ σπέρμα σου τὰς πόλεις τῶν ὑπεναντίων·
Then he brought him outside and said to him, "Look up to heaven, and number the stars, if you will be able to count them." And he said, "So shall your offspring be."	. . . seeing that God promised that "**your offspring** shall be **as *the stars* of heaven**."	I will indeed bless you with blessings, and I will make **your offspring** as numerously numerous **as *the stars* of heaven** and as the sand that is by the seashore, and your offspring shall possess the cities of their adversaries.

13. See Hagner, *Use of the Old and New Testaments*, 55–6; A. Lindemann, *Die Clemensbriefe* (AV, 1; Tübingen: Mohr Siebeck, 1992), 99.

Although Gen. 22:17 is linguistically primary, the contribution of Gen. 15:5 is important not only because it contributes unique wording to the quotation but because Gen. 15:5 is the first instance of the promise to Abraham.[14]

1 Clement's citation parallels discussion of these Genesis texts in both Romans 4 and Galatians 3. While Paul discusses these texts in close contact with one another, *1 Clement* combines them into a single promise, summarizing the larger narrative context.[15] What is more interesting, however, is that *1 Clement* understands this promise as implying both a *quantitative* increase and a *qualitative* increase in greatness.[16] While the quantitative reading of the Abrahamic promise is common (cf. Deut. 1:10; 10:22; 1 Chron. 27:23; Neh. 9:23), some early Jewish and Christian interpreters found this reading limited because it failed to distinguish Abraham from other figures in the narrative.[17] For example, Hagar receives a promise through the angel of the Lord that "I will so greatly multiply your offspring that they cannot be counted for multitude" (Gen. 16:10). How is Abraham's promise unique? Why will his descendants be "as the stars" (ὡς οἱ ἀστέρες)?

Several early Jewish (e.g., *Jub.* 25:15-16; Sir. 44:21) and Christian (e.g., Rom. 4:18) texts bear witness to a qualitative reading of the Genesis text. Noteworthy is Philo, who explicitly rejects the quantitive reading:

> When the Lord led him [= Abraham] outside He said "Look up into heaven and count the stars, if thou canst count their sum. So shall be thy seed" (Gen. xv. 5). Well does the text say "so" not "so many," that is, "of equal number to the stars." For He wishes to suggest not number merely, but a multitude of other things, such as tend to happiness perfect and complete. The seed shall be, He says, as the ethereal sight spread out before him, celestial as that is, full of light unshadowed and pure as that is, for night is banished from heaven and darkness from ether. It shall be the very likeness of the stars.
>
> *Rer. Div. Her.* 86–7 [LCL]

14. Hagner, *Use of the Old and New Testaments*, 56, may be correct that texts are conflated due to memory quotation. However, this is by no means an assured conclusion given the practice of composite quotations in other writers of the time.

15. On summarizing or condensing quotations, see S.A. Adams and S.M. Ehorn, "Introduction", in *Composite Citations in Antiquity*, Vol. 2: *New Testament Uses*, eds. S.A. Adams et al. (LNTS, 593; London: Bloomsbury T&T Clark, 2018), 1–15 (4–5); Hagner, *Use of the Old and New Testaments*, 56, believes that Clement is quoting from memory.

16. *Pace* Lindemann, *Die Clemensbriefe*, 100, who emphasizes only the quantitative reading: "die 'nicht geringe δοξα' bezöge sich dann auf die zahlenmäßige Größe der Stämme."

17. See M. Theissen, *Paul and the Gentile Problem* (Oxford: Oxford University Press, 2016), 135–6.

Here Philo employs a lexical strategy where he explores the possible meanings of "so" (οὕτως) in the quoted part of the Abraham narrative. Significant for present purposes, Philo not only rejects the quantitative reading but he suggests that Abraham's seed "shall be the very likeness of the stars" (ἔσται ... ἀστεροειδέστατον).[18]

The author of *1 Clement* shares a similar perspective. In particular, the combined quotation of Gen. 15:5 and 22:17 in *1 Clem.* 32.2 is surrounded by δόξα-terminology to describe the quality of those who inherit Abraham's promise: "τὰ δὲ λοιπὰ σκῆπτρα αὐτοῦ οὐκ ἐν μικρᾷ <u>δόξῃ</u> ὑπάρχουσιν, ὡς ἐπαγγειλαμένου τοῦ θεοῦ ὅτι ἔσται τὸ σπέρμα σου ὡς οἱ ἀστέρες τοῦ οὐρανοῦ. πάντες οὖν <u>ἐδοξάσθησαν</u> καὶ ἐμεγαλύνθησαν" (and his other tribes are held in no small <u>honor</u>, seeing that God promised that "your seed shall be as the stars of heaven." All, therefore, were <u>glorified</u> and magnified) (32.2c-3a). *1 Clement* is not simply comparing the growth of Abraham's seed with vast number of stars. Rather, he is noting the "star-like" quality of Abraham's seed.[19] Here the author uses δόξα in one of its common senses to refer to "a [transcendent] being deserving of honor."[20] In the late second century CE, Irenaeus picks up this theme as well, noting that, in addition to the numerical growth, Abraham "might also know the *glory* of his seed ... God led him outside at night and said to him, 'look toward heaven and see if you can count the stars of heaven; so shall be your seed'" (*Epid.* 24).[21] Following Theissen, this "star-like" quality is connected to angelic beings, who are depicted as pneumatic and not simply corporal beings (e.g., LXX Ps. 103:4; cf. Heb. 1:7).

The overall point for *1 Clement* is that God's promise to Abraham that "your seed shall be as the stars of the heaven" is not simply a recognition of numerical growth, rather, it is a recognition of "magnificence of the gifts that are given by [God]" (μεγαλεῖα τῶν ὑπ' αὐτοῦ δεδομένων δωρεῶν, 32.1). Here, the promise to Abraham is not set aside or abandoned, but it is understood to play an integral part in the shaping of Christian identity for *1 Clement*'s readers.

In summary, *1 Clement* uses Abraham to motivate readers toward righteous behavior (10.1–7) by following the example of Abraham, who fixed his eyes on God (17.2). Moreover, as Abraham's seed, Christians are "glorified and magnified" in accordance with God's will (32.3), which is a partial realization of God's promise to Abraham (32.2).

18. Ibid, 136–7.

19. Ibid, 138; cf. D.A. Burnett, "'So Shall Your Seed Be': Paul's Use of Genesis 15:5 in Romans 4:18 in Light of Early Jewish Deification Traditions", *JSPL* 5, no.2 (2015): 211–36.

20. F.W. Danker, W. Bauer, W.F. Arndt, and F.W. Gingrich. *Greek-English Lexicon of the New Testament and Other Early Christian Literature* (3rd ed.; Chicago: University of Chicago Press, 2000), 257.4.

21. Cited in Theissen, *Paul and the Gentile Problem*, 138.

Abraham in Ignatius

It is generally agreed upon that Ignatius of Antioch was killed during Trajan's reign (*c.* 110 CE).[22] Prior to his death (likely martyrdom), he wrote letters to multiple churches, including one to the Philadelphians. The one brief reference to Abraham in Ignatius's writing occurs within a letter that is highly polemical against Ἰουδαϊσμός (Ignatius, *Phld.* 6.1). Ignatius encourages his readers not to listen "if someone expounds Judaism to you" (ἐὰν δέ τις Ἰουδαϊσμὸν ἑρμηνεύῃ ὑμῖν).[23]

This broader polemical context helps to make sense of Ignatius's reference to Abraham in *Phld.* 9.1. In context, Ignatius notes that some people are contrasting what is found "in the archives" (ἐν τοῖς ἀρχείοις, 8.2) with what is found "in the gospel" (ἐν τῷ εὐαγγελίῳ, 8.2).[24] Ignatius, then, equates Jesus Christ with the archives (ἐμοὶ δὲ ἀρχεῖά ἐστιν Ἰησοῦς Χριστός, 8.2). This discussion ultimately leads Ignatius to evoke Abraham in *Phld.* 9.1:

> αὐτὸς ὢν θύρα τοῦ πατρός, δι᾽ ἧς εἰσέρχονται Ἀβραὰμ καὶ Ἰσαὰκ καὶ Ἰακὼβ καὶ οἱ προφῆται καὶ οἱ ἀπόστολοι καὶ ἡ ἐκκλησία. πάντα ταῦτα εἰς ἑνότητα θεοῦ.
>
> for he himself is the door of the Father, through which Abraham and Isaac and Jacob and the prophets and the apostles and the church enter in. All these come together in the unity of God.

Here Abraham (and the other patriarchs) are said to approach God through "him" (αὐτός), i.e., Christ. Because Abraham enters through "the door" of Christ (cf. *Phld.* 8.2), he "seems essentially to be a Christian," a least for Ignatius.[25] Of importance for Ignatius' readers, then, is that they understand the broad message of Christ: "It is enough to recognize the sufficiency of Jesus Christ and to know that Scripture pointed forward to him."[26]

22. J.B. Lightfoot, *The Apostolic Fathers: Clement, Ignatius, and Polycarp* (Peabody, MA: Hendrickson, 1989), Vol. 2.2, 435–72 is still the best treatment of introductory issues. See also P. Foster, "The Epistles of Ignatius of Antioch", in *The Writings of the Apostolic Fathers*, ed. P. Foster (London: Bloomsbury T&T Clark, 2007), 81–107.

23. Although addressing only pre-Christian uses of Ἰουδαϊσμός, still see M.V. Novenson, "Paul's Former Occupation in *Ioudaismos*", in *Galatians and Christian Theology: Justification, The Gospel, and Ethics in Paul's Letters*, eds. M.W. Elliott et al. (Grand Rapids: Baker, 2014), 24–39.

24. W.R. Schoedel, *Ignatius of Antioch: A Commentary on the Letters of Ignatius of Antioch* (Philadelphia: Fortress, 1985), 208, notes that "archives" should be taken as a reference to (OT) Scripture (cf. Philo, *Congr.* 175; *Fug.* 132; *Somn.* 1.33, 48; 2.265, 301; *Praem. Poen.* 2).

25. J.S. Siker, *Disinheriting the Jews: Abraham in Early Christian Controversy* (Louisville: Westminster John Knox, 1991), 151.

26. Schoedel, *Ignatius*, 210.

Abraham in Barnabas

Because the epistle of *Barnabas* is a pseudepigraphic letter, we cannot date it precisely, but it is generally accepted to be from within the range of 70 CE to 135 CE.[27] Taken broadly within this timeframe, *Barnabas* presents readers with a fascinating window into early Christian biblical interpretation. The overall argument of *Barnabas* seeks to demonstrate how Christians, not Jews, are the true heirs of God's covenant.[28] In two instances, Abraham is evoked as a witness to Christ (*Barn.* 8.1–4; 9.7–8); in two other instances Abraham is associated with God's promise *for the nations* (6.8) and as "the father of the nations who believe in God without being circumcised" (πατέρα ἐθνῶν τῶν πιστευόντων δι' ἀκροβυστίας τῷ θεῷ, 13.7).

Barnabas *6.8*

The text of *Barn.* 6.8 is a condensed quotation of Exod. 33:1-3, which evokes the land promise made to Abraham, Isaac, and Jacob.[29]

Exod. 33:1-3	***Barn.* 6.8**
Καὶ εἶπεν κύριος πρὸς Μωυσῆν Πορεύου ἀνάβηθι ἐντεῦθεν σὺ καὶ ὁ λαός σου, οὓς ἐξήγαγες ἐκ γῆς Αἰγύπτου, εἰς τὴν γῆν, ἣν *ὤμοσα* τῷ Αβρααμ καὶ Ισαακ καὶ Ιακωβ λέγων Τῷ σπέρματι ὑμῶν δώσω αὐτήν. 2 καὶ συναποστελῶ τὸν ἄγγελόν μου πρὸ προσώπου σου, καὶ ἐκβαλεῖ τὸν Αμορραῖον καὶ Χετταῖον καὶ Φερεζαῖον καὶ Γεργεσαῖον καὶ Ευαῖον καὶ Ιεβουσαῖον. 3 καὶ εἰσάξω σε εἰς γῆν ῥέουσαν γάλα καὶ μέλι· οὐ γὰρ μὴ συναναβῶ μετὰ σοῦ διὰ τὸ λαὸν σκληροτράχηλόν σε εἶναι, ἵνα μὴ ἐξαναλώσω σε ἐν τῇ ὁδῷ.	τί λέγει ὁ ἄλλος προφήτης Μωϋσῆς αὐτοῖς; Ἰδού, τάδε λέγει κύριος ὁ θεός· Εἰσέλθατε εἰς τὴν γῆν τὴν ἀγαθήν, ἣν *ὤμοσεν* κύριος τῷ Ἀβραὰμ καὶ Ἰσαὰκ καὶ Ἰακώβ, καὶ κατακληρονομήσατε αὐτήν, γῆν ῥέουσαν γάλα καὶ μέλι.
And the Lord said to Moyses, "Go, ascend from here, you and your people, whom you brought out of the land of Egypt, into the land that *I swore* to Abraam, Isaak and Iakob, saying, 'To your seed I will give it.' 2 And I will send along my angel before you, and he will cast out the Amorrite and Chettite and Pherezite and Gergesite and Heuite and Iebousite. 3 And he will lead you into a land flowing with milk and honey. For I shall never go up together with you because you are a stiff-necked people, lest I exterminate you in the way."	What does the other prophet, Moses, say to them? "Behold, thus says the Lord God: 'Enter into the good land, which the Lord *promised by oath* to Abraham and Isaac and Jacob, and take possession of it as an inheritance, a land flowing with milk and honey.'?"

27. J.C. Paget, "The *Epistle of Barnabas*", in *The Writings of the Apostolic Fathers*, ed. P. Foster (London: Bloomsbury T&T Clark, 2007), 72–80; more extensively, see J.C. Paget, *Epistle of Barnabas: Outlook and Background* (WUNT, 2/64; Tübingen: Mohr Siebeck, 1994), 9–30.

28. A helpful discussion of critical introductory issues is found in Holmes, *Apostolic Fathers*, 370–9.

29. See esp. N.A. Dahl, "La terre où coulent le lait et le miel selon Barnabé 6, 8–19", in *Aux sources de la tradition chrétienne*, ed. M.M. Goguel (Neuchâtel-Paris: Delachaux & Niestle 1950), 62–70.

The following context of *Barnabas* provides interpretive comments on several of the key phrases from 6.8. It is significant that "a land flowing with milk and honey" is spiritualized, referring to how a child is nourished with honey first, then milk (πρῶτον τὸ παιδίον μέλιτι, εἶτα γάλακτι, 6.17). And, in the spiritual possession of this land, Christian readers (= Gentiles) take possession of "the good land" (6.16). This is where the condensing of the passage is extremely convenient for *Barnabas*'s reading of the text. Exod. 33:2 states that God will send "my messenger" (ἄγγελόν μου) to remove the Gentile inhabitants from the land: ἐκβαλεῖ τὸν Αμορραῖον καὶ Χετταῖον καὶ Φερεζαῖον καὶ Γεργεσαῖον καὶ Ευαῖον καὶ Ιεβουσαῖον. The verb ἐκβάλλω is used here, as elsewhere, to describe the act of sending someone or a group of people away, often with force (e.g., Gen. 3:24; 21:10; Exod. 6:1; etc.). Because *Barnabas* is interested in presenting the Gentiles as the true heirs of the land, it seems likely that the author omitted (or found agreeable the omission of) key wording from this passage.[30] This selective condensing—removing the inconvenient fact that various Gentile groups were removed from the land—is very amenable to *Barnabas*' wider theological perspective, where it is the Gentiles who receive an inheritance rather than the Jews (cf. 5.13).[31]

In *Barn.* 6.8 the promise made to Abraham is (re-)interpreted to refer to Gentile Christian readers. *Barnabas* supports this with a condensed biblical quotation and creative biblical interpretation that follows the quotation. It is noteworthy that, in the mid-second century, Justin Martyr offered a similar interpretation of the land promise. Most clearly, in *Dial.* 119.5, Justin states that "along with Abraham *we* shall inherit the holy land, when we shall receive the inheritance for an endless eternity, being children of Abraham through the like faith." Here Justin, not unlike *Barnabas*, "takes the divine promises to Abraham in Genesis and redefines them so that they apply exclusively to Christians."[32]

Barnabas *8.1–4*

Throughout much of *Barnabas* 7–8 the author demonstrates various *types* of Christ in Israel's Scriptures (cf. τύπος in 7.3, 7, 10, 11; 8.1 [twice]). This includes Isaac as

30. It is commonly held that *Barn.* 6.8–19 is comprised of traditional materials that pre-date *Barnabas*. See P. Prigent, *Les Testimonia dans le christianisme primitif. L'Épître de Barnabé I–XVI et ses sources* (Ebib; Paris: Gabalda, 1961), 84–90. Given how amenable this modified text is to *Barnabas*' argument, I am sceptical that he depends solely on a borrowed text. It seems just as likely that *Barnabas* has modified this quotation, tailoring it exactly to suit his purposes.

31. Modification of the Abraham story is common in extant sources. E.g., in 1QapGen ar 19: 18–21, God (and not Abraham!) initiates the deception of the Egyptians by telling them that Sarah is Abraham's sister.

32. Siker, *Disinheriting the Jews*, 178; cf. O. Skarsaune, *The Proof from Prophecy—A Study in Justin Martyr's Proof-Text Tradition: Text-Type, Provenance, Theological Profile* (NovTSup, 56; Leiden: Brill, 1987), 336.

a type of Christ (7.3), sacrificial goats that are burnt and cursed (7.7, 10), scarlet wool and wood (7.11), and the red heifer from Num. 19:17-22 (*Barn.* 8.11). Each of these types are evoked by *Barnabas* in order to connect Jesus and his suffering with Israel's Scriptures.

It is within the typology of the red heifer that *Barnabas* evokes Abraham. He is recalled because the "three children" (τρεῖς παῖδες) who sprinkled water and ashes (cf. Num. 19:17-19) appeared "as a witness" (εἰς μαρτύριον) to Abraham, Isaac, and Jacob because (ὅτι) these three were great in God's sight (*Barn.* 8.4).[33] Abraham is portrayed here as one of several biblical figures who "preached to us the good news about the forgiveness of sins and the purification of the heart" (*Barn.* 8.3). Just as quickly as he appears, Abraham fades away in the argument. Yet, as noted earlier about *Barn.* 6.8, Abraham's significance for Gentiles has been underscored.[34]

Barnabas 9.7–8

Barnabas 9 is an argument about the nature of circumcision. *Barnabas* describes circumcision of the heart (9.1) and ears (9.4) and he contrasts these with a more traditional Jewish understanding of circumcision: "the circumcision in which they have trusted has been abolished, for he declared that circumcision was not a matter of the flesh" (ἡ περιτομὴ ἐφ' ᾗ πεποίθασιν κατήργηται, περιτομὴν γὰρ εἴρηκεν οὐ σαρκὸς γενηθῆναι, 9.4). Part of his rationale for rejecting a standard Jewish definition of circumcision involves a consideration of Abraham. As noted by Hvalvik, this is a risky move because Abraham himself was given the covenant of circumcision and, according to Genesis, practiced it as a physical rite.[35] *Barnabas*' reading of Abraham's circumcision, then, is typological and this allows him to read it as an anticipation of the cross of Christ.

The main interpretive move appears in *Barn.* 9.7–8, where *Barnabas* offers a striking interpretation of the number 318, which he refers to as "the teaching of the three letters" (τριῶν γραμμάτων δόγματα). The entire interpretation finds its basis in a quotation from the Abraham narrative, combining wording from Gen. 14:14 and 17:23 into a single text form.[36]

33. F.R. Prostmeier, *Der Barnabasbrief* (KAV, 8; Göttingen: Vandenhoeck & Ruprecht, 1999), 329.

34. Ibid., 330, rightly notes that "V 4 beansprucht also die Patriarchen für die Kirche."

35. R. Hvalvik, *The Struggle for Scripture and Covenant: The Purpose of the Epistles of Barnabas and Jewish-Christian Competition in the Second Century* (WUNT 2/82; Tübingen: Mohr Siebeck, 1996), 186.

36. Prostmeier, *Der Barnabasbrief*, 368, refers to this as a "Mischzitat aus Gen 17,23 und Gen 14,14." See the discussion of conflated text forms in various chapters of S.A. Adams and S.M. Ehorn, *Composite Citations in Antiquity*, Vol. 1, *Jewish, Graeco-Roman, and Early Christian Uses* (LNTS, 525; London: Bloomsbury T&T Clark, 2016).

Gen. 14:14	*Barn.* 9.8	Gen. 17:23
ἀκούσας δὲ Αβραμ ὅτι ᾐχμαλώτευται Λωτ ὁ ἀδελφὸς αὐτοῦ, ἠρίθμησεν τοὺς ἰδίους οἰκογενεῖς αὐτοῦ, τριακοσίους *δέκα καὶ ὀκτώ*, καὶ κατεδίωξεν ὀπίσω αὐτῶν ἕως Δαν.	λέγει γάρ· **καὶ περιέτεμεν Ἀβραὰμ *ἐκ τοῦ οἴκου αὐτοῦ ἄνδρας*** δεκαοκτὼ καὶ τριακοσίους.	Καὶ ἔλαβεν Αβρααμ Ισμαηλ τὸν υἱὸν αὐτοῦ καὶ πάντας τοὺς οἰκογενεῖς αὐτοῦ καὶ πάντας τοὺς ἀργυρωνήτους καὶ πᾶν ἄρσεν ***τῶν ἀνδρῶν τῶν ἐν τῷ οἴκῳ*** **Αβρααμ καὶ περιέτεμεν** τὰς ἀκροβυστίας αὐτῶν ἐν τῷ καιρῷ τῆς ἡμέρας ἐκείνης, καθὰ ἐλάλησεν αὐτῷ ὁ θεός.
And when Abram heard that his kinsman Lot had been taken captive, he counted his own homebreds, three hundred eighteen, and chased after them as far as Dan.	For it says: "**And Abraham circumcised** ten and eight and three hundred ***men of his household***."	And Abraam took his son Ismael and all his homebreds and all the ones bought with money and every male ***of the men that were in Abraam's house***, **and he circumcised** their foreskins at the opportune time of that day, as God had said to him.

As Clayton Jefford notes, "[n]ew revelations quickly arose for interpreters who combined various scriptural texts on the basis of key words shared by those texts and then extracted hidden interpretations from these new combinations."[37] In this instance, the combination of these two scriptural contexts seems to be warranted by a shared reference to Abraham's own "homebreds" (οἰκογενής).[38] In Gen. 17:23 Abraham circumcises "all his homebreds" (πάντας τοὺς οἰκογενεῖς αὐτοῦ) along with Ishmael and the slaves owned by his household. However, Gen. 17:23 provides no indication of the size of this group. It is from Gen. 14:14 that "his own homebreds" (τοὺς ἰδίους οἰκογενεῖς) are specifically numbered to 318. Of particular importance is that *Barnabas* latches onto the significance of the number, represented in Greek by TIH (T = 300; IH = 18). These letters, *Barnabas* tells us, have symbolic significance: "As for the 'ten and eight', the I is ten and the H is eight; thus you have 'Jesus'. And because the cross, which is shaped like the T, was destined to convey grace, it mentions also the 'three hundred'. So he reveals Jesus in the two letters, and the cross in the other" (*Barn.* 9.8). The name "Jesus" is understood from the abbreviated form IH, a common *nomen sacrum* in early Christian manuscripts.[39] Similarly, *Barnabas* understands the Greek letter

37. C.N. Jefford, *Reading the Apostolic Fathers: A Student's Introduction* (Grand Rapids: Baker, 2012), 17.

38. On the phenomenon of conflating scriptural narratives, see esp. S. Docherty, "Composite Citations and Conflation of Scriptural Narratives in Hebrews", in *Composite Citations in Antiquity*, Vol. 2, *New Testament Uses*, eds. S.A. Adams et al. (LNTS, 593; London: Bloomsbury T&T Clark, 2018), 190–208, here 200–2.

39. Hvalvik, *The Struggle for Scripture and Covenant*, 126; L.W. Hurtado, *The Earliest Christian Artifacts: Manuscripts and Christian Origins* (Grand Rapids: Eerdmans, 2006), 95–134, here 97. Cf. R. Hvalvik, "Barnabas 9,7–9 and the Use of Gematria", *NTS* 33 (1987): 276–82.

tau (T) as a reference to Jesus's cross. On two occasions, Justin Martyr mentions that early Christians saw references to Jesus by appealing to the shape of the letter *tau* (*1 Apol.* 55; 66). *Barnabas*'s overall interpretation of 318 is also shared by Clement of Alexandria (*Strom.* 6.278–80).

Whereas most readers understand the Genesis narrative as the foundational text that gives the command of literal circumcision to the Jews, *Barnabas* interprets the Abraham text typologically, turning it into a witness to Jesus's death. Moreover, *Barnabas* makes a distinction between Abraham's physical circumcision (including the 318 of his household) and the circumcision practiced by Jews, which he claims was taught to them by "an evil angel" (*Barn.* 9.4). By associating physical circumcision with demonic activity rather than divine promise, *Barnabas* spurns the typical Jewish practice of circumcision in his own day because it puts false hope in the flesh.[40] Thus, *Barnabas* speaks positively about circumcision but *only* about Abraham's because it bears witness to Christ.

Barnabas *13.7*

Whereas the earlier evocations of Abraham in *Barnabas* give the story a decidedly Christian flavor, *Barn.* 13.7 moves a step beyond this by claiming the patriarch for Gentile Christians exclusively. This can be seen most clearly by reading 13.7 in its immediate and wider literary context.

> Observe how by these means he has ordained that this people should be first, and heir of the covenant. Now if in addition to this the same point is also made through Abraham, we add the final touch to our knowledge. What, then, does he say to Abraham, when he alone believed and was established in righteousness? "Behold, I have established you, Abraham, as the father of the nations who believe in God without being circumcised."
>
> *Barn.* 13.6–7

The language of "covenant" (διαθήκη) is employed frequently in *Barnabas* in reference to Gentile Christians inheriting God's covenant (e.g., 4.3; 6.19; 13.1, 6; 14.4, 5). As the argument of *Barnabas* 13 begins, the author asks "let us see whether this people or the former people is the heir, and whether the covenant is for us or for them." This culminates in *Barnabas*'s clear statement that Abraham has been "established ... as the father of the nations who believe in God without being circumcised" (τέθεικά ... πατέρα ἐθνῶν τῶν πιστευόντων δι᾽ ἀκροβυστίας τῷ θεῷ).

40. Due to *Barnabas*' waffling between perspectives, many scholars argue that *Barn.* 9.7–9 is an interpolation. But, following, F. Scorza-Barcellona, *Epistola di Barnaba* (CP, 1; Turin: Società Editrice Internazionale, 1975), 147–8, it is more likely that *Barnabas* distinguishes Abraham's physical circumcision (an inconvenient truth) with circumcision practiced more widely by Jews.

The citation that *Barnabas* adduces here is provocative because of its departure from the wording and meaning of his putative sources. The covenant from Genesis is clearly in view, but it likely includes a strand of interpretation connected with the Pauline tradition.[41]

Gen. 15:6; 17:4-5	***Barn.* 13.7**	**Rom. 4:11, 17**
καὶ ἐπίστευσεν Αβραμ τῷ θεῷ, καὶ ἐλογίσθη αὐτῷ εἰς δικαιοσύνην. Καὶ ἐγὼ ἰδοὺ ἡ διαθήκη μου μετὰ σοῦ, καὶ ἔσῃ πατὴρ πλήθους ἐθνῶν. [5] καὶ οὐ κληθήσεται ἔτι τὸ ὄνομά σου Αβραμ, ἀλλ᾽ ἔσται τὸ ὄνομά σου Αβρααμ, ὅτι πατέρα πολλῶν ἐθνῶν τέθεικά σε.	τί οὖν λέγει τῷ Ἀβραάμ, ὅτε μόνος πιστεύσας ἐτέθη εἰς δικαιοσύνην; Ἰδού, **τέθεικά σε**, Ἀβραάμ, **πατέρα ἐθνῶν τῶν πιστευόντων δι᾽ ἀκροβυστίας** τῷ θεῷ.	καὶ σημεῖον ἔλαβεν περιτομῆς σφραγῖδα τῆς δικαιοσύνης τῆς πίστεως τῆς ἐν τῇ ἀκροβυστίᾳ, εἰς τὸ εἶναι αὐτὸν **πατέρα** πάντων **τῶν πιστευόντων δι᾽ ἀκροβυστίας**, εἰς τὸ λογισθῆναι [καὶ] αὐτοῖς [τὴν] δικαιοσύνην, καθὼς γέγραπται ὅτι **πατέρα** πολλῶν **ἐθνῶν τέθεικά σε**, κατέναντι οὗ ἐπίστευσεν θεοῦ τοῦ ζῳοποιοῦντος τοὺς νεκροὺς καὶ καλοῦντος τὰ μὴ ὄντα ὡς ὄντα.
And Abram believed God, and it was reckoned to him as righteousness. "And as for me, see, my covenant is with you, and you shall be an ancestor of a multitude of nations. [5] And no longer shall your name be called Abram, but your name shall be Abraam, for I have made you an ancestor of many nations.	What, then, does he say to Abraham, when he alone believed and was established in righteousness? "Behold, **I have established you**, Abraham, **as the father of the nations** who believe in God without being circumcised."	He received the sign of circumcision as a seal of the righteousness that he had by faith while he was still uncircumcised. The purpose was to make him the **ancestor** of all **who believe without being circumcised** and who thus have righteousness reckoned to them, as it is written, "**I have made you the father** of many **nations**")—in the presence of the God in whom he believed, who gives life to the dead and calls into existence the things that do not exist.

Although ostensibly borrowing language from Paul, *Barnabas* departs from Paul's argument by rejecting its ultimate trajectory. Whereas Paul argues in Romans 4 that Abraham is the ancestor of *both* Jews and Gentiles (cf. Rom. 4:12), *Barnabas* denies this fact in his appeal to Abraham. Abraham is presented as the father of the nations *and not the Jews.*

This claim coheres with *Barnabas*'s wider agenda. Specifically, in *Barn.* 4.14, the author clearly states the Jews have been "abandoned" (ἐγκαταλείπω) by God; and in 5.7, the author notes that God is preparing "the new people" (τὸν λαὸν τὸν

41. Paget, *Epistle of Barnabas*, 164–5.

καινὸν). Gentiles, then, are depicted as the true heirs of God's covenant and the promises to Abraham.[42]

Conclusion

The adoption of Abraham as a central figure in the developing Christian narrative is a curious feature that has its origins, it seems, in the apostle Paul. Rather than abandon the Patriarch altogether, ceding him to his opponents, Paul develops an argument that even the Gentiles must become children of Abraham, just not through the natural or "fleshy" means. By developing this argument, Paul lays the groundwork for later Christians to pick up the Abraham story for themselves in diverse ways. As noted above, this use of Abraham and his story ranged from picking out small examples from Abraham's life to be emulated, to the wholesale co-opting of the Abrahamic narrative for Gentiles.

Some of the texts surveyed above are letters: either real or pseudepigraphic. This, no doubt, influences how Abraham is evoked within these texts. For, as is common in ancient letters, ancient figures/characters can be produced as examples for current readers. Additionally, *Barnabas* is likely a polemical essay placed within an epistolary framework.[43] As such, it contains complex (if not convoluted) arguments that appeal to Scripture, including the Abraham narrative. Comparison with the book of Hebrews is instructive, where one finds a sermon or word of exhortation couched within an epistolary framework. Both Hebrews and *Barnabas* make extensive appeals to Scripture in support of their different arguments.

In *1 Clement* we saw that Abraham's faith, and especially his hospitality, were employed to motivate Christian faithfulness (*1 Clem.* 10.2). Abraham is, likewise, an example of humility in *1 Clem.* 17.2 and provides the model of one who fixed his eyes on God from which later Christians can learn (*1 Clem.* 7.4; 9.2; 19.2; 36.2). Moreover, reflecting an emerging Jewish and Christian interpretation of the Abraham story, *1 Clem.* 32.2 associates the Abrahamic promise with "star-like" qualities of the recipients of the promise. For *1 Clement*, this is part of the magnificence of God's gifts to his people that shape who they are and how they should live.

The one brief reference to Abraham in Ignatius' *Letter to the Philadelphians* represents a different trajectory than *1 Clement*. There is an overt conflict *adversus Judaeos* in Ignatius's letter, and this frames the way he engages with the Abraham story. For Ignatius, Abraham is basically a Christian who "enters through the door" of Christ (Ignatius, *Phld.* 9.1–2). While Ignatius has not gone as far as *Barnabas* in denying Abrahamic paternity to the Jews, his Christianizing of Abraham is broadly amenable to that perspective.

42. Siker, *Disinheriting the Jews*, 151.

43. Although, judging by the scholarly literature on *Barnabas*, the question of genre is much debated.

The notion that Abraham was the father of many nations is well-attested in Jewish literature (e.g., Sir. 44:19; *Jub.* 15:6-8),[44] but *Barnabas*'s use of this idea makes a noticeable departure. Whereas some were willing to universalize Abraham's significance for the nations, *Barnabas* co-opts Abraham, seizing him from Jewish tradition and claiming him for the Gentiles and, emphatically, not for the Jews. This idea comes through most clearly in *Barn.* 13.6–7, but is seen also in 6.8 when Gentiles are the ones who inherit the land.

In order to arrive at these conclusions, *Barnabas* does not reject Israel's Scripture overtly. However, he does perform (or inherit) revisionary readings by blending multiple texts together to form new conclusions (e.g., *Barn.* 9.8), by condensing a text to omit inconvenient parts (e.g., 6.8), and by reading typologically to find Abraham as a witness to Christ (e.g., 8.1–4).

Before concluding, I note also that other key figures from the Abraham narrative do not make an appearance in the Apostolic Fathers. Neither Sarah nor Hagar are mentioned at all, even when texts that have been associated with one (or both) of them are quoted and discussed at some length (e.g., *2 Clem.* 2.1 quotes Isa. 54:1; cf. Gal. 4:27). It is difficult to make inferences about what is not there, but perhaps we can say, at minimum, that the desire to connect Gentiles to Abraham might have led some authors to avoid mentioning Sarah and Hagar, especially because these characters both provided connections to Abraham that have been exploited in different trajectories: Sarah (children of the promise, i.e., Jews) and Hagar (children of the flesh, i.e., Gentiles). However, given the general silence of the sources, this can only be a tentative suggestion.

Throughout the Apostolic Fathers we see examples of Christian authors grappling with Israel's Scriptures and the key figures contained within them. Although Abraham is but one of many examples of this, he is a significant example because to him belongs the significant scriptural promises of inheritance and land.

44. Perhaps most universal is the idea in Mt. 3:9 that God can create children of Abraham from stones!

Chapter 10

ABRAHAM IN CONTEMPORARY GREEK AND LATIN AUTHORS

Margaret Williams

Survey of the Ancient Literature

Abraham does not receive so much as a mention in either of the surviving surveys in Greek of Jewish history and customs: those written by, respectively, the historian, Diodorus Siculus (second half of the first century BCE) and the geographer, Strabo of Amaseia (active around the beginning of the Common Era).[1] The reason for this omission is that both these scholars believed that the key foundational figure of Judaism was Moses. This conception of Jewish history—though surfacing for the first time in surviving Graeco-Roman literature only in their respective works[2]—was considerably older. Its first appearance in a classical text had been *c.* 300 BCE, the approximate date of Hecataeus of Abdera's pioneering study of the Jews, the first to be written by a Greek in Greek.[3] That Hecataeus should have found no room for Abraham in his account of the origins, institutions, and practices of the Jews is not surprising. Viewing Jewish history from a wholly Hellenic perspective, he saw in Moses a typical founder/lawgiver figure: i.e., an *oikistes/nomothetes.*[4]

1. For these two scholars, see *OCD*[3], *s.v.v.* Diodorus (3) and Strabo. For their ethnographic surveys of the Jews, see M. Stern, *Greek and Latin Authors on Jews and Judaism*, 3 vols., (Jerusalem: The Israel Academy of Sciences and Humanities, 1974–84) [hereafter, *GLAJJ*], Vol. 1, 11 and 115.

2. Diodorus Siculus, *Bibl.* 40.3.3–8; Strabo, *Geogr.* 16.2.35–6.

3. For a full discussion of Hecataeus' work, see B. Bar-Kochva, *The Image of the Jews in Greek Literature: The Hellenistic Period* (Berkeley: University of California Press, 2010), 90–135.

4. The work by Hecataeus on Abraham, mentioned by Josephus, *Ant.* 1.159 is unanimously agreed to be a late Hellenistic Jewish forgery. See Bar-Kochva, *Image of the Jews*, 93–4 and 135.

In the principal surviving account in Latin of Jewish origins, customs, and history, that of Tacitus (early second century CE), the same view of Jewish history is also to be found. Sharing the general Roman lack of interest in ethnographic matters,[5] Tacitus was happy simply to accept what he had found in his Greek sources, hence his attribution also of the Jews' distinctive social and religious practices to Moses.[6] At no point does he mention Abraham.

This absence of Abraham from Hecataeus' ethnography and the principal surviving surveys of Jewish origins and customs by Greek and Latin authors, does not mean, however, that Abraham does not figure at all in Greek and Latin literature. Although Hecataeus' ground-breaking study of the Jews initially had the field to itself, and remained hugely influential for a long time,[7] in due course it was joined by other works in Greek that dealt in varying degrees with Jewish customs, personalities, and history. Bar-Kochva lists around a dozen such writings, several of them authored by individuals of enormous intellectual stature within Hellenic society.[8] It is in the fragments of some of these works, preserved as citations in the works of later authors, that the hitherto neglected figure of Abraham makes a brief appearance.[9]

But it is not just writers of Hellenic ethnicity who wrote works in Greek in the period after Hecataeus. With the diffusion of Jews from the late fourth century BCE onwards throughout the territories that had, prior to Alexander the Great, formed part of the Persian empire, other ethnic groups, such as Babylonians and Egyptians, became increasingly aware of the Jews in their midst. With awareness came curiosity, and with curiosity, first, a gathering of knowledge and then a desire to put that knowledge into the public domain. Since Greek had now replaced Aramaic as the lingua franca of empire, it was through the medium of Greek that they operated.

Not all of this work was friendly; for many non-Jews, the Jews themselves came over as an uncongenial people whose socio-religious practices seemed distinctly peculiar, even offensive. Consequently, when it was discovered that the author of those practices had been a certain Moses, then he became the subject of particular

5. R.S. Bloch, *Antike Vorstellungen vom Judentum: Der Judenexkurs des Tacitus im Rahmen der griechisch-römischen Ethnographie* (Historia-Einzelschriften 160; Stuttgart: Franz Steiner, 2002), 176–85.

6. Tacitus, *Hist.* 5.4.

7. According to Bar-Kochva, *Image of the Jews*, 90, it became "a sort of vulgate on which later authors drew for information on the Jews."

8. Bar-Kochva, *Image of the Jews*, 3–4. Of these now largely lost works, the one most to be regretted is that of Posidonius, the author in the late first/early second century BCE of an idealizing study of the Jews, thought to be Strabo's main source at *GLAJJ*, Vol. 1, 115. For an in-depth study of Posidonius and his works, see Bar-Kochva, *Image of the Jews*, chapters 10–13.

9. For a comprehensive list of the Graeco-Roman authors mentioning Abraham, see J.S. Siker, "Abraham in Graeco-Roman Paganism", *JSJ* 18 (1997): 188–208.

vilification.[10] In turn, such vilification provoked a spirited Jewish backlash, the consequences of which were not only a vigorous defense of Moses by Hellenized Diaspora Jews, but their energetic championing of other, no less distinguished, figures from the Jewish past. Notable among these cultural heroes was Abraham, an individual whose origins (Chaldaean), and therefore implied skills (astrological know-how), made him a far more sympathetic and "marketable" figure than Moses.

Most of these writers in Greek, no matter what their ethnic origin, can hardly be classed as household names, as will become apparent below.[11] Indeed, so little interest did some of these writers evoke, even in antiquity, that their works almost certainly would have vanished without a trace had it not been for the efforts largely of one man: a Milesian freedman active in Rome in the first half of the first century BCE, Cornelius Alexander, more commonly known as Alexander Polyhistor. An indefatigable researcher and harvester of quotations and historical facts (whence his nickname[12]), he produced a vast number of compilations (now largely lost) on a wide range of subjects, one of which concerned itself solely with the Jews: the Περὶ Ἰουδαίων (*On the Jews*).[13] Rescued from total oblivion, mostly because the early Christian historian Eusebius of Caesarea found portions of this wide-ranging collection of Jewish material particularly useful for his propagandist tract, the *Praeparatio Evangelica* (*Preparation for the Gospel*), Polyhistor's Περὶ Ἰουδαίων furnishes us with some of the most colorful material about Abraham to survive from the whole of Graeco-Roman antiquity.

In comparison with the some of the Hellenistic writing about Abraham, the material on him by authors of the Roman imperial period seems rather tame. Tameness aside, it is not without its merits. The sources, being more substantial[14] and more precisely datable,[15] enable us to perceive with unprecedented clarity the close relationship that existed between the presentation of Abraham, on the one hand, and societal needs and values, on the other. Since none of these things

10. A pioneer of this form of abuse was the third-century Egyptian priest, Manetho, for whom see *GLAJJ*, Vol. 1, 62–5.

11. So obscure are some of them (e.g., Cleodemus Malchus) that even the most basic things about them (e.g., their date and ethnicity) cannot be precisely determined.

12. See, for instance, Suetonius, *Gram. et Rhet.* 20.1 (Cornelium Alexandrum, grammaticum Graecum, quem propter antiquitatis notitiam Polyhistorem multi, quidam Historiam vocabant). While "Polyhistor" ("much-inquiring"/"very learned") occurs commonly in references to Alexander, "Historia" ("Mr History") is found only in this passage. For full discussion, see R.A. Kaster, ed., *C. Suetonius Tranquillus—De Grammaticis et Rhetoribus* (Oxford: Clarendon, 1995), 210.

13. On Polyhistor generally, see E. Rawson, *Intellectual Life in the Late Roman Republic* (London: Duckworth, 1985), 8, 44, 55, 61–2, 69–70, 249, 256, 267, 293–4, 299 and 309.

14. The only complete texts with which we shall be dealing here, the astrological treatises of Vettius Valens and Firmicus Maternus, both come from this period.

15. The emperor Julian's anti-Christian polemic, *Contra Galilaeos*, for instance, can be dated precisely to the winter of 362/3 CE.

remained static, it is not surprising that the depiction of Abraham changed in response to changes within Graeco-Roman society, the most momentous of which was the increasingly Christian nature of the Roman Empire from the time of Constantine onwards.

In order to appreciate the changing ways in which Abraham was portrayed by Greek and Latin writers over the long period under consideration here, it will be best to deal with the evidence in a linear fashion, starting with the Greek writers of the middle and late Hellenistic periods and ending with the Roman writers of the fourth century CE. To proceed in a strict chronological order is not possible, given the uncertain dating of many of the authors, especially those active in the period before Alexander Polyhistor.

Hellenistic Writers on Abraham

Hellenic Authors

Out of the many Hellenic authors of the middle and late Hellenistic periods whose work contained a Jewish element, only three actually mentioned Abraham and so are of relevance here. The earliest of these is Hermippus of Smyrna, a scholar with primarily philosophical interests, whose professional life was spent at Alexandria's world-renowned research institute, the Museum, during the latter half of the third century BCE.[16] Second in chronological order comes the internationally famous rhetorician and teacher of rhetoric, Apollonius Molon. Originally from Alabanda in Caria, he plied his craft in the first half of the first century BCE mostly in the republic of Rhodes, where he was visited by, among other elite young Romans, the budding orator and politician Marcus Tullius Cicero.[17] Slightly later in the same century comes Nicolaus of Damascus. A one-time tutor of the children of Cleopatra VII by Marcus Antonius, he subsequently became a key figure at the court of Herod the Great and the highly regarded author of numerous works of literature. Among these was a 144-book universal history, a substantial part of which, perhaps thirty books or more, was devoted to the rise to power and reign of his patron, Herod.[18]

Originating from areas with established Jewish communities, and conducting their professional lives in cities which not only contained substantial Jewish populations but also provided plentiful opportunities for research,[19] each of these

16. For Hermippus' dates, see J. Bollansée, *Hermippos of Smyrna and His Biographical Writings: A Reappraisal* (Leuven: Peters, 1999), 14–15.

17. Bar-Kochva, *Image of the Jews*, 469–516.

18. B. Wacholder, *Nicolaus of Damascus* (Berkeley: University of California Press, 1962), 62.

19. For the core evidence relating to Jewish settlement in each of these places, see F. Millar's "geographical survey", in E. Schürer, *The History of the Jewish People in the Age of Jesus Christ*, 3 vols. (revised by G. Vermes et al., Edinburgh: T&T Clark, 1973–87), Vol. 3.1, 3–86.

distinguished scholars came, over time, to view the course of Jewish history rather differently from Hecataeus. From the various sources to which they had access, many of them not available to Hecataeus himself, they came to realize that Moses, though clearly a figure of importance, was not the fount of all things Jewish. Their researches showed them that before Moses a whole line of characterful and influential leaders had existed, prominent among whom had been the patriarch Abraham.

Since these scholars were operating in different parts of the Graeco-Roman world, were utilizing different sources, were motivated by different agendas, and had different attitudes towards the Jews, unsurprisingly the portraits that they present of Abraham vary considerably.

For Hermippus, almost certainly drawing upon materials generated in Egyptian Jewish circles (on which, more below), "the most wonderful Abraham" (ὁ θαυμασιώτατος Ἄβραμος) was an astrological authority to be revered and cited.[20] That Hermippus should have viewed Abraham so positively is not a surprise. Citations from his works by Josephus and Origen show that he held Judaism, in his eyes a philosophical system, in high regard.[21]

Nicolaus of Damascus was no less positive about Abraham, something only to be expected given that his patron and employer at the time of the composition of the universal history was the Jewish king, Herod the Great. Depicting Abraham in the fourth book of that work as a kind of proto-Hellenistic monarch, Nicolaus has him invading Syria from the Land of the Chaldees (i.e., Babylonia), capturing its main city with the backing of an army (σὺν στρατῷ) and then ruling over it as its king.[22] Since Herod had within living memory established his rule over Judaea in an almost identical manner (37 BCE),[23] it is not difficult to see what is driving the presentation of Abraham here. Clearly the latter is intended to be seen as a prototype for Herod: the successful ruler in the manner of Alexander the Great of "spear-won territory" (γῆ δορίκτητος).[24]

So much for Nicolaus' motivation. What about his sources? That he was at least acquainted with the biblical version of Abraham's life is shown by the reference to the latter's Chaldaic origin.[25] For the Damascene part of his tale, however, his source almost certainly will have been more immediate. Among his erstwhile fellow citizens the Damascenes, there was a lively oral tradition, probably of local

20. *GLAJJ*, Vol. 2, 339. This reference, known only from its citation by the second-century CE astrological writer Vettius Valens, will be discussed below in the section on that writer.

21. *GLAJJ*, Vol. 1, 25 and 26.

22. Josephus, *Ant.* 1.159.

23. Josephus, *Ant.* 14.394–486. On Nicolaus as the most likely source for the narrative here, see Wacholder, *Nicolaus of Damascus*, 60–2.

24. For the Hellenistic concept of spear-won territory, see P. Green, *From Alexander to Actium: The Hellenistic Age* (London: Thames and Hudson, 1990), 187 and 194.

25. Gen. 11:28 and 31; 15:7.

Jewish origin,[26] that Abraham had once dwelt in their city. Nicolaus almost certainly will have known of this tradition, as there still existed in his day, in the vicinity of Damascus, a village which was called Abraham's Abode after that patriarch.[27]

In contrast to the wholly favorable depictions of Abraham by Hermippus and Nicolaus, Apollonius Molon's portrayal of the patriarch in his monograph on the Jews appears to be rather negative, notwithstanding the view expressed recently by Bar-Kochva that Molon's treatment of Abraham and the early patriarchal period is "unbiased."[28] Since I need to defend, not merely assert, my divergent view here, I now supply as an aid to the discussion a translation of my own of the evidence at issue: a citation by Eusebius at *Praep. Ev.* 9.19 of an earlier citation by Polyhistor from a work by Molon:

> But Molon, the one who wrote the abusive work against the Jews, says that after the Flood the man who had survived (i.e., Noah) departed from Armenia with his sons, having been driven from his home by the people of the country. Having crossed the intervening territory, he came to the mountainous part of Syria which was uninhabited. After three generations Abraham was born, whose name by interpretation means "father-loving". Becoming/being wise, he sought the desert. After taking two wives, one, a local (and) a relative, the other, an Egyptian (and) a slave, he had twelve sons by the Egyptian, who, departing for Arabia, divided up the land among themselves and were the first to rule as kings over the people of that country. As a result of this, (even) in our day there are twelve kings of the Arabians, having the same names as them (i.e., Abraham's sons). From his wife, he had one son whose name in Greek was Gelos (Laughter). Abraham died of old age. From Gelos (= Isaac) and his native wife there were born eleven sons and a twelfth, Joseph, and from him, in the third generation, Moses. So writes Polyhistor.

On the face of it, this passage is not noticeably anti-Semitic: the genealogy of the Jews from the Flood until Moses, although full of errors, some of them egregious (e.g., making the twelve tribal leaders of the Jews the sons of Isaac rather than Jacob), is rendered in a very matter-of-fact way. Further, the portrait of Abraham, the central character in Molon's narrative, is not overtly negative. Indeed, in a clear echo of Hecataeus' portrait of Moses,[29] Abraham is described as wise. If we probe beneath the surface, however, a rather different picture can be discerned.

26. Bar-Kochva, *Image of the Jews*, 488 n.57.

27. That was still the case almost a century later. See Josephus, *Ant.* 1.160: "The name of Abraham is still celebrated in the region of Damascus, and a village is pointed out that is called after him Abraham's Abode."

28. Bar-Kochva, *Image of the Jews*, 470–1.

29. See Diodorus, *Bibl.* 40.3.3 = *GLAJJ*, Vol. 1, 11.

Although there can be no doubt that Molon's main source was, albeit somewhat distantly, the narrative found in Genesis of the early patriarchal period, it clearly has become distorted through being blended with material of less benign origin. For at several points in this passage unmistakable traces of themes common in the anti-Semitic literature of the period—most of them emanating from Graeco-Egyptian circles—can be detected.

Ignoring the favorable account of Abraham's origins—that he had come from the Land of the Chaldees (i.e., Babylonia), a country whose inhabitants were renowned for their astronomical and astrological skills[30]—Molon invents an altogether less prestigious background for him. By transferring to the early patriarchal period elements of the hostile Graeco-Egyptian portrayal of the Exodus, according to which that seminal event had been the result of a *xenelasia*, a driving out of undesirable foreigners,[31] he subtly but deliberately denigrates the early patriarchs, the most prominent of whom, at least in this passage, was Abraham. Further, in order to strengthen the association between Abraham and that first "national" humiliation, he shortens the interval between Noah and Abraham, making it a mere three generations, instead of the biblical ten.[32]

This is not the only instance, however, of Molon transferring to Abraham elements from the Graeco-Roman version of the Moses story. From Hecataeus onwards, it was a feature of Graeco-Roman writing on the Jews to comment upon their excessive numbers, their *polyandria*, and to blame Moses for this situation, the latter having criminalized infanticide.[33] A striking feature of this passage is the focus on the philoprogenitiveness of Abraham and his offspring. Not only is Abraham (incorrectly) said to have fathered no fewer than twelve sons by his Egyptian slave, but Gelos/Isaac, equally incorrectly, is claimed to have produced another dozen.

The negativity of this passage does not come about, however, solely from the transference to Abraham of elements from the hostile Graeco-Roman tradition relating to Moses. Some of it almost certainly arises from Molon's own well documented antipathy to Jews. According to Josephus, the main transmitter of citations from Molon's writings, the latter had not only accused Moses of being a charlatan and an impostor (*Apion* 2.145) but he had also described the Jews as "the

30. In antiquity, the two disciplines enjoyed a parity of status, astrology being seen as "the application of astronomy . . . to the sublunary environment." See *OCD*^{3}, *s.v.* astrology.

31. For a survey of the Greek and Latin texts in which this view is expressed, see P. Schäfer, *Judeophobia: Attitudes towards the Jews in the Ancient World* (Cambridge, MA: Harvard University Press, 1997), 15–33. On Molon's allusion to this tradition, see Schäfer, *Judeophobia*, 21.

32. Gen. 11:10-26 for the ancestry of Abraham.

33. See, for instance, Tacitus, *Hist.* 5.5.3: "augendae tamen multitudini consulitur . . . hinc generandi amor" = however, they take thought to increase their numbers. Hence their passion for begetting children. On the negative connotations here of *multitudo*, see Bloch, *Antike Vorstellungen*, 87 n.54.

most inferior of the barbarians,"[34] a sentiment later echoed by the most distinguished of his elite pupils, Cicero, who at one point described the Jews as a nation born to be slaves.[35]

Given such contempt for the Jews, it is not surprising that in this extract the semi-servile status of the majority of Abraham's offspring, the twelve sons by the anonymous Egyptian slave-girl, is greatly emphasized, and most of his close family members are not even dignified with a personal name. That the responsibility for this omission of names lies with Molon rather than his excerptor can safely be deduced from other citations made by that scholar;[36] omitting personal names in the interests of succinctness clearly was not Polyhistor's regular practice.

From the foregoing, the conclusion seems inescapable that Molon's depiction of Abraham, far from being unbiased, is on the whole quite negative. Indeed, it would be amazing if it were to be anything else, given Eusebius's description of Molon's monograph as "an abusive work against the Jews"[37] and Molon's own reputation in antiquity as a dyed-in-the-wool anti-Semite.[38]

Works in Greek by Non-Hellenic Scholars

It was not solely in works by scholars of Hellenic origin, however, that Jews made an appearance in the Greek literature of the later Hellenistic period. Hellenized intellectuals from a variety of ethnic backgrounds, Babylonian, Egyptian, Jewish, also produced works in that language that dealt wholly or in part with Jewish matters. In several of these works Abraham appears.

Whether the reference by the nationalistic Babylonian historian, the priest Berossus, to "the just and great man versed in celestial lore who lived among the Chaldaeans in the tenth generation after the flood" is actually an allusion to Abraham is disputed. Although Josephus (*Ant.* 1.158) was of the opinion that "our father Abraham" (ὁ πατὴρ ἡμῶν Ἄβραμος) was meant by these words, Stern was not convinced by this interpretation, and so excluded this reference from his collection.[39] Siker, by contrast, believes that "the convergence of three elements in this passage traditionally associated with Abraham as one who was *dikaios*, *para Chaldaios*, and *ta ourania empeiros* seems to point quite naturally to Abraham,"[40] a conclusion with which I find it hard to disagree. For even if Josephus had drawn

34. *Apion* 2.148, adding that "they were the only people who had made no useful contribution to civilisation."

35. *De prov. cos.* 5.10 = *GLAJJ*, Vol. 1, 70.

36. See, for instance, Polyhistor's citation from the works of Demetrius the Chronographer, quoted by Eusebius (*Praep. Ev.* 9.21). On the general accuracy of Polyhistor's citations, see Bar-Kochva, *Image of the Jews*, 480.

37. *Praep. Ev.* 9.19.

38. Josephus, *Apion* 2.145 and 236.

39. Stern, *GLAJJ*, Vol. 1, 55.

40. Siker, "Abraham in Graeco-Roman Paganism", 189 n.3.

this equation from Jewish-Hellenistic circles (Stern's sole grounds for rejecting this passage), that does not necessarily invalidate the equation itself.

No such doubt, however, attaches to the testimonies of Eupolemus, Artapanus and Cleodemus Malchus, for all three writers are cited by Eusebius precisely because they specifically mention Abraham, and so provide proof that he was not simply a Christian invention.[41] Although there has been much debate in the past as to who precisely these writers were,[42] Gruen is surely right in arguing that all three could have been Jewish.[43] The most striking feature of the citations from their respective works is the clear determination shown to utilize and to embellish the biblical traditions relating to the more charismatic of the ancient ancestors of the Jews. And who but Jews would have had any interest in doing that or the knowledge and expertise to carry that out? But we can go further than this. Since the ancestral episodes that are written up never relate to the Land of Canaan (i.e., Judaea) but in every case are concerned with an area densely inhabited by Jews by the middle of the Hellenistic period (i.e., Egypt, or Phoenicia, or Libya), it surely is safe to infer that both the creators of this material and the people at whom it was aimed (mainly Diaspora Jews?) are likely to have had some association with those areas too.

Thus we find Artapanus,[44] exploiting the tradition that Abraham had actually met and been honored by the Pharaoh during his sojourn in Egypt,[45] to make the case for the cultural superiority of the Jews of his native Egypt[46] over both the indigenous inhabitants of that country and its ruling Graeco-Macedonian elite. Not only does he claim that this famous ancestor of the Jews, the man after whom they were named,[47] introduced the Egyptians in general to the esteemed "science"

41. See Eusebius, *Praep. Ev.* 9.17–18 and 20.

42. With regard to Eupolemus, I here follow those who believe that the material ascribed to him by Polyhistor/Eusebius was actually written by a totally different, anonymous author. For a succinct discussion of this complicated issue, see M. Goodman, "Prose Literature about the Past", in Schürer, *History* (revised), Vol. 3.1, 517–20 and 528–30.

43. E.S. Gruen, *Heritage and Hellenism: The Reinvention of Jewish Tradition* (Berkeley: University of California Press, 1998), 146–53. The least certain of the three is Cleodemus Malchus. However, even if he himself was not Jewish, his material with its strong *interpretatio Judaica* clearly was. So Gruen, *Heritage and Hellenism*, 152.

44. As cited by Eusebius at *Praep. Ev.* 9.18.1

45. Gen. 12:10-20.

46. From the strongly Egyptian focus of all the surviving fragments of Artapanus, as well as the knowledge shown of the Septuagint, scholars unanimously conclude that he must have been an Egyptian Jew. For full discussion, see for instance, Goodman "Prose Literature", in Schürer, *History* (revised), Vol. 3.1, 521–4; J.J. Collins, "Artapanus", in *Old Testament Pseudepigrapha*, ed. J. H. Charlesworth, Vol. 2 (Garden City, NY: Doubleday, 1985 and 1985), 889–95.

47. "Καλεῖσθαι δὲ αὐτοὺς ἀπὸ Ἀβραάμου": Eusebius, *Praep. Ev.* 9.18.1. The basis for this is probably Gen. 14:13, according to Goodman "Prose Literature", in Schürer, *History* (revised), Vol. 3.1, 523.

of astrology, but he even has Abraham giving instruction in that subject to the Pharaoh himself!

Bold as the claims of Artapanus are, they are as nothing compared with those of Eupolemus. Elaborating upon the stories in Genesis of Abraham's experiences in the Land of the Philistines,[48] Eupolemus portrays him not only as an instructor of the Phoenicians in heavenly matters, teaching them "the changes of the sun and moon, and all things of that kind," but also as a successful military commander, a man skilled in conflict-resolution, and a firm favorite with the local ruler.[49] Nor did he allow Abraham's achievements to rest there. Following a famine-induced migration to Egypt, Abraham is claimed to have made a considerable mark upon the culture of that country too. During a period of cohabitation with Egyptian priests at Heliopolis, a major cult center and a renowned seat of learning,[50] he is said to have introduced that elite group "*both* to astronomy *and* to the other sciences."[51]

With Cleodemus Malchus, we move into another part of the Jewish world, North Africa (Libya), an area where Jewish military settlement started in the early Ptolemaic period,[52] and from where Cleodemus Malchus himself may have come.[53] In the solitary passage from his work that has come down to us, a citation made by Polyhistor and preserved, with slight variations, in both Josephus and Eusebius,[54] Abraham himself does not play an active role, the main *dramatis personae* being three of his sons by his second wife/concubine Ketturah, the suggestively named Assur, Afra, and Afer.[55] Notwithstanding Abraham's absence from the action, Heracles's legendary expedition against the North African giant, Antaeus, the reader is able to infer from the successful part played by his sons in that enterprise, a great deal about Abraham himself. Not only had these sons helped Heracles to defeat the giant, but their contribution to the whole enterprise had been considered so significant that one of them, Afra, had been rewarded with a marriage-connection with the great man himself!

48. Genesis 20 and 21.

49. Eusebius, *Praep. Ev.* 9.17.4–5. Goodman "Prose Literature", in Schürer, *History* (revised), Vol. 3.1, 529 sees here a midrash on Genesis 14.

50. It is worth noting here that it was at Heliopolis that Manetho, the Jews' arch-critic, was a priest.

51. Eusebius, *Praep. Ev.* 9.17.8.

52. See Millar "geographical survey", in Schürer, *History* (revised), Vol. 3.1, 60.

53. For speculation about this writer's place of origin, see R. Doran, "Cleodemus Malchus", in *Old Testament Pseudepigrapha* (Garden City, NY: Doubleday, 1983 and 1985), Vol. 2, 882–6, here 885.

54. Josephus, *Ant.* 1.239–41; Eusebius, *Praep. Ev.* 9.20.2–4.

55. Assur, recalling Assyria, and the other two, Afra and Afer, a city Afra and the country Africa. So Eusebius at *Praep Ev.* 9.20. In Genesis (25:1-4), the names of the sons of Abraham and Ketturah are entirely different.

Given the widespread belief at that time that the qualities exhibited by a man's sons must have been inherited from their father,[56] much is implied about Abraham here. The military feats of the sons allow, indeed positively encourage, the reader to infer that their father too must have been a warrior of the highest caliber. Like them, he is also to be seen as a champion of civilization against barbarism, and so a justification for the powerful presence, from the third century BCE onwards, of the Jews in North Africa.[57] Through the link that is forged through the marriage of Afra's daughter to Heracles, Abraham himself can be depicted as the social equal of the very best in the non-Jewish world. Finally, through the aetiological names he had given to his sons, it is to be inferred that the Jews' great ancestor had entertained suitably grand ambitions for his people!

Writers of the Roman Imperial Period on Abraham

Compared with these extravagances, the material supplied about Abraham by writers of the Roman imperial period is distinctly unexciting. Further, it cannot be denied that some of their references to Abraham contribute virtually nothing to the discussion here. Counterbalancing these negatives, however, are some important positives. Firstly, the identity of the authors for the most part is far more certain than was the case in the Hellenistic period and the evidence, in consequence, more precisely datable. Secondly, the material about Abraham is more directly accessible, as on the whole we are dealing with works that are either fully extant or surviving in substantial quantities rather than, as earlier, with short citations whose original context is lost. Together these factors make it far easier than heretofore to appreciate how the portraiture of Abraham was influenced by the social situation in which it was created.

For the most striking aspect of the evidence to be presented in this section, is the way in which the depiction of Abraham changes over time. While the focus at the start of the Roman imperial period is very much on Abraham as a secular figure, the later writers, i.e., those active in the third and the fourth centuries CE, tend to dwell more on his religiosity, depicting him in one case, as a scrupulous performer of ritual practices[58] and in another as a man so holy that he merited personal worship.[59] This shift in emphasis from the secular to the religious is

56. L.H. Feldman, "Hellenizations in Josephus' Jewish Antiquities: The Portrait of Abraham", in *Josephus, Judaism, and Christianity*, eds. L. H. Feldman et al. (Leiden: Brill, 1987), 133–53, here 147–8.

57. On the military origins of Jewish settlement in North Africa (Libya), see Josephus, *Apion* 2.44.

58. Of particular note is the emperor Julian's comment at *Contra Galilaeos* 356C (= *GLAJJ*, Vol. 2, 481a): "For Abraham used to sacrifice even as we (*sc*. Greeks and Romans) do, always and continually."

59. *SHA*, Alexander Severus 29.2 (= *GLAJJ*, Vol. 2, 522).

largely a reflection of the changing character of Graeco-Roman society at that time, a period which saw not only the emergence of a variety of entirely new cults in various parts of the empire, but the triumph of Christianity over the whole of it. In this new, increasingly Christianized environment, religious identity and behavior, hitherto largely taken for granted, at least by elite Graeco-Roman writers, became a matter of paramount interest. Hence the entirely new focus upon the religious side of Abraham and the complete disappearance from the record (at least as we have it) of Abraham as a military and regal figure.

What does not change, however, is the respect accorded Abraham as an astrological authority. This neatly reflects the continuing regard in which Chaldaean lore—i.e., the art of astrology first developed by the Babylonians—was held. Notwithstanding the occasional show of hostility by the Roman authorities against its practitioners,[60] in general astrology was taken very seriously in Graeco-Roman society, at all levels and at all periods.[61]

Early Imperial Writers In the earliest text to be considered here, an extract from the *Historiae Philippicae* (*Philippic History*)—a history of the post-Alexander Hellenistic world written in Latin in Rome during the reign of Augustus by the Romanized Gallic scholar, Pompeius Trogus[62]—the secular Abraham is still very much in evidence in the form of a kingly ruler of Damascus. However, the presentation of Abraham in that role by Trogus is rather different from that found in Nicolaus' universal history. Whereas the latter had depicted Abraham as an invader from Babylonia who had gained control of that city by force of arms, Trogus, using a source that claimed a Damascene origin for the Jews,[63] sees him as an indigenous ruler. And whereas there is no hint in Nicolaus' text of Abraham being part of any Damascene dynasty—indeed it is claimed there that "not long after" his capture of Damascus, Abraham left with his followers for the Land of Canaan[64]—that is not the case with Trogus. He states explicitly that after Abraham's death, his son (sic) Israhel (i.e., Jacob) ruled over the city in his place.[65]

60. On the intermittent expulsions of astrologers from Rome and Italy, see F.H. Cramer, *Astrology in Roman Law and Politics* (Philadelphia: The American Philosophical Society, 1954), 233–48.

61. T. Barton, *Ancient Astrology* (London: Routledge, 1994).

62. Probably between the years 2 BCE and 2 CE. See J. M. Alonso-Núñez, "An Augustan World History: The "Historiae Philippicae" of Pompeius Trogus", *Greece and Rome* 34, no.1 (1987): 56–72, here 60–1. The text that we have, however, is not the original but an abridged version, produced probably in the third/fourth century CE, by a certain Justin. See Stern at *GLAJJ*, Vol.1, 332–3 and no. 127.

63. *Hist. Phil.* 36.2.1, *Iudaeis origo Damascena.*

64. As cited at Josephus, *Ant.* 1.159.

65. *Hist. Phil.* 36.2.3. For an illuminating discussion of Trogus' Jewish excursus, see Bloch, *Antike Vorstellungen*, 59–61.

That Trogus should present a version of Abraham's relations with Damascus so different from that of Nicolaus is not at all surprising. As a desk-bound researcher in Rome, he will have had no access to the oral Damascene traditions with which Nicolaus, a native of that city, can be assumed to have had an easy familiarity. Instead, Trogus will have had to rely upon Greek written sources, of which at least three are discernible in his brief excursus on the Jews. Stern has characterized these as "a biblical version, a Damascene version and a hostile Graeco-Egyptian version."[66] That it has not proved possible to precisely identify the authors of these versions, despite vigorous scholarly attempts to do so, matters not a jot here.[67] Far more significant is the fact that the version that had started as a local, probably Jewish, tradition in Damascus,[68] had become an established part of Graeco-Roman literature on the Jews.

With Vettius Valens, writing a century and a half after Trogus during the reign of Antoninus Pius (138–161 CE), the secular Abraham still remains very much to the fore. Here, however, it is Abraham the astrologer who is the subject of interest in his nine-book treatise *Anthologia*, not Abraham the king. That we should find this to be the case here is not surprising. As well as being a specialist writer on the subject of astrology, Valens was also a life-long practitioner of that art.[69]

While Valens' focus on Abraham as an astrologer in an astrological treatise is not surprising, his presentation of him in that role is. Whereas for Artapanus and Eupolemus, Abraham was simply a *teacher* of astrology—admittedly to the elite and the very great—in Valens we meet him for the first time as a *writer* on the subject. Not only does Valens refer to Abraham's written works but he even quotes from them. Thus at *Anthologia* 2.28 we find the following "The most wonderful Abramos has shown us about this position (on travelling) in his books (ἐν τοῖς βιβλίοις αὐτοῦ)."

Although it is only with this citation that *we* first hear of Abraham as a writer on astrology, clearly the belief that Abraham was an author of books on the subject is much older, for Valens' citation comes at second-hand from a much earlier writer, none other than Hermippus of Smyrna/Alexandria.[70] Since Hermippus was writing in the second half of the third century BCE, it shows that the tradition must have become well established in academic circles in Alexandria by that time: testimony surely to the success of Egyptian Jews in promoting their ancestor as a cultural hero.

Astonishing as this information is about the existence of these presumably pseudonymous texts and at such an early date, it needs to be taken seriously. For

66. *GLAJJ*, Vol. 1, 332.

67. Useful discussion at Bar-Kochva, *Image of the Jews*, 489 n.58, and Bloch, *Antike Vorstellungen*, 58–9.

68. Bar-Kochva, *Image of the Jews*, 488 n.57.

69. See M. Riley, *A Survey of Vettius Valens*: http://www.csus.edu/indiv/r/rileymt/PDF_folder/VettiusValens.PDF, accessed July 9, 2018.

70. *GLAJJ*, Vol. 1, 339: "On travelling, from the works of Hermippus . . ."

both Hermippus and Valens were very serious scholars, the former a much-admired philosopher, and the latter an astrological authority of paramount importance not only during his lifetime but long after his death. Until well into the Middle Ages, Valens' astrological treatise was treated as a veritable *vade mecum* by astrologers and even today his work is taken very seriously, the *Anthologia* being regarded by scholars researching ancient astrology as the most important work on that subject to survive from antiquity.[71]

With the third and final author in this section, the distinguished Antonine politician and writer of a 44-book universal history, Aulus Claudius Charax of Pergamum,[72] the focus is still on the secular Abraham. Here, however, he appears neither as an astrologer nor as a king but the man who gave the distinctive name, Hebrews, to the Jewish people. The evidence, preserved as an entry in Stephanus of Byzantium's (sixth century CE) ethnographic/geographic dictionary, could not be more succinct. Under the heading *Hebraioi* (Hebrews), the following definition is to be found: "This is the name Jews get from Abraham, as Charax says."[73] Since, as we saw above, Polyhistor cites Artapanus to precisely the same effect,[74] it would be easy simply to dismiss out of hand Charax's evidence here. However, it may have had a greater value for his readers than for us. While Polyhistor's work appears to have made very little impact on the reading public of the (pagan) Roman world,[75] Charax's now lost universal history is known to have been widely read in antiquity.[76] Consequently, his notice about the Abrahamic origins of the term *Hebraioi*, even if it is not news to us, may have been the first information that some Roman readers attained on this point.

Later Imperial Writers The first of the three writers to be considered in this section is Fermicus Maternus, a retired Roman lawyer from the age of Constantine, and the author of the last substantial treatise on astrology to be written in classical times: the eight-book *Mathesis* (*Learning*).[77] Given the subject matter of this work, it is not surprising that it is as an astrological authority that Abraham features in it: his last

71. *OCD*[3], *s.v.* Vettius Valens.

72. For this distinguished member of the Roman governing class—who early in his career helped Q. Lollius Urbicus to conquer Scotland for the emperor, Antoninus Pius—see A.R. Birley, *The Roman Government of Britain* (Oxford: Oxford University Press, 2005), 253–4.

73. Stephanus Byzantius, *Lex. s.v. Ἑβραῖοι = GLAJJ*, Vol. 2, 335 (Εβραῖοι. οὕτως Ἰουδαῖοι ἀπὸ Ἀβράμωνος ὥς φησι Χάραξ.)

74. See n.47 above.

75. Rawson, *Intellectual Life*, 62.

76. *OCD*[3], *s.v.* Claudius Charax, Aulus.

77. For a full translation of this work, see J.R. Bram, *Ancient Astrology Theory and Practice:* Matheseos Libri VIII *by Firmicus Maternus* (Park Ridge, NJ: Noyes Press, 1975). For Firmicus Maternus himself, see D. McCann, "Julius Firmicus Maternus: Profile of a Roman Astrologer": http://www.skyscript.co.uk/firmicus.html, accessed July 9, 2018.

appearance in that role in classical antiquity. Clearly Maternus has considerable regard for this figure from the remote past. Well acquainted with Abraham's writings, he not only refers to them at several points in his own work,[78] but he even claims to have included an appendix containing an extract from Abraham's very own books (*ex Abrahae libris*) to prove the veracity of what he has been saying.[79]

Maternus' admiration for Abraham, however, goes beyond merely quoting from his work. He puts it firmly on record that he counts him among the "greats" of the art. For in the *prooemium* to *Mathesis* 4 we find him placing Abraham in the company of the legendary fathers of astrology: Hermes, Orpheus, and the revered Egyptian *astrologi*, Petosiris and Nechepso.[80] Had Artapanus and Abraham's other Diaspora champions still been alive they surely would have been amazed, and perhaps a little discomfited, at the success of their campaign to promote their great ancestor as a cultural icon. In the eyes of Maternus, Abraham was literally a god: *divinus ille Abram* is how he describes him at *Mathesis* 4.17.2.[81]

In our two remaining sources a different kind of Abraham is in evidence. In these, he is presented as a religious, not a secular figure.[82] In the pseudonymous and thoroughly unreliable biography of the emperor Alexander Severus (222–235 CE) purportedly written by Aelius Lampridius,[83] Abraham makes a fleeting appearance as one of those "holy souls" worshipped daily by that emperor:

> His manner of living was as follows: first of all . . . in the early morning hours he would perform cultic acts (*rem divinam faciebat*) at his private shrine (*lararium*). In this he kept statues of deified emperors—of whom, however, only the best had been selected—and also of certain holy souls, among them Apollonius (of

78. *Math.* 4.17.2; 4.17.5; 4.18.1 (= *GLAJJ*, Vol. 2, 474–6).

79. *Math.* 8.3.5, a passage overlooked by Stern.

80. *GLAJJ*, Vol. 2, 473. According to Stern, this pair were believed in antiquity to be not only the joint authors of an astrological handbook but also the writers under their own names of other astrological works. All these works, like the writings attributed to Abraham, were, of course, pseudepigraphic.

81. See *GLAJJ*, Vol. 2, 474.

82. I have decided to exclude from the discussion here the passage in which the Neoplatonist philosopher, Alexander of Lycopolis in Egypt (second half of the third century CE), refers to Abraham's readiness to sacrifice his son to God (*Contra Manichaei Opiniones Disputatio* 24 = *GLAJJ*, Vol. 2, 468). Detailed analysis of the vocabulary, syntax, and content of this passage indicates that it was almost certainly a Christian interpolation. See M.J. Edwards, "A Christian Addition to Alexander of Lycopolis", *Mnemosyne* 42 (1989), 483–7.

83. This work is one of the series of pseudonymous imperial biographies belonging to the work generally referred to as the *Scriptores Historiae Augustae* (Writers of the Augustan History). Although these biographies purportedly were written by six individuals, modern scholarship is unanimous in believing that it was the work of one man, a late fourth century CE hoaxer. For a recent discussion of this hugely controversial work, see A. Cameron, *The Last Pagans of Rome* (Oxford: Oxford University Press, 2011), chapter 20.

> Tyana), and, according to a contemporary writer, Christ, Abraham, Orpheus and others of that nature, as well as portraits of his ancestors.[84]

Given the universally accepted unreliability of this source, it is hard to know how much credence to give either to the contents in general of this extract or to Abraham's cultic status in particular. Admittedly, there are several other passages in this biography where reference is made to this emperor's religious inclusivity,[85] but this may all be part and parcel of the writer's clear attempt to present Alexander Severus as a model ruler.[86] Consequently, without hard evidence independent of Lampridius for the religious beliefs and behavior of this emperor, it would probably be wiser to suspend belief about both his religious eclecticism and Abraham's divine status.

With our final source, the evidence for Abraham as a religious figure is much stronger. This is the anti-Christian polemic of the emperor Julian, the *Contra Galilaeos*, a work penned at Antioch in the winter of 362/3 CE, and recoverable in parts from the spirited rebuttal of it by Bishop Cyril of Alexandria in the early fifth century CE.[87] Drawing upon the LXX version of Genesis, a text in which he was well versed owing to his upbringing as a Christian, Julian berates his former co-religionists for the error of their ways. These included their refusal both to build altars of sacrifice and to pay proper attention to divine signals, such as the flight of birds and the appearance of abnormal celestial phenomena.[88] Since Abraham could, at a stretch,[89] be shown to have done all these things, his conduct is presented by Julian as a model of correct religious behavior.

Conclusion

From the foregoing it will have been seen that Abraham was a far more "malleable" figure than the law-giver, Moses.[90] In consequence, he was also a far more useful

84. *SHA*, Alexander Severus 29.2 (trans. M. Williams) For the Latin text, see *GLAJJ*, Vol. 2, 522.

85. See, for instance, *SHA*, Alexander Severus 22.4, with sympathy for both Jews and Christians.

86. R. Syme, *Emperors and Biography: Studies in the "Historia Augusta"* (Oxford: Clarendon, 1971), 155, who elsewhere in this study (e.g., 276) dismisses the reference to Severus' "domestic chapel" as a fable.

87. *GLAJJ*, Vol. 2, 481a and W.C. Wright, *The Works of the Emperor Julian*, 3 vols. (London: Heinemann, 1923), Vol. 3, 313–17.

88. *Contra Galilaeos* 354A–356C.

89. Although Abraham's sacrificial activity can be documented convincingly, as at Gen. 12:7-8 and 22:9, the evidence for his interpretation of shooting stars and the flight of birds is extraordinarily weak. The only possible references are Gen. 15:5 (stars) and 15:11 (birds).

90. Gruen's term for Abraham. See his *Heritage and Hellenism*, 151.

one. For his story could be manipulated by all manner of people for all manner of positive purposes, such as by Jewish apologists of Diaspora origin, such as Artapanus, to boost their cultural standing vis-à-vis their non-Jewish neighbors. Also, Abraham could be used by the courtier Nicolaus of Damascus, primarily to flatter his patron, and by the anti-Christian polemicist Julian the Apostate, to attack that sect. Hence, there is a largely favorable picture that emerges of this Jewish patriarch from our sources (the only rather negative voice is that of Apollonius Molon whose antipathy to the Jews was notorious).

There were, of course, features in the Abraham story that would not have played well with a Graeco-Roman audience: the preparations the latter made, albeit reluctantly, to sacrifice his son at the behest of his god,[91] and his willingness to undergo circumcision personally, and to agree to the divine command that henceforth it should be the defining mark of his people.[92] Hence the studious avoidance in the sources discussed above of both these key episodes in the Abrahamic narrative. Although infanticide was widely practiced in both Greek and Roman society, the sacrifice of a child who had been accepted into the family and become an established part of it, was regarded as especially abhorrent.[93] No less barbaric did circumcision seem to both Greeks and Romans. The former, for whom the male body in its natural state represented the epitome of perfection, deplored the practice largely on aesthetic grounds.[94] As for the latter, such was the revulsion with which Romans viewed this "mutilation of the genitals,"[95] that they actually made circumcision a criminal offence, punishable by exile or death.[96] Given such attitudes towards child-sacrifice and circumcision, it is hardly surprising that Abraham's readiness to contemplate the killing of his son and to

91. Genesis 22.

92. Genesis 17.

93. W.V. Harris, "Child-Exposure in the Roman Empire", *Journal of Roman Studies* 84 (1994): 1–22, here 2–3. Illustrative of the revulsion with which child-sacrifice was viewed, is the prominence accorded the story of Agamemnon's sacrifice of his daughter, Iphigeneia, in both Greek and Latin literature (e.g., Aeschylus' *Oresteia* and Lucretius' *De Rerum Natura* 1.84–100) and classical art (e.g., the "Iphigeneia" fresco from the House of the Tragic Poet at Pompeii). On this material, see the discussions at *PW*, Vol. 9.2, *s.v.* Iphigenia; and J.-M. Croisille, "Le sacrifice d'Iphigénie dans l'art romain et la littérature latine", *Latomus* 22 (1963): 209–25 (esp. plates XXV–XXX).

94. Schäfer, *Judeophobia*, 105; and K.J. Dover, *Greek Homosexuality* (Cambridge, MA: Harvard University Press, 1978), 127–30 (with full discussion at 128–9 of the circumcised penis as a marker of servile and barbarian status in Greek vase-painting).

95. *SHA*, Hadrianus 14.2 = *GLAJJ*, Vol. 2, 511.

96. The offender's social status determined the penalty. For this legislation and the Jews' exemption from it, see A. Linder, *The Jews in Roman Imperial Legislation* (Detroit, MI: Wayne State University Press and Jerusalem: The Israel Academy of Sciences and Humanities, 1987), 99–102.

commit his people in perpetuity to the rite of cutting off their foreskins, are not so much as hinted at in the texts discussed above. In the view of their authors it was far better to play up qualities that were admired in Graeco-Roman society, hence their focus on Abraham as a successful military man and, above all, as an astrological authority. The ability to interpret celestial phenomena remained a widely admired skill throughout the entire period considered here, and indeed well beyond.

Chapter 11

THE FIGURE OF ABRAHAM IN THE ANCIENT GNOSIS[1]

Csaba Ötvös

καὶ ἐγένετο μετὰ τὰ ῥήματα ταῦτα
ὁ θεὸς ἐπείραζεν τὸν Ἀβραάμ

— Gen. 22:1 LXX

The subject of this paper is the figure of Abraham in the so-called ancient Gnostic systems. At first sight, the topic is seemingly obvious and straightforward, but before turning to the question more closely, it is necessary to introduce, as concisely as possible, this rich, ambiguous, and complex source material under examination.

The never-ending questions that surround the religious, theological-philosophical, and mythological phenomenon of the ancient Gnosis are well known.[2] Without being distracted by the disputes over the definition, as well as the temporal and dogmatic limitations of the ancient Gnosis, I use this term as a common denominator for the second- and third-century theo-mythological dualist systems that are detectable in the codices from the Nag Hammadi Library[3]

1. First and foremost I would like to express my gratitude and my heartfelt thanks to the editors of this volume for their kind invitation. The research for this chapter was supported by the Project OTKA PD 112421.

2. For a general introduction and basic questions, see e.g., K.L. King, *What is Gnosticism?* (Cambridge, MA: Harvard University Press, 2003); Ch. Markschies, *Die Gnosis* (Munich: Beck, 2001, 2006); K. Rudolph, *Gnosis: The Nature and History of Gnosticism* (trans. R. Wilson; San Francisco: Harper San Francisco, 1987); K.W. Tröger, *Die Gnosis. Heilslehre und Ketzerglaube* (Freiburg: Herder Verlag: 2001), M.A. Williams, *Rethinking "Gnosticism": An Argument for Dismantling a Dubious Category* (Princeton: Princeton University Press, 1996).

3. The facsimile editions of the codices from Nag Hammadi were published by Brill between 1972–9.

and related codicological materials,[4] as well as the systems which were labeled as pseudo-Gnostics, and which belong to this category in the refutations of the Church Fathers.[5] Because of this flexible, indefinite, but far from indisputable grouping, one is unable to handle the sources together, and only the particular features, that will be introduced later, could fill in and strengthen this apparently dubious category of Gnostic. In the course of this analysis, the categories of Gnostic and Christian are re-evaluated, along with their complex relationship. Furthermore this investigation will offer clear evidence for continuity between these heterogeneous materials and, despite divergences and contradictions within the corpus, the evaluation of these Gnostic systems together is not only possible, but also a necessity.[6]

In light of these suggestions (in place of a strict definition and unmentioned significant features), I will attempt to survey relevant Gnostic passages that mention the figure of the Patriarch Abraham in order to delineate how his person and his biblical stories were interpreted and used in these writings. One has to note that for the known and anonymous Gnostic authors, Abraham was not as central a figure as other Biblical characters, such as Adam or Seth, and so he is rarely mentioned in the primary and secondary sources. The *opinio communis* is well expressed by Bethge: "So gehen etwa die Zeugnisse des Sethianismus aufälligerweise auf die Patriarchenüberlieferung entweder gar nicht oder nur im Zusammenhang mit den Ereignissen von Sodom und Gomorra ein, haben aber z.B. an der Gestalt des Abraham überhaupt kein Interesse."[7] Accepting in part this evaluation of

4. We have four codices: the *Papyrus Berolinensis 8502* (see: W. Till, trans., *Die gnostischen Schriften des koptischen Papyrus Berolinensis 8502* (Berlin: Akademie-Verlag, 1955)., erw. Aufl. bearb. von H.M. Schenke (TU 60; Berlin, 1972); the *Codex Askewianus* (see: V. Macdermot and C. Schmidt, trans. and eds., *Pistis Sophia* (NHS 9; Leiden: Brill, 1978); the *Codex Brucianus* (see: V. Macdermot and C. Schmidt trans. and eds., *The Books of Jeu and the Untitled Text in the Bruce codex* (NHS 13; Leiden: Brill, 1978); and the *Codex Tschacos* (see: J. Brankaer and H.G. Bethge, eds., *The Codex Tschacos: Text und Analysen* (TU 161; Berlin: de Gruyter, 2007).

5. The Manicheans and Mandeans are not part of this research and we will not refer to philosophical critics and refutations because neither Celsus nor Plotinus were interested in the biblical figure of Abraham, even though Celsus mentions Abraham's name, knows about circumcision, and his begetting children. For this topic, see E.J. Young, "Celsus and the Old Testament", *Westminster Theological Journal* 6, no.2 (1994): 166–97. On the other side, Origen tells us that Abraham's name occurs in magical formulas, invocations, exorcist formulas etc., in the formula "the God of Abraham, the God of Isaac" (e.g., *C. Cels.*, 4.33).

6. This idea is not a new one: see e.g., S. Pétrement, *Le Dieu separe. Les origines du gnosticisme* (Paris: Cerf, 1984).

7. H.G. Bethge, "Die Ambivalenz alttestamentlicher Geschichstraditionen in der Gnosis", in *Altes Testament-Frühjudentum-Gnosis. Neue Studien zu "Gnosis und Bibel"*, ed. K.W. Tröger (Berlin: Evangelsiche Verlagsantalt, 1980), 89–109, here 99.

Sethian writings, in what follows I attempt to modify this position and show how these authors engaged with the character of Abraham.

In order to reach this aim, I will begin by evaluating the relevant primary quotations and their mythological background. Then, turning to the secondary sources belonging to the Christian theologians and Church Fathers, I shall attempt to replace this deficient picture with a more complete one. In doing so, I hope to provide a compilation of materials comparable with the Christian examples. Lastly, I will briefly point out how these examples could serve to describe the developments of the allegoric exegesis and the movement of the ancient Gnosis.

Primary Sources

The figure of Abraham in the primary sources of the ancient Gnosis is not only present in its biblical texts, but was also used and commented on by anonymous writers. There is no Gnostic writing where the whole Abrahamic story occurs, instead, parts of it—sentences or allusions—are witnesses for the author's knowledge of the biblical narrative. These examples not only represent different Gnostic theological concepts and different purposes, but also reflect the contemporary Jewish and Christian theological ideas concerning the Father of the Faith. In every case, their wider context indicates the given author's or school's relationship to specific Jewish and Christian traditions, especially to those related to Genesis 6–9.[8]

Exegesis Animae *(NHC II.6)*

The *Exegesis Animae* (ExAn) is the sixth treatise of the Nag Hammadi Codex II. It was composed in the second half of the second century and provides a short account of the Gnostic myth of the feminine soul, from her fall into a body and the world to the return to her heavenly place.[9] The main elements of the narrative are the soul's fall into a body, her defilement, desolation, repentance, regeneration, and marriage to the bridegroom, her brother sent from heaven, and, as a result of this salvation, her ascent to the Father.

8. For the background of our question, see the recent, general, and detailed overview of L. Jaan, *Gnosis und Judentum. Alttestamentliche und jüdische Motiven der gnostischen Literatur und das Ursprungsproblem der Gnosis* (NHMS 75; Leiden: Brill, 2012).

9. M. Scopello, *L'Exégèse de L'Âme, Nag Hammadi Codex II,6. Introduction, traduction et commentaire* (NHS 25; Leiden: Brill, 1985); C. Kulawik, *Die Erzählung über die Seele* (TU 155; Berlin: de Gruyter, 2005); L. Roig Lanzillotta, "'Come out of Your Country and Your Kinsfolk': Abraham's Command and Ascent of the Soul in the Exegesis on the Soul (NHC II,6)", in *Abraham, the Nations, and the Hagarites. Jewish, Christian, and Islamic Perspectives on Kinship with Abraham*, eds. M. Goodman et al. (Leiden: Brill, 2010), 401–20.

Turning closer to the text, the significant sentences come from the middle of the mythological story, as the soul starts to recognize her brother.[10] The following passage reveals also the methodology of the writer[11]:

> Then gradually she recognized him, and she rejoiced once more, weeping before him as she remembered the disgrace of her former widowhood. And she adorned herself still more so that he might be pleased to stay with her. And the prophet said in the Psalms: "Hear, my daughter, and see and incline your ear and forget your people and your father's house, for the king has desired your beauty, for he is your lord.
>
> "For he requires her to turn her face from her people and the multitude of her adulterers, in whose midst she once was, to devote herself only to her king, her real lord, and to forget the house of the earthly father, with whom things went badly for her, but to remember her father who is in heaven. Thus also it was said to Abraham: 'Come out from your country and your kinsfolk and from your father's house' ⲁⲙⲟⲩ ⲉⲃⲟⲗ ϩⲙ̄ ⲡⲉ̀ⲕⲕⲁϩ ⲙⲛ̄ ⲧⲉⲕⲥⲩⲛⲅⲉⲛⲉⲓⲁ ⲁⲩⲱ ⲉⲃⲟⲗ ϩⲙ̄ⲡⲏ[ⲉ]ⲓ̣ ⲙ̄ⲡⲉ̀ⲕⲓⲱⲧ̀."
>
> 133.10–31[12]

The quotation includes two units with the same structure. In both, the argumentation starts with the mythological story, manifesting the Gnostic background on the actual state of the soul and is followed by an explanation, or rather verification, from Scripture.[13] The first quotation from Ps. 45:10-11 reinforces the soul's repentance and its turning back to her Father. This usage of biblical verses presents the personification and interiorization of the Psalm as the marriage of the nation/the church and its Savior, as it is known in the Jewish and early Christian exegetical traditions (e.g., Origen's spiritual exegesis on the Song of Songs: Ambrose, *De virginibus* 1.31).[14]

10. This happens by the will of the heavenly Father and regeneration starts with a cleansing from pollution that could be identified with the rite of baptism: see, ExAn 131, 27–34. For this motive see B. Layton, "The Soul as a Dirty Garment", *Mus* 91 (1978): 155–69.

11. The Coptic text is from the Coptic Workplace 1.1. Silver Mountain Software, Canada, 1983.

12. The translation is from Robinson, in B. Layton ed., *Nag Hammadi Codex II, 2-7 Together with XIII,2, Brit Lib.Or.4926(1), and P. Oxy. 1,654, 655* (NHS 21; Leiden: Brill, 1989) 157 and 159 with small modifications.

13. R.McL. Wilson, "Old Testament Exegesis in the Gnostic Exegesis on the Soul", in *Essays on the Nag Hammadi Texts in Honour of Pahor Labib*, ed. M. Krause (Brill: Leiden, 1975), 217–24.

14. For Ambrose and the Latin tradition of the history of the Psalm's interpretation, see D.G. Hunter, "The Virgin, the Bride and the Church. Reading Psalm 45 in Ambrose, Jerome and Augustine", *Church History* 69, no.2 (2000): 281–303.

The second part of the quotation mentions the figure of Abraham and, thus, the same mythological thinking arises. The new features are the real Lord and the king, the heavenly father with the original "house"; all these elements were used as symbols of mythological thinking. On the one hand, the writer creates a theological duality (hinting at a heavenly father[15]) in the present, worldly state, while he also describes why the *metanoia* of the soul is needed. The quotation comes from Gen. 12:1, but with significant alterations related to the biblical story, these being: it is not the Lord who commands Abraham (a simple passive form of the verb appears); and the reference to a promised land that will be shown to him, in the biblical story, is omitted.

The common motif between the two units is the departure from the country by the soul which is only apparently her own. For this concept, both references from the Old Testament fit well. As far as the structure of the passage is concerned, the mythological method of thinking reveals first its own story line and then uses the Scriptures in order to exemplify it. On the one hand, the line of the myth runs on the soul, while on the other, the Scriptures relate the story of Abraham. At this point, I conclude that there is no real exegesis of the biblical passages, and the biblical story is not the source for the narrative here. On the contrary, the writer has his own concept and proceedings on the line of his own story, while supporting its successive steps by different biblical quotations, that is, by the authority of Scripture.

In this passage, the story of Abraham was used to illustrate the state of the soul. The anonymous writer used the biblical story[16] and the example of the Patriarch in order to present his own theological perspective on repentance and the returning of the soul to her original place: her authentic, celestial origin.[17]

15. It could be a sign of the duality of the first God and the creator god, but also of the earthly and heavenly father. The former is the opinion of Scopello, *L'Exégèse*, 144. According to the opinion of other scholars, this passage is insufficient evidence to argue for a theological dualism, e.g., Kulawik, *Die Erzählung*, 204.

16. Before ending this analysis, one should mention that the author of the treatise not only used the Bible (the Old and New Testament), but also introduced frequent quotations from Homer, and, in weaving together the biblical and the classical traditions, he created an original symbolism about the Gnostic story of the Soul. For this, see M. Scopello, "Les citations d'Homère dans le Traité de L'Exégèse de l'âme", in *Gnosis and Gnosticism*, ed. M. Krause (Leiden: Brill, 1977), 3–12.

17. It is worth noting the conclusion of Lanzillotta discussing the possible parallels from the Christian tradition: "Origen and Didymus consequently not only provide exactly the same interpretation of the Genesis passage as the Exegesis on the Soul; they also combine Gen. 12:1 with the same quotation from Psalms. Even more interesting, however, is the fact that all three texts artificially introduce a gloss in order for the quotes to fit in their respective contexts": Roig Lanzillotta, "Come out of your Country", 417.

The Gospel of Philip *(NHC II.3)*

The *Gospel of Philip* belongs to the Valentinian tradition[18] and was written around the second half of the second century or the first half of the third century.[19] Its writer uses not only the name, but also the story of Abraham in its accounts of controversies on religious practices, presenting detail that had not been mentioned previously:

"When Abraham [rejoiced/laughed[20]] for him to see what he would see, [he] circumcised the flesh of the foreskin (ⲚⲦⲤⲀⲢⲜ ⲚⲦⲀⲔⲢⲞⲂⲨⲤⲦⲒⲀ), [teaching/telling] us that it is necessary to destroy the flesh (ⲚⲦⲤⲀⲢⲜ)" (82.26–8).[21]

This short fragmentary sentence provides an unique interpretation of the practice of circumcision. It is not an exact quotation from the Old Testament, but one can state with certainty that it is a witness to the author's knowledge of the Old Testament and use of allegorical exegesis.

As far as its links to the biblical sources are concerned, the thoughts of Evans, Webb, and Wiebe seem correct.[22] They suggest that the first half of the sentence with the supposed Coptic word (ⲢⲀϢⲈ, rejoiced)[23] could come from Jn 8:56 (in agreement with Schenke and the translators who followed him e.g., Menard and Janssens),[24]

18. For this Valentinian school, see the collection of B. Layton, ed., *The Rediscovery of Gnosticism. I. The School of Valentinus. Studies in the History of Religions* 41 (Supplements to Numen; Leiden: Brill, 1980); and E. Thomassen, *The Spiritual Seed: The Church of the "Valentinians"* (NHMS 60; Leiden: Brill, 1980, 2006); and Ch. Markschies, "Valentinian Gnosticism. Toward the Anatomy of a School," in *The Nag Hammadi Library after Fifty Years: Proceedings of the 1995 Society of Biblical Literature Commemoration*, eds. J.D. Turner et al. (NHMS XLIV; Leiden: Brill, 1980), 401–38.

19. For the writing see e.g., W.W. Isenberg, "The Coptic Gospel According to Philip", PhD. diss., The University of Chicago, 1968; H.M. Schenke, *Das Philippus-Evangelium (Nag-Hammadi-Codex II,3)* (TU 143; Berlin: Akademie Verlag, 1997); and R.McL Wilson, *The Gospel of Philip. Translated from the Coptic Text, with an Introduction and Commentary* (New York: Evanston, 1962).

20. Layton's addition in B. Layton ed., *Nag Hammadi Codex II,2–7 Together with XIII,2, Brit Lib.Or.4926(1), and P. Oxy. 1,654, 655* (NHS 20; Leiden: Brill, 1989), 206 and Schenke's in his first translation ("sich freute") in H.M. Schenke, "Das Evangelium nach Philippus", *ThLZ* 84, no.1 (1959): 1–26, here 23.

21. Translation from Isenberg, *The Coptic Gospel According to Philip,* with minor modifications.

22. C.A. Evans, R.A. Wiebe, and R.L. Webb, *Nag Hammadi Texts and the Bible: A Synopsis and Index* (New Testament Tools & Studies; Leiden: Brill, 1993).

23. The verb ⲢⲀϢⲈ could be the translation of the Greek χαίρειν, ἱλαρύνειν, εὐφραίνειν. W.E. Crum, *A Coptic Dictionary* (Oxford: Clarendon Press, 1939) 308B.

24. Schenke, "Das Evangelium nach Philippus", 23 and Schenke, *Das Philippus-Evangelium*, 501; J.E. Menard, *L'évangile selon Philippe: Introduction, texte, traduction, commentaire* (Strassburg-Paris: Letuzey et Ane, 1967) 109 ("se réjouit"); Y. Janssen, "L'Évangile selon Philippe", *Mus* 81 (1968): 407–14.

while the second half resembles Gen. 17:24.[25] On the reconstruction of this fragmented passage, it should be noted that there are scholars who argue that the suggested Coptic word ⲣⲁϣⲉ should be "laughed" instead of "rejoiced" (e.g., Wilson).[26] According to Wilson, if this was the case, the source could have been Gen. 17:17 (where Abraham "laughed"): "since Philip does not appear to share completely the Gnostic aversion to the Old Testament."[27] On the question of the reconstruction we could also follow Segelberg's opinion on the treatise: "These references clearly show that the author or authors of the Gospel of Philip had access to basic Old Testament teaching about the beginning of the world and of the elect people of God in Abraham".[28]

In order to understand the symbolism of the passage, it is worth noting that, behind the narrative, it represents an anthropological dualism that lies between the soul and the body, and a theological dualism between the first God and the creator archon. These concepts explain the sharp rejection of the body as it was created by the archon. In spite of this dualist framework, the figure of Abraham and his acts have a positive evaluation, but this attitude to the Old Testament is rare in the writings of the Valentinian tradition as well as in other Gnostic texts. The reason for this positivism is that the writer finds a parallel between circumcision and his concept of rejection and devaluation of the body; in this way, the biblical example finds its way into the argumentation seen in Gnostic writing. In short, according to the interpretation of the writer, the meaning of the Old Testament scene is that Abraham mortifies the flesh to attain the spirit. Going further, based on these aforementioned reasons, we should mention the author's invention connecting the motive behind the laughter and circumcision, as this invention also supports the author's implied belief concerning the body. At the same time, we should note that the main alteration in this excerpt from the biblical story, that is the omission of the covenant, is because the writer does not need it within his theological perspective.

Siker interprets the part of the sentence, ("that he was to see what [or whom] he was to see") as a clear reference to Christ.[29] In this reading—based on the supposed influence of Jn 8:56-58—Abraham's action foreshadows and anticipates the meaning of Christ's advent. This solution could be true and fits well within the context of the writing. However, I incline to the more cautious opinion of Lundhaug who writes: "While the text does not explicitly state that Abraham saw God, it emphasizes that circumcision was necessary in order for him to see what he was going to see."[30] In addition, Wolfson argues:

25. For this see Evans, Webb, and Wiebe, *Nag Hammadi Texts and the Bible*, 169.

26. Wilson, *The Gospel of Philip*, 186.

27. Ibid.

28. E. Segelberg, "The Coptic-Gospel According to Philip and its Sacramental System", *Numen* 7, no.2 (1960): 189–200.

29. J.S. Siker, "Gnostic Views on Jews and Christians in the Gospel of Philip", *NovT* 31 (1989): 275–88, here 282.

30. H. Lundhaug, *Images of Rebirth* (NHMS 73; Leiden: Brill, 2010), 262.

> The motif of Abraham's circumcision occasioning a vision of the divine—based on the exegesis of the juxtaposition of Abraham circumcising himself, Ishmael, and every other male in his household, to the epiphany of the Lord by the terebinths of Mamre and the subsequent vision of three men/angels at the entrance to his tent—is a well attested topos in midrashic and kabbalistic sources.[31]

In contemporary Jewish and Christian traditions, Abraham's circumcision received similar, but not identical interpretations. In Philo (*Migr. Abr.* 89–93) the foreskin is the symbol of the bodily passions ("excision of pleasure and all passions"). The main differences are that Philo retains the role of bodily circumcision in God's covenant with the Jews and he is critical of some Jews who want to spiritualize circumcision completely and renounce the actual rite itself. Of the earliest witness of the Christian tradition, the author of Col. 2:11 makes another allegorical interpretation: "in whom also ye are circumcised with the circumcision made without hands, in putting off the body of the sins of the flesh by the circumcision of Christ" (ἐν ᾧ καὶ περιετμήθητε περιτομῇ ἀχειροποιήτῳ ἐν τῇ ἀπεκδύσει τοῦ σώματος τῆς σαρκός, ἐν τῇ περιτομῇ τοῦ Χριστοῦ). The Epistle pairs circumcision with baptism (Col. 2:12), creating the basis for the later Christian understanding of the gesture. In Justin Martyr's writings, these two rituals pertain to the same sacrament (see *Dialogue with Trypho* 19).[32]

Thus, we could state that the story of Abraham in this Gnostic passage was not only known before the Valentinian writer but he positively used it without a literal quotation of the Old or New Testament. From this point a new question could emerge: was the author a Jewish Christian, who affirmed the legitimacy of circumcision based on the Jewish tradition, but who added a new spiritual significance to it, or was he rather a Gentile Christian, who attempted to replace the circumcision of the flesh with the circumcision of the spirit following the Pauline understanding?[33] It is well-known that the figure of Abraham and his circumcision was a central element of the controversy over religious practices between Jews and Christians, as well as amongst early Christians. Thus, the meaning and the significance of this passage—just as those elsewhere in this "gospel"—should be assessed in the context of this dispute. In this way, we can suppose that the writing on Abraham's circumcision occupies the position of the bodily understanding ("it is necessary to destroy the flesh (ⲚⲦⲤⲀⲢⲜ")) but it is used as a prerequisite for his spiritual experience).

31. E.R. Wolfson, "Becoming Invisible: Rending the Veil and the Hermeneutic of Secrecy in the Gospel of Philip", in *Practicing Gnosis. Ritual, Magic, Theurgy and Liturgy in Nag Hammadi, Manichaean and Other Ancient Literature. Essays in Honor of Birger A. Pearson*, eds. A.D. DeConick et al. (Leiden: Brill, 2013), 118–35, here 118–19.

32. For this, with other occurrences see R. Jensen, *Baptismal Imagery in Early Christianity: Ritual, Visual and Theological Dimension* (Ada, MI: Baker, 2012), 86.

33. For this question I am indebted to Wolfson, *Becoming Invisible*, 119.

The Second Treatise of the Great Seth (NHC VII.2)

This writing exemplifies so-called Sethian literature,[34] from Codex VII of the Nag Hammadi Library. Along with the pattern of Sethian thinking in the treatise, there is a significant Christian influence, including the part describing a revelation delivered by the ascended Savior Christ to his followers, who are "from the height." The revelation describes the heavenly triad in a heavenly world of light, with the heavenly church. Further, it covers the history of the redemption: the role of the Savior as the heavenly Son from his descent into the world of creation that is ruled by Jaldabaoth and his archons, taking the body of an earthly man, the docetic passion during the crucifixion and his return to the celestial home, to the end-time wedding feast. The writing is polemical, standing in opposition to the Christians of the church ("the few and uninstructed") while using motifs of Christian revelation.[35]

In the second half of the text, the polemical attitude prevails, and becomes stronger. The target of the rejection is not only the Christian faith and its practices, but the text addresses Jews and some Gnostic schools and their doctrines:

> For Adam was a laughingstock, since he was created from the image of type of man by the Hebdomad, as if he had become stronger than me and my brothers. We are innocent with respect to him, since we have not sinned. And Abraham and Isaac and Jacob were a laughingstock, since they were given a name by the Hebdomad, the counterfeit fathers, as if he had become stronger than my brothers and me. We are innocent with respect to him, since we have not sinned.[36]
>
> 62.27–63.3

The use of antithetical pairs between the Old Testament figures and the writer's group illustrates precisely the negative relationship with the tradition of the Old

34. H.M. Schenke, "Das sethianische System nach Nag-Hammadi-Handschriften", in *Studia Coptica*, ed. P. Nagel (Berliner Byzantinistiche Arbeiten 45; Berlin: Akademie-Verlag, 1974), 165–73; and H.M. Schenke, "The Phenomenon and Significance of Gnostic Sethianism", in *The Rediscovery of Gnosticism*, Vol. 2: *Sethian Gnosticism*, ed. B. Layton (Studies in the History of Religions 41; Supplements to Numen; Leiden: E. J. Brill, 1981), 588–616; and J. Turner, *Sethian Gnosticism and the Platonic Tradition* (Bibliothèque Copte de Nag Hammadi, Section: «Études» 6; Québec: Les Presses de l'Université Laval; Leuven: Peeters, 2001).

35. According to van den Broek, it implies that the writing "was written after the rift between gnostic and non-gnostic Christians had become a fact and the two groups had started to exclude each other from the true Church" and for this reason could be dated to the last decade of the second or the first decade of the third century. For this see R. van den Broek, *Gnostic Religion in Antiquity* (Cambridge: Cambridge University Press, 2013), 111.

36. The translation is from G. Riley, "Second Treatise of the Great Seth" (with minor modifications), in *Nag Hammadi Codex VII*, ed. B.A. Pearson, (NHMS 30; Leiden: Brill, 1996), 129–200, here 181–3.

Testament. The list begins with Adam, continues with the Patriarchs and ends with the names of David, Solomon, the 12 prophets, Moses, and John the Baptist (63.4–34). They are the main characters of the Old Testament for the anonymous author.

For the concept of rejection under investigation, one could assume that the saying which comprises the three Patriarch's names could be a shortened form of self-revelation, namely how God makes himself known in this form as God of Abraham, of Isaac, and of Jacob (e.g., Exod. 3:15). This scriptural tradition could be the source for the name-giving of the Patriarchs referenced in the quotation ("they were given a name by the Hebdomad", ⲉⲁⲩϯ ⲣⲁⲛ ⲉⲣⲟⲟⲩ ⲉⲃⲟⲗ ϩⲓⲧⲙ̄ ⲡⲓⲙⲉϩⲥⲁϣϥ). If this hypothesis is true, a trace of the theophany found in Exodus 3 or its history of reception can be unveiled in the present treatise. In any case, one is able to understand accurately why and how the writer used the tradition of the Old (or New) Testament.

In scholarly literature, this treatise has a prominent place, especially due to its relation to Old Testament material, but opinions vary. S.E. Robinson argues: "As elsewhere in Gnosticism, the God of the Old Testament is here identified with an inferior being, and those who serve him or observe his Law, including Adam, Abraham, Isaac, Jacob, David, Moses, and the other prophets and John the Baptist, are called laughingstocks."[37] Nagel creates a categorization, where he quotes this present passage (in its first type),[38] arguing: "die offene, höhnische Absage an Gestalten und Begebenheiten des Alten Testaments."[39] In Tröger's explanation this passage is "ein markantes Beispiel für die polemische Behandlung biblischer Traditionen,"[40] while Bethge argues "Es gibt auch keine Uminterpretation, sondern nur totale Ablehnung und Konfrontation."[41]

37. S.E. Robinson, "Second Treatise of the Great Seth", in *Claremont Coptic Encyclopedia*, ed. A.S. Atiya, Vol, 7, 2117b-2118b. On the website: http://ccdl.libraries.claremont.edu/cdm/ref/collection/cce/id/1726

38. Nagel differentiated six types of interpretation of the OT: 1. a clear rejection of figures and events from the Old Testament (e.g., The Second Discourse of the Great Seth, The Testimony of Truth); 2. an interpretation that changes the roles and functions of OT characters and events (The Hypostasis of the Archons, On the Origin of the World, The Apocalypse of Adam); 3. a corrective interpretation is closely related to point 2 (The Apocryphon of John); 4. a neutral and allegorical interpretation (Justin's Baruch, Pistis Sophia); 5. the quoting of a single Old Testament verse, is order to support Gnostic teachings or practices (the Valentinians); 6. etiological and typological interpretations of the Old Testament, sometimes with a soteriological tendency (Gospel of Philip, The Tripartite Tractate, Gospel of Truth, The Exegesis on the Soul, Pistis Sophia). See: P. Nagel, "Die Auslegung der Paradieserzählung in der Gnosis", in *Altes Testament, Frühjudentum, Gnosis*, ed. K.W. Tröger (Berlin: Evangelische Verlagsanstalt, 1980), 49–70.

39. Nagel, "Die Auslegung der Paradieserzählung".

40. See Tröger, *Die Gnosis*, 120; Similarly, Bethge, "Die Ambivalenz", 106.

41. Bethge, "Die Ambivalenz", 106.

The mythical background of the passage is worth exploring. In the Sethian tradition, there is the aforementioned theological dualism between the first God and the inferior Creator. In the quotation mentioned above, the Creator and his brothers or his creatures, the archons, can be found in the sphere of Seven and they constitute it. It could also signify only Jaldabaoth, the first archon, as mentioned e.g., in the account of Irenaeus (*Adv Haer.* 1.5.2). According to the ancient cosmological view, the seven planets are the seven personified spherical powers,[42] but in these systems, as is well-known from other Gnostic systems, the archons are hostile powers, since they work against the created man and his salvation, keeping humanity in slavery and ignorance. According to this, salvation comes from above, from the eighth sphere, with the coming of the Savior in the form of the heavenly Christ.[43]

Considering this essential duality, the radical rejection of the Old Testament, as it was known in the roughly contemporary Marcion school and other Gnostic schools, becomes more understandable. According to this view, all the events and persons that are positive in the Old Testament are negative and should be rejected and eliminated. Consequently, because of the devaluation of the Jewish biblical tradition, its significance lies with this negative attitude and its presentation of the negative side of the author's own line of tradition. From this twisted perspective, the biblical creation of Adam could be interpreted as a fake creation by the Hebdomad, and the Old Testament Patriarchs could be considered as *counterfeit fathers*. In this way the writer constructs a reverse historical timeline of Israel's history and heroes and, in doing so, subverts the tradition, with his own version developing on the basis seen in the Bible (e.g., in Hebrews).[44]

To sum up, from this Sethian perspective, in the earthly cosmos that is ruled by the archons, the Patriarchs and the prophets of the Old Testament belong to the hostile powers, and, since they are lead astray by the archons, they preached their Law and rules. Thus, only with the rejection of the Old Testament tradition and

42. For astrological theories in late antiquity, see H. Bietenhard, *Die himmlische Welt im Urchristentum und Spätjudentum* (Tübingen: J.C.B. Mohr, 1951). For Gnostics see e.g., N.D. Lewis, *Cosmology and Fate in Gnosticism and Graeco-Roman Antiquity* (NHMS 81; Leiden: Brill, 2013).

43. It is the reason why we could find the identification between their heavenly figures, e.g. in Epiphanius of Salamis, *Panarion* 40.7.4. For this see Riley, introduction to "Second Treatise of the Great Seth" (with minor modifications), in *Nag Hammadi Codex VII*, ed. B.A. Pearson, (NHMS 30; Leiden: Brill, 1996), 131.

44. Other similar lists can be found in Josh. 24:1-15, Ezek. 20:2-38, Neh. 9:6-38, Pss. 135:1-26 and 77:1-72. Hellenistic Judaism contributes Jdt. 5:5-21, Wis.10:16–11:14, 1 Macc. 2:51-59, *4 Macc.* 16.2–25, and most impressively of all, the "Now let us praise famous men" set piece in Sir. 44:1–50:24. For this list, see: R.A. Kitchen, "Making the Imperfect Perfect. The Adaptation of Hebrews 11 in the 9th Mēmrā of the Syriac Book of Steps", in *The Reception and Interpretation of the Bible in Late Antiquity: Proceedings of the Montreal Colloquium in Honour of Charles Kannengiesser, 11–13 October 2006*, eds. L. DiTommaso et al. (Leiden: Brill, 2008), 235.

with dismissing these persons (i.e., the chosen race) could the audience of the tractate correctly understand the message of the Savior and reach the heavenly bridal chamber. In this explanation, theological and mythological reasoning are amalgamated into the establishing story of origin, and serve as a basis for the exegetical methodology that inevitably leads to the rejection of the Old Testament and the figures of the Patriarchs.

Apocalypse of Adam *(NHC V.5)*

The *Apocalypse of Adam* is the final treatise in Codex V of Nag Hammadi, and indeed Epiphanius mentions the "apocalypses of Adam" that were used by the Gnostics (*Pan.* 26.8.1),[45] thus it may have existed beyond the Library corpus. It is a part of so-called Adam literature.[46]

Concerning its content, the work presents itself as an apocalypse that was given to Adam after the fall. He taught it to Seth, while explaining their creation, the fall, the hostile creator God and his archons, and the work of the Savior: the Illuminator. The story of the revelation here tells us in some detail the transmission, loss, and recovery of redemptive knowledge: the gnosis. The account of this revelation is significant: Adam receives it in dream as a vision ("Now I slept in the thought of my heart"). Then in his discourse the sentence continues:

> "And I saw three men before me whose likeness I was unable to recognise."[47]
>
> 65.26–9

According to the *opinio communis* of scholars, this short sentence is a witness of the biblical story of the three visitors of Abraham at Mamre.[48] If this is the

45. For an introduction to the treatise see e.g., G.V. MacRae, "Introduction", in *Nag Hammadi Codices V, 2–5 and VI: With Papyrus Berolinensis 8502, 1 and 4*, ed. D. M. Parrott (Leiden: Brill 1979), 151–3; and F. Morard, "L'Apocalypse d'Adam de Nag Hammadi. Un essai d'interprétation", in *Gnosis and Gnosticism. Papers Read at the Seventh International Conference on Patristic Studies Oxford 1975*, ed. M. Krause (NHS 8; Leiden: Brill, 1977), 35–42. See also: G.W.E. Nickelsburg, "Some Related Traditions in the Apocalypse of Gnosticism", in *The Rediscovery of Gnosticism. Proceedings of the International Conference on Gnosticism at Yale New Haven, Connecticut, 1978. Bd. 2: Sethian Gnosticism*, ed. B. Layton (SHR 41; Leiden: Brill, 1981), 515–39.

46. For good introductions to the literature, its categorization, and main questions, see M. Stone, *A History of the Literature of Adam and Eve* (Atlanta, GA: SBL 1992); M. De Jonge and J. Tromp, eds., *The Life of Adam and Eve and Related Literature* (Sheffield: Sheffield Academic Press, 1997); G.A. Anderson, M.E. Stone, and J. Tromp, eds., *Literature on Adam and Eve: Collected Essays* (Leiden: Brill, 2000).

47. The translation is from MacRae, in Parrott, *Nag Hammadi Codices*, 159.

48. See G.M. Shellrude, "Nag Hammadi Apocalypses: A Study of the Relationship of Selected Texts to the Traditional Apocalypse", PhD diss., University of St Andrews, 1986.

case, the text alludes to Gen. 18:2, and thus is another witness to the story of Abraham.

Further, the text reveals the meaning and the relevance of this short sentence. The passage quoted above continues with the explanation: "because they were not from the powers of god who created us." (65.29–32). Here, the story returns to its Gnostic context and introduces the theological duality of the first God and the creator god on the one hand, and the different types of creatures on the other, using a quotation from Gen. 1:26 and the biblical story of creation. Thus, one can suppose that the three visitors were not created by the creator god through his power, and for this reason they have another likeness (ⲉⲓⲛⲉ in Coptic). Unfortunately, the next lines are so fragmentary that only a few words are readable (e.g., they surpassed, glory), thus no conclusion can be drawn for certain about these three men. Based on these details, I am only able to suggest that the text's topic is the three visitors coming from the heavenly world, and one or all three of them are the mediator(s) of the revelation: the saving knowledge.

The genre of this tract is a contemporary revelatory account, starting with a circumstantial setting (the dream), continuing with the angelic visitors and the mediation of the knowledge, with reference to their indescribable appearance.[49]

The sentences do not offer us any other indications for identifying with certainty the source or any contemporary traditions related to the Mamre theophany. The Jewish allegoric interpretation, expressed by Philo, *Abr.* 121—according to whom it was a vision of God's powers, both creative and royal—has to be excluded. Most Christian interpretations, in which the Church Fathers saw either one God, the Word, or the Lord among the three visitors (e.g., Justin, Tertullian, Clement of Alexandria, Origen, Irenaeus), or *the holy and consubstantial Trinity* (e.g., Cyril of Alexandria, Augustine, Athanasius of Sinai, Ambrose of Milan, Maximus the Confessor), have to be excluded as well.[50]

In the sixth century, Procopius of Gaza mentions that in the interpretation of the biblical story, "Some take the three men as three angels" (*Comm. Gen.* 18 [PG 87/1:364B]), probably supported by LXX Ps. 78:25 ("man ate the bread of the angels,"). The same interpretation was also used in Late Second Temple Judaism (e.g. Josephus, *Ant.* 1.196, Philo, *Abr.* 115).[51] In light of these interpretations, it

49. Ibid., 293.

50. For the Jewish and Christian interpretations see A.E. Arterbury, *Entertaining Angels. Early Christian Hospitality in its Mediterranean Setting* (Sheffield: Sheffield Phoenix Press, 2005), esp. 59–70. See also E. Grypeou and H. Spurling, "Abraham's Angels: Jewish and Christian Exegesis of Genesis 18–19", in *The Exegetical Encounter Between Jews and Christians in Late Antiquity*, eds. E. Grypeou et al. (Leiden: Brill, 2009), 181–202; and B.B. Bucur, "The Early Christian Reception of Genesis 18: From Theophany to Trinitarian Symbolism", *Journal of Early Christian Studies* 23, no.2 (2015): 245–72.

51. K.P. Sullivan, *Wrestling with Angels: A Study of the Relationship Between Angels and Humans in Ancient Jewish Literature and the New Testament* (Leiden: Brill, 2004), esp. ch. 2.1.

seems the example quoted above has similarities to this reading. Thus, the early Jewish or Christian angelological traditions that identified the three visitors with three angelic beings could have been the source of the text, since its writer could have been acquainted with this type of interpretation of the story of the visitors of Abraham.

Pistis Sophia

Pistis Sophia was written in the third to fourth century and presents a fully developed Gnostic system. In it the resurrected Savior explains the mysteries of the heavenly world, the creation, and salvation for the disciples. In the dialogue between Mary and Jesus on the fate of the Patriarchs, the Savior says[52]:

> I forgave Abraham, and Isaac and Jacob, all their sins and iniquities, and I gave to them the mystery of light in the aeons and I put them in the place of Jabraoth and all the archons who have repented. And when I go to the height and I am about to go to the light I will carry their souls with me to the light.
>
> III.135[53]

The Patriarchs and the Prophets belong to the part of Jabraoth (who is the brother of Sabaoth Adamas and rules over six aeons); after the repentance the Savior gives them the possibility to return to the middle-place. In this strongly mythologized but theological concept that is far away from the Old Testament narratives, we are facing an interpretation where Abraham is among the fallen ones but in the two-stage process of redemption; with the Savior's help he is lifted up to the kingdom of light, that is the perfect and ultimate redemption. The process starts with the repentance and the practice of the mysteries of light and they are rewarded by being placed in the location of Jabraoth together with the rulers, and are waiting until the Savior Jesus takes them into the place of light.[54] Undoubtedly, the figure of Abraham does not play an active role as an independent person, but exemplifies repentance and the belief that characterizes other Old Testament figures (who are linked with the figure of Jabraoth) as well. Going further, we can suppose that the quotation demonstrates the underlying positive evaluation of the Old Testament, or at least the main characters in it, among them Abraham.

52. Macdermot and Schmidt, *Pistis Sophia*, 702.

53. The translation is from Macdermot and Schmidt, *Pistis Sophia*, 703, with minor amendments.

54. For the cosmological system in the Pistis Sophia, see E.M. Evans, "The Books of Jeu and the Pistis Sophia. System, Practice, and Development of a Religious Group", PhD diss., University of Edinburgh, 2011, esp. ch. 3.

Secondary Sources

Marcion (Irenaeus, Adv Haer. *4.8.1.)*

Marcion was not only regarded as a heretic thinker, theologian, and radical exegete of the Gospel in the early second century CE, but he was also a founder of a church. Although his doctrines are sometimes separated from the category of the ancient Gnosis, there are reasons for which we must include him.[55] Justin Martyr's *Apology* (*c.* 153/154) mentions Marcion's name for the first time and describes his activity and teachings. The two main sources for the reconstruction of his system come from Irenaeus' *Adversus Haereses* and Epiphanius in his *Panarion* (*c.* 375), who refute his school and church. Although Marcion's theology was refuted and attacked by the Church Fathers, the Marcionite church in the East and traces of Marcionite groups are found in Arabic sources as late as the tenth century.[56]

It is not necessary to assess the rich scholarly literature on the sources and assessment of Marcionite teachings here,[57] but even though they do not provide a coherent picture of Marcionite doctrine or its alterations by its disciples, there is no doubt that his teaching focuses on theological dualism. Concerning the author's exegetical methodology and the source's critical methodology, it is also beyond dispute that he created his own canon from the Gospel of Luke and the *Corpus Paulinum*. Equally though, he does not accept the Old Testament in his canon; he treats it as the testimony of the Creator who is opposed to the Father of Jesus Christ.[58] In this theological dualism, according to which the God of Jesus had been totally unknown before his first appearance and miracle, Marcion concluded that there could be no connection between Jesus and the Hebrew Scriptures. Thus, although in the case of Marcion one is unable to find a reference to the person or the biblical story of Abraham, Marcion and his school need to be mentioned since he created a dualist system with theological reasoning that is paradigmatic in the evaluation of other heretical examples.

In Irenaeus' refutation of Marcion, this theological dualism was the reason why he rejected Marcion's opinion and the exclusion of the Patriarchs (Abel, Enoch, Noah, and Abraham) from salvation. According to Irenaeus, behind this theological conviction there was a simple logical argumentation which points to an opposition

55. Markschies left him outside of the Gnosis: Ch. Markschies, *Die Gnosis* (Munich: C.H. Beck, 2001).

56. M. Frenschkowski, "Marcion in arabischen Quellen", in *Marcion und seine kirchengeschichtliche Wirkung/Marcion and His Impact on Church History*, eds. G. May et al. (Berlin: Walter de Gruyter, 2002), 39–63.

57. For the present state of the literature see, S. Moll, "At the Left Hand of Christ: The Arch-Heretic Marcion", PhD diss., University of Edinburgh, 2009.

58. For the Marcionite revisions of the Scripture we accept the conclusions of Schmid; in the case of the Pauline corpus the deletions are in fact the only safe textual changes we may assume for Marcion: U. Schmid, *Marcion und sein Apostolos* (Berlin: de Gruyter, 1995).

to the original Christian message, with this reverse logic leading to mistaken conclusions. Following the rhetorical strategy of Irenaeus, Marcionite theology fails to reach the meaning of the salvation:

> Saying all things in direct opposition to the truth, that Cain, and those like him, and the Sodomites, and the Egyptians, and others like them, and, in fine, all the nations who walked in all sorts of abomination, were saved by the Lord, on His descending into Hades but on the other side: the serpent which was in Marcion declared that Abel, and Enoch, and Noah, and those other righteous men who sprang from the patriarch Abraham, with all the prophets, and those who were pleasing to God, did not partake in salvation. For since these men, he says, knew that their God was constantly tempting them, so now they suspected that He was tempting them, and did not run to Jesus, or believe His announcement: and for this reason he declared that their souls remained in Hades.
>
> *Adv. Haer.* 1.27.3[59]

The source of this story is an early Christian teaching where the Patriarchs, prophets, and the Jews are in Hades and are waiting for the coming of the Savior. However, Marcion gave it an opposite meaning based on his theological teaching on the unknown God. He made a distinction not only between the two gods, but between two Messiahs also, "one who appeared under Tiberius, another who is promised by the Creator."[60] The Patriarchs and the prophets saw the descended Savior but did not believe in him and so they remained in Hades, waiting because they knew that their God was always tempting them, and so they suspected that he was tempting them again (*Adv. Haer.* 1.27.3).[61] This understanding could be a consequence of the literal interpretation. This non-allegorical, non-figurative interpretation of the prophets and, indeed, of all the Hebrew Scriptures occurs in some other refutations (e.g., Origen, *De Princ.* 2.5.2). It is worth mentioning a further passage from Irenaeus (*Adv.Haer.* 4.8.1):

> Vain, too, is [the effort of] Marcion and his followers when they [seek to] exclude Abraham from the inheritance, to whom the Spirit through many men, and now by Paul, bears witness, that "he believed God, and it was imputed unto him for righteousness." (Rom. 4:3). And the Lord [also bears witness to him,] in the first place, indeed, by raising up children to him from the stones, and making his seed as the stars of heaven, saying, "They shall come from the east and from the west, from the north and from the south, and shall recline with Abraham, and Isaac,

59. The translation is from A. Roberts and W. Rambaut, trans., *Ante-Nicene Fathers*, Vol. 1., eds. A. Roberts et al. (Buffalo, NY: Christian Literature Publishing, 1885).

60. Tertullian, *Adv. Marc.* 1.15.6.

61. For this, see Moll ibid, who notes that Epiphanius also reports this story, but in his version the reason is other: they do not follow Christ because they stuck to their own God (*Pan.* 42.4.3–4).

and Jacob in the kingdom of heaven;" (Mt. 8:11) and then again by saying to the Jews, "When ye shall see Abraham, and Isaac, and Jacob, and all the prophets in the kingdom of heaven, but you yourselves cast out." (Lk. 13:28). This, then, is a clear point, that those who disallow his salvation, and frame the idea of another God besides Him who made the promise to Abraham, are outside the kingdom of God, and are disinherited from [the gift of] incorruption, setting at naught and blaspheming God, who introduces, through Jesus Christ, Abraham to the kingdom of heaven, and his seed, that is, the Church, upon which also is conferred the adoption and the inheritance promised to Abraham.[62]

In this passage the Church Father Irenaeus refutes Marcion with arguments from New Testament verses. He not only insists that the testimony of the Old Testament has the same authority with the one of the New Testament, but he also uses the authoritative sayings of the Lord and Saint Paul, who referred to righteous ones, and among them, to Abraham. Thus, Irenaeus proclaims his own teaching, arguing for universal salvation and, at the same time, for the unity of the God of the Old and New Testaments. The verses on the promise that serve and prove the unity of the Old and the New Testament, form also the basis of the theological doctrines on the heavenly kingdom. This idea is in opposition with Marcion's teaching that neglects not only the Old Testament with the figure of Abraham, but also the validity of universal salvation.[63]

Ophites and Sethians (Irenaeus, Adv. Haer. *1.30.10)*

Irenaeus' account of the mythological story of the Ophites[64] and Sethians includes some details that were missing from the aforementioned examples. The main actors are Jaldabaoth and Sophia, both of whom operate in the worldly sphere and participate actively in forming and constructing the history of humanity as if it would be a history of their and their parts' struggle for reaching and possessing the fallen divine light:

62. The translation is from Roberts and Rambaut, *Ante-Nicene Fathers*, with minor modifications.

63. From later refutations we can refer to the example of Theodoret of Cyrus, because, according to him, Marcion calls the patriarchs and prophets lawbreakers (*Haer. fab. com.* 24.41).

64. The evaluation of this section of Irenaeus leads us into the complex history of traditions from the writings of the Library, from Origen (*Contra Celsum*) and from the Ophite Diagrams. For recent scholarly opinion about this account and its connection to other heretical movements and writings from Nag Hammadi, see, T. Rasimus, *Paradise Reconsidered in Gnostic Mythmaking: Rethinking Sethianism in Light of the Ophite Evidence* (NHMS 68; Leiden: Brill, 2009).

> Jaldabaoth himself chose a certain man named Abraham from among these, and made a covenant with him, to the effect that, if his seed continued to serve him, he would give to them the earth for an inheritance. Afterwards, by means of Moses, he brought forth Abraham's descendants from Egypt, and gave them the law, and made them the Jews.
>
> *Adv.Haer.* 1.30.10

As in the aforementioned writings, Jaldabaoth represents the creator god, the God of the Old Testament. This broad identification is clearly detectable from an earlier passage where Jaldabaoth claims vainly to be the only God in words that are reminiscent of YHWH's monotheistic claim (*Adv.Haer.* 1.30.6). The new—and until now unmentioned—motif that occurs in this quotation is the covenant. Corresponding to the biblical accounts, the creator God chooses Abraham to give him the entire earth. But the author goes further and uses this motive to explain the nation's origin; through Moses he creates the Jewish nation out of his descendants.

According to the source that Irenaeus uses, the Ophites (and Sethians) rewrite the Old Testament in order to create their own mythological story of origin and destiny. As mentioned before, in this mythological history Abraham, among other important figures, has a negative role, similar to the figures who were subservient to the archons. This understanding was well known in Sethian thinking (e.g., 2LogSeth), but was also present in some Valentinian writings and in the texts belonging to the other Gnostic schools, such as the Marcionite.[65]

Heracleon

Heracleon was a Valentinian author who wrote the first extant, systematic commentary on the Gospel of John in the second half of the second century.[66] Scholars have different opinions concerning the place of his activity; Pagels situates him in Alexandria, but according to Rudolf he was active in Rome.[67]

His commentary is lost but some fragments are preserved in Origen's similar work, since he quoted, commented, and refuted the opinion of Heracleon.[68]

65. In Irenaeus there is another example from the Gnostics whose arithmological speculation mentions Abraham's tribes (*Adv. Haer.* 1.18.3).

66. A.E. Brooke, *The Fragments of Heracleon* (Cambridge: Cambridge University Press, 1891) and T.J. Pettipiece, "Heracleon: Fragments of Early Valentinian Exegesis. Text, Translation, and Commentary", PhD diss., Wilfrid Laurier University, 2002.

67. E. Pagels, *Johannine Gospel in Gnostic Exegesis: Heracleon's Commentary on John* (Nashville: Abingdon Press, 1973), 29; Rudolph, *Gnosis. The Nature and History of Gnosticism*, 323.

68. In the Commentary of Origen there are 48 fragments from Heracleon, next to them there are two others, in Clem.Al., *Strom.* 6.71–3; Photius, *Ep.* 143).

Thomassen states, based on the list of the fragments, that "It is uncertain whether Heracleon's Commentary covered the whole text of the gospel."[69] The relevant fragment is a part of smaller group that is concerned with the dispute of Jesus with the Jews (Frgs. 44–9). Fragment 44 comes from Origen's work 20.168–70 as a commentary on John 8:43-4[70]:

> Heracleon, however, attempts to give a reason for why they are not able to hear the word of Jesus nor understand his language in that passage: "you are from your father the devil" (ὑμεῖς ἐκ *τοῦ πατρὸς τοῦ* διαβόλου ἐστέ). He says with these words: Why are you not able to hear what I say? Or that "you are from your father the devil? (Διατί δε οὐ δύνασθε ἀκούειν τὸν λόγον τὸν ἐμόν ἤ ὅτι ὑμεῖς ἐκ τοῦ πατρὸς τοῦ διαβόλου ἐστέ) Showing them their nature "from the substance of the devil" (ἐκ τῆς οὐσίας τοῦ διαβόλου) and proclaims to them that they are not children of Abraham for they would not hate him, nor of God for they would not love him.[71]

Unlike our other examples, this text focuses on the words of the Savior in the Gospel. By means of allegorical exegesis and by his interpretation of Jesus' words, Heracleon demonstrates his doctrine on the three, pneumatic, psychic, and bodily natures.[72] Accepting the results of Thomassen, who doubts this evaluation of Heracleon's teaching,[73] I am inclined to think that Heracleon, keeping his tripartite teaching, considered the different response to the Savior's call as an explanation of these different categories. Thus, salvation is for all, but people's response to it reveals their human natures.[74] In this way, in Heracleon's understanding, the οὐσία explains rejection of Jesus by the Pharisees as a consequence of their "substance."

By means of this teaching, Heracleon was able to make a new distinction between the Jews and the Christians, and to formulate a special teaching about the

69. E. Thomassen, "Herakleon", in *The Legacy of John. Second Century Reception of the Fourth Gospel* (Leiden: Brill, 2010), 176.

70. The Greek text is from Pettipiece, "Heracleon", 143.

71. Translation from Pettipiece, "Heracleon", 143 with minor modifications.

72. For the Valentinian understanding of the three natures, see I. Dunderberg, "The School of Valentinus", in *A Companion to Second-Century Christian "Heretics"*, eds. A. Marjanen et al. (Leiden: Brill, 2005), 68–70.

73. E.g., B. Aland, "Erwählungstheologie und Menschenklassen-lehre: Die Theologie des Herakleon als Schlüssel zum Verständnis der christlichen Gnosis", in *Gnosis and Gnosticism*, ed. Martin Krause (NHS 8; Leiden: Brill, 1977), 148–81; A. Wucherpfennig, *Heracleon Philologus: Gnostiche Johannesexegese im zweiten Jahrhundert* (WUZNT 142; Tübingen: Mohr Siebeck, 2002); J. Holzhausen, "Die Seelenlehre des Gnostikers Herakleon", in *Psyche—Seele—Anima: Festschrift für Karin Alt*, ed. G. Buch (Beiträge zur Altertumskunde 109; Stuttgart: Teubner, 1998), 279–300.

74. Thomassen, *Herakleon*.

origin of the Pharisees from the substance of evil (in this construction the matter has no *physis*). Further, the Jews are presented as the children of Abraham, the psychics, in accordance with Heracleon's understanding. This is different from the widespread Valentinian understanding where the church belongs to this category and is identified with the psychics (e.g., *Gosp. Truth*; *Interp. Know.*).

The genre of the text is a genealogy, rooted in the tradition of Abraham as ancestor of the Jews. This idea is widespread and occurs not only in Jewish writings (e.g., as father of the Jews according to Josephus, *Ant.* 1.158; as forefather in Josephus, *War* 5.380), but also in Christian writings (e.g. Rom. 4:1; Eusebius, *Praep. Evang.* 9.19.2–3), and even in pagan texts (e.g., Apollonius Molon).[75]

In the passage quoted, this widespread motif is used in a totally different way than in the previous accounts examined so far. Based on the structure of the fragment, its source is the words spoken by the Lord in the Gospel. Moreover, from them the author derived their allegorical interpretation, in which the Jews are independent from the Pharisees, with their own origin. Also, at a new interpretative level in this Valentinian context, the category of Abraham's children received its symbolic understanding as representative of the psychic nature.

Theodotus

Theodotus, a contemporary of Valentinus, provides another example of how the figure of Abraham was used in eastern Valentinianism.[76] Nothing is known about Theodotus' life and doctrines, except for what Clement of Alexandria's *Excerpts from Theodotus and of the so-called eastern doctrine of Valentinianism* mentions.[77] This work is a compilation of different authentic writings interwoven with the comments of Clement. In *Exc.* 18, Clement mentions:

> When the Saviour descended, he was seen by the angels and so they proclaimed him. But he was also seen by Abraham and the other righteous men who are in Paradise on his right hand. For he says, "He rejoiced to see my day," (Ηγαλλιάσατο γάρ, φησίν, ἵνα ἴδῃ τὴν ἡμέραν τὴν ἐμήν) that is the advent in the flesh. Wherefore, the risen Lord preached the good tidings to the righteous who are in Paradise, and moved them and translated them and they shall all "live under his shadow"

75. For these examples and other occurrences see B. van der Lans, "Belonging to Abraham's Kin: Genealogical Appeals to Abraham as a Possible Background for Paul's Abrahamic Argument", in *Abraham, the Nations, and the Hagarites: Jewish, Christian, and Islamic Perspectives on Kinship with Abraham*, eds. M. Goodman et al. (Leiden: Brill, 2010), 307–18.

76. F. Sagnard, *Clément d' Alexandrie: Extraits ex Theodote* (SC 23, Paris : Editions du Cerf, 1970).

77. R.P. Casey, ed. and trans., *The Excerpta ex Theodoto of Clement of Alexandria* (London/Cambridge: Christophers, 1934).

(ἐν τῇ σκιᾷ αὐτοῦ ζήσονται). For the advent here is a shadow of the Saviour's glory which is with the Father, and a shadow of light is not darkness but illumination (φωτὸς δὲ σκιὰ οὐ σκότος, ἀλλὰ φωτισμός ἐστιν).

The passage is a testimony of Theodotus' exegesis of Jn 8:56. Jesus' sentence in the Gospel implies Abraham's name, while the Valentinian writer mentions it later, together with reference to the righteous. In the first sentence, there is a particular early Christian teaching on the descent of the Savior, who gradually takes the form of the beings and identifies with them. Further, the text hints at the incarnation, the embodiment (the advent in flesh), and to the transfiguration and resurrection, when he preached the gospel in Paradise. Moreover, in the last sentence the text identifies the antediluvian condition of creation with the saved condition, through the symbol of the shadow, which hints at the Garden of Paradise.[78]

If we look more closely at the methodology of Theodotus, it seems that the location of the Savior's speech is Paradise, where Abraham is placed with other righteous men. This verse starts the exegesis to express a particular Valentinian teaching on redemption and illumination. The author uses the figure of Abraham so that his speculation corresponds with the biblical concept of Paradise as Abraham's bosom (cf. Lk. 16:22). This motive can reveal the main and radical alteration to the standard narrative, because this Paradise is not the final place where people reside, but rather a transitionary one where the Savior preaches the Gospel and from where the Savior moved and translated the righteous ones to his light. With the symbol of a light's shadow, the narrative turns back to the Mosaic creation account and receives a new focus, through which the author is able to create his own interpretation. To present his theological concept one more change needs to be applied, namely the advent of the Savior takes the place of the advent of God; that is a change between judgement and redemption and illumination.

The Refutatio *on One Valentinian Teaching*

The *Refutatio*[79] gives a radical allegorical interpretation that supports a unique understanding of Abraham. As a part of the Valentinian allegorical interpretation and arithmology in VI.34, the anonymous author mentions Abraham in this way:

> In this manner these subdivide the parts within the Pleroma. Now likewise the parts in the Ogdoad have been subdivided, and there has been projected Sophia, which is according to them, the mother of all living creatures (μήτηρ πάντων τῶν ζώντων), and the joint fruit of the Pleroma who is the Logos, and the other aeons who are the celestial angels that have citizenship in Jerusalem which is above, which is in heaven (Ιερουσαλὴμ τῇ ἄνω, τῇ ἐν οὐρανοῖς). For this

78. This description is supported by references to Heb. 1:3 and 2 Cor. 4:6.

79. The authorship is debated in scholarly literature, but this is beyond the scope of this paper.

> Jerusalem is Sophia, she is outside (the Pleroma) and her spouse is the joint fruit of the Pleroma. And the Demiurge projected souls, for this (Sophia) is the essence of souls (οὐσία ψυχῶν). This (the Demiurge), according to them is Abraham and these (the souls) are the children of Abraham (οὗτός ἐστι κατ' αὐτοὺς Ἀβρα<ὰ>μ καὶ ταύτα<ς> τοῦ Ἀβραὰμ τὰ τέκνα).
>
> *Ref.* 6.34.3.3–6.34.5.1

The introduction to this chapter reports that the sphere of the creator is the sphere of the Soul. This teaching, coming from a Platonic interpretation of the world's Soul, provides the key for understanding the last sentences, according to which Abraham and his descendants belong to the psychics. This is the first main alteration compared to other Valentinian accounts. Thus, I support Dundenberg's evaluation: "Thus, it seems that the psychic offspring is especially associated with the Jews rather than with 'Church Christians' mentioned in Irenaeus."[80] This type of interpretation is not unknown in the Valentinian exegetical tradition, but this version exemplifies a new, unusual stratum which deepens the allegorical interpretation and identifies Abraham with the Creator: the Demiurge.

Conclusion

To conclude, this review of the figure of Abraham and his biblical stories in the Gnostic traditions reveals a unique, polymorphic, and complex mix of traditions that are both interrelated and interconnected. Although there is no common, one-sided picture of the Old Testament, nor a common attitude to the biblical tradition, a commonly accepted methodology for the interpretation of the texts, nor a common genre, the late antique writers used the name and the story of the Patriarch Abraham regardless of the school to which they belonged. The surviving texts, which belong to the Valentinian, Sethian, and the Marcionian schools, show that their authors were acquainted with the Patriarch. Nevertheless, for them, Abraham was not as central an Old Testament character compared to others, such as Adam and Seth. However, in spite of his relative absence, the material related to him characterizes not only the different Gnostic schools, but also their divergent exegetical methods.

For Böhlig, the reason for Abraham's absence, from a theological viewpoint, is that: "Seth, der Sohn Adams, hat sich im Synkretismus des Hellenismus einen hervorragenden Platz erobert. Er ist der spiritualisierte Abraham."[81] This statement could be applied to some Sethian writings, where Seth has a central and essential

80. I. Dunderberg, *Beyond Gnosticism. Myth, Lifestyle and Society in the School of Valentinus* (New York: Columbia University Press, 2008), 141.

81. A. Böhlig, "Zur Frage nach den Typen des Gnostizismus und seines Schrifttums", in *Gnosis und Synkretismus. Gesammelte Aufsätze zur spätantiken Religionsgeschichte*, ed. A. Böhlig (Tübingen: Mohr Siebeck, 1989), 225.

role, but we cannot prove this. The examples we have looked at testify not only to the presence of Abraham but his relevance in creating and articulating Gnostic ideas. In addition, in some cases, the figure of Abraham is a spiritualized one, but he still has his own character, independent of the negative or positive role that he plays within these texts.

These writings use a plethora of methodological strategies, which vary from literal to ethical and allegorical exegesis. Besides this variety, which indicates the manner in which the authors considered their own theological doctrines, the presence of Old Testament writings, regardless of how radically the writers used them, is significant. Naturally, there is no doubt as to the compound influence of the New Testament as well on these texts, and both signify not only the main source here, but also the authority of Scripture for these Gnostic writings. It is also beyond question that the nature of this "authority" varies wildly, from complete aversion to a positive evaluation of Scripture.

Further, in the examples quoted above, the writers reflect on contemporary controversies over differing religious and theological questions, such as circumcision, the command of God for a religious calling and conversion (*metanoia*), hospitality, or the name of the Patriarchs. All these theological topics were part of acrimonious disputes between movements and schools in the first Christian centuries and, if my hypothesis is right, all of them are reflected in early Christianity. The status of the Old Testament is questioned primarily through the figure of Abraham, but these examples and writings belong firmly within the Christian tradition. From this theological perspective, these passages are significant for their mythological context and expressions and, hopefully, now, after this short investigation, these are more clearly understandable.

One should also mention that some other Abrahamic episodes are missing from the quoted texts. These are the story of Melchizedek (although a revelatory text under his name exists [NHC IX.1] it does not mention Abraham), the episodes in which his wife appears, or his children, his prayers, the *Akedah*, etc. Although this chapter does not aim to investigate their absence, it would appear that the authors did not need these Abrahamic narratives to express their theological argument.

In spite of the different strategies of argumentation, theological contents, and mythological backgrounds of these Gnostic texts, they have some common features. This seemingly arbitrary selection, with all its inconveniences and weaknesses, displays the following characteristics: (1) in all the examples the rejection of the God of the Old Testament occurs; (2) the supposition that evil and/or inferior power(s) created and rule the world is present; (3) the texts have their own teaching about Jesus, which differs from the teaching of the church (in some cases it is definitely docetic Christology); and, lastly (4) the adherents claim, through these examples, that they have been liberated from obedience to the evil angels and/or the creator, through knowledge. All these features together offer the possibility for raising a minimum definition of ancient Gnosis.

BIBLIOGRAPHY

Primary Sources

Adams, S.A., *Baruch and the Epistle of Jeremiah: A Commentary Based on the Texts in Codex Vaticanus* (SCS; Leiden: Brill, 2014).

Brankaer, J. and H.G. Bethge., eds., *Codex Tschacos: Texte und Analysen* (TU 161; Berlin: de Gruyter, 2007).

Broshi, M., E. Eshel, J. Fitzmeyer, E. Larson, C. Newsom, L. Schiffman, M. Smith, M. Stone, J. Strugnell, and A. Yardeni, *Qumran Cave 4: XIV, Parabiblical Texts, Part 2* (DJD 19. Oxford: Clarendon Press, 1995).

Casey, R.P., ed. and trans., *The Excerpta ex Theodoto of Clement of Alexandria* (London/Cambridge: Christophers, 1934).

Charlesworth, J.H., ed., *The Old Testament Pseudepigrapha* (Garden City, NY: Doubleday, 1983 and 1985).

Crum, W.E., *A Coptic Dictionary* (Oxford: Clarendon Press, 1939).

Das, A.A., *Galatians. Concordia Commentary* (Saint Louis, MO: Concordia Publishing House, 2014).

De Boer, M.C., *Galatians: A Commentary* (The New Testament Library; Louisville, Ky.: Westminster John Knox Press, 2011).

deSilva, D.A., *4 Maccabees: Introduction and Commentary on the Greek Text in Codex Sinaiticus* (SCS; Leiden: Brill, 2006).

Feldman, L.H., *Judean Antiquities Books 1–4. Flavius Josephus: Translation and Commentary 3* (Leiden: Brill, 2000).

Friedman, R.E., *Commentary on the Torah* (New York, NY: HarperCollins, 2001).

Hossfeld, F-L and E. Zenger., *Psalms 2: A Commentary on Psalms 51–100* (Hermeneia; Minneapolis: Fortress Press, 2005).

International Encyclopedia of Unified Science, 2 vols. (Chicago: University of Chicago Press, 1962).

Jacobson, H., *A Commentary on Pseudo-Philo's Liber Antiquitatum Biblicarum with Latin Text and English Translation,* 2 vols. (AGAJU 31; Leiden: Brill, 1996).

Jewett, R., *Romans: A Commentary* (Minneapolis: Fortress, 2007).

Johnson, L.T., *Hebrews: A Commentary* (Louisville, KY: Westminster John Knox, 2012).

Kaster, R.A., ed., *C. Suetonius Tranquillus—De Grammaticis et Rhetoribus* (Oxford: Clarendon, 1995).

Keener, C.S., *Acts: An Exegetical Commentary: 3:1–14:28*, Vol. 2 (Grand Rapids: Baker Academic, 2013).

Krause, M., ed., *The Coptic Encyclopedia* (London: Macmillan, 1991).

Lane, W.L., *Hebrews 1–8. Word Biblical Commentary* (Dallas: Word, 1998).

Littman, R.J., *Tobit: The Book of Tobit in Codex Sinaiticus* (SCS. Leiden: Brill, 2008).

Luz, U., *Matthew 1–7: A Commentary* (trans. W.C. Linss; Minneapolis: Augsburg, 1985).

Macdermot, V and C. Schmidt, trans. and eds., *Codex Askewianus. Pistis Sophia* (NHS 9; Leiden: Brill, 1978).

Macdermot, V. and C. Schmidt, trans. and eds., *The Books of Jeu and the Untitled Text in the Bruce Codex* (NIHS 13; Leiden: Brill, 1978).
Martyn, J.L., *Galatians: A New Translation with Introduction and Commentary* (AB; London: Doubleday, 1997).
Menard, J.E., *L'évangile selon Philippe: Introduction, texte, traduction, commentaire* (Strasbourg/Paris: Letuzey et Ane, 1967).
Moo, D.J., *Galatians: Baker Exegetical Commentary on the New Testament* (Grand Rapids: Baker Academic, 2013).
Pagels, E., *Johannine Gospel in Gnostic Exegesis. Heracleon's Commentary on John* (Nashville: Abingdon Press, 1973).
Parrott, D.M., *Nag Hammadi Codices V, 2–5 and VI: With Papyrus Berolinensis 8502, 1 and 4* (Leiden: Brill, 1979).
Pauly, A.F., A.G. Wissowa, W. Kroll, K. Witte, K. Mittelhaus, and K. Ziegler, eds. *Paulys Realencyclopädie der classischen Altertumswissenschaft: neue Bearbeitung*, 83 vols. (Stuttgart: J. B. Metzler, 1894–1980).
Pearson, B.A., ed., *Nag Hammadi Codex VII* (NHMS 30; Leiden: Brill, 1996).
Perrot, C. and P.M. Bogaert, *Les antiquités bibliques. Tome 2: introduction littéraire, commentaire et index* (SC 230; Paris: Editions du Cerf, 1976).
Pettipiece, T.J., "Heracleon: Fragments of Early Valentinian Exegesis. Text, Translation, and Commentary", PhD diss., Wilfrid Laurier University, 2002.
Piovanelli, P., "The Story of Melchizedek with the Melchizedek Legend from the Chronicon Paschale. A New Translation and Introduction", in *Old Testament Pseudepigrapha: More Noncanonical Scriptures,* Vol. 1, eds. R. Bauckham, J.R. Davila, and A. Panayotov (Grand Rapids, MI: William B. Eerdmans, 2013), 64–81.
Sarna, N.M., ed., *The JPS Torah Commentary: Genesis* (Philadelphia: The Jewish Publication Society, 1994).
Schoedel, W.R., *Ignatius of Antioch: A Commentary on the Letters of Ignatius of Antioch* (Philadelphia: Fortress, 1985).
Terian, A., "Philonis De visione trium angelorum ad Abraham: A New Translation of the Mistitled De Deo", *SPhA* 28 (2016): 77–107.
Von Rad, G., *Genesis. A Commentary. Revised edition* (Philadelphia: The Westminster Press, 1972).
Wilson, R. McL., *The Gospel of Philip. Translated from the Coptic Text, with an Introduction and Commentary* (New York: Evanston, 1962).
Wright, N.T., "The Letter to the Romans. Introduction, Commentary, and Reflections", in *The New Interpreter's Bible*, ed. L.E. Keck (Nashville: Abingdon, 2002), 393–770.
Wucherpfennig, A., *Heracleon Philologus: Gnostiche Johannesexegese im zweiten Jahrhundert* (WUZNT 142; Tübingen: Mohr Siebeck, 2002).

Secondary Sources

Ackerman, S., "Women in Ancient Israel and the Hebrew Bible", *Oxford Research Encyclopedia of Religion*, http://religion.oxfordre.com/view/10.1093/acrefore/9780199340378.001.0001/acrefore-9780199340378-e-45.
Adams, S.A., "Reframing Scripture: A Fresh Look at Baruch's So-Called 'Citations'", in *Scriptural Authority in Early Judaism and Ancient Christianity*, eds. I. Kalimi, T. Nicklas, and G.G. Xeravits (Berlin: de Gruyter, 2013) 63–83.

Adams, S.A., "The Characterization of Disciples in Acts: Genre, Method, and Quality", in *Characters and Characterization in Luke-Acts*, eds. F. Dicken and J. Snyder (LNTS 548; London: Bloomsbury, 2016), 155–68.

Adams, S.A. and S.M. Ehorn, eds., *Composite Citations in Antiquity:* Vol.1: *Jewish, Graeco-Roman, and Early Christian Uses* (LNTS 525; London: Bloomsbury/T&T Clark, 2016).

Adams, S.A. and S.M. Ehorn, eds., *Composite Citations in Antiquity:* Vol. 2: *New Testament Uses* (LNTS 593; London: Bloomsbury/T&T Clark, 2018).

Adams, S.A., "Movement and Travel in Philo's Migration of Abraham: The Adaptation of Genesis and the Introduction of Metaphor", *SPhA* 30 (2018): 47–70.

Adams, S.V., *The Reality of God and Historical Method: Apocalyptic Theology in Conversation with N.T. Wright* (Downers Grove, IL.: IVP Academic, 2015).

Aland, B., "Erwählungstheologie und Menschenklassen-lehre: Die Theologie des Herakleon als Schlüssel zum Verständnis der christlichen Gnosis", in *Gnosis and Gnosticism*, ed. M. Krause (Leiden: Brill, 1977), 148–81.

Alexander, P.S., "Retelling the Old Testament", in *It Is Written: Scripture Citing Scripture. Essays in Honour of Barnabas Lindars*, eds. D.A. Carson and H.G.M. Williamson (Cambridge: Cambridge University Press, 1988), 99–118.

Allison, Jr., D.C., *Testament of Abraham* (Berlin/New York: de Gruyter, 2003).

Alonso-Núñez, J.M., "An Augustan World History: The 'Historiae Philippicae' of Pompeius Trogus", *Greece and Rome* 34, no.1 (1987): 56–72.

Alter, R., *The Art of Biblical Narrative* (New York: Basic Books, 1981).

Andersen, S.M., and S. Chen, "The Relational Self: An Interpersonal Social-Cognitive Theory", *Psychological Review* 109, no.4 (2002): 619–45.

Anderson, G.A., and J.S. Kaminsky, eds., *The Call of Abraham: Essays on the Election of Israel in Honor of Jon D. Levenson* (CJAS 19; Notre Dame: University of Notre Dame Press, 2013).

Anderson. G.A., M.E. Stone and J. Tromp, eds., *Literature on Adam and Eve: Collected Essays* (Leiden: Brill, 2000).

Arterbury, A.E., *Entertaining Angels. Early Christian Hospitality in its Mediterranean Setting* (Sheffield: Sheffield Phoenix Press, 2005).

Arterbury, A.E., "Zacchaeus: 'A Son of Abraham'?", in *Biblical Interpretation in Early Christian Gospels:* Vol.3: *The Gospel of Luke*, ed. T. Hatina (LNTS 376; London/New York: T&T Clark, 2010), 18–31.

Ashton, J., *Understanding the Fourth Gospel* (2nd edn.; Oxford: Oxford University Press, 2007).

Auerbach, E., *Mimesis: The Representation of Reality in Western Literature* (trans. W. Trask; Princeton: Princeton University Press, 1953).

Avioz, M., "Josephus's Portrayal of Lot and His Family", *JSP* 16, no.1 (2006): 3–13.

Avioz, M. "Josephus' Land Theology: A Reappraisal", in *The Gift of the Land and the Fate of the Canaanites in Jewish Thought*, eds. K. Berthelot, J.E. David, and M. Hirshman (New York: Oxford University Press, 2014) 36–49.

Avioz, M., *Josephus' Interpretation of the Books of Samuel* (LSTS 86; London: Bloomsbury, 2015).

Bakhos, C., *The Family of Abraham: Jewish, Christian, and Muslim Interpretations* (Cambridge, MA: Harvard University Press, 2014).

Balz, H., and G. Schneider, eds., *The Exegetical Dictionary of the New Testament* (Grand Rapids: Eerdmans, 1993).

Bar-Kochva, B., *The Image of the Jews in Greek Literature: The Hellenistic Period* (Berkeley: University of California Press, 2010).

Bar Kochva, B., "On Abraham and the Egyptians: A Hellenistic-Greek or a Hellenistic-Jewish Composition", *Tarbiz* 70 (2011): 327–52.
Barclay, J.M., *Paul and the Gift* (Grand Rapids: Eerdmans, 2015).
Barth, K., *The Epistle to the Romans* (trans. E. C. Hoskyns; Oxford: Oxford University Press, 1968).
Barthes, R., *Image-Music-Text*, ed. and trans. S. Heath (New York: Farrar, Straus and Giroux, Hill and Wang, 1977).
Bartlett, J. R., *1 Maccabees* (Sheffield: Sheffield Academic Press, 1998).
Barton, T., *Ancient Astrology* (London: Routledge, 1994).
Bauckham, R., "The Dispute over Abraham. A New Translation and Introduction", in *Old Testament Pseudepigrapha: More Noncanonical Scriptures,* Vol. 1., eds. R. Bauckham, J.R. Davila, and A. Panayotoy (Grand Rapids, MI: William B. Eerdmans, 2013), 53–8.
Bauckham, R., "The Inquiry of Abraham (A Possible Allusion to the Apocalypse of Abraham). A New Translation and Introduction", in *Old Testament Pseudepigrapha: More Noncanonical Scriptures,* Vol. 1., eds. R. Bauckham, J.R. Davila, and A. Panayotoy (Grand Rapids, MI: William B. Eerdmans, 2013), 59–63.
Bechmann, U., "Genesis 12 and the Abraham-Paradigm Concerning the Promised Land", *Ecumenical Review* 68, no. 1 (2016): 62–80: https://doi.org/10.1111/erev.12199.
Beentjes, P.C., "Ben Sira 44:19–23—The Patriarchs: Text, Tradition, Theology", in *Studies in the Book of Ben Sira*, eds. G.G. Xeravits and J. Zsengellér (JSJSup 127; Leiden: Brill, 2008), 209–28.
Begg, C.T. "The 'Classical Prophets' in Josephus' 'Antiquities.'" *Louvain Studies* 13, no.4 (1988): 341–57.
Begg, C.T., "Josephus' Retelling of 1 Kings 1 for a Graeco-Roman Audience", *TynBull* 57, no.1 (2006): 85–108.
Begg, C.T., "Genesis in Josephus", in *The Book of Genesis: Composition, Reception, and Interpretation*, eds. C.A. Evans, J.N. Lohr, and D.L. Peterson (Leiden: Brill, 2012), 303–29.
Bennema, C., *A Theory of Character in New Testament Narrative* (Minneapolis: Fortress Press, 2014).
Berger, P.L., and T. Luckmann, *The Social Construction of Reality: A Treatise in the Sociology of Knowledge* (Garden City, New York: Doubleday Anchor, 1967).
Bernstein, M.J., "4Q252: From Re-Written Bible to Biblical Commentary", *JJS* 45, no.1 (1994): 1–27.
Bernstein, M.J., "'Rewritten Bible': A Generic Category Which Has Outlived its Usefulness?", *Textus* 22, no.1 (2005): 169–96.
Bernstein, M.J., "The Genesis Apocryphon: Compositional and Interpretive Perspectives", in *A Companion to Biblical Interpretation in Early Judaism*, ed. M. Henze (Grand Rapids: Eerdmans, 2012), 157–79.
Berthelot, K., *In Search of the Promised Land? The Hasmonean Dynasty Between Biblical Models and Hellenistic Diplomacy* (JAJSup 24; Göttingen: Vandenhoeck & Ruprecht, 2017).
Bethge, H.G., "Die Ambivalenz alttestamentlicher Geschichstraditionen in der Gnosis", in *Altes Testament-Frühjudentum-Gnosis: Neue Studien zu Gnosis und Bibel*, ed. K.W. Tröger (Berlin: Evangelsiche Verlagsantalt, 1980), 89–109.
Bickerman, E.J., "A Jewish Festal Letter of 124 B.C.E. (2 Macc 1:1–9)", in *Studies in Jewish and Christian History*, Vol. 1 (Leiden: Brill, 2007).
Bietenhard, H., *Die himmlische Welt im Urchristentum und Spätjudentum* (Tübingen: J.C.B. Mohr, 1951).

Birley, A.R., *The Roman Government of Britain* (Oxford: Oxford University Press, 2005).

Birnbaum, E., *The Place of Judaism in Philo's Thought: Israel, Jews, and Proselytes* (BJS 290; Atlanta, GA: SBL, 1996).

Birnbaum, E., "Exegetical Building Blocks in Philo's Interpretation of the Patriarchs", in *From Judaism to Christianity: Tradition and Transition: A Festschrift for Tomas H. Tobin, S.J., on the Occasion of His Sixty-fifth Birthday*, ed. P. Walters (Leiden: Brill, 2010), 69–92.

Birnbaum, E., "What in the Name of God Led Philo to Interpret Abraham, Isaac, and Jacob as Leaning, Nature, and Practice?", *SPhA* 28 (2016): 273–96.

Blenkinsopp, J., *Abraham: The Story of a Life* (Grand Rapids, MI: Wm B. Eerdmans, 2015).

Bloch, R.S., *Antike Vorstellungen vom Judentum: Der Judenexkurs des Tacitus im Rahmen der griechisch-römischen Ethnographie* (Historia-Einzelschriften 160; Stuttgart: Franz Steiner, 2002).

Boda, M.J., D.K. Falk, and R.A. Werline, eds., *Seeking the Favor of God*, Vol. 1: *The Origins of Penitential Prayer in Second Temple Judaism* (SBLEJL 21; Atlanta, GA: SBL, 2006).

Boda, M.J., D.K. Falk, and R.A. Werline, eds., *Seeking the Favor of God*, Vol. 2: *The Development of Penitential Prayer in Second Temple Judaism* (SBLEJL 22; Atlanta, GA: SBL, 2007).

Boda, M.J., D.K. Falk, and R.A. Werline, eds., *Seeking the Favor of God*, Vol. 3: *The Impact of Penitential Prayer beyond Second Temple Judaism* (SBLEJL 23 ; Atlanta, GA: SBL, 2008).

Bogaert, P-M., *Abraham dans la Bible at dans la tradition Juive* (Brussels: Institutum Iudaicum, 1977).

Böhlig, A., *Gnosis und Synkretismus: Gesammelte Aufsätze zur spätantiken Religionsgeschichte* (Tübingen: Mohr Siebeck, 1989).

Bohm, M., *Rezeption und Funktion der Vatererzahlungen bei Philo von Alexandria: Zum Zusammenhang von Kontext, Hermeneutik und Exegese im fruhen Judentum* (BZNW 128; Berlin: De Gruyter, 2005).

Bollansée, J., *Hermippos of Smyrna and His Biographical Writings: A Reappraisal* (Leuven: Peters, 1999).

Borgen, P., *Philo of Alexandria: An Exegete For His Time* (NovTSup 86; Leiden: Brill, 1997).

Bos, A.P., "Abraham and the Enkyklios Paideia in Philo of Alexandria", in *Abraham, the Nations, and the Hagarites: Jewish, Christian, and Islamic Perspectives on Kinship with Abraham*, eds. M. Goodman, G.H. van Kooten, and J.T.A.G.M. van Ruiten (Leiden: Brill, 2010), 163–75.

Bram, J.R., *Ancient Astrology Theory and Practice: Matheseos Libri VIII by Firmicus Maternus* (Park Ridge, NJ: Noyes Press, 1975).

Brawley, R.E., "Abrahamic Covenant Traditions and the Characterization of God in Luke-Acts", in *The Unity of Luke-Acts*, ed. J. Verheyden (BETL 142; Leuven: Leuven University Press, 1999), 109–32.

Brawley, R.L., *Luke-Acts and the Jews: Conflict, Apology, and Conciliation* (SBLDS 33; Atlanta, GA: SBL 1987).

Brock, S.P., "Abraham and the Ravens: A Syriac Counterpart to Jubilees 11–12 and its Implications", *JSJ* 9, no.1 (1978): 132–52.

Brock, S.P., "Creating Women's Voices: Sarah and Tamar in Some Syriac Narrative Poems", in *The Exegetical Encounter between Jews and Christians in Late Antiquity*, eds. E. Grypeou and H. Spurling (Leiden: Brill, 2009), 125–41.

Brooke, A.E., *The Fragments of Heracleon* (Cambridge University Press: Cambridge, 1891).

Brueggemann, W., *A Commentary on Jeremiah: Exile and Homecoming* (Grand Rapids, MI: William B. Erdmans, 1998).

Bucur, B.B., "The Early Christian Reception of Genesis 18: From Theophany to Trinitarian Symbolism", *JECS* 23, no.2 (2015): 245–72.

Burnett, D.A., "'So Shall Your Seed Be': Paul's Use of Genesis 15:5 in Romans 4:18 in Light of Early Jewish Deification Traditions", *Journal for the Study of Paul and his Letters* 5, no.2 (2015): 211–36.

Callaway, J.A., "Burials in Ancient Palestine: From the Stone Age to Abraham", *The Biblical Archaeologist* 26, no.3 (1963): 73–91.

Calvert, N.L., "Abraham", in *Dictionary of Paul and His Letters*, eds. G.F. Hawthorne, R.P. Martin, and D.G. Reid (Leicester: IVP, 1993), 1–8.

Calvert-Koyzis, N., *Paul, Monotheism and the People of God: The Significance of Abraham Traditions for Early Judaism and Christianity* (JSNTSupp 273; London: T&T Clark, 2004).

Cameron, A.,. *The Last Pagans of Rome* (Oxford: Oxford University Press, 2011).

Campbell, C.R., *Paul and Union with Christ: An Exegetical and Theological Study* (Grand Rapids: Zondervan, 2012).

Campbell, D.A., "The Story of Jesus in Romans and Galatians", in *Narrative Dynamics in Paul: A Critical Assessment*, ed. B.W. Longenecker (Louisville, Ky: Westminster John Knox, 2002), 97–124.

Campbell, D.A., *The Quest for Paul's Gospel: A Suggested Strategy* (London: T&T Clark, 2005).

Campbell, D.A., *The Deliverance of God: An Apocalyptic Rereading of Justification in Paul* (Grand Rapids: Eerdmans, 2009).

Campbell, D.A., *Paul: An Apostle's Journey* (Grand Rapids: Eerdmans, 2018).

Carden, M., *Sodomy: A History of a Christian Biblical Myth* (London: Equinox, 2004).

Carroll, R.P., *From Chaos to Covenant: Use of Prophecy in the Book of Jeremiah* (London: SCM, 1981).

Cazeaux, J., *La trame et la chaine: ou les structures littéraires et l'exégèse dans cinq des traités de Philon d'Alexandrie* (ALGHJ 15; Leiden: Brill, 1983).

Chadwick, H., "Justification by Faith and Hospitality", in *Studia Patristica*, Vol. 4, ed. F.L. Cross (T.U. 79; Berlin: Akademie-Verlag, 1961), 281–5.

Charlesworth, J.H., ed., *The Old Testament Pseudepigrapha* (Garden City, NY: Doubleday, 1983 and 1985).

Charlesworth, J.H., and G.S. Oegema, *The Pseudepigrapha and Christian Origins: Essays From the Studiorum Novi Testamenti Societas* (New York: T&T Clark International, 2008).

Chatman, S., *Story and Discourse: Narrative Structure in Fiction and Film* (Ithaca: Cornell University Press, 1978).

Clement Hoskyns, E., *The Fourth Gospel* (London: Faber and Faber, 1947).

Clines, D., *The Theme of the Pentateuch* (JSOTSup 10; Sheffield: Sheffield Academic Press, 1989).

Coats, G.W., "Abraham's Sacrifice of Faith: A Form-Critical Study of Genesis 22", *Interpretation: A Journal of Bible and Theology* 27, no. 4 (1973): 389–400.

Cohen, S.J.D., *Josephus in Galilee and Rome: His Vita and Development as a Historian* (Leiden: Brill, 2002).

Cole, Z., *Numerals in Early Greek New Testament Manuscripts* (NTTSD 53. Leiden: Brill, 2017).

Collins, J.J., "Artapanus", in *The Old Testament Pseudepigrapha*, ed. J.H. Charlesworth (Garden City, NY: Doubleday, 1983 and 1985), 889–903.

Collins, J.J., "A Syntactical Note (Genesis 3:15): Is the Woman's Seed Singular or Plural?", *TynBull* 48, no. 1 (1997): 139–48.

Cover, M., "Philo's De mutatione nominum: Sample Commentary, Exegetical Structure, and Its Place in the 'Abrahamic Cycle' of the Allegorical Commentary", paper presented at the SBL Annual Meeting, San Antonio, November 2016: http://torreys.org/philo_seminar_papers/.

Cramer, F.H., *Astrology in Roman Law and Politics* (Philadelphia: The American Philosophical Society, 1954).

Crawford, C.D., "On the Exegetical Function of the Abraham/Ravens Tradition in Jubilees 11", *HTR* 97, no.1 (2004): 91–7.

Croisille, J-M., "Le sacrifice d'Iphigénie dans l'art romain et la littérature latine", *Latomus* 22 (1963): 209–25.

Crüsemann, F., *Das Alte Testament als Wahrheitsraum des Neuen: die neue Sicht der christlichen Bibel* (Gütersloh: Gütersloher Verlagshaus, 2011).

Dahl, N.A., "La terre où coulent le lait et le miel selon Barnabé 6, 8–19", in *Aux Sources de la tradition chrétienne*, ed. M.M. Goguel (Neuchâtel-Paris: Delachaux & Niestle, 1950), 62–70.

Dahl, N.A., "The Story of Abraham in Luke-Acts", in *Studies in Luke-Acts*, eds. L.E. Keck and J.L. Martyn (Mifflintown, PA: Sigler Press, 1966), 139–58.

Daly, R.J., "The Soteriological Significance of the Sacrifice of Isaac", *CBQ* 39, no.1 (1977): 45–75.

Darr, J.A., *On Character Building: The Reading and the Rhetoric of Characterization in Luke-Acts* (LCBI; Louisville: Westminster/John Knox Press, 1992).

Davies, E.W., "The Inheritance of the Firstborn in Israel and the Ancient Near East", *Journal of Semitic Studies* 38, no. 2 (1993): 175–91.

De Jonge, M. and J. Tromp, *The Life of Adam and Eve and Related Literature* (Sheffield: Sheffield Academic Press, 1997).

De Temmerman, K. and E. van Emde Boas, eds., *Characterization in Ancient Greek Literature: Studies in Ancient Greek Narrative*, Vol.4 (MneSup 411; Leiden: Brill, 2018).

Delaney, C., *Abraham on Trial: The Social Legacy of Biblical Myth* (Princeton: Princeton University Press, 1998).

Dèmare-Lafont, S., "The Status of Women in the Legal Texts of the Ancient Near East", in *The Bible and Women: An Encyclopedia of Exegesis and Cultural History—Torah*, eds. I. Fischer, M. Navarro Puerto, A. Taschl-Erber, and J. Økland (Atlanta: SBL, 2011), 109–32.

deSilva, D.A., *Perseverance in Gratitude: A Socio-Rhetorical Commentary on the Epistle "to the Hebrews"* (Grand Rapids: Eerdmans, 2000).

Desmond Alexander, T., *Abraham in the Negev: A Source Critical Investigation of Genesis 20:1–22:19* (Carlisle: Paternoster, 1997).

Di Lella, A.A., "The Deuteronomic Background of the Farewell Discourse in Tob 14:3–11", *CBQ* 41 (1979): 382–3.

Docherty, S.E., *The Jewish Pseudepigrapha* (London: SPCK, 2014).

Docherty, S.E., "Why So Much Talk? Direct Speech as a Literary and Exegetical Device in Rewritten Bible with Special Reference to Pseudo-Philo's Biblical Antiquities", *Svensk Exegetisk Årsbok* 82 (2017): 52–75.

Docherty, S.E., "Composite Citations and Conflation of Scriptural Narratives in Hebrews", in *Composite Citations in Antiquity*: Vol. 2: *New Testament Uses*, eds. S.A. Adams and S.M. Ehorn (LNTS 593; London: Bloomsbury T&T Clark, 2018) 190–208.

Doran, R., "Cleodemus Malchus", in *The Old Testament Pseudepigrapha*, ed. J.H. Charlesworth (Garden City, NY: Doubleday, 1983 and 1985), 882–6.

Dover, K.J., *Greek Homosexuality* (Cambridge, MA: Harvard University Press, 1978).

Dunderberg, I., "The School of Valentinus", in *A Companion to Second-Century Christian "Heretics"*, eds. A. Marjanen and P. Luomanen (Leiden: Brill, 2005), 64–99.

Dunderberg, I., *Beyond Gnosticism. Myth, Lifestyle and Society in the School of Valentinus* (New York: Columbia University Press, 2008).

Eco, U., *A Theory of Semiotics* (Bloomington: Indiana University Press, 1976).

Edwards, M.J., "A Christian Addition to Alexander of Lycopolis", *Mnemosyne* 42 (1989): 483–7.

Ehorn, S.M., "Galatians 1:8 and Paul's Reading of Abraham's Story", *JTS* 64, no.2 (2013): 439–44.

Endres, J.C., *Biblical Interpretation in the Book of Jubilees* (CBQMS 18; Washington: Catholic Biblical Association of America, 1987).

Erlemann, K., "Die Datierung des ersten Klemensbriefes—Anfragen an eine Communis Opinio", *NTS* 44 (1998): 591–607.

Evans, C.A., R.A. Wiebe, and R.L. Webb, eds., *Nag Hammadi Texts and the Bible: A Synopsis and Index* (New Testament Tools & Studies; Leiden: Brill, 1993).

Evans, E.M., "The Books of Jeu and the Pistis Sophia. System, Practice, and Development of a Religious Group", PhD Diss., University of Edinburgh, 2011.

Exum, J.C., *Fragmented Women: Feminist (Sub)versions of Biblical Narratives* (2nd edn.; London: Bloomsbury/T&T Clark, 2016).

Fatehi, M., *The Spirit's Relation to the Risen Lord in Paul: An Examination of Its Christological Implications* (Tübingen: Mohr Siebeck, 2000).

Feldman, L.H., "Hellenizations in Josephus' Jewish Antiquities: The Portrait of Abraham", in *Josephus, Judaism, and Christianity*, eds. L. H. Feldman and G. Hata (Leiden: Brill, 1987), 133–53.

Feldman, L.H., *Josephus's Interpretation of the Bible* (HCS 27; Berkeley: UCLA Press, 1998).

Feldman, L.H., "The Destruction of Sodom and Gomorrah according to Philo, Pseudo-Philo and Josephus", *Henoch* 23 (2001): 185–98.

Fisk, B.N., "Offering Isaac Again and Again: Pseudo-Philo's Use of the Aqedah as Intertext", *CBQ* 62, no.3 (2000): 481–507.

Fitzmyer, J.A., *Tobit* (CEJL; Berlin: de Gruyter, 2003).

Forster, E.M., *Aspects of the Novel* (New York: Harcourt, 1927).

Foster, P., "The Epistles of Ignatius of Antioch", in *The Writings of the Apostolic Fathers*, ed. P. Foster (London: Bloomsbury/T&T Clark, 2007), 81, 107.

Foster, R.B., *Renaming Abraham's Children: Election, Ethnicity, and the Interpretation of Scripture in Romans 9* (WUNT II; Tübingen: Mohr Siebeck, 2016).

Foster, R.J., *The Significance of Exemplars for the Interpretation of the Letter of James* (WUNT II, 376; Tübingen: Mohr Siebeck, 2014).

Franxman, T.W., *Genesis and the Jewish Antiquities of Flavius Josephus* (Rome: Pontifical Biblical Institute, 1979).

Frenschkowski, M., "Marcion in arabischen Quellen", in *Marcion und seine kirchengeschichtliche Wirkung/Marcion and His Impact on Church History*, eds. G. May and K. Greschat (Berlin: de Gruyter, 2002), 39–63.

Frow, J., *Character and Person* (Oxford: Oxford University Press, 2014).

Fuchs, E., "The Literary Characterisation of Mothers and Sexual Politics in the Hebrew Bible", in *Women in the Hebrew Bible: a Reader*, ed. A. Bach (New York/London: Routledge, 1999) 127–40.

Fuller, M.E., *The Restoration of Israel: Israel's Re-gathering and the Fate of the Nations in Early Jewish Literature and Luke-Acts* (BZNW 138; Berlin: de Gruyter, 2012).
Gathercole, S.J., *Where is Boasting? Early Jewish Soteriology and Paul's Response in Romans 1-5* (Grand Rapids: Eerdmans, 2002).
Gaventa, B.R., "The Singularity of the Gospel: A Reading of Galatians", in *Pauline Theology, Vol. 1: Thessalonians, Philippians, Galatians, Philemon*, ed. J.M. Bassler (Minneapolis: Fortress, 1991), 147–59.
Geertz, C., *The Interpretation of Cultures; Selected Essays* (New York: Basic, 1973).
Geljon, A-C., "Abraham in Egypt: Philo's Interpretation of Gen 12:10–20", *SPhA* 28 (2016): 297–319.
Gera, D.L., *Judith* (CEJL; Berlin: de Gruyter, 2014).
Ginzberg, L., *The Legends of the Jews, (Vol. I-V11)* (Philadelphia: Jewish Publication Society, 1909–38).
Gilmour, R., *Juxtaposition and the Elisha Cycle* (LHBOTS 594; London: Bloomsbury/T&T Clark, 2014).
Glicksman, A.T., *Wisdom of Solomon 10: A Jewish Hellenistic Reinterpretation of Early Israelite History through Sapiential Lenses* (DCLS 9; Berlin: de Gruyter, 2011).
Gnuse, R., *Dreams and Dream Reports in the Writings of Josephus: A Traditio-Historical Analysis* (Leiden: Brill, 1996).
Goldstein, J.A., *I Maccabees* (AB 41; New York: Doubleday, 1976).
Goldstein, J.A., *II Maccabees* (AB 41A; New York: Doubleday, 1983).
Goodman, M., G.H. van Kooten, and J.T.A.G.M. van Ruiten, eds., *Abraham, the Nations, and the Hagarites: Jewish, Christian, and Islamic Perspectives on Kinship with Abraham* (TBN 13; Leiden: Brill, 2010).
Gossai, H., *Power and Marginality in the Abraham Narrative* (2nd edn.; Eugene: OR: Pickwick Publications, 2010).
Grabbe, L.L., *Etymology in Early Jewish Interpretation: The Hebrew Names in Philo* (BJS 115; Atlanta, GA: SBL, 1988).
Green, J.B., "The Problem of a Beginning: Israel's Scriptures in Luke 1–2", *BBR* 4 (1994): 61–86.
Green, J.B., "Jesus and a Daughter of Abraham (Luke 13:10–17): Test Case for a Lucan Perspective on Jesus' Miracles", *CBQ* 51 (1989): 643–54.
Green, P., *From Alexander to Actium: The Hellenistic Age* (London: Thames and Hudson, 1990).
Gregory, A.F., "1 Clement: An Introduction", in *The Writings of the Apostolic Fathers*, ed. P. Foster (London: Bloomsbury T&T Clark, 2007), 21–31.
Gregory, A.F., "1 Clement and the Writings that Later Formed the New Testament", in *The Reception of the New Testament in the Apostolic Fathers*, eds. A.F. Gregory and C.M. Tuckett (Oxford: Oxford University Press, 2007), 129–58.
Gregory, B.C., "Abraham as the Jewish Ideal: Exegetical Traditions in Sirach 44:19–21", *CBQ* 70 (2008): 66–81.
Griffith, T., *Keep Yourselves from Idols: A New Look at 1 John* (JSNTSup 233; London: Sheffield Academic Press, 2002).
Griffith, T. "'The Jews Who Had Believed in Him' (John 8:31) and the Motif of Apostasy in the Gospel of John", in *The Gospel of John and Christian Theology*, eds. R. Bauckham and C. Mosser (Grand Rapids: Eerdmans, 2008), 183–92.
Grogan, G.W., "The Old Testament Concept of Solidarity in Hebrews", *TynBull* 49, no. 1 (1998): 159–73.
Grossman, J., *Abram to Abraham: A Literary Analysis of the Abraham Narrative* (Bern: Peter Lang, 2016).

Gruen, E.S., *Heritage and Hellenism: The Reinvention of Jewish Tradition* (Berkeley: University of California Press, 1998).

Gruen, E.S., *Diaspora. Jews Amidst Greeks and Romans* (Boston: Harvard University Press, 2004).

Grypeou, E., and H. Spurling, "Abraham's Angels: Jewish and Christian Exegesis of Genesis 18–19", in *The Exegetical Encounter Between Jews and Christians in Late Antiquity*, eds. E. Grypeou and H. Spurling (Leiden: Brill, 2009), 181–202.

Gunther, J.J., *Saint Paul's Opponents and Their Background* (Leiden: Brill, 1973).

Haglund, E., *Historical Motifs in the Psalms* (Coniectanea Biblical, OTS 23; Uppsala: CWK Gleerup, 1984).

Hagner, D.A., *The Use of the Old and New Testaments in Clement of Rome* (NovTSup 34 Leiden: Brill, 1973).

Halpern-Amaru, B., *Rewriting the Bible: Land and Covenant in Postbiblical Jewish Literature* (Valley Forge: Trinity Press International, 1994).

Hamley, I., "'Dis(re)membered and Unaccounted For': פִּילֶגֶשׁ in the Hebrew Bible", *JSOT* 42, no. 4 (2018): 415–34.

Hamm, D., "Luke 19:8 Once Again: Does Zacchaeus Defend or Resolve?", *JBL* 107 (1988): 431–7.

Hanhart, R., *Text und Textgeschichte des Buches Tobit* (MSU 17; Göttingen: Vandenhoeck & Ruprecht, 1984).

Hansen, G.W., *Abraham in Galatians: Epistolary and Rhetorical Contexts* (JSNTSup 29; Sheffield: JSOT, 1989).

Harmelink, B.L., "Exploring the Syntactic, Semantic, and Pragmatic Uses of ויהי in Biblical Hebrew", PhD diss., Westminster Theological Seminary, 2004.

Harrington, D.J., "Pseudo-Philo", in *The Old Testament Pseudepigrapha*, Vol. 2, ed. J.H. Charlesworth (New York: Doubleday, 1985), 297–377.

Harris, W.V. "Child-Exposure in the Roman Empire", *Journal of Roman Studies* 84 (1994): 1–22.

Harvey, W.J., *Character and the Novel* (Ithaca: Cornell University Press, 1965).

Hay, D.M., "Philo's References to Other Allegorists", *SPhilo* 6 (1979–80): 41–75.

Hays, R.B., "'Have We Found Abraham to Be Our Forefather According to the Flesh?' A Reconsideration of Romans 4:1", *NovT* 27 (1985): 76–98.

Hays, R.B., *Echoes of Scripture in the Gospels* (Waco, TX: Baylor University Press, 2016).

Heliso, D., *Pistis and the Righteous One: A Study of Romans 1:17 Against the Background of Scripture and Second Temple Jewish Literature* (WUNT II. Tübingen: Mohr Siebeck, 2007).

Hendel, R., *Remembering Abraham: Culture, Memory and History in the Hebrew Bible* (Oxford: Oxford University Press, 2005).

Hieke, T., "Endogamy in the Book of Tobit, Genesis, and Ezra-Nehemiah", in *The Book of Tobit: Text, Tradition, Theology*, eds. G.G. Xeravits and J. Zsengellér (JSJSup 98; Leiden: Brill, 2005), 103–20.

Hieke, T., "The Role of Scripture in the Last Words of Mattathias (1 Macc 2:49–70)", in *The Books of the Maccabees: History, Theology, Ideology*, eds. G.G. Xeravits and J. Zsengellér (JSJSup 118; Leiden: Brill, 2007), 61–74.

Hildebrandt, T., "A Song of Our Father Abraham: Psalm 150", in *Perspectives on Our Father Abraham: Essays in Honor of Marvin. R. Wilson*, ed. S.A. Hunt (Michigan: Wm. B. Eerdmans, 2012), 44–67.

Hirth, V., *Gottes Boten im Alten Testament* (Theologische Arbeiten 32; Berlin: Evangelische Verlagsanstalt, 1975).

Hochman, B., *Character in Literature* (Ithaca: Cornell University Press, 1985).
Holmes, M.W., *The Apostolic Fathers: Greek Texts and English Translations* (3rd edn.; Grand Rapids: Baker, 2007).
Holzhausen, J., "Die Seelenlehre des Gnostikers Herakleon", in *Psyche—Seele—Anima: Festschrift fur Karin Alt*, ed. G. Buch (Beiträge zur Altertumskunde 109; Stuttgart: Teubner, 1998), 279–300.
Hood, J.B., *The Messiah, His Brothers, and the Nations: Matthew 1.1—17* (LNTS 441; New York: T&T Clark, 2011).
Huizenga, L.A., *The New Isaac: Tradition and Intertextuality in the Gospel of Matthew* (NovTSup 131; Leiden: Brill, 2009).
Hunt, S.A., "And the Word Became Flesh—Again? Jesus and Abraham in John 8:31–59", in *Perspectives on Our Father Abraham: Essays in Honor of Marvin R. Wilson*, ed. S.A. Hunt (Grand Rapids: Eerdmans, 2012), 81–109.
Hunter, D.G., "The Virgin, the Bride and the Church. Reading Psalm 45 in Ambrose, Jerome and Augustine", *Church History* 69, no.2 (2000): 281–303.
Hurtado, L.W., *The Earliest Christian Artifacts: Manuscripts and Christian Origins* (Grand Rapids: Eerdmans, 2006).
Hvalvik, R., "Barnabas 9,7–9 and the Use of Gematria", *NTS* 33 (1987): 276–82.
Hvalvik, R., *The Struggle for Scripture and Covenant: The Purpose of the Epistles of Barnabas and Jewish-Christian Competition in the Second Century* (WUNT 2/82; Tübingen: Mohr Siebeck, 1996).
Ilan, T., "The Torah of the Jews of Ancient Rome", *JSQ* 16 (2009): 363–95.
Isenberg, W.W., "The Coptic Gospel According to Philip", PhD diss., The University of Chicago, 1968.
Jaan, L., *Gnosis und Judentum. Alttestamentliche und jüdische Motiven der gnostischen Literatur und das Ursprungsproblem der Gnosis* (NHMS 75; Leiden: Brill, 2012).
Janssen, Y., "L'Evangile selon Phillipe", *Mus* 81 (1968): 407–14.
Jefford, C.N., *Reading the Apostolic Fathers: A Student's Introduction* (Grand Rapids: Baker, 2012).
Jensen, R., *Baptismal Imagery in Early Christianity: Ritual, Visual and Theological Dimension* (Ada, MI: Baker, 2012).
Jervell, J., *Luke and the People of God* (Eugene, OR: Wipf & Stock, 2002).
Jeska, J., *Die Geschicte Israels in der Sicht des Lukas: Apg 7,2b-53 und 13,17–25 im Kontext antic-jüdischer Summarien der Geschichte Israels* (Göttingen: Vandenhoeck and Ruprecht, 2001).
Jipp, J.W., "Rereading the Story of Abraham, Isaac, and 'Us' in Romans 4", *JSNT* 32 (2010): 217–42.
Jipp, J., *Divine Visitations and Hospitality to Strangers in Luke-Acts: An Interpretation of the Malta Episode in Acts 28:1–10* (NovTSup 153; Leiden: Brill, 2013).
Jipp, J.W., "What Are the Implications of the Ethnic Identity of Paul's Interlocutor? Continuing the Conversation", in *The So-Called Jew in Paul's Letter to Romans*, eds. R. Rodriguez and M. Theissen (Minneapolis: Fortress Press, 2016), 183–203.
Jipp, J., *Saved by Faith and Hospitality* (Grand Rapids: Eerdmans, 2017).
Kaster, R.A., ed., *C. Suetonius Tranquillus–De Grammaticis et Rhetoribus* (Oxford: Clarendon, 1995).
Kee, H.C., "Testaments of the Twelve Patriarchs", in *The Old Testament Pseudepigrapha*, Vol. 1, ed. J.H. Charlesworth (Garden City, NY: Doubleday & Company, Inc., 1983), 775–828.
Kessler, E., *Bound by the Bible: Jews, Christians and the Sacrifice of Isaac* (Cambridge: Cambridge University Press, 2004).

King, K.L., *What is Gnosticism?* (Cambridge, MA: The Belknap Press of Harvard University Press, 2003).

Kister, M., "Observations on Aspects of Exegesis, Tradition, and Theology in Midrash, Pseudepigrapha, and Other Jewish Writings", in *Tracing the Threads: Studies in the Vitality of the Jewish Pseudepigrapha*, ed. J. Reeves (SBLEJL 6; Atlanta, GA: SBL, 1994), 1–34.

Kitchen, R.A., "Making the Imperfect Perfect. The Adaptation of Hebrews 11 in the 9th Mēmrā of the Syriac Book of Steps", in *The Reception and Interpretation of the Bible in Late Antiquity: Proceedings of the Montreal Colloquium in Honour of Charles Kannengiesser, 11–13 October 2006*, eds. L. DiTommaso and L. Turcescu (Leiden: Brill, 2008), 227–51.

Kitzberger, I.R., "Synoptic Women in John: Interfigural Readings", in *Transformative Encounters: Jesus and Women Re-viewed*, ed. I.R. Kitzberger (BIS 43; Leiden: Brill, 2000), 77–111.

Klopper, F., "Interpretation is All We Have. A Feminist Perspective on the Objective Fallacy", *Old Testament Essays* 22, no. 1 (2009): 88–101.

Knoblock, F.W., "Adoption in the Old Testament and ANE", *ABD* I (1992): 76–9.

Knowles, M.P., "Abram and the Birds in Jubilees 11: A Subtext for the Parable of the Sower?", *NTS* 41 (1995): 145–51.

Konradt, M., *Israel, Church, and the Gentiles in the Gospel of Matthew* (trans. K. Ess; Baylor-Mohr Siebeck Studies in Early Christianity; Waco, TX: Baylor University Press, 2014).

Kraemer, D., *Jewish Eating and Identity through the Ages* (London: Routledge, 2007).

Kugel, J.L., *Traditions of the Bible* (Cambridge, MA: Harvard University Press, 1998).

Kugel, J.L., "Early Interpretation: The Common Background of Late Forms of Biblical Exegesis", in *Early Biblical Interpretation*, eds. J.L. Kugel and R.A. Greer (Library of Early Christianity 3. Philadelphia: Westminster Press, 1986), 9–106.

Kuhn, T.S., *The Structure of Scientific Revolutions*, Vol. 2: No. 2 (Foundations of the Unity of Science; Chicago: University of Chicago Press, 1967).

Kuhn, T.S., and I. Hacking, *The Structure of Scientific Revolutions: 50th Anniversary Edition* (Chicago: University of Chicago Press, 2012).

Kulawik, C., *Die Erzählung über die Seele* (TU 155; Berlin: de Gruyter, 2005).

Law, T.M., *When God Spoke Greek: The Septuagint and the Making of the Christian Bible* (Oxford: Oxford University Press, 2013).

Layton, B., "The Soul as a Dirty Garment", *Mus* 91 (1978): 155–69.

Layton, B., ed., *The Rediscovery of Gnosticism. I. The School of Valentinus* (Studies in the History of Religions 41; Supplements to Numen; Leiden: Brill, 1980).

LeDonne, A., *The Historiographical Jesus: Memory, Typology, and the Son of David* (Waco, TX: Baylor University Press, 2009).

Lee, T.R., *Studies in the Form of Sirach 44–50* (SBLDS 75; Atlanta, GA: SBL, 1986).

Levenson, J.D., *Resurrection and the Restoration of Israel: The Ultimate Victory of the God of Life* (New Haven, CT: Yale University Press, 2006).

Levenson, J.D., *Abraham Between Torah and Gospel* (The Pere Marquette Lecture in Theology; Milwaukee: Marquette University Press, 2011).

Levenson, J.D., *Inheriting Abraham: The Legacy of the Patriarch in Judaism, Christianity, and Islam* (Princeton: Princeton University Press 2012).

Lewis, N.D., *Cosmology and Fate in Gnosticism and Graeco-Roman Antiquity* (NHMS 81; Leiden: Brill, 2013).

Lichtenberger, H., "Das Tora-Verständnis im Judentum zur Zeit des Paulus", in *Paul and the Mosaic Law*, ed. J.D.G. Dunn (Tübingen: Mohr Siebeck, 1996), 7–24.

Lightfoot, J.B., *The Apostolic Fathers: Clement, Ignatius, and Polycarp* (Peabody, MA: Hendrickson, 1989).
Lincicum, D., "A Preliminary Index to Philo's Non-Biblical Citations and Allusions", *SPhA* 25 (2013): 139–67.
Linder, A., *The Jews in Roman Imperial Legislation* (The Israel Academy of Sciences and Humanities; Detroit, MI: Wayne State University Press and Jerusalem, 1987).
Liong-Seng Phua, R., *Idolatry and Authority. A Study of Corinthians 8.1–11.1 in the Light of the Jewish Diaspora* (London/New York: T. & T. Clark, 2005).
Littman, R.J., *Tobit: The Book of Tobit in Codex Sinaiticus* (SCS; Leiden: Brill 2008).
Livneh, A., "Deborah's New Song: The Historical Résumé in LAB 32:1–11 in Context", *JSJ* 48 (2017): 203–45.
Loader, J.A., *A Tale of Two Cities: Sodom and Gomorrah in the Old Testament, Early Jewish and Early Christian Traditions* (CBET 1; Kampen: Kok Publishing House, 1990).
Lombaard, C., "The Strange Case of the Patriarchs in Jeremiah 33:26", *Acta Theologica* 35, no. 2 (2015): 36–49.
Lona, H.E., *Der Erste Clemensbrief* (KAV 2; Göttingen: Vandenhoeck & Ruprecht, 1998).
Longenecker, R.N., *The Epistle to the Romans* (NIGTC; Grand Rapids: Eerdmans, 2016).
Ludlow, J., *Abraham Meets Death: Narrative Humor in the Testament of Abraham* (Sheffield Academic Press, 2002).
Ludlow, J., "Humor and Paradox in the Characterization of Abraham in the Testament of Abraham", in *Ancient Fiction: The Matrix of Early Christian and Jewish Narrative*, eds. J.A. Brant, C.W. Hedrick, and C. Shea (SBL Symposium Series 32; Atlanta, GA: SBL, 2005), 199–216.
Lundhaug, H., *Images of Rebirth* (NHMS 73; Leiden: Brill, 2010).
Macaskill, G., *Union with Christ in the New Testament* (Oxford: Oxford University Press, 2018).
Macatangay, F.M., *The Wisdom Instructions in the Book of Tobit* (DCLS 12; Berlin: de Gruyter, 2011).
Macdermot, V., *Pistis Sophia,* ed. C. Schmidt (NHS 9; Leiden: Brill, 1978).
Machiela, D.A., *The Dead Sea Genesis Apocryphon: A New Text and Translation with Introduction and Special Treatment of Columns 13–17* (Leiden: Brill, 2009).
Malina, B.J., *The New Testament World: Insights from Cultural Anthropology* (3rd edn.; Louisville: Westminster John Knox, 2001).
Marcus, J., *Mark 8–16* (AYBC 27A; New Haven: Yale University Press, 2009).
Markschies, C., *Die Gnosis* (Munich: Beck, 2001, 2006).
Markschies, C., "Valentinian Gnosticism. Toward the Anatomy of a School", in *The Nag Hammadi Library after Fifty Years: Proceedings of the 1995 Society of Biblical Literature Commemoration*, eds. J.D. Turner and A. McGuire (NHMS XLIV; Leiden: Brill, 1997), 401–38.
Marttila, M., *Foreign Nations in the Wisdom of Ben Sira: A Jewish Sage between Opposition and Assimilation* (DCLS 13; Berlin: de Gruyter, 2012).
Marzouk, S., *Egypt as a Monster in the Book of Ezekiel* (Tübingen: Mohr Siebeck, 2015).
Mason, S., "The 'Contra Apionem' in Social and Literary Context: An Invitation to Judean Philosophy", in *Josephus' "Contra Apionem": Studies in Its Character and Context with a Latin Concordance to the Portion Missing in Greek*, eds. L.H. Feldman and J.R. Levison (Leiden: Brill, 1996), 187–228.
Matthews, D., *Royal Motifs in the Pentateuchal Portrayal of Moses* (LHBOTS 571; London: T & T Clark, 2012).

McCann, D., "Julius Firmicus Maternus: Profile of a Roman Astrologer", http://www.skyscript.co.uk/firmicus.html.
McDonald, J., "Searching for Sarah in the Second Temple Era: Portraits in the Hebrew Bible and Second Temple Narratives", PhD diss., Brite Divinity School, 2015.
Meeks, W.A., *The Prophet-King: Moses Traditions and the Johannine Christology* (NovTSup 14; Leiden: Brill, 1967).
Mendelson, A., *Secular Education in Philo of Alexandria* (Cincinnati: HUC Press, 1982).
Mirguet, F., *An Early History of Compassion: Emotion and Imagination in Hellenistic Judaism* (New York: Cambridge University Press, 2017).
Moessner, D.P., *Luke the Historian of Israel's Legacy, Theologian of Israel's "Christ": A New Reading of the 'Gospel Acts' of Luke* (BZNW 182; Berlin: de Gruyter, 2016).
Moll, S., "At the Left Hand of Christ: The Arch-Heretic Marcion", PhD diss., University of Edinburgh, 2009.
Momigliano, A., "The Date of the 1st Book of Maccabees", in *L'Italie préromaine et la Rome républicaine: Mélanges offerts à J. Heurgon* (Rome: École Française de Rome, 1976), 657–61.
Moo, D.J., *The Epistle to the Romans* (Grand Rapids: Eerdmans, 1996).
Morard, F., "L'Apocalypse d'Adam de Nag Hammadi. Un essai d'interprétation", in *Gnosis and Gnosticism. Papers Read at the Seventh International Conference on Patristic Studies Oxford 1975*, ed. M. Krause (NHS 8; Leiden: Brill, 1977), 35–42.
Moyise, S., *Paul and Scripture* (London: SPCK, 2010).
Muffs, Y., *Love and Joy: Law, Language and Religion in Ancient Israel* (New York: Jewish Theological Seminary, 1992).
Mühling, A., "*Blickt auf Abraham, euren Vater": Abraham als Identifikationsfigur des Judentums in der Zeit des Exils und des Zweiten Tempels* (FRLANT 236; Göttingen: Vandenhoeck & Ruprecht, 2011).
Mukenge, A.K., *L'unité littéraire du Livre de Baruch* (Etudes Bibliques N.S. 38; Paris: Gabalda, 1998).
Mulder, O., *Simon the High Priest in Sirach 50: An Exegetical Study of the Significance of Simon the High Priest as Climax to the Praise of the Fathers in Ben Sira's Concept of the History of Israel* (JSJSup 78; Leiden: Brill, 2003).
Müller, W.G., "Interfigurality: A Study of the Interdependence of Literary Figures", in *Intertextuality*, ed. H.F. Plett (Berlin: De Gruyter, 1991), 101–21.
Murphy, F.J., *Pseudo-Philo: Rewriting the Bible* (New York: Oxford University Press, 1993).
Myers, A.C., *Characterizing Jesus: A Rhetorical Analysis of the Fourth Gospel's Use of Scripture in its Presentation of Jesus* (LNTS 458; London: T&T Clark, 2012).
Nagel, P., "Die Auslegung der Paradieserzählung in der Gnosis", in *Altes Testament, Frühjudentum, Gnosis*, ed. K.W. Tröger (Berlin: Evangelische Verlagsanstalt, 1980), 49–70.
Nagy, V.K., "Die Beziehung der Makkabäer zu fremden Nationen—die Bündnisse mit Rom und Sparta", in *The Stranger in Ancient and Mediaeval Jewish Tradition*, eds. G.G. Xeravits and J. Dušek (DCLS 4; Berlin: de Gruyter, 2010), 107–17.
Newsom, C., "Angels", in *ABD*, Vol 1, ed. D.N. Freedman (New York: Doubleday, 1992), 250.
Nickelsburg, G.W.E., and J.J. Collins, eds., *Ideal Figures in Ancient Judaism* (Ann Arbor: Scholars Press, 1980).
Nickelsburg, G.W.E., "Some Related Traditions in the Apocalypse of Gnosticism", in *The Rediscovery of Gnosticism. Proceedings of the International Conference on Gnosticism at Yale New Haven, Connecticut, 1978*, ed. B. Layton (SHR 41; Leiden: Brill, 1981), 515–93.

Nickelsburg, G.W.E., "The Bible Rewritten and Expanded", in *Jewish Writings of the Second Temple Period*, ed. M.E. Stone (Assen: Van Gorcum/Philadelphia: Fortress, 1984) 89–156.
Nicol, G.G., "Story-Patterning in Genesis", in *Text as Pretext: Essays in Honour of Robert Davidson*, ed. R.P. Carroll (Sheffield: JSOT Press, 2009), 215–33.
Niehoff, M., *The Figure of Joseph in Post-Biblical Jewish Literature* (AGJU 16; Leiden: Brill, 1992).
Noort, E. and E.J. Tigchelaar, eds., *The Sacrifice of Isaac: The Aqedah (Genesis 22) and Its Interpretations* (TBN 4; Leiden: Brill, 2002).
Noort, E., "Abraham and the Nations", in *Abraham, the Nations, and the Hagarites: Jewish, Christian and Islamic Perspectives on Kinship with Abraham*, eds. M. Goodman, G.H. van Kooten, and J.T.A.G.M. van Ruiten (Themes in Biblical Narrative Jewish and Christian Traditions; Leiden: Brill, 2010), 3–31.
Noort, E. and E.J. Tigchelaar eds., *Sodom's Sins: Genesis 18–19 and its Interpretations* (Leiden: Brill, 2004).
Novakovic, L., *Raised from the Dead According to Scripture: The Role of Israel's Scripture in the Early Christian Interpretations of Jesus' Resurrection* (London/New York: Bloomsbury T&T Clark, 2012).
Novenson, M.V., "Paul's Former Occupation in Ioudaismos", in *Galatians and Christian Theology: Justification, The Gospel, and Ethics in Paul's Letters*, eds. M.W. Elliott, S. J. Haffemann, N.T. Wright, and J. Frederick (Grand Rapids: Baker, 2014), 24–39.
Novick, T., "Biblicized Narrative: On Tobit and Genesis 22", *JBL* 126 (2007): 755–64.
Nünlist, R., *The Ancient Critic at Work: Terms and Concepts of Literary Criticism in Greek Scholia* (Cambridge: Cambridge University Press, 2009).
Oswalt, J.N., "Abraham's Experience of Yahweh: An Argument for the Historicity of the Patriarchal Narratives", in *Perspectives on Our Father Abraham: Essays in Honour of Marvin R. Wilson*, ed. S.A. Hunt (Grand Rapids, MI/Cambridge: William B. Eerdmans, 2010), 33–43.
Paget, J.C., "The Epistle of Barnabas", in *The Writings of the Apostolic Fathers*, ed. P. Foster (London: Bloomsbury/T&T Clark, 2007), 72–80.
Paget, J.C., *Epistle of Barnabas: Outlook and Background* (WUNT 2/64; Tübingen: Mohr Siebeck, 1994).
Parker, V., "The Letters in II Maccabees: Reflexions on the Book's Composition", *ZAW* 119 (2007): 386–90.
Parsons, M., *Body and Character in Luke-Acts: The Subversion of Physiognomy in Early Christianity* (Grand Rapids: Baker Academic, 2006).
Peleg, Y., "Was the Ancestress of Israel in Danger? Did Pharaoh Touch (נגע) Sarai?", *ZAW* 118 (2006): 197–208.
Pelling, C.B.R., ed. *Characterization and Individuality in Greek Literature* (Oxford: Clarendon Press, 1990).
Pétrement, S., *Le Dieu separe. Les origines du gnosticisme* (Paris: Cerf, 1984).
Pikor, W., *The Land of Israel in the Book of Ezekiel* (LHBOTS 667; London: T & T Clark, 2018).
Piotrowksi, N.G., *Matthew's New David at the end of Exile: A Socio-Rhetorical Study of Scriptural Quotations* (NovTSup 170; Leiden: Brill, 2016).
Pohl, C.D., *Making Room: Recovering Hospitality as a Christian Tradition* (Grand Rapids: Eerdmans, 1999).
Porter, S.E., ed., *Paul and His Opponents* (Pauline Studies, Vol. 2; Leiden: Brill, 2005).
Preuss, H.D., *Old Testament Theology* (OTL; Louisville: WJK, 1995).

Prigent, P., *Les testimonia dans le christianisme primitif. L'Épitre de Barnabé I-XVI et ses sources, Ebib* (Paris: Gabalda, 1961).

Propp, V., *Morphology of the Folktale* (2nd edn.; trans. L. Scott; Austin: University of Texas Press, 1968).

Prostmeier, F.R., *Der Barnabasbrief* (KAV 8; Göttingen: Vandenhoeck & Ruprecht, 1999).

Rakel, C., *Judit—über Schönheit, Macht und Widerstand im Krieg: Eine feministisch-intertextuelle Lektüre* (BZAW 334; Berlin: de Gruyter 2003).

Rasimus, T., *Paradise Reconsidered in Gnostic Mythmaking: Rethinking Sethianism in Light of the Ophite Evidence* (NHMS 68; Leiden: E. J. Brill, 2009).

Rawson, E., *Intellectual Life in the Late Roman Republic* (London: Duckworth, 1985).

Reed, A.Y., "The Construction of Subversion of Patriarchal Perfection: Abraham and Exemplarity in Philo, Josephus, and the Testament of Abraham", *JSJ* 40 (2009): 185–212.

Reed, A.Y., "Abraham as Chaldean Scientist and Father of the Jews: Josephus, Ant. 1.154–168, and the Greco-Roman Discourse about Astronomy/Astrology", *JSJ* 35 (2004): 119–58.

Reese, J.M., "Plan and Structure in the Book of Wisdom", *CBQ* 27 (1965): 391–9.

Reinhartz, A., "John 8:31–59 From a Jewish Perspective", in *Remembering for the Future 2000: The Holocaust in an Age of Genocides*, 2 vols., eds. J.K. Roth and E. Maxwell-Meynard (London: Palgrave, 2001), 787–97.

Reiterer, F.V., "Die Vergangenheit als Basis für die Zukunft. Mattatias' Lehre für seine Söhne aus der Geschichte in 1 Makk 2:52–60", in *The Books of the Maccabees: History, Theology, Ideology*, eds. G. Xeravits and J. Zsengellér (Leiden: Brill, 2007), 75–100.

Riley, M., "A Survey of Vettius Valens", http://www.csus.edu/indiv/r/rileymt/PDF_folder/VettiusValens.PDF.

Roberts, A. and W. Rambaut trans., *Ante-Nicene Fathers*, Vol. 1., eds. A. Roberts and J. Donaldson (Buffalo, NY: Christian Literature Publishing, 1885).

Roig Lanzillotta, L., "'Come out of Your Country and Your Kinsfolk': Abraham's Command and Ascent of the Soul in the Exegesis on the Soul (NHC II,6)", in *Abraham, the Nations, and the Hagarites. Jewish, Christian, and Islamic Perspectives on Kinship with Abraham*, eds. M. Goodman, G.H. van Kooten, and J.T.A.G.M. van Ruiten (Leiden: Brill, 2010), 401–20.

Roitman, A.D., "The Traditions about Abraham's Early Life in the Book of Judith (5:6–9)", in *Things Revealed: Studies in Early Jewish and Christian Literature in Honor of Michael E. Stone*, eds. E. Chazon, D. Satran, and R. Clements (JSJSup 89; Leiden: Brill, 2004), 73–87.

Römer, T., "Abraham Traditions in the Hebrew Bible Outside the Book of Genesis", in *The Book of Genesis: Composition, Reception, and Interpretation*, eds. C.A. Evans, J.N. Lorh, and D.L. Peterson (VTSup 152; Leiden: Brill, 2012), 159–80.

Royse, J.R., "The Works of Philo", in *The Cambridge Companion to Philo*, ed. A. Kamesar (Cambridge: Cambridge University Press, 2009), 32–64.

Rudolph, K., *Gnosis: The Nature and History of Gnosticism* (trans. R. Wilson; San Francisco: Harper San Francisco, 1987).

Runesson, A., *Divine Wrath and Salvation in Matthew: The Narrative World of the First Gospel* (Minneapolis: Fortress Press, 2016).

Runia, D.T., "The Place of De Abrahamo in Philo's Œuvre", *SPhilo* 20 (2008): 133–50.

Runia, D.T., "The Structure of Philo's Allegorical Treatises: A Review of Two Recent Studies and Some Additional Comments", *Vigiliae Christianae* 38 (1984): 209–56.

Runia, D.T., *Philo of Alexandria and the Timaeus of Plato* (PhilASup 44; Leiden: Brill, 1986).

Ryu, J., *Knowledge of God in Philo of Alexandria* (WUNT 2.405; Tübingen: Mohr Siebeck, 2015).

Sagnard, F., *Clément d'Alexandrie: Extraits ex Theodote* (SC 23; Paris: Editions du Cerf, 1970).

Samely, A., *Rabbinic Interpretation of Scripture in the Mishnah* (Oxford: Oxford University Press, 2002).

Sandmel, S., *Philo's Place in Judaism: A Study of Conceptions of Abraham in Jewish Literature* (New York: Ktav, 1971).

Sarna, N.M., "Genesis Chapter 23: The Cave of Machpelah", *HS* 23 (1982): 17–21.

Scott, J.M., ed., *Restoration: Old Testament, Jewish, and Christian Perspectives* (JSJSup 72; Leiden: Brill, 2001).

Schäfer, P., *Judeophobia: Attitudes towards the Jews in the Ancient World* (Cambridge, MA: Harvard University Press, 1997).

Schenke, H.M., "Das sethianische System nach Nag-Hammadi-Handschriften", *Studia Coptica*, ed. P. Nagel (Berliner Byzantinistiche Arbeiten 45; Berlin: Akademie-Verlag, 1974), 165–73.

Schenke, H.M., "The Phenomenon and Significance of Gnostic Sethianism", in *The Rediscovery of Gnosticism*, Vol. 2: *Sethian Gnosticism*, ed. B. Layton (Studies in the History of Religions 41; Supplements to Numen; Leiden: E. J. Brill, 1981), 588–616.

Schenke, H.M., *Das Philippus-Evangelium (Nag-Hammadi-Codex 11,3)* (TU 143; Berlin: Akademie-Verlag 1997).

Schmid, U., *Marcion und sein Apostolos* (Berlin: de Gruyter, 1995).

Schürer, E., *The History of the Jewish People in the Age of Jesus Christ*, 3 vols. (revised by G. Vermes, F. Millar and M. Black; Edinburgh: T&T Clark, 1973–87).

Schwartz, D.R., *2 Maccabees* (CEJL; Berlin: de Gruyter 2008).

Schwartz, D.R., "Josephus, Catullus, Divine Providence, and the Date of the Judean War", in *Flavius Josephus: Interpretation and History*, eds. J. Pastor, P. Stern, and M. Mor (Leiden: Brill, 2011), 331–52.

Scopello, M., "Las citations d'Homère dans le Traité de L'Exégèse de l'âme", in *Gnosis and Gnosticism*, ed. M. Krause (Leiden: Brill, 1977), 3–12.

Scopello, M., *L'Exégèse De L'Âme, Nag Hammadi Codex II,6. Introduction, traduction et commentaire* (NHS 25; Leiden: Brill, 1985).

Scorza-Barcellona, F., *Epistola di Barnaba* (CP 1; Turin: Società Editrice Internazionale, 1975).

Segelberg, E., "The Coptic-Gospel According to Philip and its Sacramental System", *Numen* 7, no.2 (1960): 189–200.

Shinan, A. and Y. Zakovitch, *Abram and Sarai in Egypt, Gen. 12.10–20 in the Bible, the Old Versions and the Ancient Jewish Literature* (Jerusalem: The Hebrew University, 1983).

Shinan, A. and Y. Zakovitch, "'Why is "A" Placed Next to "B"? Juxtaposition in the Bible and Beyond", in *Tradition, Transmission, and Transformation from Second Temple Literature through Judaism and Christianity in Late Antiquity*, eds. M. Kister, H. Newman, M. Segal, and R. Clements (STDJ 113; Leiden: Brill, 2015), 322–42.

Siegert, F., "'Und er hob seine Augen auf, und siehe': Abrahams Gottesvision (Gen 18) im hellenistischen Judentum", in *'Abraham, unser Vater': die gemeinsamen Wurzeln von Judentum, Christentum und Islam*, eds. R.G. Kratz and T. Nagel (Göttingen: Wallstein Verlag, 2003), 67–85.

Sievers, J., "Josephus, First Maccabees, Sparta, the Three haireseis—and Cicero", *JSJ* 32 (2001): 241–51.

Siker, J.S., "Abraham in Graeco-Roman Paganism", *JSJ* 18 (1987): 188–208.

Siker, J.S., "Gnostic Views on Jews and Christians in the Gospel of Philip", *NovT* 31 (1989): 275–88.

Siker, J.S., *Disinheriting the Jews: Abraham in Early Christian Controversy* (Louisville, KY: Westminster/John Knox Press, 1991).

Skarsaune, O., *The Proof from Prophecy—A Study in Justin Martyr's Proof-Text Tradition: Text-Type, Provenance, Theological Profile* (NovTSup 56; Leiden: Brill, 1987).

Skehan, P.W. and A.A. Di Lella, *The Wisdom of Ben Sira* (AB 39; New York: Doubleday 1987).

Skinner, C.W., *Reading John* (Cascade Companions; Eugene, OR: Cascade, 2015).

Sly, D., *Philo's Perception of Women* (BJS 209; Atlanta, GA: SBL, 1990).

Smit, P-B., *Fellowship and Food in the Kingdom: Eschatological Meals and Scenes of Utopian Abundance in the New Testament* (WUNT 2.234; Tübingen: Mohr-Siebeck, 2008).

Somov, A., and V. Voinov, "'Abraham's Bosom' (Luke 16:22–23) as a Key Metaphor in the Overall Composition of the Parable of the Rich Man and Lazarus", *CBQ* 79 (2017): 615–33.

Spilsbury, P., *The Image of the Jew in Flavius Josephus' Paraphrase of the Bible* (Tübingen: Mohr Siebeck, 1998).

Squires, J.T., *The Plan of God in Luke-Acts* (SNTS Monograph Series 76; Cambridge: Cambridge University Press, 1993).

Stavrakopoulou, F., *Land of our Fathers: The Roles of Ancestor Veneration in Biblical Land Claims* (London: T&T Clark, 2010).

Stemberger, G., "Genesis 15 in Rabbinic and Patristic Interpretation", in *The Exegetical Encounter between Jews and Christians in Late Antiquity*, eds. E. Grypeou and H. Spurling (JCPS 18; Leiden: Brill, 2009), 143–62.

Sterling, G.E., *Historiography and Self Definition, Josephus, Luke-Acts and Apologetic Historiography* (Leiden: Brill, 1992).

Sterling, G.E., "'Opening the Scriptures': The Legitimation of the Jewish Diaspora and the Early Christian Mission", in *Jesus and the Heritage of Israel: Luke's Narrative Claim upon Israel's Legacy*, ed. D.P. Moessner (Harrisburg, PA: Trinity Press International, 1999), 199–217.

Sterling, G.E., "'The Queen of the Virtues': Piety in Philo of Alexandria", *SPhA* 18 (2006): 103–23.

Sterling, G.E., "When the Beginning Is the End: The Place of Genesis in the Commentaries of Philo", in *The Book of Genesis: Composition, Reception, and Interpretation*, eds. C.A. Evans, J.N. Lohr, and D.L. Petersen (VTSup 152; Leiden: Brill, 2012), 427–46.

Sterling, G.E., "The People of the Covenant or the People of God: Exodus in Philo of Alexandria", in *The Book of Exodus: Composition, Reception, and Interpretation*, eds. T.B. Dozeman, C.A. Evans, and J.N. Lohr (VTSup 164; Leiden: Brill, 2014), 404–39.

Stern, M., *Greek and Latin Authors on Jews and Judaism*, 3 vols. (Jerusalem: The Israel Academy of Sciences and Humanities, 1974–84).

Stone, M., *A History of the Literature of Adam and Eve* (Atlanta, GA: SBL, 1992).

Stowers, S.K. *A Rereading of Romans: Justice, Jews, and Gentiles* (New Haven: Yale University Press, 1994).

Stuckenbruck, L.T., "Apocrypha and Septuagint. Exploring the Christian Canon", in *Die Septuaginta und das frühe Christentum—The Septuagint and Christian Origins*, eds. S. Caulley and H. Lichtenberger (WUNT 277; Tübingen: Mohr Siebeck, 2011), 177–204.

Sullivan, K.P., *Wrestling With Angels. A Study of the Relationship Between Angels and Humans in Ancient Jewish Literature and the New Testament* (Leiden: Brill, 2004).

Swetnam, J., "The Meaning of πεπιστευκότας in John 8,31", *Biblica* 61 (1980): 106–9.
Swetnam, J., *Jesus and Isaac: A Study of the Epistle to the Hebrews in the Light of the Aqedah* (AB 94; Rome: Biblical Institute Press, 1981).
Syme, R., *Emperors and Biography: Studies in the "Historia Augusta"* (Oxford: Clarendon, 1971).
Taylor, J.E., and D. Hay, "Astrology in Philo of Alexandria's De Vita Contemplativa", *ARAM Periodical* 24 (2012): 56–74.
Terian, A., "Philonis De vision trium angelorum ad Abraham: A New Translation of the Mistitled De Deo", *SPhA* 28 (2016): 77–107.
Theissen, M., *Paul and the Gentile Problem* (Oxford: Oxford University Press, 2016).
Theophilos, M.P., "John 15.14 and the ΦΙΛ- Lexeme in Light of Numismatic Evidence: Friendship or Obedience?", *NTS* 64, no. 1 (2018): 33–43.
Thiselton, A.C., *New Horizons in Hermeneutics: The Theory and Practice of Transforming Biblical Reading* (Grand Rapids: Zondervan, 1992).
Thomassen, E., *The Spiritual Seed: The Church of the "Valentinians"* (NHMS 60; Leiden: Brill, 1980).
Thomassen, E., "*Herakleon*". In *The Legacy of John. Second Century Reception of the Fourth Gospel* (Leiden: Brill, 2010).
Till, W., trans., *Die gnostischen Schriften des koptischen Papyrus Berolinensis 8502* (Berlin: Akademie-Verlag, 1955).
Tilling, C., *Paul's Divine Christology* (Grand Rapids: Eerdmans, 2015).
Tilling, C., "Paul and the Faithfulness of God. A Review Essay (Part 2)", *Anvil* 31, no. 1 (March 2015): 57–69.
Tilling, C., "From Adams's Critique of Wright's Historiography to Barth's Critique of Religion: A Review Essay of Sam Adams's The Reality of God and Historical Method", *Theology Today* 73, no. 2 (2016): 168–77.
Tilling, C., "Paul, Christ, and Narrative Time", in *Christ and the Created Order: Perspectives from Theology, Philosophy, and Science*, eds. A.B. Torrance and T.H. McCall (Grand Rapids: Zondervan, 2018) 151–66.
Tilling, C., "Paul the Trinitarian", in *Essays on the Trinity*, ed. L. Harvey (Eugene, Or.: Cascade, 2018) 36–62.
Tobin, T., "The Beginning of Philo's Legum allegoriae I", *SPhA* 12 (2000): 29–43.
Tooman, W.A., *Gog of Magog: Reuse of Scripture and Compositional Technique in Ezekiel 38–39* (FAT 2.52; Tübingen: Mohr Siebeck, 2011).
Torrance, A.J., "Reclaiming the Continuing Priesthood of Christ: Implications and Challenges", in *Christology Ancient and Modern: Explorations in Constructive Dogmatics*, eds. O.D. Crisp and F. Sanders (Grand Rapids: Zondervan, 2013), 184–204.
Trible, P., "Genesis 22: The Sacrifice of Sarah", in *Women and the Hebrew Bible: a Reader*, ed. A. Bach (New York: Routledge, 1999), 271–90.
Tröger, K.W., *Die Gnosis. Heilslehre und Ketzerglaube* (Freiburg: Herder Verlag, 2001).
Tropper, A.D., *Rewriting Ancient Jewish History: The History of the Jews in Roman Times and the New Historical Method* (London and New York: Routledge, 2016).
Turner, J., *Sethian Gnosticism and the Platonic Tradition, Bibliothèque Copte de Nag Hammadi, Section: «Études» 6.* (Québec; Les Presses de l'Université Laval; Leuven: Peeters, 2001).
Van den Broek, R., *Gnostic Religion in Antiquity* (Cambridge: Cambridge University Press, 2013).
Van der Horst, P.W., *Studies in Ancient Judaism and Early Christianity* (Leiden: Brill, 2014).

Van der Lans, B.,"Belonging to Abraham's Kin: Genealogical Appeals to Abraham as a Possible Background for Paul's Abrahamic Argument", in *Abraham, the Nations, and the Hagarites: Jewish, Christian, and Islamic Perspectives on Kinship with Abraham*, eds. M. Goodman, G.H. van Kooten, and J.T.A.G.M. van Ruiten (Leiden: Brill, 2010), 307–18.

Van Henten, J.W., "Judith as a Female Moses: Judith 7–13 in the light of Exodus 17; Numbers 20 and Deuteronomy 33:8–11", in *Reflections on Theology and Gender*, eds. A. Brenner and F. van Dijk-Hemmes (Kampen: Kok, 1994), 33–48.

Van Nuffelen, P., "De migratione Abrahami und die antike Exilliteratur", in *Abrahams Aufbruch: Philon von Alexandria: De migratione Abraham*, eds. M. Niehoff and R. Feldmeier (SAPERE 30; Tübingen: Mohr Siebeck, 2017), 203–18.

Van Ruiten, J.T.A.G.M., "Abraham, Job and the Book of Jubilees: The Intertextual Relationship of Genesis 22:1–19, Job 1:1–2:13 and Jubilees 17:15–18:19", in *The Sacrifice of Isaac: The Aqedah (Genesis 22) and its Interpretations*, eds. E. Noort and E. Tigchelaar (TBN 4; Leiden: Brill, 2001) 58–85.

Van Ruiten. J.T.A.G.M., "Lot Versus Abraham: The Interpretation of Genesis 18:1–19:38 in Jubilees 16:1–9", in *Sodom's Sin: Genesis 18–19 and its Interpretations*, eds. E. Noort and E. Tigchelaar (TBN 7; Leiden: Brill, 2004), 29–46.

Van Ruiten, J.T.A.G.M., *Abraham in the Book of Jubilees: The Rewriting of Genesis 11:26–25:10 in the Book of Jubilees 11:14–23:8* (Leiden: Brill, 2012).

Van Seters, J., "The Problem of Childlessness in Near Eastern Law and the Patriarchs of Israel", *JBL* 87, no. 4 (1968): 401–8.

Vanderkam, J.C., "Enoch Traditions in Jubilees and Other Second Century Sources", in *SBL Seminar Papers 13*, ed. P.J. Achtemeier (Missoula: Scholars Press, 1987), 229–51.

Vanderkam, J.C., "The Aqedah, Jubilees and Pseudojubilees", in *The Quest for Context and Meaning: Studies in Biblical Intertextuality in Honor of James A. Sanders*, eds. C.A. Evans and S. Talmon (Biblical Interpretation Series 28; Leiden: Brill, 1987), 241–62.

Vanderkam, J.C., *The Book of Jubilees*, 2 vols. (Corpus Scriptorum Christianorum Orientalium, 510–11; Scriptores Aethiopici, 87–88; Leuven: Peeters, 1989).

Vanderkam, J.C. and J.T. Milik, "The First Jubilees Manuscript From Qumran Cave 4: A Preliminary Publication", *JBL* 110 (1991): 243–70.

Vanderkam, J.C., *The Book of Jubilees* (Sheffield: Sheffield Academic Press, 2001).

Vermes, G., *Scripture and Tradition in Israel* (SPB 4. Leiden: Brill, 1961).

Vermes, G., *Post-Biblical Jewish Studies* (Leiden: Brill, 1975).

Von Heijne, C.H., *The Messenger of the Lord in Early Jewish Interpretations of Genesis* (BZAW 412; Berlin: de Gruyter, 2010).

Wacholder, B-Z., *Nicolaus of Damascus* (Berkeley: University of California Press, 1962).

Wacholder, B-Z., "Pseudo-Eupolemus' Two Greek Fragments on the Life of Abraham", *Hebrew Union College Annual* 34 (1963): 83–113.

Wacholder, B-Z., "How Long Did Abram Stay in Egypt? A Study in Hellenistic, Qumran, and Rabbinic Chronology", *HUCA* 35 (1964): 43–56.

Wahl, H.M., "Ester, das adoptierte Waisenkind. Zur Adoption im Alten Testament", *Biblica* 80 (1999): 78–99.

Wallace, D.B., *Greek Grammar Beyond the Basics* (Grand Rapids: Zondervan, 1996).

Ward, R.B., "The Works of Abraham. James 2:14–26", *Harvard Theological Review* 61, no. 2 (1968): 283–90.

Watson, F., *Paul and the Hermeneutics of Faith* (London: T&T Clark, 2004).

Wegner, J.R., "Philo's Portrayal of Women: Hebraic or Hellenic?", in *"Women Like This": New Perspectives on Jewish Women in the Greco-Roman World*, ed. A.J. Levine (SEJL 1; Atlanta, GA: SBL, 1991), 41–66.

Wendel, S., *Scriptural Interpretation and Community Self-Definition in Luke-Acts and the Writings of Justin Martyr* (NovTSup 139; Leiden: Brill, 2011).
Werman, C. and A. Shemesh, "The Halakha in the Dead Sea Scrolls", in *The Dead Sea Scrolls*, ed. M. Kister (Jerusalem: Yad ben Zvi, 2009), 409–33.
Westerholm, S., *Perspectives Old and New on Paul: The "Lutheran" Paul and His Critics* (Grand Rapids: Eerdmans, 2004).
White Crawford, S., *Rewriting Scripture in Second Temple Times* (Grand Rapids: Eerdmans, 2008).
Williams, C.H., "Patriarchs and Prophets Remembered: Framing Israel's Past in the Gospel of John", in *Abiding Words: The Use of Scripture in the Gospel of John*, eds. A.D. Myers and B.G. Schuchard (Atlanta: SBL, 2015), 187–212.
Williams, M.A., *Rethinking "Gnosticism": An Argument for Dismantling a Dubious Category* (Princeton: Princeton University Press, 1996).
Williamson, H.G., "Abraham in Exile", in *Perspectives on Our Father Abraham: Essays in Honor of Marvin R. Wilson*, ed. S.A. Hunt (Michigan: Wm. B. Eerdmans, 2010), 68–79.
Williamson, P.R., *Abraham, Israel and the Nations: The Patriarchal Promise and its Covenantal Development in Genesis* (JSOTSup 315; Sheffield: Sheffield Academic Press 2000).
Wills, L.M., "Jewish Novellas in a Greek and Roman Age: Fiction and Identity", *JSJ* 42 (2011): 141–65.
Wilson, R. McL., "Old Testament Exegesis in the Gnostic Exegesis on the Soul", in *Essays on the Nag Hammadi Texts in Honour of Pahor Labib*, ed. M. Krause (Brill: Leiden, 1975), 217–24.
Wimsatt, W.K., and M.C. Beardsley, "The Intentional Fallacy", in *20th Century Criticism*, ed. D. Lodge (London: Longman, 1972), 334–45.
Wintermute, O.S., "Jubilees: A New Translation and Introduction", in *The Old Testament Pseudepigrapha*, ed. J.H. Charlesworth, Vol. 2 (New York: Doubleday, 1985), 41–3.
Winston, D., *The Wisdom of Solomon* (AB 43; New York: Doubleday, 1979).
Wisdom, R., *Blessing for the Nations and the Curse of the Law: Paul's Citation of Genesis and Deuteronomy in Gal 3.8–10* (Tübingen: Mohr Siebeck, 2001).
Wolfson, E.R., "Becoming Invisible: Rending the Veil and the Hermeneutic of Secrecy in the Gospel of Philip", in *Practicing Gnosis. Ritual, Magic, Theurgy and Liturgy in Nag Hammadi, Manichaean and Other Ancient Literature. Essays in Honor of Birger A. Pearson*, eds. A.D. DeConick, G. Shaw, and J.D. Turner (Leiden: Brill, 2013), 113–36.
Woloch, A., *The One vs. the Many: Minor Characters and the Space of the Protagonist in the Novel* (Princeton: Princeton University Press, 2003).
Wolter, M., *Der Brief am die Römer. Teilband 1: Röm 1–8. EKK* (Neukirchen-Vluyn: Neukirchener Verlagsgesellschaft, 2014).
Wright, A.G., "The Structure of Wisdom 11–19", *CBQ* 27 (1965): 28–34.
Wright, A.G., "The Structure of the Book of Wisdom", *Biblica* 48, no.2 (1967): 165–84.
Wright, N.T., *Paul and the Faithfulness of God* (Minneapolis: Fortress Press, 2013).
Wright, N.T., *Pauline Perspectives: Essays on Paul, 1978–2013* (Minneapolis, MN: Fortress Press, 2013).
Wright, W.C., *The Works of the Emperor Julian*, 3 vols. (London: Heinemann, 1923).
Yinger, K.L., *The New Perspective on Paul: An Introduction* (Eugene, OR: Cascade Books, 2011).
Young, E.J., "Celsus and the Old Testament", *Westminster Theological Journal* 6, no. 2 (1994): 166–97.

Zakovitch, Y., "Juxtaposition in the Abraham Cycle", in *Pomegranates and Golden Bells: Studies in Biblical, Jewish, and Near Eastern Ritual, Law, and Literature in Honor of Jacob Milgrom*, eds. D.P. Wright, D.N. Freedman, and A. Hurvitz (Winona Lake, IN: Eisenbrauns, 1995), 509–24.

Zsengellér, J., "Judith as a Female David: Beauty and Body in Religious Context", in *A Pious Seductress: Studies in the Book of Judith*, ed. G.G. Xeravits (DCLS 14; Berlin: de Gruyter 2012), 186–210.

Index of Ancient Sources

Hebrew Bible/Old Testament

Old Testament Pseudepigrapha

Early Christian Writings

Rabbinic and Related Works

Dead Sea Scrolls

Greek and Latin Authors

Nag Hammadi Codex

INDEX OF AUTHORS